INTERPRETING STATE CONSTITUTIONS

INTERPRETING
STATE CONSTITUTIONS

A JURISPRUDENCE OF FUNCTION
IN A FEDERAL SYSTEM

James A. Gardner

THE UNIVERSITY OF CHICAGO PRESS

CHICAGO AND LONDON

James A. Gardner is professor at the State University of New York, University at Buffalo Law School. He is the author of *Legal Argument: The Structure and Language of Effective Advocacy* (1993) and editor of *State Expansion of Federal Constitutional Liberties: Individual Rights in a Dual Constitutional System* (1999).

The University of Chicago Press, Chicago 60637
The University of Chicago Press, Ltd., London
© 2005 by The University of Chicago
All rights reserved. Published 2005
Printed in the United States of America

14 13 12 11 10 09 08 07 06 05   1 2 3 4 5

ISBN: 0-226-28337-2 (cloth)

Library of Congress Cataloging-in-Publication Data

Gardner, James A. 1959–
   Interpreting state constitutions : a jurisprudence of function in a federal
system / James A. Gardner.
     p. cm.
   Includes bibliographical references and index.
   ISBN 0-226-28337-2 (cloth : alk. paper)
   1. Constitutional law—United States—States. 2. Constitutional law—United
States—States—Interpretation and construction. I. Title.
   KF4552.G37 2005
   342.7302—dc22

                                      2004022689

⊗ The paper used in this publication meets the minimum requirements of the American National Standard for Information Sciences—Permanence of Paper for Printed Library Materials, ANSI Z39.48-1992.

To my parents

CONTENTS

Like most people who study state constitutional law, I came to the field by accident. A long-standing interest in law and democracy led me to a decision by the New York Court of Appeals upholding the legality under the New York Constitution of the legislative practice of hiring employees, at public expense, to work on partisan political campaigns—a practice I was convinced ought to be unconstitutional under any reasonable conception of basic democratic principles. In studying its opinion, I incidentally noticed that the court had relied for its construction of the New York Constitution almost entirely on decisions of the U.S. Supreme Court construing the U.S. Constitution. This seemed puzzling: why would the decisions of a federal court construing the federal Constitution furnish the main body of precedent in a state law case arising under structural provisions of that state's constitution?

This question initially piqued my interest not as a scholar, but as a lawyer. Obviously, the lawyer defending the legislature had offered the New York court federal case law to support the challenged practice. Why? Why not New York case law? And in any event, how could the lawyer challenging the practice have allowed the court to accept these decisions as authoritative? Didn't he or she argue against the relevance or persuasiveness of federal law? As I dug further into New York constitutional law, I found that the Court of Appeals often relied on federal constitutional decisions when construing provisions of the state constitution. Sometimes it followed federal decisions, and sometimes it rejected them. Yet I could find no coherent explanation why the court so frequently used federal constitutional law as its point of departure, nor could I discern any pattern among the cases that might indicate when the Court of Appeals would accept federal decisions and when it would not.

As a former litigator, I was bothered immensely by this. If I were litigating a case involving the New York Constitution, how would I know what body of law a New York court would consider authoritative? What arguments could I make—what words could I address to the court—to persuade it to follow or to reject decisions of the U.S. Supreme Court interpreting analogous provisions of the U.S. Constitution? After reading well over a thousand state constitutional decisions from many states and thoroughly investigating the scholarly literature of state constitutional interpretation, I found myself no closer to a satisfying answer.

This lawyer's interest in the language of judicial persuasion has, as much as any scholarly curiosity, driven my inquiry into state constitutional law. The lack of a satisfying language in which to discuss something is a sure sign of distress; it suggests some disjunction between what people think they ought to do and what they think may acceptably be said. The main attempt to bridge this gap has thus far been made by scholars and judges associated with the New Judicial Federalism movement. Members of this group most commonly argue that a state constitution should be approached and interpreted precisely in the way one would approach and interpret the national Constitution—that is, as an independent, free-standing body of positive constitutional law. This prescription rests, however, on a methodological analogy that implicitly treats states as equivalent to nations and state polities as equivalent to national polities. While this might be an accurate way to think of states in a confederacy such as existed under the Articles of Confederation, or under a Calhounian compact theory of national union, it seems plainly inadequate as an account of what states are under the complex system of federalism we actually have. For this reason, I have long found the language of state constitutional argument offered by the New Judicial Federalism to be unpersuasive. That state courts generally have been unwilling to change their adjudicatory practices in response to these kinds of arguments suggests that they may harbor similar doubts.

This book is an attempt to devise a new and different language in which to address and persuade state courts in cases arising under state constitutions. The language I offer here is one not of methodological convention, but of function—the functions that state constitutions serve in a system of federalism. Those functions are far more complicated, and ambiguous, than students of the subject have sometimes been willing to acknowledge. Putting function at the center of a theory of constitutional interpretation, I believe, puts the horse before the cart. The methodological conventions of constitutional interpretation do not precede, but rather follow from, the functions that a constitutional document serves within a legal system. Although its practitioners have made enormous strides in advancing our understanding of state constitutions, the New Judicial Federalism has sometimes faltered by beginning with interpretational conventions and from them deducing the functions of state power, when the analysis should be the other way around.

* * *

This book has taken shape over the course of more than a decade, during which time I have accumulated more debts than I can possibly acknowledge. Robert Schapiro, who read pieces of the book on more than one occasion and then read and commented on the entire manuscript, has been a wonderful sounding board and has offered many valuable ideas and suggestions. I am also indebted to Jay Mootz for his unflagging willingness over many years to engage and discuss the ideas that went into the book and many of the articles that preceded it. Guyora Binder offered much insightful commentary on the main ideas of the book and many valuable suggestions on a draft of the manuscript. Lynn Mather, director of the Christopher Baldy Center for Law and Social Policy, not only gave me very useful comments on the manuscript but also arranged a manuscript development workshop in which I received much valuable feedback from the participants. Portions of the manuscript have also benefited from workshops at the University at Buffalo Law School, Indiana University School of Law (Indianapolis), Roger Williams University School of Law, and Western New England College School of Law, and from the comments of an anonymous reviewer for the University of Chicago Press. Among the many research assistants who have provided valuable help over the years, I owe the largest debts to Stephanie Lebowitz and Jesse Baldwin.

I wish to acknowledge a special debt to my friend Bob Williams, the dean of state constitutional legal scholars. When as a newly minted academic I first began to write about state constitutional law, Bob immediately embraced me as a colleague even though my work criticized some of his own. A lesser spirit might have taken offense at these nips about the heels, but Bob instead welcomed me into what he has always viewed as a large-scale collaborative effort by many heads and hands to make sense of this stubbornly difficult field. I have benefited from his insights, his generosity, and his camaraderie ever since. Finally, I must thank my wife, Lise Gelernter, and my daughter Sarah for their patient and enthusiastic support of this project as it has finally come to fruition.

In writing this book, I have drawn in several places on previously published work. Some material in the introduction appeared originally in "The Failed Discourse of State Constitutionalism," 90 *Michigan Law Review* 761 (1992). Portions of the introduction and chapter 1 first appeared in "The Positivist Revolution That Wasn't: Constitutional Universalism in the States," 4 *Roger Williams University Law Review* 109 (1998). Portions of chapter 1 have been modified from my "Introduction" to *State Expansion of Federal Constitutional Liberties: Individual Rights in a Dual Constitutional System* (New York: Garland Publishing, 1999). Portions of chapter 2 appeared, in a different form, in "Federalism and the Problem of Political Subcommunities," in David E. Carney, ed., *To Promote the General Welfare: A Communitarian Legal Reader* (New York: Lexington Books 1999). Some material in chapters 2 and 4 first appeared in "Southern Character, Confederate Nationalism, and the Interpretation of State Constitutions: A Case Study in Constitutional Argument," 76 *Texas Law Review* 1219 (1998). Material in chapter 3 has been modified from "State Constitutional Rights as Resistance to National Power: Toward a Functional Theory of State Constitutions," 91 *Georgetown Law Journal* 1003 (2003). Small amounts of material in chapters 4 and 5 first appeared in "Madison's Hope: Virtue, Self-Interest, and the Design of Electoral Systems," 86 *Iowa Law Review* 87 (2000), and "Devolution and the Paradox of Democratic Unresponsiveness," 40 *South Texas Law Review* 759 (1999). Chapter 6 was originally published, in modified form, as "State Courts as Agents of Federalism: Power and Interpretation in State Constitutional Law," 44 *William & Mary Law Review* 1725 (2003). I thank the publishers of all these works for permission to use this material.

The Problem of State Constitutional Interpretation

W HEN PEOPLE who are familiar with American constitutional law learn that some scholars, lawyers, and judges devote considerable time and effort to the problem of interpreting state constitutions, they are sometimes skeptical. How, they ask, can state constitutions pose interpretational problems that differ in any way from the well-worn interpretational issues that have long dominated the study of federal constitutional law? "It's a constitution," these skeptics announce. "It has words. Interpret it. What's the big deal?"

This is an understandable reaction. In our legal system, the way one interprets a legal document depends to a great degree on what kind of document it is. We have rules and conventions governing the interpretation of contracts, wills, deeds, judicial opinions, statutes, regulations, and many other classes of documents. Although these bodies of interpretational rules bear some noticeable family resemblances, they have evolved over long periods of time to serve different purposes, and thus in many cases differ from one another substantively in significant ways. Indeed, as any teacher of law well knows, the thoughtless application of a set of interpretational conventions developed for one class of legal documents to a different class of documents constitutes a rudimentary legal error. This is not necessarily to say that interpretational approaches suitable for one kind of legal document can never be applied to other kinds. It does mean, however, that the use of interpretational tools across categorical boundaries and in settings for which they were not originally designed must be soundly justified before it can be accepted as legitimate.

By what conventions ought the constitution of an American state be interpreted? To the skeptic, this looks like an easy question. A state constitution has the word "constitution" emblazoned prominently across the top of it. That seems like a bit of a hint. State constitutions have preambles and bills of rights. They contain articles dealing with the powers and organization of the legislative, executive, and judicial branches of government. They have been drafted by constitutional conventions and ratified by the people of the state. They look for all the world exactly like . . . well, constitutions. Clearly it must follow that they should be approached and interpreted using the methods and techniques of constitutional law as we know it, which is to say, federal constitutional law. Thus, to interpret a state constitution, one simply turns to the text, structure, history, precedent, purposes, framers' intentions, values of the polity, and all the other tools and conventions familiar from our well-developed tradition of federal constitutional interpretation.

On closer inspection, however, things turn out to be considerably more complicated. The problem is not that standard conventions of constitutional interpretation are unsuitable for application to state constitutions—clearly, they are a great help in illuminating the meaning of these documents. Rather, the difficulty is that the application of the conventions of federal constitutional interpretation to a state—or "subnational"—constitution, particularly within the structure of dual sovereignty established by a system of federalism, is rarely as straightforward as it would be to the constitution of a nation. Consider a typical problem that arises frequently in the interpretation of state constitutions. The U.S. Supreme Court tells us that the starting point in interpreting any constitutional provision is the text. Fair enough. Here is the text of Article I, § 12, clause 1, of the New York Constitution:

> The right of the people to be secure in their persons, houses, papers and effects, against unreasonable searches and seizures, shall not be violated, and no warrants shall issue, but upon probable cause, supported by oath or affirmation, and particularly describing the place to be searched, and the persons or things to be seized.

Anyone who knows constitutional law will notice immediately that the language looks familiar. It is in fact identical, word for word, to the Fourth Amendment of the U.S. Constitution, and was obviously copied directly from that document. What is the meaning of this text?

One obvious inference is that because it uses the same words as the Fourth Amendment, Article I, § 12 of the New York Constitution means precisely the same thing. But on what basis might such a conclusion rest? The meaning of the Fourth Amendment was established slowly, over many years, by decisions of the U.S. Supreme Court, especially in its decisions elucidating the meaning of the words "unreasonable," "searches," and "probable cause." Does Article I, § 12 of the New York Constitution have the same meaning the Supreme Court has given to the Fourth Amendment because words like "unreasonable" and "search," when used in certain combinations, simply *have* a particular meaning whenever they are used in a document purporting to be a constitution? That seems unlikely. According to conventions of constitutional interpretation worked out by the Supreme Court in the early twentieth century, constitutional words and phrases are not to be given their meaning according to some set of hypothesized principles of natural law. On the contrary, a constitution, as the Court has long maintained, must be understood as a unique positive enactment, to be given the meaning that it actually and contingently has, not the meaning that it in any sense "should" have.

If the text itself is inconclusive, the Supreme Court has told us that constitutional meaning also is illuminated by precedent. To see the problems here, it is useful to consider a concrete factual setting. Suppose that New York State troopers begin to look for marijuana farms in rural areas by using aerial surveillance. Because the surveillance is indiscriminate—the troopers look at everything they can see from the air—they cannot demonstrate probable cause and thus neither seek nor obtain a warrant. Suppose that by this surveillance state police find marijuana and charge someone with growing it, and a New York court is presented for the first time with the question of whether Article I, § 12 of the New York Constitution demands that police obtain a warrant before engaging in aerial drug surveillance.

The U.S. Supreme Court has held, in construing the identical language of the Fourth Amendment, that aerial surveillance is not a "search" within the meaning of the Constitution.[1] Clearly, this precedent is not controlling under the New York Constitution. But there is a more interesting question: is it even relevant, and if so, in what way? The language of the state constitution was copied, obviously deliberately, from the federal constitutional provision. This seems to suggest that New Yorkers included this language because they liked the federal provision and wanted something similar in their own constitution. But similar to what? When the U.S. Supreme Court construes the Fourth Amendment, it is construing a provision that was ratified in 1791 and has been in continuous existence ever since. The present New York Constitution was adopted in 1938; prior versions contained no protection whatsoever against unreasonable searches and seizures.[2] Which version of the Fourth Amendment, then, did New Yorkers admire and adopt—the version that was initially

1. California v. Ciraolo, 476 U.S. 207 (1986).
2. Galie, *The New York State Constitution,* 59.

drafted in 1791 or the version that, by 1938, it had been become after 147 years of authoritative construction by the U.S. Supreme Court? Or did New York write into its state constitution the meaning of the Fourth Amendment independently of how it had been construed by federal courts? Did New York, in other words, incorporate into its constitution the meaning of the Fourth Amendment's text as it "really" is, separate and apart from the body of federal jurisprudence construing it? But must we not, consistent with standard federal conventions, reject as a legitimate aide to constitutional interpretation the notion that constitutional language has a universal, natural meaning independent of judicial construction? Or could that rejection be too hasty? Might different rules of construction apply to state constitutions? And even if constitutional language has a true meaning independent of what judges may make of it, surely the Supreme Court of the United States is equally obliged to give the provision its "real" meaning, in which case its decisions ought to be given some respect, even deference.

Conversely, might the New York Constitution's word-for-word adoption of a federal constitutional provision be understood to evince a desire to link New York's constitutional law of search and seizure to the Fourth Amendment, however it might henceforth be authoritatively construed by the Supreme Court? The New York Court of Appeals, New York's highest court, has sometimes suggested as much.[3] But if judicial review under a constitution is justifiable at all, is it not justified mainly by the presence of a backup democratic check on judicial decisionmaking, whether by direct election of judges or, indirectly, through their appointment by other officials who are themselves democratically elected? Why would the people of a state wish to make the meaning of their own constitution depend upon the decisions of a court over which they exercise no meaningful democratic control?

But there's more; the constitutional appropriation of text raises a whole family of different problems. Under the U.S. Constitution's "incorporation" doc-

3. People v. Harris, 570 N.E.2d 1051, 1053 (N.Y. 1991) ("Because the language of the Fourth Amendment of the United States Constitution and section 12 of article I of the New York State Constitution prohibiting unreasonable searches and seizures is identical, it may be assumed, as a general proposition, that the two provisions confer similar rights."). Regarding aerial surveillance, the New York Court of Appeals has said that "the identity of language in the two clauses supports a policy of uniformity in both State and Federal courts," and it has interpreted the two provisions to require the same result. People v. Reynolds, 523 N.E.2d 291, 293 (N.Y. 1988). But see People v. Scott, 593 N.E.2d 1328 (N.Y. 1992) (rejecting open fields exception for posted land).

trine, the prohibition on unreasonable searches and seizures embodied in the Fourth Amendment independently restrains New York State officials by operation of the Fourteenth Amendment's Due Process Clause. Yet that would seem to render Article I, § 12 of the New York Constitution utterly superfluous if it means substantially the same thing as the Fourth Amendment: if the two have the same meaning, then the Fourth Amendment, which applies mandatorily under the Supremacy Clause, controls the outcome and makes Article I, § 12 irrelevant. One of the basic canons of federal constitutional interpretation requires courts to give effect to every word of a constitution if it is at all possible to do so. If the New York Constitution is a constitution, and both it and the U.S. Constitution are part of a single nationwide constitutional scheme of federalism, then the principle of avoiding constitutional redundancy seemingly ought to apply. But if the principle does apply, the only way to comply with it, and thus to give independent effect to Article I, § 12, is to interpret the New York provision to mean something different from the Fourth Amendment. Yet this would result in a paradoxical rule of construction requiring that the more closely a state constitutional provision resembles a federal constitutional provision, the more different the meaning it must be given. That seems to make little sense.

State constitutional interpretation seems to raise problems at every turn. Suppose we resort, as the U.S. Supreme Court often does, to history; perhaps New York's experience with unreasonable searches and seizures by government officials can provide some insight into the problems Article I, § 12 was designed to guard against. But can New York's historical experience of highhanded government searches and seizures be much different from the nation's? The people of the United States adopted the Fourth Amendment mainly to prevent any repetition of their experience of British general warrants, which were used to search indiscriminately for evidence of colonial tax evasion. These intensely disliked warrants were executed in major commercial centers—including New York City.[4] Indeed, New York's experience of search and seizure is an important aspect of the *national* experience of search and seizure. Can its experience, then, really provide sufficient traction for a distinctive interpretation of identical constitutional language?

Other problems arise if we consult the intentions of the drafters and rati-

4. See, e.g., Dickerson, *Writs of Assistance as a Cause of the Revolution,* 54–58; Levy, *Original Intent and the Framers' Constitution,* 233; Cuddihy and Hardy, "A Man's House Was Not His Castle," 391.

fiers of Article I, § 12. It is possible, of course, that records of the 1938 New York constitutional convention might show that the intentions of the drafters of Article I, § 12 differed sufficiently from the intentions of the drafters of the Fourth Amendment to justify giving it a different meaning (the records, by the way, show nothing of the sort).[5] Yet this possibility is not without its difficulties, for those who drafted and ratified the New York Constitution were not just New Yorkers but also Americans, who lived under, and whose consent sustained the legitimacy of, the Constitution of the United States. Is it really plausible that New Yorkers could simultaneously will the words "unreasonable" and "probable cause" to have one meaning under the U.S. Constitution and a different meaning under the New York Constitution?

At this point the skeptic might say, "All right, state constitutional interpretation raises some unique difficulties for provisions copied directly from the U.S. Constitution, but most provisions of state constitutions are not duplicative, and for these the usual methods of constitutional analysis may be straightforwardly applied." That is partly true, but only partly. First, as chapter 1 explains, the individual rights provisions of state constitutions have been the focus of by far the greatest attention and controversy. Many of them exhibit problems of overlap and duplication, making the handling of such provisions one of the central problems of state constitutional interpretation. Second, even though most provisions of state constitutions have not been pilfered from the U.S. Constitution, they have typically been pilfered from the constitutions of other states. For two centuries, constitutional drafting in the American states has proceeded mainly through a process of borrowing, swapping, and copying from somebody else's constitution.[6] This simply replicates many of the difficulties caused by copying federal constitutional law, but with the constitutional text, precedent, and traditions of another state as the problematic point of reference.

Most important, however, state constitutional law does not come only from state constitutions; it comes also, and perhaps preponderantly, from judicial decisions interpreting state constitutions. When analyzed by the standards and conventions that govern the interpretation of the U.S. Constitution, the actual practices of state courts are puzzling and raise a host of additional questions.

In the first place, state courts often appropriate and adopt federal constitutional doctrine as the rule of decision for state constitutional provisions not

5. See Galie, *The New York State Constitution*, 58–62.
6. Tarr, *Understanding State Constitutions*, 50–55.

only when the state constitutional text is identical to its federal counterpart, but even when it differs in potentially significant ways. For example, the Massachusetts Constitution's provision against unreasonable searches and seizures provides:

> Every subject has a right to be secure from all unreasonable searches, and seizures, of his person, his houses, his papers, and all his possessions. All warrants, therefore, are contrary to this right, if the cause or foundation of them be not previously supported by oath or affirmation; and if the order in the warrant to a civil officer, to make search in suspected places, or to arrest one or more suspected persons, or to seize their property, be not accompanied with a special designation of the persons or objects of search, arrest, or seizure: and no warrant ought to be issued but in cases, and with the formalities prescribed by the laws.[7]

This language differs in obvious respects from the language of the Fourth Amendment: it lacks the term "probable cause," for example, and establishes the "formalities" of "the laws" as the reference point for evaluating the constitutionality of warrants. In spite of these differences, the Massachusetts Supreme Judicial Court has construed it to be identical to the Fourth Amendment in virtually all respects and for virtually all purposes.[8]

The Religion Clauses of the First Amendment of the U.S. Constitution provide: "Congress shall make no law respecting an establishment of religion, or prohibiting the free exercise thereof. . . ." The religious freedom provision of the Virginia Constitution could not be more different. It provides:

> That religion or the duty which we owe our Creator, and the manner of discharging it, can be directed only by reason and conviction, not by force or violence; and, therefore, all men are equally entitled to the free exercise of religion, according to the dictates of conscience; and that it is the mutual duty of all to practice Christian forbearance, love, and charity towards each other. No man shall be compelled

7. Mass. Const. Part the First, art. XIV.

8. In a small number of cases, the Supreme Judicial Court has construed the Massachusetts Constitution to provide broader protection than does the Fourth Amendment. For example, the court has held that the state provision requires a more demanding showing of probable cause to issue a search warrant on the testimony of informants, Commonwealth v. Upton, 476 N.E.2d 548 (Mass. 1985), and that police pursuit of a person constitutes a seizure within the meaning of the provision, Commonwealth v. Stoute, 665 N.E.2d 93 (Mass. 1996).

to frequent or support any religious worship, place, or ministry whatsoever, nor shall be enforced, restrained, molested, or burthened in his body or goods, nor shall otherwise suffer on account of his religious opinions or belief; but all men shall be free to profess and by argument to maintain their opinions in matters of religion, and the same shall in nowise diminish, enlarge, or affect their civil capacities. And the General Assembly shall not prescribe any religious test whatever, or confer any peculiar privileges or advantages on any sect or denomination, or pass any law requiring or authorizing any religious society, or the people of any district within this Commonwealth, to levy on themselves or others, any tax for the erection or repair of any house of public worship, or for the support of any church or ministry; but it shall be left free to every person to select his religious instructor, and to make for his support such private contract as he shall please.[9]

Despite these vast and obvious differences, the Virginia Supreme Court has treated the state and federal provisions as essentially the same, and in construing the Virginia provision has drawn freely on U.S. Supreme Court cases construing the federal First Amendment.[10]

Indeed, state courts have occasionally been so eager to rely upon and adopt federal constitutional rulings for purposes of construing their state constitutions that they have treated the state constitutional text as completely irrelevant to the adjudicatory process. For example, until it was amended in 2003, the Delaware Constitution contained no express protection for the freedom of speech. Its most nearly relevant clause protected only the freedom of the press: "The press shall be free to every citizen who undertakes to examine the official conduct of men acting in a public capacity; and any citizen may print on any subject, being responsible for the abuse of that liberty."[11] Despite the conspicuous absence of a speech clause, Delaware courts construing this provision typically proceeded as though the missing language were present, and relied heavily in their analyses on U.S. Supreme Court cases construing the Speech Clause of the First Amendment.[12]

Conversely, state courts often ignore the presence of text or even entire provisions in the state constitution that might decisively affect the outcome,

---

9. Va. Const. art. I, § 16.

10. E.g., Reid v. Gholson, 327 S.E.2d 107 (Va. 1985).

11. Del. Const. art. I, § 5 (1897).

12. E.g., State v. Ceci, 255 A.2d 700 (Del. Super. Ct. 1969); Ramada Inns, Inc. v. Dow Jones & Co., Inc., 1988 Del. Super. LEXIS 29; 15 Media L. Rep. 1586 (Del. Super. Ct. 1988).

relying instead on U.S. Supreme Court decisions construing entirely different and much less relevant provisions of the U.S. Constitution. For example, the U.S. Constitution makes no mention of education, a fact that figured prominently in a leading U.S. Supreme Court decision refusing to recognize education as a fundamental right for purposes of federal equal protection analysis.[13] The Georgia Constitution, in contrast, provides: "The provision of an adequate public education for the citizens shall be a primary obligation of the State of Georgia."[14] One might think this language worthy of attention, yet in a case raising the same question under the Georgia Constitution, the Georgia Supreme Court chose to rely heavily on the U.S. Supreme Court's earlier ruling, notwithstanding that it rested on a construction of the Equal Protection Clause of an entirely different constitution that altogether lacked an education clause. "[T]he fact that education is not a 'fundamental right' under the U.S. Constitution," the Georgia Supreme Court explained, opaquely, "provides some guidance to the states. Consistency in constitutional adjudication, though not demanded, is preferred."[15] It is puzzling indeed that the desirability of such consistency should tempt a state court to overlook stark, potentially relevant textual differences between the state and federal constitutions.

One might think from these examples that state courts adopt federal doctrine and reasoning when interpreting state constitutional *rights* provisions because, after all, the business of protecting individual rights has been largely federalized as a result of the incorporation doctrine. Because state law must conform to the U.S. Constitution in one way or another, perhaps there is some logic to the way in which these courts have proceeded. In fact, however, state courts have been quick to embrace federal constitutional doctrines and reasoning even when construing provisions of the state constitution to which neither the Fourteenth Amendment nor the Supremacy Clause has the slightest relevance.

For example, in decisions concerning the separation of powers under state constitutions, state courts often rely to a surprising degree on federal constitutional doctrine. The Connecticut Supreme Court, for instance, has adopted as a matter of Connecticut constitutional law the federal political question

---

13. San Antonio Independent School District v. Rodriguez, 411 U.S. 1 (1973).

14. Ga. Const. art. VIII, § 1.

15. McDaniel v. Thomas, 285 S.E.2d 156, 167 (Ga. 1981). The constitutional language at issue in this case differed slightly from that quoted in the text, which reflects changes made in 1983. The substance was not materially altered, however.

doctrine, which holds that Article III of the U.S. Constitution limits the power of federal courts to adjudicate certain kinds of disputes.[16] The Rhode Island Supreme Court has adopted the majority opinion in the U.S. Supreme Court's ruling in *INS v. Chadha,* a prominent federal separation of powers case, in the course of upholding revolving-door restrictions on state employment.[17] Recently, the Georgia Supreme Court relied heavily on federal separation of powers doctrine in a decision interpreting the state constitution's allocation of authority between the governor and the independently elected state attorney general—an allocation of power with no counterpart in the U.S. Constitution.[18]

What makes these opinions especially puzzling is that the separation of powers under state constitutions often bears only a passing resemblance to the divisions of power created under the U.S. Constitution. Unlike the federal Constitution, many state constitutions have provisions specifically addressing the separation of powers that might suggest the need for a different approach. The Rhode Island Constitution, to give just one example, provides: "The powers of the government shall be distributed into three departments: the legislative, executive and judicial."[19] State constitutions also frequently differ structurally from the federal Constitution. All but four states provide for independent popular election of lower executive branch officials such as the state's attorney general or chief financial officer, and many provide for popular election to numerous other cabinet-level executive offices. The independent election of these officials gives them an autonomy that lower executive branch officials of the United States lack, thereby removing from the governor significant powers that the president of the United States retains. In addition, the constitutions of many states provide for popular election of at least some state judges, diminishing their independence but increasing their accountability in ways unknown in the federal system. Furthermore, state power under state constitutions is generally understood to be plenary except as limited, while power under the U.S. Constitution is withheld except as specifically

16. Pellegrino v. O'Neill, 480 A.2d 476, 481–83 (Conn. 1984).

17. In re Advisory from the Governor, 633 A.2d 664, 674 (R.I. 1993). For many other examples, see Gardner, "The Positivist Revolution That Wasn't."

18. Perdue v. Baker, 2003 Ga. Lexis 700 (Ga. Sup. Ct., Sept. 4, 2003).

19. R.I. Const. art. V. Courts in some states that have such provisions have interpreted them to require a stricter separation of powers than does the U.S. Constitution. See Alexander v. State, 441 So. 2d 1329 (Miss. 1983). Others have not attached great significance to such language. See Department of Transportation v. Armacost, 532 A.2d 1056, 1064–65 (Md. 1987).

granted.[20] This might provide the state legislature with an advantage in inter-branch disputes that on the federal level Congress would be unable to claim. Conversely, governors often have an item veto, increasing gubernatorial power in comparison to presidential power. State legislatures also are typically less professionalized than Congress and have fewer resources, potentially giving the governor another advantage as compared to the president. These differences surely have ramifications for the precise ways in which the balance of power among the branches of government ought to be struck, and might be thought to undermine to a considerable extent the relevance of federal separation of powers jurisprudence, yet they are almost universally ignored in judicial analyses of the separation of powers under state constitutions in favor of direct appropriation of federal doctrine.

Another puzzling adjudicatory practice of state courts is their general unwillingness to address the intentions of the drafters and ratifiers of the state constitution. The conventions of federal constitutional interpretation make judicial consultation of the intent of the framers a frequently desirable, and sometimes mandatory, strategy. Consequently, even a casual student of federal constitutional law is able to learn much about the main participants in the constitutional founding and their thinking on constitutionally significant issues simply by reading judicial decisions; and experienced federal constitutional litigators generally need to be fairly well versed in the history of the founding period to mount credible arguments. The same typically cannot be said about the constitutional jurisprudence of any state. Even a serious student of state constitutions would be hard pressed to extract from state judicial rulings the slightest impression of who drafted the various state constitutions or influenced the constitutional debates, the kinds of problems that concerned the framers, or the historical setting in which state constitutions were drafted.

The Massachusetts Constitution, for instance, dates to 1780 and is the oldest continuously operating constitution in the world. It was drafted almost single-handedly by John Adams, a pivotal figure in the nation's founding and the author of a treatise on constitutional law that deeply influenced thinking about constitutions during the period following independence. One might expect Adams's views to occupy a significant place in the interpretation of the Massachusetts Constitution, yet in the course of the entire twentieth century the Massachusetts Supreme Judicial Court invoked Adams's name a grand

---

20. Compare McCulloch v. Maryland, 17 U.S. 316 (1819), with Pratt v. Allen, 13 Conn. 119, 124–25 (1839). See also Tarr, *Understanding State Constitutions*, 6–9.

total of fifteen times, seriously engaging his thought on even fewer occasions. Similarly, the Virginia Supreme Court has consulted the views of George Mason, the principal drafter of its famous Declaration of Rights, exactly three times in its entire history of more than two hundred years. The thinking of Thomas Jefferson likewise plays no meaningful role in the Virginia Supreme Court's state constitutional jurisprudence.[21] If these giants of state constitutional foundings are ignored, one can easily, and accurately, imagine how often state courts consult the thought of lesser figures.

Finally, perhaps the strangest adjudicatory practice of state courts in cases construing the state constitution is their frequent unwillingness to explain or to attempt to justify the kinds of interpretive practices I have just described. If a state court thinks, for instance, that federal constitutional doctrine should supply the rule of decision in cases brought under a similar provision of the state constitution (to say nothing of a dissimilar provision), it ought, one might think, to explain why. State courts have been surprisingly reluctant to do this. More often, they offer only conclusory assertions: "we refuse to give any broader interpretation [to the state constitution's due process guarantee]";[22] the state constitution affords "the same protections" as,[23] or is "identical in scope" to,[24] the federal Constitution; "no justification for breaking new ground as to [the state] clause . . . is sufficiently advanced."[25] These kinds of dismissive statements fill the state reporters, suggesting that state courts not only have little interest in engaging in intensive and independent interpretation of their state constitutions, but also that they see no particular benefit in explaining to the bar and to lower courts why state constitutional adjudication should be performed in this perfunctory manner.

* * *

The many conceptual difficulties that arise in interpreting state constitutions, and the odd and seemingly unsatisfactory practices of state courts when they

21. These data were obtained by a search of the Lexis database, unrestricted by date, for the names of these individuals.

22. R. G. Moore Bldg. Corp. v. Committee for the Repeal of Ordinance R(C)-88-13, 391 S.E.2d 587, 591 (Va. 1990).

23. In re Petition of Lucas, 789 P.2d 1157, 1160 (Kan. 1990).

24. State ex rel. Love v. One 1967 Chevrolet El Camino, 799 P.2d 1043, 1048 (Kan. 1990).

25. People v. Hernandez, 552 N.E.2d 621, 624 (N.Y. 1990).

interpret state constitutions, has conventionally been understood in the following way:

The practice of state constitutional interpretation poses certain conceptual challenges, to be sure. These challenges make the task of interpreting state constitutions less straightforward than its federal counterpart, but the practice remains nonetheless a part of the same basic enterprise of constitutional interpretation. Whatever challenges state courts face are thus far from insurmountable, and it is the duty of state courts when interpreting state constitutions to grapple with and ultimately to resolve these problems. It follows that the main problem facing state constitutional law today is the unwillingness, or perhaps even the inability, of state courts to rise to the challenge. They fail to understand their role, no matter how many times it is called to their attention by critics, and they routinely insist on taking the lazy way out by relying willy-nilly on federal law, ignoring peculiarities of local text, history and political values, and generally closing their eyes to the complexities of state constitutional interpretation, as it is properly understood.

This is, without a doubt, the dominant view. Many academics and a few enterprising state judges have long criticized state courts for the often perfunctory character of their state constitutional analyses, and for their apparently general unwillingness to take state constitutional interpretation as seriously as their critics think it ought to be taken. State courts have responded to this kind of criticism in several ways. A few have taken it to heart and made serious attempts to reform their interpretive practices, although many of these have apparently found it difficult to sustain the effort over time and across the entire body of state constitutional jurisprudence. Such reform efforts often seem to depend upon the persistence and institutional leadership of a very small number of state judges who individually have committed themselves to the project of adjudicatory reform. The retirement of these judges, or their distraction with administrative tasks as they have gained seniority, has often resulted in a reversion by the courts on which they sit to the same approach to state constitutional interpretation that prompted the original criticism.

A second way in which some state courts have reacted to criticism has been to embrace the freedom promised by their critics' exhortations to state constitutional independence, but to exercise that freedom only substantively, without any corresponding methodological reform. In a typical pattern, the court begins its analysis by invoking the jurisprudential independence of state from federal constitutional law, and then proceeds to announce, in the same perfunctory manner and without significant supporting analysis, that the state constitution means something different from the U.S. Constitution. Often in such cases, the state constitutional provision in question turns out to mean what a dissenting justice in a U.S. Supreme Court case unsuccessfully claimed was the meaning of the corresponding federal constitutional provision, or what the corresponding federal provision used to mean under Warren Court rulings, before the Burger or Rehnquist Courts cut back on its scope.

This kind of response has earned state courts that have employed it a second and perhaps even more intense round of criticism in which they have been accused of deliberately manipulating the meaning of the state constitution for the purpose of engaging in ideological warfare against the U.S. Supreme Court. You've missed the point, these critics contend. The point is not to interpret the state constitution to mean something different than the U.S. Constitution merely because one disagrees with how the federal document has been construed by federal courts. That's just as lazy and inappropriate as interpreting the state constitution identically because one likes the federal result. The point, rather, is that state constitutional interpretation, like its federal counterpart, does not take the meaning of some other constitution as the reference point for analysis. Instead, each constitution must be *interpreted,* and that means taking it on its own terms, through independent analysis of the text, history, controlling precedent, and so on. The problem with mindless adoption of federal doctrine, these critics argue, is not necessarily the adoption of federal doctrine, but the mindlessness.

This "mere disagreement" approach to state constitutional interpretation is, however, only a variant of what has been by far the most common response on the part of state courts to academic critiques of their interpretational practices: to ignore the criticism altogether. Notwithstanding a considerable and still-growing literature criticizing the way state courts interpret state constitutions, most state courts today continue to employ the same basic approach: they routinely begin and end their analysis by adopting rules of decision developed by the U.S. Supreme Court for use under the U.S. Constitution; engage in no meaningfully independent analysis of the state constitution; and offer little in the way of explanation for their actions. From time to time, the bolder of the state courts may reach a result that differs from one the U.S. Supreme Court has reached under the federal Constitution, but in a way that suggests the result was dictated by the state court's disagreement with the federal outcome.

According to this dominant understanding that I have been describing, the enterprise of state constitutional interpretation has now reached something of an impasse. Academic and judicial critics have repeatedly explained to state courts what they ought to be doing, and a few committed judges have even provided workmanlike demonstrations in a small number of exemplary cases. The word is out. Yet despite the criticism, the explanations, and the demonstrations, state courts by and large do not seem to hear the message; they adhere to their old, incorrect ways and thus fail routinely to interpret state constitutions as they should.

This understanding of state constitutional interpretation—the dominant one, as I have said—should make us suspicious. When such otherwise mature and presumably rational government officials as state judges refuse consistently to behave in the ways prescribed by some theory of adjudication, it is worth considering whether something is amiss with the theory rather than with the actors whose behavior it fails either accurately to describe or meaningfully to influence. I believe there is a different and better way to understand what is happening in state constitutional law, one that provides a better description of what state courts are actually doing, a better framework for evaluating what state courts ought to be doing, and a better explanation of the relationship between the observed behavior of state courts and their theoretical obligations. The purpose of this book is to lay out that understanding.

* * *

The main problem with most current understandings of state constitutional interpretation, and the critiques of state constitutional adjudicatory practices on which they are based, is that they tacitly assume—wrongly, and without justification—that the interpretation of state constitutions ought to proceed under and to be evaluated according to the prevailing conventions of federal constitutional interpretation. They adopt, that is to say, the skeptic's stance: "Hey, it's a constitution; what's the big deal?" From this perspective, state courts do indeed appear to come up short. But what if state courts interpreting state constitutions ought to be doing something other than what federal courts do when they interpret the federal Constitution? What if their actions should be evaluated by different standards?

Lawyers and judges decide how to interpret a legal document by first assigning it to a recognized legal category—will, deed, contract, statute, constitution, and so on—and then applying to it the conventions that, by general agreement, are understood to be appropriate to the interpretation of that particular class of documents. Critics of state constitutional interpretation have generally assumed, perhaps understandably enough, that state constitutions belong in the class of documents labeled "constitutions." To put this another way, they have assumed that a state constitution is a "constitution" in the same way that the U.S. Constitution is a "constitution," and that the two kinds of documents therefore belong to the same legal genus for purposes of interpretation.

More important than the label, however, is what follows from the labeling, and here the critics of state constitutional interpretation typically go on to make an additional and much more important assumption about the interpretational conventions appropriate to constitutions: they assume that the correct methodology for interpreting any constitution consists exclusively of the collection of techniques that federal courts routinely employ when interpreting the U.S. Constitution. Here, I believe, lies the critics' fundamental error, an error that derives from their assumption that the conventions governing the interpretation of the U.S. Constitution are the conventions of constitutional interpretation generally. As a working hypothesis, this will certainly do. Unfortunately, the hypothesis seems badly undermined by the evidence. As I have indicated, not only do state constitutions routinely pose interpretational difficulties for which federal constitutional analysis offers at best remote and indirect guidance, but state courts seem only rarely to follow the federal interpretational model despite a constant stream of academic exhortations to do so. These phenomena ought to lead us to question whether the conventions of federal constitutional interpretation really can be applied successfully to the interpretation of state or other subnational constitutions. Perhaps state courts fail routinely to employ the conventions of federal constitutional interpretation because they find that those conventions simply don't work very well, or don't comport with state courts' understanding of what they are supposed to be doing when they interpret state constitutions, or require them to say or do things that simply don't make sense to them.

To raise such questions, however, is really to raise another and much more fundamental one: if the conventions of federal constitutional interpretation are not well suited to the interpretation of state constitutions, might this not indicate that state constitutions ought not to be considered "constitutions" in the same sense as the national Constitution? After all, interpretational conventions grow up around a class of legal documents only because they actually help interpreters discern the meaning of documents of that class; they survive and flourish because they work. Yet interpretational conventions in large measure derive their power to illuminate the meaning of a class of documents from their sensitivity to the context in which legal actors use the documents; they respond to the purposes for which the documents are created, for example, and the functions they are meant to serve. To question whether state constitutions are appropriate objects of federal interpretational methodology is thus to question whether state constitutions are created for the same purposes and serve the same functions as the U.S. Constitution. But if a constitution is created for somewhat different purposes than the federal Constitution, serves somewhat different functions and is used somewhat differently than the U.S. Constitution, in what sense, precisely, does it deserve to be called a "constitution"?

For academic and judicial critics of state constitutional interpretation, this seems to be the sticking point: in trying to make sense of what state courts do, virtually no one wants to abandon the one piece of seemingly firm ground in the whole arena of inquiry. "This sure is a strange and puzzling area of law," they seem to say, "but at least I know what a constitution is." Yet that is precisely what I wish to call into question—indeed, it is precisely what *must* be called into question if any progress is to made in explaining the mysteriously stubborn and contrary behavior of state courts. Such an inquiry yields rewards, for, as it turns out, the constitutions of the American states differ from the national Constitution not only in the obvious and largely superficial ways so often described in the literature, but also in more fundamental ways that justify thinking of them as a somewhat different species of constitution than their federal cousin.

Function, I believe, provides the key to distinguishing state from national constitutions. All constitutions, contemplated at a certain level of abstraction, serve similar purposes; they lay out the structure and powers of government, for example, and contain mechanisms designed to secure the liberties of the citizenry. But it does not follow that all constitutions serve these abstract purposes in precisely the same way. This is especially true within the American system of federalism, which, by dividing sovereignty, creates two distinct species of government. Again, conceived at a sufficiently abstract level, the national and state governments all serve similar purposes. Nevertheless, federalism assigns to each level of government a somewhat different role and, correspondingly, a set of distinct functions within the larger federal plan. Indeed, for federalism to work at all, the state and national governments must of necessity serve different functions; no sign of trouble in the federal system could be surer than the indiscriminate swapping of functions by the two levels of government. But if the state and national governments themselves serve different functions, surely it is inevitable that their respective constitutions, which assign and order the very powers that these governments possess and deploy, should also serve somewhat different functions.

Where function differs, interpretational conventions also must differ. Reduced to its essence, the basic and entirely unoriginal message of this book is that interpretation follows function: the ways in which we determine the meaning of a document depend greatly on the functions that document is meant to serve by those who use it. This principle holds true whether the document is a grocery list or a constitution. Only by opening ourselves to the possibility that not all constitutions are functionally equivalent—and specifically that subnational constitutions might serve importantly different functions than national constitutions—can we clear the fog that has for too long surrounded the practice of state constitutional interpretation, and begin to arrive at an account of the practice that is both descriptively accurate and theoretically satisfying.

THE ARGUMENT OF THE BOOK

In this book, I present an alternative account of state constitutions and state constitutional interpretation that proceeds, in brief, along the following lines. A realistic account of states and their powers must begin from the recognition that the American states are not free-standing, independent polities, but rather are embedded in a nationally created system of federalism. The apparatus of federalism exists for a purpose: to protect the liberty of all Americans. Federalism does so by constructing two levels of government, state and national; granting each level considerable overlapping authority; and charging each level of government with a duty not only to monitor the behavior of the other, but actively to resist it when it takes actions that threaten public welfare. Although it is by no means the only purpose for which state power exists, the appropriate resistance of national tyranny is clearly one of the most important goals to which state power may be directed.

State constitutions, in turn, exist for the purpose of creating, limiting, and regulating state power and the governmental organs that exercise it. If a properly functioning system of federalism requires states to possess certain kinds of power and to deploy it in certain circumstances against the national government to resist national tyranny, then one of the functions a well-crafted state constitution must perform is to ensure that state officials have the necessary authority. In crafting their constitutions, state polities will inevitably balance the need to create a state government capable of discharging its responsibilities to federalism against many other goals that they might legitimately wish to pursue in designing constitutional institutions. However, while we may thus expect state constitutions to fulfill their responsibilities to a well-functioning federalism in a great variety of ways, we may reasonably expect every state constitution to be concerned to some degree with the achievement of this goal.

One important variable that state constitutional designers must confront is whether they wish to allocate to the state judicial branch any authority to participate in state resistance to abuses of national power. While we normally think of courts as passive institutions not well suited for engaging in intergovernmental power struggles, state courts are capable of using their powers against the national government in at least two ways, both of which involve their role in interpreting the state constitution. First, state courts may directly resist certain abuses of national power, particularly abuses of national judicial power, by construing state constitutional rights guarantees more (and in some cases less) generously than federal courts have construed parallel provisions of the national Constitution. Second, they may resist national power indirectly by construing the state constitution in ways that facilitate resistance by other organs of state government. When state courts act in these ways, they act, I shall say, as "agents of federalism."

Acting as an agent of federalism, however, requires a state court to interpret its state constitutions instrumentally—that is, to interpret it with the deliberate purpose of undermining acts of the national government that the state court believes threaten liberty. Although instrumental interpretation runs counter to certain well-known conventions of constitutional interpretation, these conventions evolved to guide interpretation of the national Constitution, and thus have no necessary application to the interpretation of state constitutions, which occupy a very different institutional position in the federalism framework. Whether a state court has the authority to act as an agent of federalism, then, is to be determined by reference not to prevailing conventions of federal constitutional interpretation, but to the contingent decisions of state polities to grant to or to withhold from their courts that specific form of authority—it is a question, in other words, of positive popular authorization. This leaves the question of how to determine whether state courts have been authorized to act as agents of federalism, a question that should be resolved, I argue, by way of a rebuttable presumption in favor of such authority.

This account of state constitutional interpretation has two main advantages. First, it provides prescriptive advice to state courts designed to show them how to fulfill their responsibilities to the federal system in a way that strengthens American constitutional discourse and, by refocusing attention on the mechanisms of federalism, improves the protection of American liberty. Second, it is descriptively superior to the prevailing models of state constitutional interpretation in that it is capable of accounting for the stubborn fact that state courts by and large tend to treat state constitutional law as though it were a forum for passing judgment on federal constitutional rulings by the U.S. Supreme Court. In my account of state constitutional law, this behavior is neither puzzling nor mistaken, but rather the fulfillment of a basic responsibility that state courts bear under a well-functioning system of judicial federalism.

PLAN OF THE BOOK

The argument of the book is presented in seven chapters laid out in the following way. Chapter 1 introduces the basic problems of state constitutional interpretation. Although state constitutional provisions often closely resemble their federal counterparts, under the structure of our federal system, state constitutional law is jurisprudentially independent of federal constitutional law and need not follow or even acknowledge it. This independence gives state courts the authority to depart from federal precedent and to construe state constitutional rights provisions more broadly than the Supreme Court construes equivalent provisions of the federal Constitution. To constrain this discretion, however, state courts require a stock of disciplining jurisprudential concepts. So far, these concepts have been supplied mainly by adherents of the New Judicial Federalism movement, a loose collection of judges and scholars who understand state constitutions to be a significant source of fully independent constitutional law and tend generally to support the use of state constitutions to expand protection of individual rights.

Adherents of this movement argue that state constitutional law is independent of federal constitutional law for the same reason that federal constitutional law is independent of any other kind: because a constitution is a unique piece of positive law enacted by a politically distinct and independent polity. This contention, however, rests on a false analogy between state and national constitutions, and it has led, I argue in chapter 2, to an interpretational embrace of "romantic subnationalism," in which state constitutional devia-tions from federal law are justified mainly by purported differences in values and character of the peoples of the state and nation, respectively. The bulk of chapter 2 refutes romantic subnationalism both conceptually and empiri-cally, paving the way for a different state constitutional jurisprudence.

Chapter 3 lays the groundwork for such a jurisprudence by going back to basics and examining the workings of the federal system. Extracting the prac-tical mechanics of federalism yields two important insights: states and state power exist not by fiat of independent state polities, but as part of a larger plan of government executed by the national polity; and they exist not primarily to give expression to the values and character of independent state polities (al-though they may incidentally serve that function), but to protect the liberty of all Americans through a system of dual enforcement of shared constitu-tional norms. Chapter 3 goes on to explain how federalism protects liberty by examining the specific mechanisms by which state and federal power are pit-ted against one another.

Chapters 4 and 5 put state constitutions in a new light by reconceptualiz-ing them in terms of the functions they serve in federalism's system of mutu-ally checking state and national power. Chapter 4 focuses on the multiple functions that state constitutions must perform within a federal system. Af-ter placing state constitutions in their functional context, chapter 4 returns briefly to the idea of romantic subnationalism to explore the circumstances in which a state constitution might serve the purposes, and thus fulfill the con-ception, of a fully independent document adopted by a distinct and politically self-conscious state polity. Chapter 5 then turns to the many different ways in which state constitutions may be structured to fulfill the several functions that state constitutions may be called upon to serve. In so doing, chapter 5 re-views many of the important choices state constitutional designers have made in practice, analyzing them in terms of the relative distrust that the people of a state feel for the state and national governments.

Chapter 6 applies the functional theory of state constitutions developed in the preceding chapters to state courts. I argue that state judicial power, like state power generally, can be deployed to protect liberty in two distinct ways. Most fundamentally, state courts can serve as agents of state power, using their powers to achieve the public good directly, or by restraining the organs of state government from abusing the state citizenry. There is, however, an-other way that state judicial power may protect liberty: by projecting outward, to protect the state polity from infringements of liberty perpetrated by the national government. The chapter goes on to argue that the degree to which a state constitution authorizes state courts to deploy judicial power against the national government will depend upon the degree of trust the people of the state choose to repose in their state courts, and reviews a variety of considerations that inform such a decision. It then takes the position that state courts may, consistent with their functions in a federal system, interpret state constitutions instrumentally when necessary to facilitate state resistance to national power. Chapter 6 argues finally that the more responsibility the people of the state give state courts to resist national tyranny, the more freely those courts may interpret the state constitution.

Chapter 7 provides guidance on how the theory developed in the book may be applied in practice. It begins by arguing that courts ought to approach the interpretation of state constitutions by applying a rebuttable presumption that state judicial power, and consequently the available methods for interpreting state constitutions, should be construed broadly. The chapter then considers the limitations that presumptively constrain the exercise of state judicial discretion in constitutional interpretation, and concludes with a discussion applying the interpretational principles developed in the book to several frequently encountered kinds of state constitutional provisions. Finally, the appendix offers a concrete example of how a court might apply the functional approach in a hypothetical case.

1

The Emergence of the Modern Debate

WHEN AMERICANS SPEAK of "constitutional law," they invariably mean the U.S. Constitution and the substantial body of federal judicial decisions construing it. The phrase typically calls to mind important liberty-protecting provisions of the national Constitution, such as the First Amendment or the Equal Protection Clause; or expansive decisions of the U.S. Supreme Court, such as *Brown v. Board of Education* or *Roe v. Wade;* or great federal judges, such as John Marshall, Louis Brandeis, or William Brennan. But one thing the phrase "constitutional law" rarely evokes is the body of law created by and under the constitutions of the various American states.

This tendency to overlook state constitutional law is, at first glance, somewhat curious. There are, after all, fifty state constitutions and only one national Constitution. The very concept of a modern, written, republican constitution aimed at establishing the powers of government and enumerating protected liberties was invented not by the framers of the U.S. Constitution at the 1787 Philadelphia convention, but eleven years earlier, by the drafters of the original constitutions of the former American colonies. The oldest continuously operating written constitution in the world today is not the U.S. Constitution, but the present Massachusetts Constitution, adopted in 1780, followed closely by the New Hampshire Constitution, in force since 1784. The Constitution of the United States receives much credit for protecting American liberties, and rightly so, yet unlike many of the state constitutions in effect between 1776 and 1787, the original federal Constitution did not even contain a Bill of Rights. When a Bill of Rights was added in 1791, its principles were not invented by its drafters but were for the most part appropriated from existing state constitutions, particularly the Virginia Declaration of Rights.

At least as far as sheer numbers and historical pedigree are concerned, then, state constitutions and state constitutional law surely ought to command some degree of public attention and respect. Yet few members of the general public even know their state has its own constitution.[1] The workings of state court systems and the rulings of state supreme courts are generally poorly understood and poorly covered by the media. Even lawyers, who might be thought to have tremendous incentives to explore state constitutional law as a potential source of rights and liberties, have traditionally been extremely reluctant even to raise state constitutional issues or, upon raising them, to brief them thoroughly.[2] Thus, despite the fact that nearly every contemporary state constitution provides explicit protection for the freedoms of speech and religion, the right to be free from intrusive government searches, the rights to equal protection and due process, and many others, it is federal constitutional law that has overwhelmingly commanded public attention and provided the focus for debates concerning the constitutional protection of liberty.

Over the last two decades, however, state constitutional law has been making steady inroads on the historical dominance of its federal counterpart. Two events have played principal roles in this transformation of the constitutional landscape. In the 1970s, the U.S. Supreme Court brought to a close an era of expansive rulings that construed the national Constitution to provide generous protection for individual liberties. A decade later, the Reagan Administration began an aggressive program to shift responsibilities from the federal government to the states, a policy pursued today with bipartisan support in the form of calls for "devolution." These developments have resulted in a blossoming of state constitutional protection of individual liberties and a rethinking of the historic relationship between the state and national governments in protecting the rights of citizens from government intrusions. These events have in turn touched off a jurisprudential crisis in state constitutional law that shows no signs of resolution.

The present era in state constitutional jurisprudence can be traced to Justice William Brennan's 1977 article in the *Harvard Law Review* calling upon state high courts to "step into the breach" left by the Supreme Court's conservative turn in constitutional decisions concerning the protection of individual liberties.[3] Brennan urged state courts to use their state constitutions to continue the expansion of constitutional protections for individual rights.

1. Advisory Commission, Changing Public Attitudes on Governments and Taxes, table 15.

2. Abrahamson, "Criminal Law and State Constitutions," 1162–63; Linde, "First Things First," 391–92.

3. Brennan, "State Constitutions and the Protection of Individual Rights," 503.

Soon liberals, who previously saw federal constitutional law as a ceaseless engine for expanding the rights of individuals against government, began turning to state courts instead. State courts have since been deluged with claims that provisions of state constitutions should be interpreted to provide broader protection for liberties than does the federal Constitution.

Many state courts have responded positively to Brennan's call, a phenomenon sometimes called the "New Judicial Federalism." For example, state courts have frequently asserted their independence in the interpretation of state constitutional protections against unreasonable searches and seizures, rejecting narrow federal rulings and in some cases adhering to Warren Court decisions that the Rehnquist Court has since repudiated. State courts have done so, moreover, despite the fact that these rulings hold state police officers to a higher standard than federal FBI or DEA agents operating alongside them within the state. This judicial independence extends across the spectrum of constitutional liberties. In the area of free speech, for example, the Oregon Supreme Court has departed from the federal path by holding that the Oregon Constitution provides direct and substantial protection for obscenity.[4] In the area of equal protection, the New Jersey Supreme Court has diverged from federal precedent by ruling that the state may not refuse to fund medically necessary abortions when it has chosen to provide funding for medically necessary procedures associated with pregnancy.[5]

The sudden importance of long-ignored state constitutions has thrown state constitutional law into a jurisprudential crisis. How should state constitutions be interpreted? In what circumstances should they be construed to provide broader protections for liberty than the federal Constitution? What is the proper role of states and state courts in policing the protection of liberties from governmental infringement?

AN OVERVIEW OF STATE CONSTITUTIONS

Every state in the union has its own constitution. In many of their most fundamental aspects, the constitutions of the states resemble one another and the federal Constitution. Every state constitution sets out the powers of government; distributes those powers among a legislative, executive and judicial

---

4. State v. Henry, 732 P.2d 9 (Or. 1987).
5. Right to Choose v. Byrne, 450 A.2d 925 (N.J. 1982).

branch; and enumerates and protects a set of common, basic liberties. Every state constitution contains a preamble setting out its goals, and establishes a process for constitutional amendment. The texts of the state constitutions are, at many critical points, similar or even identical to one another and to parallel provisions of the U.S. Constitution, for drafters of state constitutions have traditionally used prior constitutions as models and borrowed freely from them.

Yet in many other ways, state constitutions differ significantly from the national Constitution. To begin with, there are simply more of them—many more: since the nation's founding the American states have written and adopted at least 146 constitutions, an average of nearly three per state. Another obvious difference is that state constitutions tend to be considerably longer than the national Constitution: the U.S. Constitution is about 7,300 words long, whereas the average state constitution contains about 26,150 words. They range in length from the extremely terse Vermont Constitution, at 6,600 words, to the Alabama Constitution, which weighs in at an elephantine 315,000 words (nearly triple the length of this book).[6]

State constitutions tend to be longer than the federal Constitution for two reasons. First, they tend to treat a much broader scope of subject matter than the federal Constitution. For example, the typical state constitution contains provisions governing the powers and organization of local governments; restricting the powers of the state legislature and local governments to tax, borrow, and spend; and setting out governmental obligations concerning public education. Second, with the exception of the very oldest state constitutions, such as New Hampshire's, the constitutions of the states tend to go into far more detail on the subjects they treat than does the U.S. Constitution. Indeed, state constitutions have been frequently criticized for being overly "legislative" in character—that is, setting out regulated matters with such particularity as to risk undermining the gravity and dignity of the constitution.[7] The New York Constitution's article governing local finances, for example, runs on for nineteen pages and includes a provision requiring that, for purposes of calculating the indebtedness of a local government, "net revenue" must be determined either "by deducting from gross revenues of the preceding year all costs of operation, maintenance

6. Some figures are given in Sturm, "The Development of American State Constitutions," 74–75, although many are outdated due to the rapid pace of constitutional amendment in some states.

7. Note, "California's Constitutional Amendomania," 280–81; Adrian, Trends in State Constitutions; Swindler, "State Constitutions for the 20th Century," 590–99.

and repairs for such year . . . [or by] deducting from the average of the gross revenues of not to exceed five of the preceding years during which the public improvement or part thereof, or service, has been in operation, the average of all costs of operation, maintenance and repairs for the same years."[8] This is the kind of language one would expect to find in a statute, not a constitution. State constitutions sometimes also deal with topics that seem like peculiar matters for constitutionalization. The Texas Constitution, for example, contains a provision dealing with automated bank teller machines. The California Constitution contains a provision dealing with the taxation of golf courses.[9]

The broad scope and intense detail of state constitutions are themselves the result of other factors that distinguish the state constitutional environment from its federal counterpart. Certainly one of these factors is the relative ease with which state constitutions may be amended. Some state constitutions have been amended what seems like an absurd number of times: the Alabama Constitution, for example, has been amended more than seven hundred times, and the California, South Carolina, and Texas Constitutions more than four hundred times each. Even more dramatic than amendment is outright replacement of an existing constitution, something that is naturally much more difficult to accomplish than mere amendment. State constitutions are not in principle significantly easier to replace than national ones, yet state constitutions are in practice frequently discarded and replaced, something that has never even been seriously proposed on the national level. Louisiana, for example, has had eleven constitutions since it became a state; Georgia has had nine, South Carolina seven, and Virginia, Alabama, and Florida six each.[10]

Clearly at work here is an underlying attitude toward state constitutions that treats them with considerably less reverence than is accorded the Constitution of the United States. One aspect of this attitude is a strong and historically persistent belief in the desirability of solving problems of state governance directly, by popular action at the constitutional level, rather than indirectly, by using electoral processes to remove corrupt or incompetent officials. Thus, many of the provisions that pad later state constitutions in comparison to their federal and early state counterparts consist of deliberate public responses to specific acts of governmental malfeasance. For example, many state constitutions sharply restrict the state's ability to incur debt. These

8. N.Y. Const. art. VIII, § 5(C).
9. Tex. Const. art. 16, § 16; Cal. Const. art. 13, § 10.
10. Sturm, "The Development of American State Constitutions," 75–76.

restrictions date mostly from the middle third of the nineteenth century, and were adopted in response to a series of disastrous public works expenditures on canals and railroads that caused serious financial difficulty for numerous states.[11] Many state constitutions require that the title of a bill accurately reflect its subject. These provisions grew out of the infamous Yazoo scandal of 1795, in which the Georgia legislature enacted a law whose innocuous title did not accurately reflect the fact that the law's main purpose was to sell public lands to private speculators at an unconscionably low price.[12] This linkage between governmental malfeasance and constitutional reform was especially pronounced during the Progressive Era, when political reformers fought corporate influence over government by waging largely successful campaigns for such reforms as expanded suffrage, secret ballots, direct primaries, initiatives, referenda, recall, and campaign finance disclosure, among others, many of which were eventually implemented at the constitutional level.

This constant march of state constitutional reform illustrates yet another difference between state constitutions and the federal Constitution: unlike the U.S. Constitution, which was and remains a product of the late eighteenth century—and, to a lesser extent, the Civil War—state constitutions have been drafted and significantly amended during every period in American history.[13] They thus reflect the beliefs, concerns, and approaches to constitutional design characteristic of the entire spectrum of American political thought, and consequently contain a wide variety of provisions that the framers of the national document would never have thought to include. For example, New York's present constitution was adopted in 1938, just as the nation was lifting itself out of the Great Depression, and consequently contains a provision charging the state with the "aid, care and support of the needy."[14] State constitutions adopted or amended after the perfection of electronic eavesdropping technology often express a much more direct concern for the protection of privacy than does the U.S. Constitution. State constitutions adopted or amended after the birth of the environmental movement in 1970 sometimes contain provisions establishing a general right to a clean and healthful environment.

---

11. Sterk and Goldman, "Controlling Legislative Shortsightedness," 1306–10.

12. See Ruud, "No Law Shall Embrace More Than One Subject," 391–92.

13. Tarr, *Understanding State Constitutions,* 3–4; Tarr, "Interpreting the Separation of Powers in State Constitutions," 332–33.

14. N.Y. Const. art. XVII, § 1; see Tucker v. Toia, 371 N.E.2d 449 (N.Y. 1977); Hershkoff, "Rights and Freedoms under the State Constitution."

Yet it is one thing to enumerate the similarities and differences among the state and federal constitutions, and quite another to assess their legal significance. State constitutional law is state law, and state law is subordinate to federal law in many ways.[15] Even putting aside the formal legal relationship between the state and federal constitutions, the scope of individual liberties is surely a question of concern to every American, suggesting perhaps that such issues are most naturally dealt with on the national level. When these facts are considered in light of the substantial similarity of all American constitutions on many fundamental matters, it is legitimate to ask whether states are, as either a legal or practical matter, free in any meaningful sense to develop an independent body of state constitutional law. Do state constitutions have any significant role to play in the protection of the rights and liberties of Americans, and if they do, how, and subject to what constraints, may state courts oversee the development of such a body of law? And to what extent do the many differences between the state and federal constitutions either justify or even require a body of state constitutional law that is unique? These questions raise a threshold question of state power: do states have the legal authority to establish the nature and scope of constitutional protections for individual rights independently of federal constitutional law? Although the formal legal answer to this question is simple, several important historical quirks in the evolution of constitutional thought have complicated the process by which that answer has in practice been resolved.

THE JURISPRUDENTIAL BASIS FOR AN INDEPENDENT STATE CONSTITUTIONAL LAW

Throughout the 1820s, the city of Baltimore undertook a program of construction and paving during which it diverted several streams from their original course. One of these streams deposited sediment in front of a wharf owned by

15. The Supremacy Clause displaces state constitutional law to the extent that it conflicts with federal law. U.S. Const. art. VI, cl. 2. The Guarantee Clause, U.S. Const. art. IV, § 4, constrains the constitutional structure of state government, at least in theory; the constraint is perhaps more theoretical than real since the Supreme Court's ruling that issues arising under the Guarantee Clause are judicially unenforceable political questions. Luther v. Borden, 48 U.S. 1, 46 (1849). The Due Process Clause of the Fourteenth Amendment incorporates and applies to the states national constitutional standards for the protection of individual rights. See Duncan v. Louisiana, 391 U.S. 145 (1968); Mapp v. Ohio, 367 U.S. 643 (1961).

John Barron, gradually making the water so shallow that the wharf became useless. Barron sued the city, claiming that its action had taken his private property without just compensation in violation of the Fifth Amendment of the U.S. Constitution. In a decision rendered in 1833, the U.S. Supreme Court dismissed Barron's claim. The question, the Court said, was "of great importance, but not of much difficulty." Writing for the Court, Chief Justice John Marshall drew a firm distinction between the national Constitution and the constitutions of the states. The former, he said, "was ordained and established by the people of the United States for themselves, for their own government, and not for the government of the individual states."[16] To the extent that the federal Constitution limits governmental power, then, its limitations apply only to the federal government; it has no application to the powers of the states. For purposes of limiting state governmental powers, Marshall observed, "[e]ach state established a constitution for itself, and, in that constitution, provided such limitations and restrictions on the powers of its particular government as its judgment dictated."[17]

While the rule laid out in *Barron* seems perfectly clear and, as Marshall indicated, rather obvious, it has not in practice been applied with anything like the clarity Marshall anticipated. In the years since *Barron,* at least three distinct patterns of state and federal adjudication thoroughly muddied the relationship between state and federal constitutional law: a pattern of universalist state adjudicatory practices; a parallel pattern of federal universalist adjudicatory practices; and the process of Fourteenth Amendment incorporation under which the U.S. Supreme Court held many of the provisions of the federal Bill of Rights applicable to the states by operation of the Due Process Clause. These three trends so deeply confused the relationship between state and federal constitutional law that things did not get fully sorted out until the 1980s.

State Constitutional Universalism

Barron was for its time a revolutionary opinion because it rejected categorically a lengthy tradition of universalist adjudicatory practices inherited from England and colonial America, and continued unreflectively by state courts ever since. "Constitutional universalism," as I use the term here, refers to the belief that all American constitutions are drawn from the same set of universal principles of constitutional self-governance. These principles are typically understood to

16. Barron v. Mayor and City Council of Baltimore, 32 U.S. 243, 247 (1833).
17. Id.

reside in a body of natural law or in so-called general principles of law, and they are often associated with the rather Platonic belief that individual bodies of law, such as common or constitutional law, are merely imperfect corporeal approximations of transcendent legal principles binding on all humanity.[18] If the function of a constitution is merely to implement some set of universal principles, then the fact that some constitutional provision is found here or there, or expressed in this way or that, will not be of particularly great consequence.

In the event, *Barron's* insistence that each constitution be treated as a distinct body of positive law was widely ignored for about a century. For example, in an 1852 decision the Georgia Supreme Court reversed a state manslaughter conviction on the ground that admission into evidence of the victim's dying declaration violated the defendant's right to confront witnesses under the Sixth Amendment of the U.S. Constitution.[19] The Georgia Constitution then in effect contained no equivalent provision, and the state, relying on *Barron*, argued that the federal Bill of Rights was irrelevant. The Georgia Supreme Court rejected this argument. According to the court, the question was not whether the amendments in the federal Bill of Rights "were intended to operate as a restriction upon the government of the United States, but whether it is competent for a State Legislature . . . to pass an Act directly impairing the great principles of protection to person and property, embraced in these amendments [to the federal Constitution]?" The Court concluded it was not proper: "notwithstanding we may have different governments, a nation within a nation, *imperium in imperio,* we have but *one* people; . . . it is in [vain] to shield them from a blow aimed by the Federal arm, if they are liable to be prostrated by one dealt with equal fatality by their own [state]." The purpose of the federal Bill of Rights, the court held, was "to declare to the world the fixed and unalterable determination of our people, that these invaluable rights . . . should never be disturbed by *any* government."[20] Massachusetts Chief Justice Lemuel Shaw aptly summarized the universalist approach of this era when he wrote in an 1857 case:

> In considering constitutional provisions, especially those embraced in the Declaration of Rights, and the amendments of the Constitution of the United States,

18. See Gardner, "The Positivist Revolution That Wasn't," 117–28; Feldman, "From Premodern to Modern American Jurisprudence," 1394–1417; Sherry, "Natural Law in the States."

19. Campbell v. State, 11 Ga. 353 (1852).

20. Id. at 365, 366, 367.

in the nature of a bill of rights, we are rather to regard them as the annunciation of great and fundamental principles, . . . than as precise and positive directions and rules of action. . . . Many of them are so obviously dictated by natural justice and common sense, and would be so plainly obligatory upon the consciences of legislators and judges, without any express declaration, that some of the framers of state constitutions, and even the convention which formed the Constitution of the United States, did not originally prefix a declaration of rights.[21]

Federal Constitutional Universalism

State constitutional universalism obscured the authority of states to provide independently for the protection of individual liberties by suggesting that the state and federal constitutions were somehow linked, either to one another or to principles of justice that transcended both. State court decisions refusing to follow *Barron* by applying federal constitutional provisions to the states further muddied the waters by raising questions about the authority of courts to construe authoritatively their own constitutions. To these sources of confusion, however, the U.S. Supreme Court added another: rather than adhering strictly to the division of authority articulated in *Barron,* the Supreme Court between 1842 and 1938 also adopted a set of universalist adjudicatory practices that obscured the distinctions between state and federal constitutional law.

The Court embarked on this path with its 1842 decision in *Swift v. Tyson.*[22] In *Swift,* a commercial dispute arising under New York law, the Court rejected the authority of state courts to declare state law authoritatively for purposes of furnishing rules for federal courts to apply in diversity cases. The Court went on to hold that the New York courts had misconstrued "general principles" of commercial law. Rather than apply the New York courts' misinterpretation of this law, the Court identified the "correct" rule and proceeded to apply it to the facts.

The federal trend toward universalism reached its peak during the 1860s and 1870s in a set of now obscure rulings concerning municipal bonds.[23] In *Gelpcke v. Dubuque*[24] and *Olcott v. The Supervisors,*[25] the U.S. Supreme Court re-

---

21. Jones v. Robbins, 74 Mass. 329, 340 (1857).

22. 41 U.S. 1 (1842).

23. For an extremely thorough and informative discussion of these cases and their historical context, see Fairman, *Reconstruction and Reunion,* vol. 1, chs. 17–18.

24. 68 U.S. 175 (1864).

25. 83 U.S. 678 (1873).

fused, in diversity cases requiring it to apply state constitutional provisions, to follow constructions of the constitutions of Iowa and Wisconsin adopted by the highest courts of those states. This trend eventually culminated in *Pine Grove Township v. Talcott*,[26] in which the Michigan Supreme Court had ruled that the state constitution barred taxation for assisting the construction of privately owned railroads.[27] When the issue reached the U.S. Supreme Court in a subsequent diversity case, the Court went well beyond its prior rulings; here, the Court conducted an *independent* review of the Michigan Constitution and rejected the Michigan Supreme Court's interpretation of it. "With all respect for the eminent tribunal by which the judgments were pronounced," the Court said, "we must be permitted to say that they are not satisfactory to our minds."[28] The Court went on to observe that twenty-five other states permitted such laws, and that the question before it "belongs to the domain of general jurisprudence," a class of cases in which "this court is not bound by the judgment of the courts of the States where the cases arise."[29] This universalist trend was soon broadened and solidified in the area of federal constitutional law during the *Lochner* era of substantive due process decisions.

Ultimately, the universalist approach was overthrown in the federal courts by a kind of positivist revolution. By "positivist," I mean the Austinian notion that law, far from being some body of general principles upon which courts and legislators draw, is better understood as the specific commands of specific sovereigns.[30] In the area of ordinary law, this positivist revolution occurred essentially with a single stroke: the Supreme Court's 1938 decision in *Erie Railroad v. Tompkins*.[31] There, the Court overruled *Swift v. Tyson* and held that state courts are authoritative and final interpreters of state law. The parallel move to positivism in federal constitutional law has been a bit slower in coming. Evidence of this shift can be found in the intense reaction against *Lochner*, and in the embrace of textualism and originalism exemplified by their leading contemporary practitioners, U.S. Supreme Court Justices Antonin Scalia and Clarence Thomas.

26. 86 U.S. 666 (1874).

27. People ex rel. Detroit & Howell R.R. v. Township of Salem, 20 Mich. 452 (1870).

28. 86 U.S. at 677.

29. Id.

30. See Austin, *The Province of Jurisprudence Determined;* Feldman, "From Premodern to Modern American Jurisprudence."

31. 304 U.S. 64 (1938).

The Incorporation Doctrine

Even after its rediscovery of constitutional positivism, the U.S. Supreme Court continued to issue rulings that overruled and marginalized state constitutional protections of liberty, thereby casting further doubt upon the authority of states to develop an independent body of state constitutional law. The Court did so in a series of decisions construing the Due Process Clause of the Fourteenth Amendment. Unlike the federal Bill of Rights, which is addressed to the United States, the Fourteenth Amendment is addressed solely to the states: "No State shall . . . deprive any person of life, liberty, or property, without due process of law."[32] In a series of cases construing this provision, the Court held that the Due Process Clause protects a body of individual rights and liberties from infringement by the states—the so-called incorporation doctrine. Under this doctrine, the Court has held that the Due Process Clause requires states to adhere to federally established levels of protection for the rights to privacy and jury trial, and against double jeopardy, self-incrimination, and cruel and unusual punishment, among others.

These decisions purport to be straightforward interpretations of a positive federal constitutional provision, albeit one that applies directly to the states. In this respect, they do not cloud the question of state authority in the same way or to the same degree as did nineteenth-century universalist adjudicatory practices. Nevertheless, federal cases decided under the incorporation doctrine create a different kind of confusion in two distinct ways. First, these decisions implicitly criticize as inadequate the level of protection of individual liberty established by state constitutions, for if state constitutions adequately protected liberty there would be no need for federal intervention. This approach contributes to the impression that state constitutional law is irrelevant, either legally or practically, to the civil rights of American citizens. Second, these cases suggest that the Due Process Clause may have essentially federalized the entire field of constitutional protection of individual liberties, thus making state bills of rights superfluous as a matter of law.

The Modern Position

The Fourteenth Amendment incorporation process was largely complete by the early 1970s. Since then, state and federal courts, motivated partly by the vigor with which many state courts have in recent years attended to and adjudicated questions arising under their state constitutions, have reached a

32. U.S. Const. amend. XIV, § 1.

firm consensus regarding the scope of state power to develop an independent body of state constitutional law. According to the modern position, states must observe standards established by the U.S. Constitution for the protection of individual liberties, but are free, if they so choose, to provide a level of protection that exceeds federal standards, a principle often referred to as the doctrine of the "federal floor."

By introducing into the federal Constitution a broad set of constraints on state power, and by incorporating into those constraints many of the limitations that the federal Bill of Rights already applied to the federal government, the Fourteenth Amendment appeared to extend to all levels of government a single standard of constitutional protection for individual rights. This appearance was deceiving. In fact, the Fourteenth Amendment established a mandatory level of protection for individual rights that states were constrained to observe and that was enforceable by federal judicial power. So long as states complied with federal standards, however, the structure described in *Barron* remained undisturbed: states could do as they pleased. The practical consequence of this duality is that federal standards for protecting individual rights under the Fourteenth Amendment now provide a minimal level of protection—a "floor."[33] States remain free, however, to *exceed* the federal floor by providing protections for individual rights and liberties that exceed the federally mandated minimums. States, then, may accord as much or more protection for individual rights as does the U.S. Constitution, but they may not accord less.[34] To this extent, states are entirely free to develop a body of independent state constitutional law.

In sum, there is now no doubt as a jurisprudential matter that states have the power to develop a body of state constitutional law that is both indepen-

---

33. I describe this as the "practical" consequence because it is not quite an accurate description of the technical legal situation. Technically, states are as free now as they were before the Fourteenth Amendment to establish whatever level of constitutional protection for civil liberties they deem appropriate, including no protection at all. After the Fourteenth Amendment and the incorporation doctrine, however, standards set by the Fourteenth Amendment control when they come into conflict with state law by virtue of the operation of the Supremacy Clause. State protections of individual rights that fall below federal standards conflict with those standards and are preempted, but state standards that exceed federal minimums do not conflict and thus control.

34. Pruneyard Shopping Ctr. v. Robbins, 447 U.S. 74 (1980); Brennan, "State Constitutions and the Protection of Individual Rights," 500.

dent of, and more rights-protective than, federal constitutional law under the U.S. Constitution. The question is: should they?

If, by the 1970s, the jurisprudential basis for an independent state constitutional law was becoming clearer, it was by no means clear whether state courts had any reason to invest the time and effort necessary to develop such a body of law. In 1977, however, Justice William Brennan provided a reason. In a powerful article that galvanized civil libertarians and many receptive judges and scholars, Brennan sketched a vision of federalism in which state and federal courts collaborate in the enterprise of protecting the civil liberties of Americans against governmental intrusion.[35] The U.S. Supreme Court, Brennan argued, had begun to default on its responsibilities in this area. Consequently, under the federal scheme of dual protection for civil liberties, the federal retreat required state courts to shoulder the burden of protecting Americans' individual rights and liberties that had until then been borne largely by federal courts invoking the U.S. Constitution. Before turning to Justice Brennan's call to action, however, it is useful to examine briefly the condition of state constitutional law as Brennan found it at the time of his article.

State Constitutional Law in the 1970s

In 1970, it is fair to say, there was not much in any state that would today bear characterization as a body of state constitutional law. A lawyer searching through an annotated copy of just about any state constitution for judicial decisions interpreting some specific provision would very likely come up empty-handed. Such decisions as existed were likely to be either very old—from the late nineteenth century, say—and thus of extremely limited utility, or, if recent, surprisingly perfunctory and containing little actual analysis or argument. Many if not most of these decisions relied extensively on decisions of the U.S. Supreme Court construing parallel provisions of the federal Constitution, simply adopting without explanation the federal analysis. There was likely to be almost no resort to the kinds of sources that federal courts routinely turn to when analyzing the national Constitution: state history, the in-

35. Brennan, "State Constitutions and the Protection of Individual Rights."

tent of the framers of the state constitution, state precedent, or the values and traditions of the people of the state. And what was true of state constitutional rulings generally was even more true when it came to the interpretation of state constitutional rights and liberties. In the civil liberties area, state constitutional law, to the extent it existed at all, consisted primarily of a handful of decisions construing provisions in state bills of rights to have precisely the same meaning as their federal counterparts.

Although the reasons for the underdevelopment of state constitutional law are complex and have been endlessly debated by judges and scholars, the likeliest explanations for the failure of state courts to utilize their independence to develop independent bodies of state constitutional law are historical and structural. One possible explanation is the tradition of state constitutional universalism described earlier. This tradition may have predisposed state courts to approach state constitutions under the assumption that state and federal constitutional law were essentially identical, even interchangeable. Another aspect of the problem, frequently overlooked, is that constitutional law in its modern sense of a body of law providing direct protection for enumerated civil rights and liberties, is a relatively recent phenomenon in American law. Provisions of bills of rights, whether state or federal, played only an extremely limited role in controlling government actions until the civil rights revolution of the 1960s, a legal development that accompanied and was in many ways inseparable from the process of incorporation under the Fourteenth Amendment. During the early days of the Republic, the primary constitutional guarantee of individual liberties was generally thought to consist in constitutional features that limited and divided governmental powers.[36]

Moreover, even when courts were moved to provide direct protection for individual rights, historically they did not do so primarily through the vehicle of constitutional law. Before the proliferation of modern constitutional doctrines restraining governmental powers, courts relied primarily on the common law to protect the kinds of rights we now think of as constitutional. Functionally, if not theoretically, the primary source of law limiting the powers of the police to conduct searches, for example, was not the constitutional law of reasonable searches but the common law of trespass. Police powers of arrest were restrained principally not by constitutional limitations but by the com-

36. See Kagan et al., "The Business of State Supreme Courts," 133–55; Gardner, "Southern Character, Confederate Nationalism, and the Interpretation of State Constitutions," 1275–77.

mon law of false arrest and false imprisonment. Thus, state courts did not establish a body of law construing state bills of rights because constitutional bills of rights did not serve their present function until relatively recently; yet by the time bills of rights came to be understood as the primary repository of judicially enforceable restraints on government power, the U.S. Constitution had become the main engine of constitutional protection for civil liberties against both federal and state power by virtue of the Fourteenth Amendment incorporation doctrine. Whatever the reasons, state constitutional law by 1977 seemed an unlikely candidate for a leading role in any continuation of the expansion of constitutionally protected individual liberties.

Justice Brennan's Call to Action

It was against this backdrop that Justice Brennan issued his now-famous call to state courts to take up the protection of individual liberties under the state constitutions. Brennan's article began with a recitation of the federal civil rights successes of the 1960s, among which he counted cases barring state-sponsored school prayer, limiting state libel laws, affirming a constitutional right of association, and construing the Fourteenth Amendment to apply Bill of Rights standards to the states—cases that, in short, gave a liberal construction to the federal Constitution. "Of late," Brennan went on, there has been "a trend in recent opinions of the United States Supreme Court to pull back from, or at least suspend for the time being," this commitment to a liberal interpretation of the federal constitutional protection for individual rights.[37] As evidence, Brennan offered a long list of Supreme Court decisions sustaining government activity against a wide variety of constitutional challenges, including, among a number of others, challenges to the selective withdrawal of government funding for abortions; the imposition of fees for access to the judicial system; the withdrawal of government benefits without a full hearing; restrictions on speech in public forums and in their privately owned equivalents; and a variety of warrantless search and seizure practices.

Finally, Brennan contrasted these more recent Supreme Court decisions with a small number of state rulings in which state courts had affirmed their independence of federal constitutional law and rejected the Supreme Court's analysis of liberties protected independently by provisions of the state constitution. But just as he praised these scattered decisions for their protection of individual rights, Brennan also forcefully criticized the kind of unimagina-

37. Brennan, "State Constitutions and the Protection of Individual Rights," 495.

tive, overly deferential decisionmaking characteristic of most state constitutional rulings. The small body of independent, rights-expansive rulings by state supreme courts, Brennan said, "puts to rest the notion that state constitutional provisions were adopted to mirror the federal Bill of Rights." Decisions of the U.S. Supreme Court construing the federal Constitution "are not mechanically applicable to state law issues, and state court judges and the members of the bar seriously err if they so treat them." After a final invocation of federalism, Brennan concluded with the claim that federal cases foreclosing federal constitutional remedies for violations of civil liberties constitute "a clear call to state courts to step into the breach."[38]

THE NEW JUDICIAL FEDERALISM

Despite, or perhaps because of, the general underdevelopment of state constitutional law, Justice Brennan's challenge to state courts had an immediate galvanizing effect. It is not entirely clear why the article had such an impact. Perhaps Brennan's arguments came as a revelation to some judges, making them instant converts to his position. Or perhaps his challenge gave fresh expression and a concrete focus to certain widely felt but half-formulated impulses, the expression of which state judges perceived as a kind of permission to act that they had not previously sensed. Possibly, by casting state courts as major players in the protection of civil liberties, Brennan's call appealed to state judges' vanity, which had been wounded by a growing national perception of the inadequacy and consequent irrelevance of state law to the protection of individual rights.

Whatever the reason, some of the nation's leading state jurists quickly took up Brennan's message, enthusiastically repeating, emphasizing, and refining it. Justice Hans Linde of the Oregon Supreme Court, for example, was an early supporter of what soon came to be known as the "New Judicial Federalism." Linde took to the lecture circuit and the law reviews to condemn the unwillingness of state courts to "assume the same responsibility for individual rights against public authority" as the federal courts had assumed.[39] He criticized the general practice according to which "most state courts look to interpretations of the Federal Bill of Rights for the meaning of their own state constitu-

38. Id. at 501, 502, 503.
39. Linde, "First Things First," 380.

tions, in the rare cases when they consider them at all,"[40] and he urged state judges to confront the jurisprudential and methodological questions that attend the effort to develop a principled body of independent state constitutional law.

Like-minded state court judges also published articles spreading the word about state judicial independence in the constitutional arena. Justice (now Chief Justice) Shirley Abrahamson of Wisconsin and Justice Stewart Pollock of New Jersey, among others, called attention to the fact that early state constitutions preceded the federal document, and argued that the original national plan assigned to state constitutions a dominant role in protecting civil liberties, not the subordinate role they had come to play.[41] Others, such as Connecticut Chief Justice Ellen Peters, publicly placed the blame on state courts for the "generations of neglect" that state constitutional law had suffered, and called upon state courts to put things right.[42] Justice Stanley Mosk of California likewise condemned the states' "dismal record of employing their state constitutions."[43]

While these public criticisms and expressions of contrition were an important means by which the New Judicial Federalism was spread, it was on the bench, in actual decisions, that these and similarly inclined judges had the greatest impact. There they produced, with what Justice Brennan later called "marvelous enthusiasm," a sudden burst of independent, rights-protective rulings.[44] Between 1950 and 1959, according to one study, a grand total of three decisions were handed down in which a state court construed its own state's constitution to provide protection for individual rights greater than that accorded by the federal Constitution.[45] During the 1960s there were seven such rulings, followed by thirty-six more between 1970 and 1974. From there, the pace picked up dramatically. Between 1975 and 1980, state courts issued eighty-eight rights-expanding rulings. They issued 125 such rulings between 1980 and 1984, and fifty-two more in just two years, 1985 and 1986.[46] Between

40. Id. at 382–83.

41. Abrahamson, "Reincarnation of State Courts"; Pollock, "Adequate and Independent State Grounds."

42. Peters, "State Constitutional Law," 592–93.

43. Mosk, "State Constitutionalism," 1084.

44. Brennan, "The Bill of Rights and the States," 549.

45. Collins, Galie, and Kincaid, "State High Courts, State Constitutions, and Individual Rights Litigation since 1980," 142.

46. Id.

1986 and 1994, state courts extended state constitutional protections another eighty-five times in the area of criminal procedure alone.[47] These rulings, and the ones that have steadily followed, have touched on virtually every area of constitutional liberties.

The Scholarly Reception and Critique

This burst of constitutional activism by state judges, particularly as manifested in actual rights-expanding decisions by state supreme courts, was initially greeted by legal scholars with barely restrained enthusiasm. Some proudly counted the number of independent state constitutional decisions,[48] while others organized symposiums lauding the movement.[49] Yet, as one prominent student of the subject has observed, "[t]he earliest proponents of the new judicial federalism were more inclined to extol the virtues of relying on state constitutions than to explain how one should go about interpreting them."[50]

It was not long, however, before scholarly criticisms of the New Judicial Federalism began to appear. Chief among the early objections to the growing practice of independent state constitutional adjudication was the charge that such rulings were nothing more than unprincipled, result-oriented attempts to evade the force of decisions of the U.S. Supreme Court. One early critic, for example, expressed dismay at the state court practice of treating a state constitution as "little more than a handy grab bag filled with a bevy of clauses that may be exploited in order to circumvent disfavored United States Supreme Court decisions."[51] Another baldly characterized the New Judicial Federalism movement as a device for "advancing the liberal political agenda."[52] Yet another suggested that suspicion was in order even where textual differences between the state and federal constitutions were offered as the justification for a rights-expanding state ruling: textual justifications sometimes seemed like

---

47. Cauthen, "State Constitutional Policymaking in Criminal Procedure," 529.

48. E.g., Schuman, "The Right to 'Equal Privileges and Immunities,'" 221 (counting four hundred such cases).

49. E.g., "Special Section: The Connecticut Constitution"; "Symposium: The Emergence of State Constitutional Law"; Note, "Developments in State Constitutional Law"; "Symposium on the Revolution in State Constitutional Law"; "State Constitutions in a Federal System"; "Symposium on State Constitutional Jurisprudence"; "Symposium on State Constitutional Law."

50. Tarr, *Understanding State Constitutions,* 208.

51. Collins, "Reliance on State Constitutions," 2.

52. Maltz, "The Political Dynamic of the 'New Judicial Federalism,'" 233.

"the ostensible rather than the real basis for some state court decisions," and in fact, "[t]he single largest group of state cases [are] based on ideological disagreements. In these cases, the courts have used disagreement with the [Supreme Court's] reasoning . . . as primary or exclusive justification for their decisions."[53] This criticism was for the most part well taken by both judges and academics, and it precipitated a collective search for a principled independent state constitutional jurisprudence, a search that remains to this day the single major preoccupation of state constitutional theorists on and off the bench.

State Constitutional Interpretation: The Methodology Wars

Like theorists of federal constitutional law, who had long grappled with the problem of how judges could reach decisions that were based on neutral legal principles rather than on their personal and political views, state constitutional theorists began to explore the methodology by which courts might properly and legitimately adjudicate questions arising under state constitutions. Virtually every judicial and academic commentator to address this question took as his or her starting premise the illegitimacy of what was at that time by far the most common method of state constitutional interpretation: the more or less automatic interpretation of state constitutional provisions to mean the same thing as roughly corresponding provisions of the U.S. Constitution. This practice, soon pejoratively labeled "lockstep interpretation," was not only deemed improper, but indeed reviled as the very model of what a coherent practice of state constitutional interpretation must strive to avoid.

What, in the view of these theorists, was so deeply wrong about lockstep interpretation? Courts practicing lockstep interpretation tended to justify it in terms of the desirability of uniformity in state and federal constitutional law. As the Oregon Supreme Court said in one well-known case:

> There are good reasons why state courts should follow the decisions of the Supreme Court of the United States. . . . The law of search and seizure is badly in need of simplification for law enforcement personnel, lawyers and judges. . . . While [the exclusionary] rule is in effect, . . . it is important, for the guidance of law officers, that the rule be as clear and simple as may be reasonably possible, consistent with the constitutional rights of the individual. . . . Not adopting the [federal] rule . . . would add further confusion in that there would then be an "Oregon rule" and a "federal rule." Federal and state law officers frequently work together and in many in-

53. Galie, "The Other Supreme Courts," 763, 769.

stances do not know whether their efforts will result in a federal or a state prosecution or both. In these instances two different rules would cause confusion.[54]

Critics of lockstep interpretation argued in a variety of ways that a judicial yearning for simplicity and uniformity in constitutional law could not legitimately serve as the basis for construing a state constitution. To blindly follow decisions of the U.S. Supreme Court when interpreting provisions of the state constitution was, critics argued, to accord federal rulings a "presumption of correctness" to which they were not entitled.[55] As Justice Brennan pointedly observed, rulings of the U.S. Supreme Court "are not mechanically applicable to state law issues, and state court judges and the members of the bar seriously err if they so treat them."[56]

At the same time, critics of lockstep interpretation also agreed that its opposite—the interpretation of state constitutions to mean something different from the U.S. Constitution—is equally illegitimate when it rests on nothing more than mere disagreement with the way in which federal courts construe similar provisions of the federal Constitution. To reject federal constitutional doctrine because it seems objectionable was said to be just as bad as adopting it because it seems familiar or agreeable. Both approaches rest on the same fundamental conceptual error: treating state constitutions as though they are little more than forums for responding to, or expressing approval or disapproval of, developments in federal constitutional doctrine. Lockstep and rejectionist approaches to state constitutional interpretation on this view share the common defect of failing to accord state constitutions the legal and institutional autonomy with which principles of federalism and state sovereignty invest them. In using these methods, state courts improperly respond to federal constitutional doctrine when they should be engaging the state constitution on its own terms, as an independent object of legal interpretation.

54. State v. Florance, 527 P.2d 1202, 1209 (Or. 1974). While uniformity may be especially desirable in areas such as criminal procedure, where state and local law enforcement officers may need to exercise street-level discretion in ways that conform to both state and national constitutional constraints, the impulse toward uniformity has not been confined to such areas. As the Georgia Supreme Court said of its decision to follow federal rulings when construing the dimensions of the right to an education under the Georgia Constitution, "[c]onsistency in constitutional adjudication, though not demanded, is preferred." McDaniel v. Thomas, 285 S.E.2d 156, 167 (Ga. 1981).

55. Williams, "In the Supreme Court's Shadow," 356.

56. Brennan, "State Constitutions and the Protection of Individual Rights," 502.

Although proponents of the New Judicial Federalism agreed readily on the impropriety of a purely responsive state constitutional jurisprudence, whether expressed as lockstep approval or rejectionist disapproval, they sometimes disagreed on what method of state constitutional interpretation should take its place, and tended to divide into two camps. The larger group embraced what is now known as the "primacy" approach. According to this view, state courts should approach problems of state constitutional interpretation just as federal courts approach interpretational problems under the U.S. Constitution—that is, they should treat state constitutions as freestanding, wholly independent sources of positive constitutional law. This means that state courts should interpret state constitutions by bringing to bear all the traditional tools of constitutional analysis: text, structure, history, controlling state precedent, and the values of the state polity.[57] This analysis should be performed, moreover, without resort to analogous rulings by federal or other state courts except for the limited purpose of providing persuasive guidance.

The other main position, often called the "interstitial" or "supplemental" approach, holds that federal constitutional questions should be addressed first, and that state courts should turn to the state constitution only after it becomes apparent that the U.S. Constitution provides inadequate protection for the civil liberties at issue. Upon making such a determination, the state court should then examine the state constitution to determine whether it provides the additional increment of protection.[58] This approach is usually associated with a methodology of state constitutional interpretation, often labeled the "criteria" approach, that directs state courts to compare the state constitutional provision at issue to its cognate provision in the federal Constitution, and to construe it to have a different meaning from its federal counterpart only if some objective indicium supports the divergent interpretation. The indicia sufficient to support a divergent interpretation are typically said to include differences in the constitutional text, structure, or history; differences in controlling state precedent; and differences in the concerns or values of the local populace.[59]

Proponents of the primacy approach tended to reject the interstitial ap-

---

57. See Linde, "First Things First," and "E Pluribus."

58. Pollock, "State Constitutions as Separate Sources of Fundamental Rights"; Note, "Developments in the Law," 1330–31.

59. See, e.g., State v. Hunt, 450 A.2d 952 (N.J. 1982); State v. Gunwall, 720 P.2d 808 (Wash. 1986).

proach for replicating the major flaw of lockstep interpretation: taking federal constitutional law as the presumptively correct baseline from which state constitutional interpretation must proceed. Advocates of the interstitial approach sometimes responded by justifying it as better taking into account the contemporary reality of constitutional protection of individual rights—namely, that the federal Constitution has assumed the primary role in protecting such rights, and that state constitutions consequently can bear only a limited, supplemental role without calling into question their legitimacy in the legal order.[60] According to the primacy approach, however, this position is incoherent because state constitutions are not documents whose legitimacy can be called into question; they are positive legal enactments with binding force that must be given effect.

THE WORKADAY REALITY: LITTLE CHANGE

For all the brouhaha surrounding Justice Brennan's call to arms, the New Judicial Federalism response, and the increasing heat and sophistication of the methodological debates over state constitutional interpretation, those inclined to examine the actual state constitutional decisions of state courts could scarcely have failed to notice that little had actually changed. With the exception of a relatively small proportion of high-profile cases, written mostly by a small number of vocal judges on a few state courts, the workaday reality of state constitutional adjudication remained much the same as it had been before the New Judicial Federalism developed into a movement with a name.

State courts may well have issued 350 rights-expanding decisions during the decade following Justice Brennan's *Harvard Law Review* article,[61] but they also issued thousands of decisions in which they refused to construe state constitutions to provide protections for individual rights that exceed federal minimums. For every state court that has expanded the scope of constitutional lib-

---

60. Pollock, "State Constitutions as Separate Sources of Fundamental Rights," 717–18; Note, "Developments in the Law," 1357–58. One other approach has also been suggested, though with far less impact on courts and commentators: the so-called dual sovereignty approach, in which the same question is always addressed, whenever possible, under both the state and federal constitutions. See Utter, "Swimming in the Jaws of the Crocodile," 1029–41.

61. Wachtler, "Our Constitutions—Alive and Well," 397.

erties under the state constitution by refusing to follow some rights-contracting ruling of the U.S. Supreme Court, two or three state courts have followed the federal lead by construing the state constitution to provide precisely the same reduced level of protection as the federal Constitution. For example, although six state courts have expressly rejected the Supreme Court's interpretation of the First Amendment under which the public has no free speech rights in privately owned shopping malls, the courts of fourteen states have expressly followed the Supreme Court's lead and construed their state constitutions precisely as the Supreme Court has construed the First Amendment. Seven state high courts have rejected as a matter of state constitutional law the Supreme Court's ruling in *Illinois v. Gates,*[62] which made it substantially easier for police to obtain search warrants on hearsay evidence provided by informants; yet twenty-eight state courts have adopted *Gates* and construed their state constitutions to incorporate a change in search warrant standards that precisely parallels the change on the federal level. A 1991 study of state constitutional criminal procedure decisions found that state courts construe their state constitutions in conformity with federal interpretations of the federal Constitution in nearly 70 percent of all cases.[63] The same study also categorized states as "rejectionist" if they rejected federal constitutional doctrine in 75 percent or more of their independent state constitutional rulings, and "adoptionist" if they adopted federal doctrine in 75 percent or more of their independent state constitutional decisions. The study found that adoptionist states outnumbered rejectionist states twenty-two to four.[64] Many of these results were replicated in a 2000 study, which found that between 1970 and 1994 state supreme courts followed the federal analysis in 69 percent of all cases raising an issue of individual liberties.[65]

State courts have also by and large continued their pre-1970s practice of avoiding state constitutional rulings altogether. One study examined state high court decisions handed down between 1981 and 1986 that dealt with the constitutional right against self-incrimination. It found that state courts ruled exclusively on federal constitutional grounds in 78 percent of the cases.[66] Only eight state supreme courts rested their decisions on state constitutional law in

62. 462 U.S. 213 (1983).

63. Latzer, "The Hidden Conservatism of the State Court 'Revolution,'" 192.

64. Id. at 193.

65. Cauthen, "Expanding Rights Under State Constitutions."

66. Esler, "State Supreme Court Commitment to State Law," 28.

as many as half of all self-incrimination cases decided during the study period, whereas fourteen courts did not consult the state constitution in even a single self-incrimination case during the period, and another seventeen state high courts did so exactly once. Moreover, even when state courts do interpret state constitutions, their decisions frequently display many of the qualities that proponents of the New Judicial Federalism, and Justice Brennan before them, initially criticized. For example, a study of over twelve hundred state constitutional decisions issued by the highest courts of seven states during 1990 found that the great majority of these decisions were characterized by a grudging resort to the state constitution; obscurity as to whether the ruling was based on state or federal constitutional grounds; a tendency to fall into line, without offering any explanation or justification, with federal doctrine developed under the federal Constitution; and a complete absence of any discussion of state constitutional history or the intentions of the state constitution's framers.[67]

A few state courts have, not without some fanfare, self-consciously announced themselves adherents of either the primacy or interstitial approach. Yet close observation of the performance of even these courts reveals that they have rarely stuck to their methodological commitments, and have in fact often lapsed into the very kind of lockstep or reactive analysis they so deliberately committed themselves to eschew.[68] For example, in a recent article a judge of Oregon's intermediate appellate court argued candidly that "although selected Oregon decisions employ some interesting rhetoric about constitutional interpretation," a close examination of the decisions demonstrates that the Oregon Supreme Court's self-conscious methodological commitment to the primacy approach "appears to have made little difference other than to provide the courts an opportunity to arrive at different results than the application of federal law would otherwise require."[69]

THE PROBLEMS OF STATE CONSTITUTIONAL THEORY

Why don't state courts interpret state constitutions in the ways that proponents of the New Judicial Federalism prescribe? Why, even after deliberately

67. Gardner, "The Failed Discourse of State Constitutionalism," 781–94.

68. Landau, "Hurrah for Revolution"; Braithwaite, "An Analysis of the 'Divergence Factors.'"

69. Landau, "Hurrah for Revolution," 795–96.

adopting a methodological commitment to the primacy or interstitial approaches, do state courts so often abandon their self-imposed obligations and lapse into old and seemingly lazy habits, oscillating between the equally unsatisfactory extremes of marching in lockstep with the U.S. Supreme Court and reaching results that differ from federal rulings based solely on disagreement with the federal outcomes? Why, in other words, don't state courts treat state constitutions as the independent sources of positive constitutional law that the new theories of state constitutional interpretation deem them to be?

Think for a moment about what methodological critics of lockstep interpretation call upon state judges to do. According to Hans Linde's well-known formulation, state courts engaged in interpreting a state constitution must not look initially to federal constitutional law for guidance, but rather must engage the state constitution as an independent source of law by examining its text, its history, its structure, relevant state precedent, the character and values of the people of the state, and prudential considerations relating to the judicial role and the pragmatic consequences of judicial resolution of constitutional questions.[70] Linde clearly thinks that state courts taking this approach would often reach results that differ from those reached by federal courts, but that is of secondary importance to him. If such an analysis were to impel a state court to reach a result under the state constitution that is similar or even identical to the result a federal court would reach upon construing a similar provision of the U.S. Constitution, so be it; the point, precisely, is not to reach any particular result, but to engage the state constitution as an independent text and to follow the analysis wherever it leads.

But how likely is it that careful and independent examination of these factors would really lead a state court construing the state constitution to reach a result significantly different from the result the U.S. Supreme Court might reach under the U.S. Constitution? Consider the constitutional text. In 1790, the text of state and national constitutional provisions often differed significantly. Today, however, textual differences are both less common and less dramatic due to frequent state constitutional amendment and replacement, and the ubiquitous process of language-swapping. What about constitutional history? Even setting aside the obvious fact that constitutional text and constitutional history are hardly independent variables in constitutional interpre-

---

70. Linde, "E Pluribus," 181–93. In setting out these elements of constitutional adjudication, Linde relied heavily on Bobbitt, *Constitutional Fate.*

tation,[71] there are good reasons to think that the historical experiences of individual American states differ from the collective historical experiences of the United States only in rare and, in all probability, relatively minor ways. I shall have more to say about this in chapter 2, but for now it is sufficient to observe that the major episodes of American life—the colonial experience, the Revolution, the frontier, the Civil War and Reconstruction, industrialization, two world wars, the Great Depression, the rise of the social welfare state, the civil rights movement, and so on—are, from the vantage point of the present, collective, shared experiences regardless of how they may have been experienced at the time of their occurrence in different places around the nation. This is not to say that constitutional history might not differ somewhat from state to state, but that the magnitude of any such differences must be greatly reduced through the process by which American historical experience is continually collectivized.[72]

State courts attempting to follow Linde's methodology might also run into a different problem when they seek to consult relevant state constitutional precedent: there may be none, or at least there may have been none when state courts first took up issues of individual rights and liberties under their state constitutions. As I indicated earlier, state constitutional law was dramatically underdeveloped when Justice Brennan issued his call for greater attention to state constitutional protection of individual rights. State courts seeking to in-

71. Clearly, textual similarities often reflect parallel similarities in constitutional history. Because constitutional text is drafted in a particular place, at a particular time, in response to particular historical experiences or exigencies, the appearance of the same or similar text in more than one document suggests strongly that the drafters of each document were reacting independently to the same or similar historical events. Moreover, when text is initially drafted for one constitution and then later appropriated for incorporation into a different document at a different place and time, the adopted language often carries its historical pedigree with it, like a traveler with baggage. As a result, the copying of constitutional language often is understood to create a presumption that the adopted text should be given the meaning it had in its original setting, on the theory that those who copied it believed the text to provide a sound response to a set of historical problems the recurrence of which they wished to avoid. In these circumstances, the constitutional history, one might say, is vicarious, but it is incorporated nevertheless by the process of textual borrowing.

72. On the collectivization of historical memory, and its associated politics, see, e.g., Blight, *Beyond the Battlefield,* esp. 1–5.

terpret their own bills of rights often found that the provisions had never been previously construed. In contrast, they often found a highly developed body of federal constitutional law construing textually and historically similar provisions of the U.S. Constitution.

For these reasons, an approach to state constitutional interpretation that stresses jurisprudential independence may more often than not call upon state judges to give studied and independent attention to provisions of state constitutions that are textually similar or identical to their federal counterparts; that rest upon or react to historical experiences that are similar or identical to those that shape the content of federal constitutional doctrine; and for which the only available body of prior judicial analysis is found in federal case law. Certainly it is unsurprising that state judges finding themselves in such circumstances might prefer for pragmatic reasons to dispense with a laborious demonstration of a predictable doctrinal convergence and simply speed things up by adopting federal constitutional law as the presumptive rule of decision under the state constitution. Surely it is legitimate to question the utility of a theory that asks judges to do something that seems to them, perhaps not without justification, to be an unnecessary duplication of effort.

Even more damaging, however, is that the frequent congruity of guideposts to federal and state constitutional interpretation casts doubt on a fundamental premise of the New Judicial Federalism critique of lockstep interpretation: that state constitutional law is in fact, rather than merely in theory, jurisprudentially independent of federal constitutional law. If state constitutional law is not as a factual matter jurisprudentially independent of federal constitutional law—if it looks frequently to federal constitutional law not merely for inspiration but as a source of concrete legal doctrine—then the liberty-protecting justifications for treating it as independent disappear. State constitutional law would still retain its *potential* to serve as an independent and in some cases more generous source of individual liberty than national constitutional law, but this potential would remain unfulfilled due to the fact that constitutional drafters and ratifiers—the people of the states—would have chosen to adopt the federal approach, whatever it may be, for purposes of state constitutional doctrine.

By far the most serious mark against the primacy approach to state constitutional interpretation, however, is that state judges so rarely seem interested in following it. Indeed, they seem uninterested in following it not only when the relevant interpretational guideposts all point toward doctrinal convergence, but even when they do not—when the constitutional text differs from its federal counterpart; when the state constitutional history contains episodes suggesting that it might differ materially from the national historical experience; when prior, not to say ancient, state decisions construing the state constitution may give reason to think that prevailing federal doctrine may be irrelevant. Instead, whether by lockstep adoption or by rejectionist disagreement, state judges behave continually as though one of their principal functions when construing their state constitution is to pass judgment on decisions of the U.S. Supreme Court construing the national Constitution. Yet this is precisely the behavior that proponents of the New Judicial Federalism reject; to do so, they contend, is to make one of the most fundamental mistakes in law: it is to interpret the wrong document.

Even taken individually, but certainly when taken together, these difficulties with the new theoretical prescription for state constitutional interpretation call into question whether there might not be something seriously wrong with the theory. Certainly the theory fails to provide a good description of what state courts actually do—in fact, it misses by a country mile. Prescriptively, moreover, it commands state courts to do something that they might consider a waste of their time, for reasons that may have no obvious real-world application. At the same time, it tells state courts that the one thing they most consistently do when interpreting state constitutions represents an error so fundamental that it ought to be apparent to a first-year law student.

I think the critics have things backward. State courts are doing more or less what they ought to be doing. Proponents of the New Judicial Federalism are correct about the interpretational autonomy that state courts possess, but they are wrong about how state courts should go about exercising that autonomy. Passing judgment on constitutional decisions of the U.S. Supreme Court, I argue later in this book, is actually one of state courts' most important functions in the federal system. Lockstep interpretation and its rejectionist counterpart are signs of a well-functioning federalism, not a sickness in the system. My argument for this alternative understanding of state constitutional interpretation begins in chapter 3.

Before turning to that argument, however, I need to dispose of one remaining aspect of the interpretational approach advanced by the New Judicial Federalism. According to both the primacy and interstitial approaches, the meaning of state constitutions may differ from that of the U.S. Constitution because the state polities that make and adopt state constitutions may possess different fundamental values and even relevantly different character traits than the American polity collectively possesses. This aspect of state constitutional interpretation has begun to take on a disproportionate importance to courts seeking to justify reaching results that differ from federal doctrine because, as I have suggested, state constitutions so often resemble the U.S. Constitution in their relevant text, structure, and constitutional history. Consequently, sometimes the only way to comply with the primacy and interstitial interpretational approaches and still justify interpreting provisions of the state constitution to mean something different from their federal counterparts is to resort to purported differences in the character or values of the state polity. I argue in the next chapter that this approach relies on a kind of cultural romanticism that is conceptually outdated, inappropriately essentialist, and empirically insupportable. Chapter 3 then begins to lay out my argument that state courts need not justify divergences from federal doctrine for any of the reasons provided by the primacy or interstitial approaches.

2

The Dead End of Romantic Subnationalism

SUPPOSE A STATE COURT is called upon to interpret a provision of its state's constitution. After examining it, the court finds that its language is identical or very similar to a parallel provision of the U.S. Constitution, the relevant state history differs little or not at all from the history surrounding the adoption of the federal provision, and nothing in the state cases in which the provision has previously been construed provides any basis for thinking that the provision means anything different from its federal counterpart. Does this mean that the court is required to give the state provision essentially the same construction that federal courts have given the corresponding provision of the U.S. Constitution?

According to the interpretational theories of the New Judicial Federalism, the answer is no, for a divergent construction of the state provision might yet be justified based upon the character and fundamental values of the people of the state. Character-based arguments have long been employed in the interpretation of the national Constitution.[1] The plausibility of such arguments derives principally from the view that the U.S. Constitution is a self-conscious act of social definition by the American polity. Because the Constitution is a democratic expression of American aspirations for good and enduring self-government, it therefore by definition embodies the values that Americans understand themselves to hold. Character-based arguments thus appeal in some way to the belief that the best constitutional interpretation is one that "comports with the sort of people we are and the means we have chosen to solve political and customary constitutional problems."[2] It follows that if the people of the various states have demonstrably distinct characters of their own,

1. See Bobbitt, *Constitutional Fate,* 94.
2. Id. at 95.

and if state constitutions, like the national Constitution, are self-conscious expressions of the values and character of the respective state polities, then the technique of character-based interpretation may be applied with equal confidence to state and other subnational constitutions.

Both of the dominant interpretational paradigms of the New Judicial Federalism clearly and explicitly authorize the application of character-based interpretational techniques to state constitutions. Under the primacy approach, resort to the character and values of the polity is simply one of the traditionally accepted tools of constitutional interpretation generally, to be used in conjunction with other tools to bring meaning to the constitutional text. Under the interstitial approach, differences in the character or values of the state polity from those of the national polity count as one of several objective criteria to which state courts may resort when considering whether to give state constitutional language a different interpretation than similar language in the U.S. Constitution receives. In either case, proper use of the technique requires a state court first to determine that the people of the state possess some character trait or set of fundamental values that differs meaningfully from the character traits and values of the peoples of other states or of the nation, and then to discern whether and how these differences of character and values are reflected in the state constitution.

This is potentially a technique of great power, for it can justify giving different meaning even to language that is textually identical. What counts, on this view, is not the words that are used, but what their authors—the people of the state—meant by using those words. Consequently, it need not follow that commonly used words like "speech," "religion," "unreasonable search," or "cruel and unusual punishment" mean the same thing when used in a state constitution as they do when used in the national Constitution because the authors of those words may have had fundamentally differing conceptions of what those words signify.

Although reliance on the character and values of the state polity enjoys no privileged role in the interpretational methodology of either the primacy or the interstitial approaches, its attraction is obvious. First, it allows state courts to construe state constitutions to mean something different from the U.S. Constitution even when all other indicators point toward convergence, a situation that arises frequently. Second, it authorizes state courts to reach these divergent interpretations by resort to a consideration that is so indeterminate, so difficult to refute on the merits, and as to which state courts might so legitimately claim local and essentially irrebuttable expertise that decisions invoking it may be relatively insulated from subsequent criticism.

Whether for these reasons or because state judges increasingly believe in its merits as a technique of state constitutional interpretation, the resort to state character and values has come to occupy a position of disproportionate importance in the interpretational methodology of state courts, particularly when they seek to justify decisions construing their state constitutions to provide broader protection than does the U.S. Constitution for commonplace individual rights such as the freedoms of speech and privacy and the freedom from unreasonable searches and seizures. For example, the New York Court of Appeals has held that the New York Constitution's free speech clause provides greater protection of speech than does the First Amendment on the ground that "New York has a long history and tradition of fostering freedom of expression, often tolerating and supporting works which in other States would be found offensive to the community."[3] New Yorkers, in other words, are simply more tolerant of eccentric, dissenting, or distasteful speech than are Americans generally, and the state and national constitutions merely reflect the degree to which each polity possesses this particular character trait. Oregon's high court has construed the Oregon Constitution's free speech clause to provide protection for obscenity, a class of speech that the U.S. Supreme Court has found to be outside the protection of the First Amendment. The Oregon court based its interpretation in part on the fact that Oregon's settlers were "rugged and robust individuals dedicated to founding a free society unfettered by the governmental imposition of some people's views of morality on the free expression of others."[4] The Texas Supreme Court has similarly held that the state constitution must be read in view of "Texas' values, customs, and traditions," and with due regard for the "experiences and philosophies" of the state's founders, whose opinions were shaped by "years of rugged experience on the frontier."[5] The Alaska Supreme Court has justified an extremely broad construction of the state constitution's protection of privacy on the ground that Alaska "has traditionally been the home of people who prize their individuality."[6]

The burden of my argument in this book is that these kinds of rulings,

---

3. People ex rel. Arcara v. Cloud Books, 503 N.E.2d 492, 494 (N.Y. 1986).

4. State v. Henry, 732 P.2d 9, 16 (Or. 1987).

5. Davenport v. Garcia, 834 S.W.2d 4, 16 (Tex. 1992).

6. Ravin v. State, 537 P.2d 494, 504 (Alaska 1975).

which construe state constitutional provisions to provide more generous protection of individual rights than similar provisions of the federal Constitution—as well as less dramatic rulings that do nothing more than interpret similar language in the two documents to mean different things—represent in many circumstances entirely legitimate uses of state judicial power that may be easily and coherently justified. In this chapter, however, I argue that to reach such rulings by resort to some purportedly unique character or set of fundamental values of the state polity is neither necessary nor convincing. Such rulings have in common a view of the American states as distinct and cohesive political subcommunities whose inhabitants comprise peoples with integrated histories and corresponding sets of values that suffice to set them apart not only from one another, but from the national community. This view, I believe, is not only implausible on its own merits, but points us down exactly the wrong path.

COMMUNITY AND SUBCOMMUNITY

Since the dawn of the era of the modern nation-state, we have tended to think of a nation as a "community"—that is, as a "people" united by some group of distinctive interests or characteristics that sets it apart from peoples of other nations. Yet the idea that even the most internally stable and peaceful of nations comprises a single, unified community represents a gross oversimplification. Except in some kind of Platonic or Rousseauvean fantasy (or nightmare), every nation is composed not of a single uniform community but of a plethora of communities; it is inevitably a community of communities. Every individual in any actual society has numerous allegiances and ties of many different kinds—ties of family, religion, ethnicity, politics, economics. These ties are the centers of gravity for an enormous number of communities of widely differing size, membership, and focus.

The ways in which subcommunities participate in a democratic nation's political life and act on the political stage can differ greatly, depending in part on the internal structure of the nation's political institutions. At one extreme, a nation's political institutions may be heavily centralized, operating exclusively at a national level and providing neither official recognition nor power to lower-level communities. For example, the Israeli political system is unitary at the national level: all significant power is exercised at the national level, and the entire nation votes together in a single nationwide electoral district for a single national legislature.[7] At the opposite extreme, a nation's political institutions may provide formal recognition and allocate significant power to certain subcommunities. In Belgium's consociational political system, for example, the nation's major ethnolinguistic groups, the French-speaking Walloons and the Dutch-speaking Flemish, are granted what amounts to a veto power over legislation that affects their cultural autonomy.[8]

The political institution of federalism, in contrast, at least as it is practiced in the United States, stands somewhere between these two extremes. In a federal system, significant political power is formally decentralized, yet not in a way that specifically recognizes existing social groups; federalism is political rather than ethnic or linguistic. Instead, federalism recognizes the state or province as the proper receptacle for what is usually a significant amount of power. In so doing, federalism grants this power to a subcommunity defined not by ethnicity, language or religion, but by a set of geographic boundaries.

This practice raises at once an important question: what, precisely, is the nature of the community to which such political power has been allocated? Just what, in other words, is a state in a federal system? Is it, like a miniature nation, a cohesive, distinctive community characterized by some degree of internal integrity—a people in its own right? Is it distinct from other communities or peoples defined by the boundaries of neighboring states? Or are states merely lines on a map—more or less arbitrary administrative subdivisions of the nation that lack distinctive features other than the power they are entitled to wield within the spheres of their separate jurisdictions?

STATE IDENTITY AND NATIONALISM

Contemporary beliefs about the distinctiveness and coherence of the states as political communities owe an enormous debt to a set of parallel beliefs about nationalism. One model of nationalism dates to the birth, during the Enlightenment, of the modern concept of the nation. This branch of national-

---

7. See Lijphart, *Democracies,* 218. Of course, Israel has provided for political recognition of its many distinctive subcommunities by utilizing a strong system of proportional representation. Indeed, Israel has gained a reputation as a nation in which relatively small political subcommunities often exercise disproportionate power precisely as a result of significant political and social divisions among major subgroups.

8. Id. at 30; see also Lijphart, "Proportionality by Non-PR Methods."

ism, which I call "Lockean," was in historical terms radically democratic in that it "implied symbolic elevation of the populace,"[9] and "was fundamentally liberal and universal, carrying a message for all mankind and implying (if not always granting) the liberty and equality of every individual."[10] Another kind of nationalism, however, also arose from the same root. In this "Romantic" variety of nationalism, "national identity tends to be associated with and confounded with a community's sense of uniqueness and the qualities contributing to it."[11] As a result, the social, cultural, or ethnic qualities that make a people unique or identifiable to itself or others acquire special significance; the sovereign people becomes "a *unique* sovereign people."[12] Unlike the Lockean variety, in which nationality is civic and ideological, and may thus in principle be acquired, nationality of the collectivist kind is ethnic or cultural, and therefore limited to a distinct and identifiable populace. It is to this latter kind of nationalism that distinctions of language, religion, culture, and ethnicity become important.[13]

Either of these views could in principle support the conclusion that the American states are distinct societies with unique political identities. The Lockean model, however, which furnishes the dominant political ideology of American constitutionalism, is generally unconcerned with the qualities of

9. Greenfeld, *Nationalism*, 10.

10. Kohn, *The Idea of Nationalism*, 167.

11. Greenfeld, *Nationalism*, 8.

12. Id.

13. Id. at 11. Recently, some scholars have attempted to collapse the conventional distinction between civic and ethnic nationalism by arguing that what passes for civic nationalism is better described as itself an attribute of a particular kind of culture, albeit a modern, liberal one. See, e.g., Yack, "The Myth of the Civic Nation"; Miller, *Citizenship and National Identity*; Levy, *The Multiculturalism of Fear*. As Yack argues, "Distinguishing civic from ethnic understandings of nationhood is part of a larger effort by contemporary liberals to channel national sentiments in a direction—civic nationalism—that seems consistent with the commitments to individual rights and diversity that they associate with a decent political order." Yack, "The Myth of the Civic Nation," 194. These critiques are sound, and I adopt a similar position below. Nevertheless, I adhere to the traditional conceptual categories in introducing the subject because they help illuminate the historical development of contested American ideas of statehood. Ultimately, it makes no difference to my argument whether Lockean nationalism is characterized as a distinctly ideological form of nationalism or as an aspect of liberal culture; my argument focuses on the locus of collective identity, not its character.

groups that choose to form societies and governments, and thus provides no support for the notion that the polities of the states consist of distinct peoples with distinct characters and values, though it is not inconsistent with such a possibility. The Romantic model provides a much more congenial framework for a conception of state polities as meaningfully distinct, and it is easy to demonstrate the influence of this model on the development of the New Judicial Federalism by way of the American historian Frederick Jackson Turner and his subsequent admirers in political science. Yet the Romantic view is so tainted by essentialism and reductionism, and is so implausible as an empirical matter, that it must be rejected, and along with it the practice of employing its conception of unique state character and values as a factor providing much useful guidance to the practice of state constitutional interpretation.

The Lockean Model

In his *Second Treatise,* John Locke sets out what is probably the clearest account of a characteristically Enlightenment theory of the state. According to Locke's account, human society arises from the state of nature, a state in which individuals are autonomous, rational, and self-ruling as a matter of natural law. In this condition, groups of individuals voluntarily agree to band together, for their own mutual security and advantage, into a political association that Locke calls "civil society."[14] Having entered into a self-governing civil society, society's members, also known as "the people," generally find it advantageous to create a government to handle the chores associated with collective self-rule. The creation of a government, though largely a matter left to the people's discretion, involves at a minimum the appointment of a legislator to make laws binding on all members of society. The government, Locke argues, is thus no more than an agent of the people and exercises only the powers that have been delegated by them. A government duly appointed by the people and acting within the bounds of its delegated powers is "legitimate"—that is, it has the right, and not merely the power, to make laws binding on society.[15] If this account sounds familiar, it should—it is the prevailing political theory of the American nation, and it appears in all the canonical texts of American constitutionalism including the Declaration of Independence, the Preamble of the Constitution, the writings of the framers, and seminal Supreme Court decisions such as *McCulloch v. Maryland.*

14. Locke, *Second Treatise of Government,* ¶¶ 4, 87, 89.
15. Id. ¶¶ 132, 134–42, 197–98.

The Lockean model, then, conceives of the United States as a distinct civil society brought into being through the voluntary agreement of rational actors. Plainly, though, precisely the same model can be applied to the constituent states. We could just as easily say that after the American Revolution the people of the former colonies reverted to the state of nature, and that they then voluntarily reconstituted themselves into thirteen separate civil societies. Indeed, this is just how the founding generation understood the states to have come into being after 1776.[16]

Although it furnishes the dominant ideology of American constitutionalism, the Lockean model provides no support whatsoever for the proposition that the polities of the American states constitute politically distinct peoples whose citizens hold values and beliefs that differ fundamentally from the national norm. Lockean theory concerns the political legitimacy of self-government— it says nothing about the characteristics of those who choose to govern themselves. It is thus entirely consistent with the theory that like-minded groups of individuals, possessed of precisely the same basic character and fundamental values, might nevertheless choose voluntarily and rationally, for pragmatic rather than cultural reasons, to constitute themselves into different self-governing societies. Consequently, under the Lockean model, any invocation of distinctive state characters or values necessarily relies not on theoretical premises associated with the model, but on a logically independent claim concerning contingent social facts.[17] I turn shortly to the merits of such a claim, which is thoroughly unconvincing.

---

16. State constitutions written between 1776 and 1789 reveal a clear reliance on the Lockean model. See, e.g., New Hampshire Constitution (1784). The Articles of Confederation, which predate the U.S. Constitution by nine years, also suggest a view of the states as distinct civil societies of the Lockean variety. The Articles declare themselves to be the work of "Delegates of the States"; they purport to be "Articles of Confederation and Perpetual Union, between the States"; they declare the United States to be a "confederacy"; they provide that each state "shall retain its sovereignty, freedom, and independence"; and they describe the confederacy as "a firm league of friendship" among "States." This is the language of international relations and treaties, the kind of language that Lockean sovereigns use with one another.

17. Thus, even the long-rejected "compact" theory of the American union, which holds on a Lockean theory that the United States is a confederacy of independent states rather than a single polity of continental scope, furnishes at most a necessary, but by no means sufficient, condition for the presence of meaningfully distinct characters and values among the various state polities.

The Romantic Model

For the reasons just given, anyone who wants to argue that the constitutions of the American states represent fundamentally differing expressions of the distinct characters and values of distinct state polities will find a far more congenial home in the Romantic model of nationalism, the major modern competitor to the Lockean account, and it is indeed on this model that contemporary accounts of state distinctiveness rely. The Romantic model approaches the question of statehood from the perspective of the German Romanticism associated with philosophers such as Hegel and Fichte. Unlike the Lockean model, which views the polity as the product of a voluntary choice made by a collection of autonomous but ultimately independent individuals, the Romantic model conceives of the polity as an organic whole constituted not by individual choice but by the involuntary and impersonal compulsion of irresistible social and historical forces.

History, according to Hegel, is the story of the constant human march toward freedom, a freedom that can be realized only through membership in a state.[18] The form and organization of the state, however, are not, as Locke would have it, matters of collective choice. On the contrary, says Hegel, "the constitution adopted by a people makes one substance—one spirit—with its religion, its art and philosophy, or, at least, with its conceptions and thoughts—its culture generally."[19] The state, in other words, is unavoidably the concrete manifestation of the character and values—the spirit—of its people. Moreover, because this people is understood as a singular, organic whole, the state both reflects their unity and, reciprocally, unites them: "they are absolutely merged in that agency by which the totality—the soul—the individuate unity—is produced, and of which it is the result."[20] Consequently, on this view, a state is the political reification of a distinct, organic people with a unique collective spirit, and the founding of the state represents an essential step in that people's fulfillment of a historical destiny of freedom. The Romantic model, of course, provides much of the inspiration for the kind of ethnic nationalism so commonplace today around the globe.[21]

When state courts and academic commentators invoke a unique state char-

18. Hegel, *The Philosophy of History*, 38–39.

19. Id. at 45–46.

20. Id. at 47.

21. See, e.g., Connor, *Ethnonationalism*; Huntington, *The Clash of Civilizations and the Remaking of the World Order*; Ignatieff, *Blood and Belonging*; Pfaff, *The Wrath of Nations*; Smith, *National Identity*.

acter or set of indigenous fundamental values as an aid to interpreting state constitutions, they are relying, usually without knowing it, directly on the Romantic conception of nationalism. The path from nineteenth-century German historical Romanticism to the invocation of unique state character by contemporary state courts runs directly through Frederick Jackson Turner, the influential historian of the American West. Turner is best known for his "frontier thesis," first published in 1893, which holds that the essence of the American experience, and the influence that most significantly transformed European settlers into a distinctively American people, was their encounter with the constantly receding frontier.[22]

When Turner received his formal graduate education in history, in 1888–90, the dominant schools of historical method retained a heavy influence of German Romanticism, dressed up in a kind of institutional Darwinism to make them seem more scientific.[23] A crucial piece of the intellectual apparatus of the time was the so-called germ theory, which attributed the unfolding of democratic institutions to the presence of European cultural "seeds" in foreign soil. Although Turner modified the germ theory by emphasizing the influence of the physical environment of the American frontier itself, in most ways he continued to adhere to the germ theory and to Darwinian notions of historical causation and evolution. For Turner, however, the relevant germs of American character came not from Europe, but initially from the American eastern seaboard, and later from increasingly westward points in the interior as the frontier receded further into the continent.[24]

Turner's adaptation of this form of historical explanation is made clear by his account of settlement patterns in what is now the Middle West. For Turner, the starting point for analysis was the character traits possessed by the colonists who in the seventeenth century occupied, in his words, "the three well-known sections" of British North America: "New England, the Middle Region, and the South." These "different colonizing peoples," says Turner, "had distinctive psychological traits."[25] New Englanders, for example, were

the descendants of English colonists, comparatively unaffected by the variety of stocks which had occupied other parts of the country. Puritanism still laid a deep

22. Turner, *The Frontier in American History.*
23. Hofstadter, *The Progressive Historians,* 65–66.
24. Id. at 74–76; see also Bogue, *Frederick Jackson Turner,* 135.
25. Turner, *The Significance of Sections in American History,* 195.

impress upon the people. Calvinistic conceptions, a blend of individualism and social responsibility, were still at work. . . . Herein lies the explanation of much of New England's restraint, her intellectuality, and her reforming instinct.[26]

In the South, by contrast, Virginia was settled by "the American version of English country gentry," whereas South Carolina was "the offspring of a West Indian planting society, reinforced by the incisive intellects of French Huguenots and Scotch-Irishmen—self-centered, haughty, and fiery-tempered, the Hotspur of the states."[27]

From these points of origin, Turner laboriously traced the major routes of westward movement and settlement. Thus, "the prairies of the Old Northwest and the Great Lakes Basin" were settled, Turner found, predominantly by those of "New England ancestry, especially derived from those descendants who had migrated to the West from New York."[28] Indiana, in contrast, was settled by émigrés from North Carolina, Kentucky, and Tennessee,[29] the Mississippi Valley was settled mainly by migrants from the South Atlantic states,[30] and so on. For Turner, these movements explained how the distinctive characters of the peoples of the different regions were formed: migration caused a set of predictable variations in American character corresponding strongly to geographical patterns of settlement. That is why the people of Indiana have a different character from those of Kentucky or Ohio or Michigan, to say nothing of Virginia or Massachusetts. These character differences are so strong, so predictable, and so politically salient, Turner argued, that they enable us to go well beyond normative generalizations to explain observable patterns of political activity, including political party registration and voting in nineteenth-century presidential elections.[31]

Turner's reputation did not long survive his death in 1932. An "assault be-

26. Turner, *The United States, 1830–1850*, 41.

27. Id. at 147.

28. Id. at 6.

29. Turner, *The Rise of the New West*, 77.

30. Turner, *The United States, 1830–1850*, 31.

31. Id.; Turner, *The Significance of Sections*. A more plausible account of the relation between settlement patterns and partisan affiliation focuses not on character, but on habit—the habit of voting for a particular party. Key, *American State Politics*, 219–20. As Key observes, "the partisan divisions of voters" in the states are characterized by "strange sorts of blocs of votes, groups that exist for reasons not clearly associated with the political issues of the day." Id. at 219.

gan,"[32] in which "critics pummeled his work unmercifully"[33] on "counts [that are] bewilderingly numerous."[34] Notwithstanding this barrage of criticism, by the 1960s Turner had come to attract a new set of admirers—not historians this time, but political scientists.[35] Rather than reject Turner's analysis, as historians had done, these scholars not only embraced but attempted to operationalize Turner's analytic framework and to formalize his conclusions. Thus, we are told in one influential study that the character of contemporary urban politics in certain midwestern cities can be traced to one of three "subcultural stream[s] . . . carried westward by the people who were its products and the transmittors of its characteristics"; that the first stream of significance to the region under study was "the Southern stream," which flowed "northward up the numerous rivers that drain the Illinois prairie"; that as a result of this nineteenth-century pattern of movement "Southern mores have penetrated in varying degrees into the overall fabric of [midwestern urban] civic affairs"; and that these settlers "brought with them an extremely individualistic attitude toward society as a whole whereby they minimized any sense of social responsibility beyond the family circle."[36] The entire United States, on this view, consists of three different political cultures—"moralistic," "individualistic," and "traditionalistic"—corresponding to the three original stocks of eastern colonial settlement.[37]

32. Billington, "Foreword," in Turner, *The Frontier in American History,* xvii.

33. Faragher, *Rereading Frederick Jackson Turner,* 227.

34. Hofstadter, *The Progressive Historians,* 125.

35. Turner's only real contemporary heir among historians is David Hackett Fischer, who advanced a notably Turnerian theory of American cultural evolution in *Albion's Seed: Four British Folkways in America.* Fischer's book has been aggressively criticized in much the same way that Turner's work is often criticized. See, e.g., "Forum—*Albion's Seed: Four British Folkways in America*—A Symposium." Historians who study the West today, especially those associated with the New West movement, tend to distance themselves from Turner, whom they typically regard as excessively rigid and essentialist. See, e.g., Limerick, *The Legacy of Conquest;* White, "Trashing the Trails." Contemporary practitioners of regional history generally take a less deterministic view of cultural development that takes as its point of departure fairly widespread current beliefs concerning the role of social forces in the construction of civic and social identity. See, e.g., Conforti, *Imagining New England;* Pierson, "The Obstinate Concept of New England," 3–17. A more nuanced and far less essentialist adaptation of Turner's approach may be found in Etcheson, *The Emerging Midwest.*

36. Elazar, *Cities of the Prairie,* 156–57.

37. Elazar, *American Federalism,* 110–11, 106–7. For a recent expression of a very similar view, see McHugh, *Ex Uno Plura.*

From the identification of regional cultural patterns, it is of course but a short step to the notion that these organic character traits would find expression in state constitutions. Thus, for example, it has been argued that there are precisely "six constitutional patterns among the American states," and that these patterns reflect two variables: "original constitutional conceptions of the founding era plus differences among the types and goals of pioneers who first settled the Northern, Middle, and Southern colonies of the New World." Not surprisingly, these patterns of state constitutional content track geographic settlement patterns because "[s]ubsequent migrations carried the constitutional ideas of these sections westward."[38]

This body of political science scholarship eventually proved influential with early proponents of the New Judicial Federalism. Cited by influential legal scholars[39] and ultimately by state supreme courts,[40] this Turnerian-inspired political science furnished data with a seemingly scientific pedigree to support an intuition that state constitutions might properly and meaningfully be interpreted according to the character and fundamental values of state polities. Early advocates of the New Judicial Federalism thus urged state courts to treat the character and values of the people of their states as sources of constitutional meaning. Just as the character of the American people infuses the national Constitution, they claimed, so too does the character of the people of a state infuse the state charter. A state constitution was said to be a "mirror of fundamental values" of the people of the state,[41] one that expresses "the basic values of the polity."[42] A state's constitutional law becomes, on this view, "uniquely expressive of that state's own constitutional culture."[43]

This approach soon found favor with state judges. Judith Kaye, now chief judge of the New York Court of Appeals, wrote that "[m]any states today espouse cultural values distinctively their own."[44] New York's constitution, she

38. Elazar, "The Principles and Traditions Underlying State Constitutions," 18. See also Patterson, *The Political Cultures of the American States,* 206; Elazar and Zikmund, *The Ecology of American Political Culture.*

39. See, e.g., Williams, "State Constitutional Law Processes"; Fritz, "The American Constitutional Tradition Revisited."

40. See, e.g., Benning v. State of Vermont, 641 A.2d 472, 476 (Vt. 1994).

41. Howard, "State Courts and Constitutional Rights in the Day of the Burger Court," 938.

42. Macgill, "Upon a Peak in Darien," 11.

43. Teachout, "Against the Stream," 19. See also Howard, "The Renaissance of State Constitutional Law," 14.

44. Kaye, "Dual Constitutionalism in Practice and Principle," 423.

contended, "reflects the geography, history, culture and uniqueness of our state."[45] Wisconsin Supreme Court Justice (now Chief Justice) Shirley Abrahamson agreed: a state's constitution must be interpreted in light of the state's "peculiarities" including "its land, its industry, its people, its history."[46] Robert Utter, then justice of the Washington Supreme Court, made the same point: his state's constitution, he argued, must be interpreted in view of "the vast differences in culture, politics, experience, education and economic status" between the state and national founding generations.[47]

GEOGRAPHY AND DESTINY: THE RISKS OF ESSENTIALISM

It should be obvious from this account that any attempt to analyze the character and values of individual state polities, much less to attempt to discern traces of a distinctive state character in the provisions of a state constitution, runs a substantial risk of sliding into essentialism—the attribution of characteristics to groups or individuals based upon deduced first premises rather than actual observation. In a system of cultural essentialism, "objects are what they are *because* they are what they are, for once, for all time, for ontological reasons that no empirical material can either dislodge or alter."[48] As the historian George Wilson Pierson remarked about the Turnerian analysis, "Turner's views were deterministic. They were almost fatalistic.... [F]irst causes are made to lie in real estate, not state of mind."[49]

Unlike the Lockean model of nationalism, which stresses the contingencies of human rationality over fixed and impersonal environmental forces, the Romantic model taps rather easily into a naturalized view of geographic boundaries as demarcating significantly different peoples with significantly different characteristics and traditions. The potential for error and abuse is obvious:

> The Germans ... are supposed to have a disciplined, military character—exactly the opposite of that they were supposed to possess during the early Napoleonic

45. Kaye, "A Midpoint Perspective on Directions in State Constitutional Law," 19.
46. Abrahamson, "Reincarnation of State Courts," 965.
47. Utter, "Freedom and Diversity in a Federal System," 244.
48. Said, *Orientalism,* 70.
49. Pierson, "The Frontier and American Institutions," 36–38.

period. The French are thought of today as logical, cultivated . . . , pacifist lovers of freedom; exactly the opposite of what most Europeans considered them during the latter part of the Napoleonic era. [This error is made by bad historians, as well as] by contemporary two-week tourists and society editors temporarily turned foreign correspondents who set out to confirm all their prejudices and to footnote with their profound platitudes all the horrible peculiarities everyone already, of course, knows about without having investigated.[50]

Unfortunately, one need go no further for examples of the pitfalls of this approach than some of the more prominent decisions of state courts purporting to interpret their state constitutions in the mode of Romantic subnationalism. A particularly notorious example is the oft-cited case of *Ravin v. State*,[51] in which the Alaska Supreme Court held that the state constitution's protection of personal privacy required the invalidation of a state statute criminalizing the use of marijuana as applied to personal marijuana use within the home. In reaching this conclusion, the court relied explicitly on what it viewed as the unique character of Alaskans:

> The privacy amendment to the Alaska Constitution was intended to give recognition and protection to the home. Such a reading is consonant with the character of life in Alaska. Our territory and now state has traditionally been the home of people who prize their individuality and who have chosen to settle or to continue living here in order to achieve a measure of control over their own lifestyles which is now virtually unattainable in many of our sister states.[52]

Yet not long thereafter, this selfsame Alaskan people, who so prized their rugged individuality and control over personal lifestyle, overturned the court's ruling by initiative, thereby legalizing the criminal prosecution of recreational marijuana use within the home. The people of Alaska, it seems, either were not quite the rugged individualists that the court assumed them to be, or were not so distinct from the peoples of other states as to be immune from the hardening attitudes toward drug use that swept the nation during the 1980s. Indeed, according to a more recent account of life in Alaska,

50. Shafer, *Nationalism,* 230.
51. 537 P.2d 494 (Alaska 1975).
52. Id. at 503–4.

"fully half the population of more than 600,000 now lives in metropolitan Anchorage, where in most ways they might just as well be living in Minneapolis or Buffalo."[53]

The problem with the Romantic model, it must be stressed, does not lie with the notion that the American populace might in some useful way be conceived as comprising culturally distinct subcommunities. Surely it does. The problem is not even that the Turnerian brand of Romanticism links character to geography. Undoubtedly the physical characteristics of a place in which people live influence the kinds of lives they lead, and such variations might in some meaningful sense contribute to the formation of their character. Thus one might, for example, grant that city dwellers as a rule have character traits or hold values distinct from the traits or values of residents of rural areas, or that the people of one American region, such as the South, differ meaningfully from those of other regions, such as the North or West. One might even grant that climate or other physical attributes of the landscape influence the character of the residents in identifiable ways.

The problem, rather, is this: federalism does not establish borders dividing Americans into urban, suburban, and rural areas, or into multistate regions or climatic zones; it accords meaning only to the boundaries that separate one state from another. Yet no American state is exclusively urban or rural, exclusively coastal or inland, exclusively mountainous or flatland, or exclusively settled by people of one ideology or another, or who descended from one or another stock of colonial settlers. Nor does any American state contain some characteristic of landscape or populace that is not shared by at least some, and often many, other states. On the contrary, every American state contains within its borders a considerable diversity of physical and demographic attributes. The real question posed by federalism, then, is not whether geographic boundaries are capable of marking off meaningfully distinct communities—clearly they have that capacity—but whether the boundaries of the American states actually do so. Contemporary Romantic subnationalism, then, like its Lockean cousin, poses at bottom an empirical question.[54]

53. Goldberg, "Alaska Revels in Frontier Image Though Frontier Slips Away." For further discussion of the convergence of U.S. and Alaska constitutional privacy law, see Chemerinsky, "Privacy and the Alaska Constitution."

54. Wholly apart from the question of the existence of distinct American political subcommunities with distinct political cultures is the question of what behavior such distinctions might be capable of explaining. Here, the claims made on behalf of politi-

THE POROSITY OF STATE BORDERS

The claim that the populations of the various American states today constitute meaningfully distinct peoples with meaningfully distinct characters and values is dealt a serious and probably fatal blow simply by consideration of some of the most glaringly obvious features of modern American society: the ease and frequency of mobility; the dominance of mass media and mass marketing of national scope; and the increasing globalization of economic activity. These factors have made state boundaries extremely porous—indeed, for many purposes, such boundaries have become irrelevant.[55] It is difficult to imagine that any state-based political identity could maintain its integrity after an assault of this magnitude.

In 1850, Americans were flowing westward. Gold had been discovered in California the previous year, launching a wave of emigration that reached nearly half a million people by the end of the ensuing decade.[56] In that year of explosive internal migration, nearly one in four native-born Americans, 24 percent, no longer lived in the state in which he or she had been born.[57] One might expect that as the continent became settled and pioneers put down stakes, migration between states would slow dramatically. In fact, according to the U.S. Census Bureau, the number of native-born Americans living outside the state of their birth has never fallen below its 1900 level of 20.6 percent, and has risen steadily since 1940. By 1980, 31.2 percent of native-born Americans lived outside their state of birth. When the many Americans of foreign birth are included, only 64.0 percent of all Americans—fewer than two in three—still lived in their state of birth in 1980.[58] This figure includes children of all ages, who are far more likely than adults to live in the place where they were born. The percentage of American adults who have migrated from their state of birth, then, must be considerably higher.

Mobility, clearly, is a fact of American life. Each of the last five censuses

---

cal culture often exceed the bounds of logic. See Elkins and Simeon, "A Cause in Search of Its Effect," 127–45.

55. Rubin and Feeley describe state boundaries as serving today the purely administrative function of facilitating decentralized nationwide government. Rubin and Feeley, "Federalism."

56. Unruh, *The Plains Across,* 400–401.

57. Long, *Migration and Residential Mobility in the United States,* 29 (table 2.1).

58. Id.

found that about 10 percent of the entire American populace had moved from one state to another within the previous five years.[59] Since 1990, approximately 2.7 percent of the American population has moved its residence from one state to another every year. To put this in absolute numbers, between 1995 and 2000, over 35 million Americans moved from one state to another. Adding in another 7 million who immigrated from abroad, about 42 million Americans arrived in their present state of residence during this five-year period alone.[60]

As impressive as these numbers are, they hardly begin to reveal the extent to which mobility has been institutionalized in American life—or perhaps more correctly, the extent to which the states have been deprived of any ability whatsoever to exercise a fundamental prerogative of sovereign nations: the power to define the terms of state citizenship and to exclude foreigners or to treat them differently from citizens. As noted above, the Lockean model views a polity as a voluntary association of self-identified compatriots, and the Romantic model views it as an organically distinct people with some set of unique characteristics or experiences. Under either of these models, the integrity of the polity depends decisively on its ability to define for itself the scope of political membership. At a minimum, this function requires a polity to have the power to define who may and may not be a citizen, and it is often thought to require the corollary powers to exclude noncitizens from assuming certain social or political roles, or even to bar them from entering the polity's territory. These are precisely the legal powers that the U.S. Constitution denies to the American states: under the Fourteenth Amendment and the Commerce Clause, states are absolutely debarred not merely from erecting barriers to internal migration, but from refusing to extend full citizenship, and the membership in civil society it entails, to all who settle within their borders.[61]

59. Information on the 1960, 1970, and 1980 censuses appear in id. at 33 (table 2.2). Data for 1990 and 2000, as well as for earlier censuses, appear in U.S. Census Bureau, *Annual Geographical Mobility Rates*, table A-1, and can be accessed at http://www.census.gov.

60. U.S. Census Bureau, *Annual Geographical Mobility Rates*. For comparable but slightly earlier figures, see also Hansen, *Current Population Reports*, table A.

61. See The Passenger Cases, 48 U.S. 283 (1849) (persons are articles of commerce whose movement, under the Commerce Clause, states may not impede); U.S. Const. amend. 14, § 1 ("All persons born or naturalized in the United States . . . are citizens of the United States and of the State wherein they reside."); Shapiro v. Thompson, 394 U.S. 618 (1969) (Constitution recognizes fundamental personal right to interstate travel); Dunn v. Blumstein, 405 U.S. 330 (1972) (states may not refuse to grant right to vote to recent interstate migrants).

In consequence, state borders are now completely porous as a matter of constitutional law: a state cannot prohibit citizens of other states from entering the state, enjoying the benefits of state citizenship, and immediately becoming full members of the state's citizenry. Thus, not only do Americans move frequently from state to state, but they must, by constitutional entitlement, be admitted upon arrival to the full incidents of membership in the state polity. These data strongly undermine the possibility that state citizenship could define some meaningful category of social or political life. State citizenship seems more like something that Americans can, and frequently do, put on and shuck off like an old suit of clothes.

The possibility of meaningfully distinct state identities and values seems even less likely in view of the recent trends toward concentrated ownership and nationwide uniformity in the mass media.[62] The sources from which people obtain their information inevitably influence the kind of information they receive and the images and conceptions that guide their understanding of the world. At one time, Americans probably obtained most of their news of the world from a local newspaper, produced locally, by local people, who grew up in and lived the life constituted by local customs and beliefs. Today, in contrast, twenty-three corporations of nationwide reach control most of the more than twenty-five thousand media outlets—newspapers, magazines, television, books, and motion pictures—in the United States. The most competitive of these media—the daily newspaper business—is dominated by fourteen companies. The Gannett Company alone owns the national daily *USA Today* and eighty-seven other daily papers. Knight-Ridder owns the *Philadelphia Inquirer*, the *Miami Herald*, and twenty-seven other dailies. The situation is even worse in the other major media. Three companies own a majority of the nation's magazines and six own a majority of its book publishers. Three companies own a majority of television stations; four own a majority of movie studios. Control over the images that Americans see each day, the images that provide them with much of their basic stock of concepts, is concentrated in the hands of just a few national corporations.[63]

Things are much the same in the world of commerce. By the mid-1970s, fifteen thousand shopping centers had been built, accounting for nearly half of the nation's retail sales. Nearly a third of this amount was taken in by eight hundred large regional malls.[64] Surely one of the most familiar sights across America

62. Baker, "Media Concentration," 841 n.7.
63. Bagdikian, *The Media Monopoly*, 4, 18, 22, 189.
64. Frieden and Sagalyn, *Downtown, Inc.*, 69.

today is a mall containing the usual lineup of national chain stores: The Gap, The Limited, Victoria's Secret, Banana Republic, and the like. The mall has become not only a powerful economic engine, but "a national common denominator, an experience few could not relate to."[65] If local customs, beliefs, and ways of life are somehow embodied or reflected in the goods produced, sold, and consumed in a place, then it is clear that local variations across the nation are being flattened by a single consumer culture of national scale. As the journalist Peter Applebome wrote: "No one who compares the segregated, largely rural South of just three decades ago and the strip-malled South of Tex-Mex chains, bagel shops, and designer coffee kiosks today could fail to see that the South now is part of a national commercial culture in a way that it never was in the past."[66]

TRACES OF HISTORICAL DIFFERENCE?
THE ANTEBELLUM AND CONFEDERATE SOUTH

The ease and extensiveness of mobility in contemporary American life, and the uniformity of our communicative and commercial lives, cast grave doubt on the possibility that any meaningful differences in state character and identity survive. Nevertheless, constitutions are neither necessarily nor solely contemporary expressions of the values and character of the polities that live under them; they are also in significant ways backward-looking documents that carry forward to the present arrangements structured in the past by those who lived different lives, in different times. To the extent that contemporary constitutions bear the stamp of previous generations, then, it remains possible that distinctions of character and values that existed previously still demand consideration in the interpretation of extant documents.

Yet even this thinner theory of distinctive state identity is too thin and unconvincing to justify a resort to distinctive state character as a technique for the interpretation of contemporary state constitutions. Consider a single, telling example: the antebellum and Confederate South. This is a region widely believed to have been, and to remain, meaningfully different from the rest of the nation. It is also the only region in American history ever to have become so alienated from the rest of the nation as actually to dissociate itself and attempt to establish a separate nation. Yet an examination of actual southern

65. Id.
66. Applebome, *Dixie Rising*, 15.

constitutions—as opposed to southern propaganda and mythologizing on the subject of difference[67]—reveals not regional distinctiveness, but a historically stable and persistent common constitutional culture of national scope.

Consider, for example, the Constitution of the Confederate States of America (CSA). According to a frequently heard account of southern distinctiveness, secession resulted in large part from the development in the South of constitutionally significant differences of character and values.[68] Moreover, the Confederacy's act of constitutional refounding was intended, on this view, to create a new southern nation more hospitable to those distinctively southern characteristics that caused the South to find continued union with the North unacceptable. It follows that the CSA Constitution, more than any other southern constitution, ought to express the values and aspirations of a distinctive South, brought at last to full national self-consciousness.

The reality, however, is quite different: anyone hoping to find evidence of southern distinctiveness in the CSA Constitution will be sorely disappointed, for it was virtually word-for-word identical to the U.S. Constitution, from which it was quite deliberately copied. As Emory Thomas observed, "Ironically, the most striking feature of the Confederate Constitution was not its Southern orientation. The permanent Constitution prescribed for the Confederacy much the same kind of union which the Southerners had dissolved."[69] Or, as Carl Degler put it,

> what is striking about the Confederacy is how congruent its institutions and political values were with those of the United States. One searches in vain through the Confederate Constitution, for example, for those innovations and changes that would signal the arrival on the world stage of a slaveholders' republic, which repudiated the bourgeois elements characterizing the United States.[70]

Things were no different in the Confederate states themselves. Between 1776 and 1861, the eleven states of the Confederacy framed and ratified a total

67. For a full treatment of the distinctiveness hypothesis as applied to the antebellum and Confederate South, see Gardner, "Southern Character."

68. Surely no one has put this more strongly than Frank Owsley, who argued that "[t]he two sections clashed at every point. . . . What was food for one was poison for the other." Owsley, "The Irrepressible Conflict," 61, 72.

69. Thomas, *The Confederate Nation*, 64.

70. Degler, *Place Over Time*, 99.

of twenty-one constitutions. Yet these constitutions, like the Confederate Constitution, provide little evidence of any kind of southern distinctiveness. Consider, for example, the treatment of slavery. The Georgia Constitutions of 1777 and 1789, the South Carolina Constitution of 1776, and the Virginia Constitution of 1776 make no mention of slavery whatsoever. Constitutions from Louisiana, North Carolina, Tennessee, and Virginia (1830) mention slavery only indirectly, either through the use of a three-fifths clause for purposes of apportionment, as in the U.S. Constitution, or in the limitation of certain rights to freemen. To the extent that southern state constitutions restricted the rights of slaves and free blacks, they did not differ materially from many northern and western state constitutions of the same period. Thus, among non-southern states, the right to vote was restricted to whites or freemen in Connecticut, Delaware, Illinois, Indiana, Iowa, Kansas, Michigan, Ohio, Oregon, Pennsylvania, Vermont, and Wisconsin. Iowa, Kansas, and Michigan barred blacks from holding public office. Illinois, Indiana, and Oregon prohibited blacks from entering the state, and Illinois and Oregon limited due process and equality rights to freemen or whites.

FEDERALISM AND IDENTITY: A BETTER VIEW

I have argued that the polities of the American states are unlikely to comprise distinct peoples with characters and fundamental values that are meaningfully distinct from those of the national polity. It does not follow, however, that any property of the American nation or its people inevitably precludes the emergence of distinctive state polities that hold values fundamentally different from those held by the people of the nation. On the contrary, national and subnational identities so thoroughly depend upon deeply contingent historical and social conditions that any attempt to derive universally applicable principles is bound to fail. The more important point, however, is that something is deeply wrong with a conceptual structure of constitutional analysis that invites such insupportable generalizations.

A relevant difficulty with both the Lockean and Romantic models is that each model deems the polity prior to the state: the state is something that is chosen by, or somehow reflects the nature of, a preexisting group of individuals that already comprises a distinct political entity. Yet this view seems incomplete. Although distinct political groups clearly can and sometimes do act on the political stage by drawing meaningful lines around themselves, the reverse is also possible—lines drawn around some group, even those drawn initially for arbitrary reasons, can in time *become* meaningful through a process in which meaning is attached to them by the inhabitants of the places such lines divide.

In his influential work *Imagined Communities,* Benedict Anderson argues that "Nation-ness" is "the most universally legitimate value in the political life of our time." Yet a nation, he argues, is not something real and tangible that can be scientifically identified and analyzed. Rather, a nation is "an imagined political community." A key element, moreover, in the imagination of nationhood is the property of limitation: nations are imagined as limited because "[n]o nation imagines itself coterminous with mankind."[71]

The imagination of nationhood, Anderson maintains, may be stimulated by the laying down of geographic boundaries, an idea that others have applied to the status of the American states under federalism. In a widely quoted essay, for example, Russell Kirk argued that the boundaries of American states have become meaningful with time:

> [W]hile the highly arbitrary and abstract boundaries of the Western states represent nothing but cartographers' and Congressmen's convenience, still the institution and practice of territorial democracy have given to Montana and Arizona and Kansas, say, some distinct and peculiar character as political territories, by fixing loyalties and forming an enduring structure of political administration. . . . [T]he stabilizing and conservative influence of the pattern of territorial democracy has joined with increase of population and wealth to make sensible political territories of what originally were mere parallelograms of prairie and desert and forest. . . .[72]

On this view, the initially arbitrary boundaries of the western states have been invested with meaning by their inhabitants; the practice of living with boundaries has given them a social reality that they might otherwise have lacked. Indeed, Kirk's argument appears to be that the granting of political power—and in particular the power of meaningful self-governance—to territorially defined administrative units may sometimes be enough to transform a mere collec-

71. Anderson, *Imagined Communities,* 3, 6, 7.
72. Kirk, "The Prospects for Territorial Democracy in America," 42, 43 n.2.

tion of residents into a meaningful polity. The process of living together as a self-governing political unit, in other words, may eventually weld a populace into a polity.[73]

This kind of analysis finds further support in the notion of spurious or manufactured nationalism. Any kind of nationalism, whether Lockean, Romantic, or otherwise, must base itself on some kind of perceived commonality that unites the populace, yet the requisite commonalities rarely exist uniformly across the territory said to constitute the relevant nation. But because nationalism is "first and foremost a state of mind, an act of consciousness,"[74] the lack of actual commonality may not impede the imagination of a nation where the will to imagine one is sufficiently strong: "Since the nation is a self-defined rather than an other-defined grouping, a broadly held conviction concerning the group's singular origin need not and seldom will accord with factual data."[75] But if common cultural elements do not exist, "the nationalist movement may fabricate them."[76] Thus, "[d]ead languages can be revived, traditions invented, quite fictitious pristine purities restored."[77] In other words, a belief in distinctiveness may become self-fulfilling if it is held with sufficient strength. Historian David Potter has put the point well: "If the members of a population are sufficiently persuaded that they have cause to be a unified group, the conviction itself may unify them, and thus may produce the nationalism which it appears to reflect."[78]

These considerations suggest strongly that the standard models of nationalism are too simplistic and unidimensional to capture fully the complex processes by which national or subnational identity may evolve. Indeed, I think it safe to say that the process is so complex and variable that very little can be said in advance concerning the conditions that are or are not favorable to the coalescence of a meaningful group political identity along geographical or any other conventional lines of social division.[79] A better account, it seems to me, must recognize that political identity is a consequence as much as a cause

73. Briffault, "'What About the "Ism"?'" 1344–49.

74. Kohn, *The Idea of Nationalism,* 10.

75. Connor, *Ethnonationalism,* 94.

76. Potter, *The South and the Sectional Conflict,* 51.

77. Gellner, *Nations and Nationalism,* 56. See also Greenfeld, *Nationalism,* 13; Tamir, *Liberal Nationalism,* 64; Hobsbawm and Ranger, *The Invention of Tradition.*

78. Potter, *The South and the Sectional Conflict,* 53.

79. Miller, *Citizenship and National Identity,* 34 and ch. 8; Yack, "The Myth of the Civic Nation," 202; Levy, *The Multiculturalism of Fear,* ch. 3

of a group's always contingent self-understanding. A highly useful concept in contemplating this relationship is the notion that group identity is constituted, at least in part, by shared social narratives. According to a view often associated with communitarianism, "man is in his actions and practice, as well as in his fictions, essentially a story-telling animal."[80] In telling these stories to one another, groups of individuals become "interpretive communities . . . that produce meanings."[81] The narratives that a group tells about itself to express its own self-understanding, and the interpretations and meanings that it thereby produces, provide individual members of the group with a stock of concepts and characters to help explain their present situation. It is these influences that situate group members by shaping the ways in which they perceive the world. A community is thus, on the most basic level, "a group of people who tell a shared story in a shared language."[82] The community, that is to say, "talks itself into a historical identity."[83]

The content of the stories that groups tell to and about themselves, however, is never static. Narratives may at any time be rethought, revised, or even replaced by ones more congenial to the group's evolving collective self-understanding. Moreover, group narratives often reflect events in the real world outside the group's control that affect the group's position in the world and furnish it with raw material to be woven into a comprehensible narrative. This combination of changing external circumstances and constant internal narrative revision means that social narratives, and the communal self-understandings they reflect, are always to some extent in flux, always evolving and unfolding. In Robert Cover's description of this process, "the narratives that create and reveal the patterns of commitment, resistance, and understanding—patterns that constitute the dynamic between precept and material universe—are radically uncontrolled. They are subject to no formal hierarchical ordering, no centralized, authoritative provenance, no necessary pattern of acquiescence."[84] It follows from this view that any large, pluralistic society is likely to be comprised of a complicated web of subgroups, each generating its own constantly evolving understandings of its own identity, of the identity of other subgroups and the larger society, and of the relationships among

80. MacIntyre, *After Virtue,* 216.
81. Fish, *Is There a Text in This Class?* 14.
82. White, *Heracles' Bow,* 172.
83. Kahn, "Community in Contemporary Constitutional Theory," 3.
84. Cover, "Foreword: *Nomos* and Narrative," 17.

them. This process, moreover, is ultimately one that cannot be controlled or constrained by the beliefs and understandings of anyone outside the individual groups themselves.

This more nuanced view seems to me to provide a more complete and ultimately more satisfying account of the relationship between political geography and community under federalism than the models discussed earlier. Federalism establishes the nation, the states, and the boundaries that divide them, boundaries not only of geography, but of power. Because federalism is decreed by the Constitution, a shared social text that plays an integral role in constituting and unifying American society,[85] and because the precepts of federalism are enforced authoritatively by the federal judiciary, federalism's formal features are external social facts of which no American subgroup can easily refuse to take note. Nevertheless, the *interpretation* of federalism is a far more open-ended and unpredictable process. Federalism invites us to think of states as meaningful political subcommunities of internal integrity and cohesiveness. Nothing, however, requires any group—even the groups in theory defined by state boundaries—to accept this invitation. Whether the people on one side of a state boundary ultimately come to understand themselves as meaningfully different from the people on the other side of the boundary depends on a wide variety of factors—indeed, on all the many factors capable of influencing any group's narrative understanding of itself, which is to say its understanding of its purpose, origin, membership, longevity, powers, coherence, and many other characteristics.[86]

A group's self-understanding, moreover, need not be, and probably never will be, univocal. Its identity is much more likely to be complex and multilayered—it might think of itself in one way for one purpose and in another way for a different purpose. Thus, it is perfectly conceivable that the people of a state might think of themselves as an organic, meaningfully distinct society for some particular purpose, but as part of an undifferentiated society of Americans for other purposes. For example, the people of North Carolina might think of themselves as meaningfully distinct from the people of Vermont for many cultural purposes—in terms of the kinds of family life they lead, for example, or in terms of the role that food plays in some of their valued customs. Yet they might at the same time think of themselves as fundamentally the

85. See, e.g., Kammen, *A Machine That Would Go of Itself.*
86. MacIntyre, *After Virtue,* ch. 15; Taylor, *Sources of the Self.*

same in terms of their political or moral values, and thus, potentially, for purposes of making and interpreting their state constitutions.

It seems certain that at various times in our history, particularly during the founding period, Americans identified more strongly with their state governments than they did with the national government.[87] During those periods, state boundaries may have loomed larger in the self-understandings of Americans than did the boundaries of the nation, and state constitution-making during those periods sometimes seems to display the kind of deliberation and social self-identification that we associate with a genuinely constitutive societal politics.[88] Today, however, easy mobility, concentrated ownership of media and commercial enterprises, and other factors discussed earlier may provide grounds for skepticism about the present salience of state identity. A state's borders probably delineate more of a populace than a people for most significant political purposes. Yet nothing prevents the focus of American identity from shifting back to the states; federalism contemplates and functions effectively in either situation. Even so, state constitutional interpretation, if it is to be persuasive, should always rest on a contextually plausible account of state identity that comports with socially and empirically sustainable descriptions of contemporary American life. Under present social and historical circumstances, Romantic subnationalism simply does not satisfy this requirement and thus cannot sustain a plausible methodology of state constitutional interpretation. For that, we must look elsewhere.

---

87. Wood, "Foreword: State Constitution-Making in the American Revolution."
88. See Pope, "An Approach to State Constitutional Interpretation."

| 3 |

The Mechanics of Federalism

IN THE PRECEDING CHAPTERS, I hope to have demonstrated that things in the field of state constitutional law stand more or less as follows. State constitutions pose certain interpretational puzzles that lack counterparts in the interpretation of the U.S. Constitution, and for which the conventions of federal constitutional interpretation fail to provide satisfying solutions. The leading theoretical prescriptions directed specifically to the problems of state constitutional interpretation rest on questionable assumptions about the nature of states and state polities; tend, when followed, to drive state courts toward an unsatisfying jurisprudence of Romantic subnationalism; and are, in any event, routinely flouted by states courts in the day-to-day practice of state constitutional adjudication. State constitutional interpretation, in other words, seems to have lost its way.

In circumstances such as these, it is often useful to return to basics, and that is what I propose to do here. The starting point to which I return, however, is not the usual point of reference—existing practices of constitutional interpretation—but the constitutional structure of federalism. This, as I argue in the balance of the book, has been the missing ingredient in developing a satisfying solution to the problems of state constitutional interpretation. In arguing that federalism plays a critical role in establishing the functions, and thus guiding the interpretation, of state constitutions, I do not mean to suggest that anything so dramatic as a complete break with existing techniques of state constitutional interpretation is required. Without doubt, reigning models of federal constitutional interpretation provide much valuable guidance for the interpretation of state constitutions, as do efforts by proponents of the New Judicial Federalism to adapt those models to the sometimes quite different setting of state constitutional law. What I do mean to suggest, however, is that contemporary understandings of state constitutional interpretation may be improved by reading state constitutions through the lens of federalism. Federalism is, after all, a constitutional mechanism that plays a significant role in structuring the powers and functions of state governments, a fact that cannot help but be reflected in state constitutions, the purpose of which is to grant, restrain, and order the exercise of state power.

Accordingly, in this chapter I examine the federal structure in some detail, paying special attention to the mechanics of how federalism operates in actual practice. In so doing, I shall take as my starting point the conventional, Madisonian account of federalism as a constitutional structure designed to divide power for the overriding purpose of protecting liberty.

THE BASIC PRINCIPLE

"The accumulation of all powers . . . in the same hands," wrote Madison, "may justly be pronounced the very definition of tyranny."[1] To protect liberty, then, power must be divided. Federalism serves this guiding principle of American constitutional design by parceling out government powers among different levels of government, and by giving each level of government, state and national, substantial powers sufficient to allow each to monitor and check the abuses of the other. As with the horizontal separation of powers, which divides governmental power into legislative, executive, and judicial branches, each piece of government in this fragmented system is given the power and incentive to struggle against the others: "[a]mbition," as Madison put it, "must be made to counteract ambition."[2] The result is a compound federal republic in which power is deeply fragmented, reducing as far as possible by structural means the likelihood that a tyrannical measure of power can be accumulated in a single set of hands:

> In a single republic, all the power surrendered by the people is submitted to the administration of a single government; and the usurpations are guarded against by a division of the government into distinct and separate departments. In the compound republic of America, the power surrendered by the people is first divided between two distinct governments, and then the portion allotted to each

1. Madison, *The Federalist*, No. 47, 301.
2. Madison, *The Federalist*, No. 51, 322.

subdivided among distinct and separate departments. Hence a double security arises to the rights of the people. The different governments will control each other, at the same time that each will be controlled by itself.[3]

The multiplicity of power centers in the American scheme can create the impression that the system is chaotic—a pure, Hobbesian war of all against all without any purpose other than the accumulation of power. This is not the case, or at least need not be. What unifies the dispersion of governmental power, in the Framers' view, is the people, for the entire system is designed to ensure as far as possible that their wishes will be done and their liberties left intact. "The federal and State governments," Madison observed, "are in fact but different agents and trustees of the people, constituted with different powers and designed for different purposes."[4] Federalism is thus more than a passive institutionalization of social conflict. It is a dynamic system designed to be manipulated by the people to produce results they desire. Hamilton put this point clearly:

> [I]n a confederacy the people, without exaggeration, may be said to be entirely the masters of their own fate. Power being almost always the rival of power, the general government will at times stand ready to check the usurpations of the state governments, and these will have the same disposition towards the general government. The people, by throwing themselves into the scale, will infallibly make it preponderate. If their rights are invaded by either, they can make use of the other as the instrument of redress.[5]

The Framers thus expressly contemplated that popular allegiance to any government would not be fixed organically, but would ebb and flow according to that government's instrumental value to the populace at any given time. Each level of government would be given sufficient power to check any tyran-

---

3. Id. at 323.

4. Madison, *The Federalist*, No. 46, 294.

5. Madison, *The Federalist*, No. 28 (Hamilton), 180–81. See also *The Federalist*, No. 46 (Madison), 295, in which Madison, after remarking that Americans place their faith and trust primarily in their state governments, observed: "If . . . the people should in future become more partial to the federal than to the State governments, the change can only result from such manifest and irresistible proofs of a better administration as will overcome all their antecedent propensities. And in that case, the people ought not surely to be precluded from giving most of their confidence where they may discover it to be most due . . . ."

nical tendencies of the other, but when and whether to activate this checking power would be up to the people. The "double security" of which Madison spoke, then, does not arise so much from some complicated scheme of complementary powers, as is so often supposed, but from a conceptually much simpler arrangement in which the state and national governments independently police much of the same turf. To protect that turf, the people make use of whichever level of government is more capable and accommodating at any particular moment.[6]

Historically, federalism seems to have worked in much the way that the Framers anticipated. In the early days of the republic, the people identified far more strongly with their states than with the nation and looked predominantly to the states when government power was needed. The Civil War disrupted this pattern by enhancing national power and prestige throughout the North and among blacks and white unionists in the South, while driving most white southerners to even greater levels of distrust of national power. Trust in state governments enjoyed a resurgence during the late nineteenth century, particularly after public opinion turned against the northern occupation of the South and the union programs of Reconstruction. The Progressive reform movement of the early twentieth century, followed quickly by the Great Depression, two world wars, and the civil rights movement, set the nation on a path in which national power was typically far more respected and trusted than state power. By the 1980s, however, resentments against national power seemed to arise once again. Today, we may well live in an age when the American people are as close to true indifference between national and state power as they have ever been, and are willing to contemplate the exercise of power by either level of government depending upon which can more persuasively make the case that it can do the better job.[7]

6. Amar, "Of Sovereignty and Federalism"; Landau, *Federalism, Redundancy and System Reliability;* Amar, "Some New World Lessons for the Old World"; Dye, *American Federalism,* 6; Pettys, "Competing for the People's Affection."

7. Wood, "Foreword: State Constitution-Making in the American Revolution"; Foner, *Reconstruction,* 24, 582; Kramer, "Understanding Federalism," 1557–58; McDonald, *States' Rights and the Union,* 208–21; Urofsky and Finkelman, *A March of Liberty,* 1:477; Whittington, "Dismantling the Modern State?" 489–522. The events of September 11, 2001 may have changed the balance once again, shifting the focus of trust to the national government. See Nienstedt, "Social Values Emerging from the Rubble of Sept. 11"; Lightman, "Poll Tracks National Growth in Trust"; Greenhouse, "Will the Court Reassert National Authority?"

HOW FEDERALISM WORKS IN PRACTICE

State power is a vital element in federalism's design. To put the exercise of state power in context, however, I begin by examining the ways in which federalism contemplates that national power may be deployed to protect liberty. In conducting this analysis, I use the term "liberty" in a broader sense than did the founding generation, which spoke an eighteenth-century language of "liberty" and "tyranny" that does not fully capture contemporary understandings of the justifications for popular sovereignty. Even today, the concept of "liberty" is often equated with the restraint of government power—the kind of "negative" liberty that Isaiah Berlin defined as freedom from government interference with private decisionmaking.[8] While this understanding of liberty captures much of what federalism operates to protect, it is incomplete. If private decisionmaking were the sine qua non of collective life, no government would be necessary whose powers would then require restraint. Government is created and granted powers in the first instance for the purpose of helping citizens achieve some kind of good life, a good life they are by hypothesis incapable of achieving on their own, either individually or collectively in the absence of governmental organization. To fulfill this function, government needs affirmative powers, not merely restraints on those powers. Thus, although federalism contemplates the division of power to protect "liberty," I treat this conventional use of the word as a kind of synecdoche that names only one part of the broader notion of achieving, or creating, the conditions that enable citizens to obtain a substantively desirable way of life. Consequently, I use the term "liberty" interchangeably with the broader terms "public welfare" or "public good."

How the National Government Protects Liberty

Under this broad definition of liberty, the national government of the United States contributes to and protects the liberty, or public welfare, of American citizens in at least three distinct ways: (1) by using its affirmative powers in pursuit of the good,[9] (2) by internal self-restraint, and (3) by restraining state governments from impairing the ability of citizens to achieve the good.

8. Berlin, "Two Concepts of Liberty."

9. I would include in this category maintenance of physical order, see U.S. Const. preamble, although that function might also be viewed as a precondition for the existence of liberty in any social setting.

First and foremost, the national government protects the public welfare by using its affirmatively granted powers for the good of the citizenry. This conception of governmental power is broad enough to embrace any conception of the state, from a minimalist, night-watchman state to the contemporary European-style social welfare state. Whatever version of the state a society chooses to adopt, a government must exist and must possess certain powers that enable the polity collectively to achieve the goals it sets for itself. Under the U.S. Constitution, the national government has many powers that fit this description. The commerce power, spending power, and the various military powers have all been used many times to achieve through direct action by the national government objectives that the American polity has collectively decided will make it better off. The commerce power alone, for example, has given us environmental regulation, social health and welfare programs, most of the administrative state, and even much of our civil rights legislation, to name only a few of its principal uses.

Second, in the American scheme, the national government protects the liberty and welfare of the citizenry by practicing a kind of institutionalized self-restraint. In so doing, government protects the nation's citizens from itself. The U.S. Constitution contains several mechanisms that restrain the ability of the national government to do things that would make society worse off. The horizontal separation of powers, for example, restrains the amount of harm the government can do by dividing power into three branches and pitting those branches against one another, an arrangement that restricts the government's ability to take any action that does not have the broad and overlapping approval of several distinct and important constituencies. The enumeration in the Bill of Rights and elsewhere in the Constitution of specific individual rights further restrains the ability of the government to impair the welfare of the citizenry. An independent judiciary armed with the power of judicial review helps ensure that constitutional restraints are effectively observed.

The third way in which the American national government protects the liberty of its citizens is by using its powers to prevent state governments from impairing the good of the citizenry. To accomplish this purpose, the U.S. government has several tools at its disposal. Bounding the spectrum of available means for restraining state power are two methods that are perhaps best thought of as extraconstitutional. At one extreme, the national government may use force against the states to defend the welfare of its citizens. The Constitution specifically authorizes the national government to use force to defend states,[10] but nothing in the Constitution provides similar authorization for the use of force against them. Nevertheless, the principle that the national government is entitled to enforce its laws against violations and interference has long been taken to support the proposition that the use of force against states may be justified when necessary to enforce federal law.[11] This approach has been invoked on several occasions, including, most notably, the Civil War. In the twentieth century, the armed enforcement of desegregation in Little Rock, Arkansas stands out as a prominent example. Although the national government has seldom used force against a state government, the threat of it surely lurks meaningfully in the background as a reason for states to avoid persistent violations of or interference with national law.

At the other end of the spectrum lies the entirely peaceful method of ordinary political negotiation. Through political contacts and negotiation, national officials can attempt to persuade or induce state officials to act in desirable ways. Negotiation may involve anything from the simple communication of pertinent information, to persuasion and argument, to dealmaking in which each party seeks its own advantage.

Between the extraconstitutional extremes of force and talk, the national government has at its disposal at least three methods of influencing state behavior provided directly by the U.S. Constitution. First and least intrusively, the national government can use its spending power to offer states financial rewards for engaging in behavior that the national government wishes to induce, or for refraining from behavior that it wishes to discourage.[12] For example, Congress has on numerous occasions utilized the system of federal highway funding to induce states to enact legislation that Congress thought desirable by conditioning the distribution of federal funds on the enactment of the desired legislation. These conditions have included adjusting the state speed limit to conform to national guidelines, raising the state drinking age to twenty-one, requiring drivers to wear seat belts, and lowering the blood alcohol level required for a drunk driving conviction under state law.

A second and considerably more intrusive mechanism for restraining state power is the displacement of state law through the national power of preemp-

---

10. U.S. Const. art. IV, § 4 ("The United States shall . . . protect each [state] against Invasion; and on Application of the Legislature, or of the Executive (when the Legislature cannot be convened) against domestic Violence.").

11. See, e.g., The Prize Cases, 67 U.S. 635 (1863); Cooper v. Aaron, 358 U.S. 1 (1958).

12. Derthick, *The Influence of Federal Grants*.

tion. Under the Supremacy Clause, valid national legislation automatically displaces and invalidates inconsistent state law, from the lowliest administrative regulation up to the most exalted provision of the state constitution. The power to preempt state law allows Congress not only to enact at the national level legislation that it believes promotes the public good, but simultaneously to invalidate state laws and programs that, in the opinion of Congress, either are downright harmful to the public good, or do not promote it as efficaciously as the national program.

Yet another mechanism by which the national government may restrain states from using their powers in harmful ways is judicial invalidation of state law under the national Constitution. By invoking the power of judicial review, national courts may strike down state laws or invalidate state actions that violate provisions of the U.S. Constitution that apply to the states, and may issue orders forbidding state officials from repeating such violations in the future. Aside from judicial enforcement of preemptive federal law, the most common circumstance in which national courts strike down state law is when the state law violates some individual right guaranteed against state infringement by the Equal Protection or Due Process Clauses of the Fourteenth Amendment. Thus, state laws or actions infringing nationally guaranteed freedoms of speech or religion, or discriminating on the basis of race or gender, or violating restrictions governing the investigation, arrest, detention, or trial of criminal suspects, for example, have on numerous occasions been invalidated by federal courts charged with enforcing national constitutional rights against the states. In a well-known remark, Justice Holmes claimed that this kind of judicial review is of the utmost importance to the proper working of the federal scheme: "I do not think the United States would come to an end if we lost our power to declare an Act of Congress void. I do think the Union would be imperiled if we could not make that declaration as to the laws of the several States."[13]

How State Governments Protect Liberty

In the American federal system, state governments protect the liberty of the citizenry in much the same way as does the national government, although of course the influence of any individual state will be felt for the most part only within its own geographical territory and predominantly by its own citizens. Like the national government, state governments possess significant powers that they can use affirmatively in pursuit of the public good. Indeed, the scope

13. Holmes, *Collected Legal Papers,* 295.

of state power tends to be (although it need not be) broader than the scope of national power, reaching many areas of ordinary life that the national government is usually understood to lack the power to regulate. For example, state law overwhelmingly provides the controlling substantive rules in the laws of tort, contract, commercial transactions, crimes, property, wills, and family formation. Although the national government has made limited forays into all of these areas, they are most often understood to be beyond the power of the national government to regulate to any great degree. States thus have extensive resources to achieve or promote the public good directly through the exercise of affirmatively granted powers.

Similarly, state governments, like the national government, protect the liberty of their citizens by exercising a constitutionally imposed self-restraint in which the state government protects its own citizens from itself. Like the national government, every state government is constituted so as to divide governmental powers horizontally. Every state has its own bill of rights. Every state has an independent judicial branch authorized to enforce against the other branches those provisions of the state constitution that limit state power. These restrictions are designed to make the state government less dangerous to its own people.

Finally, in a mirror image of the national function, state governments protect liberty by restraining the national government from undertaking actions that, in the opinion of the officials or the polity of the state, are harmful to the public good as the people of the state understand it. The symmetry between national and state roles in this federal function, however, is limited. Unlike the national government, which has numerous directly authorized legal means at its disposal for checking abusive exercises of state power, state governments, because they are subject to the Supremacy Clause, have fewer obviously legal avenues of redress to check or impede exercises of national power that they consider detrimental to the welfare of the nation.

Illegal and quasi-legal means for checking national power. Like the national government, state governments have at their disposal certain illegal, or at least extraconstitutional, methods for checking abusive exercises of federal power. The most potent of these options is the use of force, and the most dramatic use of state force to resist national power is undoubtedly the act of secession. While the threat of state secession has not played a significant role in American politics since the Civil War, it has played an extremely potent role in many federal nations around the globe in the last few decades, including places such as Canada, the former Yugoslavia, and the former Soviet Union. The contemporary relevance of secession in global politics, often accompanied by extreme violence, suggests that its lack of relevance here ought to be treated more as a fortunate historical contingency than as evidence that secession is structurally irrelevant to American intergovernmental relations.[14]

The use of force is not, of course, limited to outright secession: states may employ force by threatening or engaging in limited armed resistance short of secession. Although it occurred against a backdrop of threatened secession, the Nullification Crisis may serve as an example of this more limited kind of resort to force.[15] In 1832, the national government enacted a protectionist tariff that many southerners felt benefited northern industrial interests at the expense of the southern economic interest in agricultural exports. The tariff caused an especially strong political reaction in South Carolina. Among the many steps South Carolina took to resist the imposition of the tariff was the mustering of a small army, which state officials threatened to deploy to block any effort by national customs officials to collect the tariff in the port of Charleston. The U.S. government responded by preparing for possible military action to enforce the tariff law. The threat of violence was eventually defused when the national government took careful steps to avoid any outright provocation, and South Carolina ultimately backed down from its threat to use force. Nevertheless, shortly after resolution of the crisis, Congress in 1834 enacted the Compromise Tariff, which phased out over a period of nine years the provisions to which South Carolinians objected. While South Carolina was not able to obtain precisely what it wanted, as quickly as it wanted, its threatened use of force clearly influenced the content of national law.

A more recent example of a state's threatened use of force is the 1957 saber-rattling of Arkansas in response to national efforts to implement a federal judicial order requiring the desegregation of Central High School in Little Rock, the state capital. Arkansas governor Orval Faubus, vowing to resist federal enforcement of the desegregation order, deployed the National Guard at the school to forcibly prevent the black students from entering the building. As a

---

14. One fortuitous factor that may account for the relative peacefulness of contemporary American federalism is the lack of a genuine homegrown ethnic nationalism. American nationalism tends to be ideological and inclusive rather than ethnic and exclusive. See, e.g., Greenfeld, *Nationalism*, 405–20, 422–23; Kohn, *The Idea of Nationalism*, 8–9; Connor, *Ethnonationalism*, 95.

15. The account here follows Freehling, *Prelude to Civil War*.

confrontation brewed, the governor withdrew the troops, leaving the students to face a white mob. President Eisenhower then sent in one thousand troops from the 101st Airborne Division, a regular U.S. military unit, to enforce the court order and keep the peace.[16] As in the Nullification Crisis, a direct, armed conflict between state and national military forces never materialized, although the threat of such a conflict was taken seriously by all sides.

Even more recently, states have threatened physical confrontation with the national government over issues of environmental policy. Prompted largely by national legislation that restricted grazing on public lands, legislatures in several western states contemplated legislation in the late 1970s and early 1980s that would have declared nationally owned lands to be the property of the states in which the land was located. In 1979, Nevada went so far as to enact legislation "declaring state sovereignty over 49 million acres of Nevada territory" owned by the national government and managed by the Bureau of Land Management.[17] Although this so-called Sagebrush Rebellion never led to organized violence against the national government by any state, a more serious incident occurred in 1988 when Idaho governor Cecil Andrus deployed state police to seize at the state border a railway shipment of radioactive waste generated at a federal nuclear facility in Colorado. Andrus had the shipment seized pursuant to a state-declared policy of refusing to accept additional nuclear waste from out of state. In 2002, the governor of South Carolina made a similar threat to block at the border trucks containing weapons-grade plutonium destined for a federal storage site in the state.

States determined to defy national law need not, of course, do so through violence or the threat of violence. Defiance can be accomplished by more peaceful means and, indeed, examples of such peaceful illegal defiance are as abundant as examples of the violent variety are rare. Once again, state resistance to national policies concerning black Americans furnishes numerous instances. During the 1850s, for example, some northern states defied the federal Fugitive Slave Act by refusing to hand over escaped slaves to federal officials and, indeed, imprisoning U.S. commissioners authorized by the Act to return fugitive slaves to their owners.[18] Half a century later, some southern states defied the Fifteenth Amendment's prohibition on denying the right to vote on account of race by

16. Branch, *Parting the Waters,* 222–24.

17. Gates, *Pressure Groups and Recent American Land Policies,* 3. See also "'Sagebrush Rebels' Are Reveling in Reagan."

18. See Cover, *Justice Accused.*

adopting constitutional amendments that disenfranchised black citizens, and by engaging in numerous tactics designed to avoid registering black voters.

There is little question but that the Framers of the U.S. Constitution contemplated and fully expected that states would express their disapproval of what they thought to be harmful national policies through precisely this kind of outright defiance of national law, including resorting to threats of force, to impede its implementation. This was, after all, the model of decentralized resistance to tyrannical central power that the Framers knew best—the model of the Revolution itself. Madison, for example, acknowledged this directly:

> [S]hould an unwarrantable measure of the federal government be unpopular in particular States, which would seldom fail to be the case, or even a warrantable measure be so, which may sometimes be the case, the means of opposition to it are powerful and at hand. The disquietude of the people; their repugnance and, perhaps, refusal to co-operate with the officers of the Union; the frowns of the executive magistracy of the State; the embarrassments created by legislative devices, which would often be added on such occasions, would oppose, in any State, difficulties not to be despised; would form, in a large State, very serious impediments; and where the sentiments of several adjoining States happened to be in unison, would present obstructions which the federal government would hardly be willing to encounter.[19]

Madison was reluctant to paint a picture of state resistance to national power that crossed the line from mere denunciation and uncooperative defiance to violence.[20] Hamilton, characteristically, was not so squeamish:

> It may safely be received as an axiom in our political system that the State governments will, in all possible contingencies, afford complete security against invasions of the public liberty by the national authority. Projects of usurpation cannot be masked under pretences so likely to escape the penetration of select bodies of men, as of the people at large. The legislatures will have better means of information. They can discover the danger at a distance; and possessing all the organs

---

19. Madison, *The Federalist*, No. 46, 297–98.

20. Later in No. 46, Madison goes so far as to compare the size of armed forces that could be raised by the state and national governments, but he clearly thought that loud public criticism of the national government would generally suffice, as evidenced by his authorship of the Virginia Resolution, in which he criticized the Alien and Sedition Acts of 1798 and pronounced them unconstitutional.

of civil power and the confidence of the people, they can at once adopt a regular plan of opposition, in which they can combine all the resources of the community. They can readily communicate with each other in the different States, and unite their common forces for the protection of their common liberty. . . . If the federal army should be able to quell the resistance in one State, the distant States would be able to make head with fresh forces. The advantages obtained in one place must be abandoned to subdue the opposition in others; and the moment the part which had been reduced to submission was left to itself, its efforts would be renewed, and its resistance revive.[21]

In addition to these outright illegal means of resisting national power, states also have at their disposal a number of what might be termed "quasi-legal" strategies for thwarting uses of national power that they consider inimical to the public good. One such strategy is a deliberate failure fully to comply with or to enforce binding federal law. Here the state does not defy national law, but nevertheless attempts, in the guise of implementing it, to undermine it by halfhearted or inappropriate measures. For example, in 1975, as part of an energy policy designed to conserve oil, Congress lowered the speed limit on all roads to fifty-five miles per hour. Most states responded by complying, and issued speeding tickets as usual to drivers who exceeded the new speed limit, levying their usual fines for violations. Montana, however, complied in an extremely halfhearted way. Instead of enforcing violations of the nationally mandated speed limit as traffic infractions, it issued five-dollar "environmental" citations to drivers traveling above fifty-five miles per hour, but below what Montana police considered a safe speed. Violations were not charged against drivers' insurance records. This kind of "enforcement" worked to undermine the congressional objective since it both declared quite plainly the state's continuing opposition to the national policy, and all but invited the public to exceed the national speed limit with impunity within the borders of the state—an invitation that drivers, predictably, took up with enthusiasm.

A similar kind of state response is to engage in deliberate foot-dragging on national initiatives that require the cooperation of state officials. A good example of this process is the continuing failure of states to comply with federal environmental laws requiring states to address the problem of "nonpoint source" water pollution. The federal Clean Water Act divides the sources of water pollution into two types: point sources and nonpoint sources. A point

21. Madison, *The Federalist,* No. 28 (Hamilton), 181.

source is a discrete and identifiable "conveyance" that discharges pollutants into the water, such as a drainpipe, ditch, or seagoing vessel.[22] Nonpoint source pollution, in contrast, refers to pollutants that enter waters from widely diffused or not clearly identifiable sources, typically as the result of rainfall runoff, snowmelt, or agricultural irrigation. Of the two, nonpoint source pollution is by far the more serious problem nationally for water quality.

In the Clean Water Act, Congress decided to leave the problem of nonpoint source pollution to the states, requiring the governor of each state to "prepare and submit to the [federal Environmental Protection Agency] for approval a management program which such State proposes to implement . . . for controlling pollution added from nonpoint sources to the navigable waters within the State and improving the quality of such waters."[23] State cooperation with the Clean Water Act's nonpoint source management program has been inconsistent at best. A summary report prepared by EPA in 1992 found, for example, that few states had included in their management plans programs addressing nonpoint source pollution of wetlands.[24] Several states had failed altogether to develop satisfactory plans long after the initial congressional deadline passed. Others complained that full compliance was impossible until EPA provided better empirical monitoring data. In the years following enactment of Section 319, some state governments evidently devoted more energy to finding ways to avoid implementing the Act's mandate than they devoted to compliance. As a result, little substantive progress has been made nationally in dealing with the environmental hazards of polluted runoff.

States have sometimes engaged in foot-dragging even when the consequences are more immediate and acute than some prospect of future environmental harm. The federal Brady Bill requires that firearms sales be conducted subject to a mandatory instant background check in which the seller consults a computerized database maintained by the FBI. The database lists people who are ineligible to buy a gun, including fugitives, convicted felons, and those involuntary committed to mental hospitals. Although the FBI maintains the database, it acquires the relevant information from the states; if states do not cooperate by supplying accurate and up-to-date information, guns may be sold to people barred by federal law from possessing them. In a few recent cases, people legally ineligible to own a gun due to a mental disability have never-

22. Federal Water Pollution Control Act (Clean Water Act), 33 U.S.C. § 1362(14).
23. Clean Water Act § 319(b)(1), 33 U.S.C. § 1329(b)(1).
24. U.S. Environmental Protection Agency, *Managing Nonpoint Source Pollution,* 32.

theless managed to buy one and use it to commit murder. The reason they were able to buy the guns, it turns out, is that their names did not appear in the FBI database. Their states had failed to supply the FBI with the names of those who had been involuntarily committed. In many instances, state officials have withheld this information because state laws aimed at protecting the privacy of the mentally ill forbid the necessary disclosures. State legislatures, caught between two important public policies, have been slow to address the problem.

Madison predicted in *The Federalist* that the national government would require the assistance and cooperation of the states to accomplish its more ambitious goals.[25] Environmental regulation and gun control seem to be areas in which Madison has been proved correct. In consequence, the refusal of states to provide the needed cooperation can be an effective means of thwarting the national government's achievement of its objectives. Where such cooperation is withheld because of a state's belief that the program for which state cooperation is sought is an abuse of national power, withholding cooperation is also a way for states to protect the welfare of the nation's citizens.

Legal means for checking national power. In addition to these illegal and quasi-legal methods, states have at least five fully legal avenues of recourse to thwart exercises of national power: (1) the use of political pressure, (2) the exercise of ordinary state power where it is not preempted, (3) refusal of national financial incentives, (4) lawsuits against the national government in federal court, and (5) setting higher standards of state conduct by granting more generous constitutional or statutory rights. This last method has received by far the greatest amount of attention in writings on state constitutional law, but it has not been heretofore understood functionally as an additional method by which states may resist abuses of national power. Before turning to this conception of state expansion of constitutionalized individual rights, however, it is useful to put this tool in context by exploring the first four methods listed above.

Much has been written about the ways in which the states may influence national legislation through political means.[26] State officials often have the capacity, for example, to press the state's congressional delegation to work for the enactment at the national level of policies favored by the state. For a decade, this view of state influence induced the U.S. Supreme Court to abandon any at-

25. Madison, *The Federalist,* No. 45.

26. Among the classic works are Wechsler, "The Political Safeguards of Federalism," and Choper, *Judicial Review and the National Political Process.*

tempt to enforce constitutional limits on the national commerce power, a position from which it has since backed away.[27] In an important recent study, Larry Kramer has suggested that political negotiation coordinated under the auspices of the national political parties has evolved into the single most important mechanism by which states influence the behavior of national officials.[28] Through such means, state officials may head off legislation of which they disapprove before it is enacted, or obtain modifications of proposed national policies that eliminate or moderate provisions to which state officials object.

Another way states may check what they perceive to be federal abuses is by using their ordinary, affirmative powers when not preempted from doing so. Power can be misused not only when it is used affirmatively for unjust ends, but also when it is withheld in circumstances that either perpetuate an unjust status quo or passively permit some individuals to behave unjustly toward others. When national power is invoked affirmatively in abusive ways, it nonetheless preempts contrary exercises of state power. In contrast, when national power is abusively withheld rather than invoked, states are often free to take corrective action. For example, state legislatures may use their affirmative powers to create state-level programs to address wrongs that the national government refuses to redress. State legislatures and courts may also create liability rules that allow individuals who are victimized by unjust private behavior to obtain injunctions against such behavior or to recover compensation for the harms it causes. Individual states may even coordinate informally with other states to create regional coalitions dedicated to correcting national omissions that rise to the level of abuses of national power.

Even where the national government has exercised its power affirmatively, however, states often are not deprived entirely of the means to ameliorate what they perceive to be negative influences of that power on the state's citizenry. As the Framers anticipated, the successful invocation of national power sometimes requires the cooperation of state officials. In recognition of this requirement of intergovernmental cooperation, Congress has frequently structured national programs so as to delegate to state officials a crucial role in the implementation and enforcement of the programs. All of the largest and most costly nonmilitary domestic national programs—social security, welfare, food

27. Compare Garcia v. San Antonio Metropolitan Transp. Auth., 469 U.S. 528 (1985), with New York v. United States, 505 U.S. 144 (1992), and Printz v. United States, 521 U.S. 898 (1997). See also United States v. Lopez, 514 U.S. 549 (1995).

28. Kramer, "Putting the Politics Back into the Political Safeguards of Federalism."

stamps, and so on—delegate much of the responsibility for the day-to-day operation of the programs to the states. State responsibility for running these programs may include setting eligibility requirements, determining benefit levels, or enforcing compliance with programmatic requirements, functions that require the exercise of a significant amount of official discretion.[29]

When the national government grants states this kind of significant responsibility for implementing national initiatives, it often does so by establishing parameters that define the outer boundaries of state discretion. Nevertheless, within these boundaries, state officials often have room to bend their implementation of national policy in ways that also serve state interests, even when those interests are opposed to successful implementation of the national program.[30] For example, if state officials believe a national program is contrary to the public good, they might set eligibility requirements as restrictively as possible so as to minimize the scope and impact of the program.[31]

29. See generally Bardach, *The Implementation Game.* Bardach calls policy implementation "the continuation of politics by other means." Id. at 85.

30. According to one study, "Washington has had, and continues to have, tremendous difficulty in executing even relatively straightforward policies precisely because state and local governments enjoy such wide latitude in deciding how best to translate federal policies into action, or whether, in fact, to follow federal policies at all. The empirical evidence on this point is simply overwhelming." DiIulio and Kettl, *Fine Print,* 18. See also Nugent, "State Implementation of Federal Policy as a Political Safeguard of Federalism," 6. But see Keiser, "Street-level Bureaucrats," 145 ("it is an unresolved empirical question whether state governments are indeed able to manipulate policy implementation to enhance their interests"); Schneider, "Governors and Health Care Policy in the American States" (arguing that governors' ability to influence state implementation of federal policy is more apparent than real).

31. For example, states have utilized their discretion to raise obstacles to siting federally subsidized low-income housing. See James v. Valtierra, 402 U.S. 137 (1971); Derthick, *New Towns In-Town.* In exercising their discretion to set eligibility requirements for federal welfare programs, midwestern and southern states "took a harder line [than federal parameters required], reflecting a tougher work ethic." Mead, *The New Politics of Poverty,* 191. About half the states have exercised federally delegated discretion to exclude from the federal food stamp program persons convicted of a drug felony. Schwartz, "A Prohibition That Frustrates the People's Will." Presently, there is mounting evidence that states are attempting to blunt the impact of the federal No Child Left Behind Act, which uses the spending power to impose regulations on school performance, by relaxing testing standards and by tinkering with the definition of what constitutes a failing school under the program. See, e.g., Dillon, "States Are Relaxing Standards on Tests to Avoid Sanctions."

Conversely, if they believe some national program is insufficient in scale to combat effectively some unjust feature of the status quo, and they are pre-empted from developing an independent state program of sufficient magni-tude, they may be able to set eligibility requirements and benefit levels within the national program much more expansively than the national government requires.[32] Thus, states may prevent what they perceive as public harm at the hands of the national government by doing good on the state level.

Sometimes, moreover, whether for political reasons or for the sake of ex-pediency, the national government seeks state cooperation not by delegating power to states in formal legislative programs, but by simply appealing to states voluntarily to cooperate with national initiatives. Here, a state that dis-likes the initiative may thus simply refuse to cooperate. Again, there are indi-cations that states may be willing to withhold cooperation even when the stakes are high. In the weeks immediately following the September 11, 2001 attacks on the World Trade Center and the Pentagon, for instance, the FBI mounted a nationwide effort to interview approximately five thousand young men of Middle Eastern descent. Police in Portland, Oregon refused to cooper-ate with the FBI's interview program on the ground that it amounted to a kind of unjustifiable racial profiling forbidden by Oregon law.[33] Since then, some two dozen cities around the nation have enacted resolutions opposing what they view as invasions of civil liberties by the national government in the pur-suit of terrorism suspects.[34] Although no state has yet passed a similar resolu-tion, these actions by localities suggest the form that similar resistance on the state level could assume.

Another common situation in which states may resist national power merely by withholding cooperation arises when the national government uses its spending power rather than its commerce power to enact nationwide pro-grams. In these instances, where the national government attempts to induce states to participate in the programs by conditioning financial rewards on state participation and compliance, states may resist abuses of national power by the simple expedient of refusing the financial incentives. Although states much more commonly accept than reject conditioned national funds, states have occasionally sacrificed such funds for the sake of rejecting policies they

32. Derthick, "American Federalism"; Thompson and Scicchitano, "OSHA, the States, and Gresham's Law," 95, 101–2; Beamer, *Creative Politics,* 5, 123–25, 130–31.

33. See Butterfield, "A Police Force Rebuffs F.B.I. on Querying Mideast Men."

34. Janofsky, "Cities Wary of Antiterror Tactics Pass Civil Liberties Resolutions."

viewed as inimical to the public good. New Hampshire, for example, has refused repeatedly to enact a mandatory seatbelt law, thereby forgoing a portion
of its allocation of federal highway maintenance and construction funds. Wisconsin has sacrificed federal highway funds by refusing to lower its statutory
threshold for drunken driving convictions to a blood alcohol level of 0.8 percent, in defiance of federal law requiring the adjustment. Kentucky recently
abolished state vehicle emission standards, threatening its ability to meet
federally mandated pollution limits, which would lead to the loss of nearly $2
billion in federal highway funds.[35]

Yet another way in which states can check abuses of power by the national
legislative and executive branches is by invoking the power of the national judicial branch against them. States have often had success suing the federal
government in federal court over alleged abuses of national authority. In 1992,
for example, New York successfully sued the United States in federal court,
obtaining a ruling invalidating a portion of the federal Low-Level Radioactive
Waste Policy Amendments Act of 1985 on the ground that one of its provisions
exceeded national authority under the Commerce Clause.[36] In subsequent
years, federal courts have at the behest of states or state agencies invalidated
numerous other federal statutes on similar grounds. In each of these cases, a
federal court has held that some piece of national legislation exceeded the
limits of enumerated national powers.

HEIGHTENED PROTECTION OF INDIVIDUAL LIBERTY

As we saw in chapter 1, state constitutions, because they are positive law independent of the U.S. Constitution, may contain protections for individual liberties that exceed the protections provided by the national Constitution. State
constitutions might thus contain provisions protecting individual rights—the
rights of free speech, or privacy, or equal protection, for example, or the rights
to be free from establishments of religion, or from unreasonable searches and
seizures—in ways that go well beyond the protections that the U.S. Constitution provides for these very same liberties. Lawyers, judges, and scholars of
state constitutional law have focused their attention overwhelmingly on this

35. Tibbetts, "Lift Seat-Belt Sanctions"; Rinard, "State Pays for Its 0.10 Standard"; Loftus, "Patton Signs Bill Abolishing Vehicle Emissions Tests."
36. New York v. United States, 505 U.S. 144 (1992).

aspect of state constitutionalism; it is, for example, the main preoccupation of the New Judicial Federalism movement. At the same time, virtually no attention has been paid to the way in which the use of state constitutions to expand the protection of individual rights might fit into the federal system of mutually checking state and national power.

In the framework I have sketched above, it might seem that a state constitutional provision protecting individual liberty ought to be understood solely as a straightforward example of state self-restraint. An individual right protected by a state constitution is enforceable only against the state. It ought to follow, then, that state constitutional liberties are to be classified, along with any separation of powers or judicial review established by the state constitution, simply as another method by which the state's people protect themselves from their own state government by restraining the scope of its powers. Unquestionably, state constitutional liberties serve exactly this purpose. Yet this view of the state constitutional protection of liberty is incomplete. Heightened state constitutional protection of individual liberty does more than merely restrain state governments from invading the liberties of their citizens. It is also a potentially significant method by which state power can be deployed to check and counteract abuses of power on the national level—particularly abuses by federal courts of national judicial power.

When we think about abuses of national power, we tend to think about rights-invasive congressional measures, such as the Alien and Sedition Act of 1798, or presidential high-handedness, such as the military internment of Japanese Americans during World War II—abuses, that is to say, by the legislative and executive branches. But power can also be abused by the judicial branch, most notably when federal courts refuse to acknowledge and accord protection to individual rights possessed by the people of the United States. Abusively stingy readings of the U.S. Constitution not only may deny litigants their rights in individual cases, but generally also provide authorization to other organs of government to invade liberties that they should be required to respect. While a state might combat this brand of judicial tyranny by invoking any of the forms of resistance mentioned earlier, state courts are especially well suited to play a role in resisting abuse of the national judicial power, and to do so through entirely peaceful and fully legal means. A powerful weapon state courts may wield in such a struggle is their authority to interpret the state constitution to provide more generous protection for individual rights than the U.S. Supreme Court has chosen to provide under the national Constitution.

State judicial rejection of excessively narrow Supreme Court precedents concerning the scope of individual rights helps check national power in at least four ways. First, whenever a state court dissents from the reasoning of a U.S. Supreme Court decision it offers a forceful and very public critique of the national ruling, which can in the long run influence the formation of public and, eventually, official opinion on the propriety of the federal ruling. Second, state rulings that depart from or criticize U.S. Supreme Court precedents can contribute to the establishment of a nationwide legal consensus at the state level, a factor that the Supreme Court sometimes considers in the course of constitutional decisionmaking. Third, generous state interpretations of individual rights can more directly check national power by prohibiting state and local governments from exercising authority permitted them under the U.S. Constitution to suppress certain kinds of private behavior. In so doing, state courts create spaces in which otherwise prohibitable behavior may flourish. Finally, rights-protective rulings by state courts can help ameliorate the harm to liberty caused by narrow national rulings by providing protection for second-best alternatives to the types of behavior that such national rulings permit governments to suppress.

Public Dissent

Whenever a state's highest court, by constitutional ruling, recognizes a level of protection for individual rights that exceeds levels of protection for those rights established under parallel provisions of the national Constitution, it registers a forceful and often very public dissent from rulings of the U.S. Supreme Court. This kind of state constitutional rejectionism makes news—not merely among members of the bar or those who follow legal affairs, but in the mainstream press as well—and such publicity inevitably influences long-term public understandings of the appropriate content of constitutionally guaranteed rights.[37]

A particularly vivid example of the newsworthiness of state constitutional rejectionism is the extensive press coverage devoted to the Georgia Supreme Court's 1998 ruling in *Powell v. State*.[38] *Powell* made news because it rejected in a highly dramatic as well as ironic fashion the U.S. Supreme Court's ruling in *Bowers v. Hardwick*.[39] In *Bowers,* the U.S. Supreme Court sustained a Georgia

37. See generally Friedman, "Dialogue and Judicial Review," 653–80.
38. 510 S.E.2d 18 (Ga. 1998).
39. 478 U.S. 186 (1986).

statute criminalizing the practice of sodomy. The law had been invoked by Georgia authorities to prosecute a gay man for engaging in consensual, homosexual sodomy within his own home. The defendant challenged the constitutionality of the state law on due process grounds, arguing that established federal constitutional rights of privacy and sexual autonomy prohibited the criminalization of sodomy between consenting adults. The Supreme Court chose to interpret this attack upon the statute in narrower terms, as seeking a judicial declaration of a due process right to engage in homosexual sodomy. The Court declined to issue such a ruling, applied a deferential standard of review, and sustained the Georgia law, holding along the way that nothing in the Due Process Clause prohibits states from enacting into law their moral condemnation of homosexuality and of gay sexual practices.

In *Powell*, the Georgia Supreme Court entertained a challenge to the very same law at issue in *Bowers*. This time, the defendant was a heterosexual male who had been convicted of engaging in sodomy with a female within the home. The defendant challenged the constitutionality of the statute under the Due Process Clause of the Georgia Constitution—a provision worded identically to the Due Process Clause of the U.S. Constitution, and which the Georgia Supreme Court had construed, like its federal counterpart, to embody a constitutional right to privacy. Rather than follow the U.S. Supreme Court's reasoning in *Bowers*, however, the Georgia Supreme Court simply brushed it aside. Pointing out that it was not bound by parallel constructions of the U.S. Constitution and could construe Georgia's Due Process Clause more generously than the U.S. Supreme Court had construed the federal Due Process Clause in *Bowers*, the Georgia Supreme Court invalidated the challenged statute. "We cannot think," the court said, "of any other activity that reasonable persons would rank as more private and more deserving of protection from governmental interference than unforced, private, adult sexual activity."[40] As it did in *Bowers*, the state attempted to justify in moral terms its invasion of the privacy interest identified by the court, but this time without success: "'it does not follow,'" said the court, "'that simply because the legislature has enacted as law what may be a moral choice of the majority, the courts are, thereafter, bound to simply acquiesce.'"[41] Finally, the Georgia Supreme Court could have attempted to harmonize its ruling with *Bowers* by invalidating the law only as applied to consensual heterosexual sodomy, preserving the statute for use against ho-

40. 510 S.E.2d. at 24.
41. Id. at 25, quoting Gryczan v. State, 942 P.2d 112, 125 (Mont. 1997).

mosexuals. Instead, in what appeared to be a deliberate rebuke to the U.S. Supreme Court, the Georgia court seemingly invalidated the state statute on its face, an action that dramatically underscored the greater rights-protectiveness of its ruling.

The ruling in *Powell* prompted an explosion of news reports, editorials, and opinion pieces. The decision was reported not only in the usual legal specialty publications such as the *National Law Journal* and *Texas Lawyer,* and not only in local papers such as the *Fulton County Daily Report* and Georgia's leading paper, the *Atlanta Journal and Constitution,* but in print media across the country. National publications such as *Time, Newsweek, USA Today,* and *Jet* all ran articles about the ruling, as did major papers with national circulation such as the *New York Times, Los Angeles Times, Washington Post, Chicago Tribune,* and *Boston Globe.* The *Powell* ruling also got extensive play in newspapers serving much smaller markets. Stories about the ruling appeared in newspapers in Houston; New Orleans; St. Louis; Seattle; Minneapolis; Baltimore; Bergen County, New Jersey; Orlando; Memphis; Austin; Jacksonville; Greensboro, North Carolina; Palm Beach; and Chattanooga, among many others.

The media response was not, however, limited merely to reporting. Editorial writers took to the editorial pages, largely to praise the Georgia Supreme Court's action. The *St. Petersburg Times,* for example, likening the U.S. Supreme Court's decision in *Bowers* to its notorious decisions in *Dred Scott* and *Plessy v. Ferguson,* praised the Georgia court for "grant[ing] Georgia residents a protection the U.S. Supreme Court should have granted all of us 12 years ago: privacy in the bedroom."[42] The *Charleston (W. Va.) Gazette* gave a "Hurrah" for *Powell,* expressed the wish that "this policy becomes standard throughout America," and took the opportunity to criticize "age-old attempt[s] by severe moralists to control how others make love."[43] In a particularly sophisticated editorial, the *Pittsburgh Post-Gazette* observed that

> [a] generation ago it was some state supreme courts that winked at fundamental violations of human rights while the U.S. Supreme Court acted boldly to correct injustices. . . . In an ironic turnabout, the Supreme Court of Georgia recently invalidated a criminal law against sodomy that the U.S. Supreme Court allowed to stand by a 5–4 vote in a notorious 1986 decision.

42. Editorial: "Get Government Out of Bedrooms."
43. Editorial: "Privacy: Leave Adults Alone."

According to the paper, the "overriding issue" in both cases "was privacy, not sex. And now, Georgia's Supreme Court has grasped that fact, putting the U.S. Supreme Court to shame."[44]

By 2003, this kind of criticism of *Bowers* had found a new and receptive audience—on the U.S. Supreme Court itself. In *Lawrence v. Texas*,[45] the Court overruled *Bowers* by a 6–3 vote, invalidating on due process grounds a criminal defendant's conviction under a Texas sodomy law for engaging in sex with another man. In reaching this decision, the majority expressly noted that "[i]n the United States criticism of *Bowers* has been substantial and continuing, disapproving of its reasoning in all respects."[46] It also cited the Georgia Supreme Court's decision in *Powell* as an example of a state court declining to follow *Bowers* in construing "provisions in their own state constitutions parallel to the Due Process Clause of the Fourteenth Amendment."[47]

Of course the *Powell* decision and the subsequent media reaction was only one event in a barrage of criticism of *Bowers* that came from many sources over a period of seventeen years, and did not by itself trigger the Supreme Court's reversal of position. The reaction to *Powell,* moreover, was certainly one of the more graphic examples of how state constitutional rejectionism may affect public opinion. However, even less significant or less well-covered state constitutional rulings may, in the long term, and when multiplied many times over, have similar impacts on public opinion and ultimately on the content of national constitutional law. Criticism of Supreme Court rulings by state courts cannot alone restrain abuses of national judicial power, of course, yet it is hardly irrelevant to such restraint. Official criticism of federal actions by holders of high state offices may from time to time find an attentive audience. And although it may take a long time, national public opinion is eventually reflected even in the rulings of Supreme Court justices who, after all, are appointed and confirmed by democratically elected and accountable national officials.[48]

44. Editorial: "Privacy Prevails: Georgia's Supreme Court Strikes Down a Sodomy Law."
45. 123 S. Ct. 2472 (2003).
46. Id. at 2483.
47. Id.
48. Dahl, "Decision-Making in a Democracy"; Carter, "The Confirmation Mess"; Segal and Cover, "Ideological Values and the Votes of U.S. Supreme Court Justices"; Segal and Spaeth, *The Supreme Court and the Attitudinal Model;* Spaeth and Segal, *Majority Rule or Minority Will;* Langer, *Judicial Review in State Supreme Courts.*

Establishment of State-Level Legal Consensus

Another way in which state courts sometimes exert an indirect influence on the exercise of national judicial power is by contributing to the establishment of a national legal consensus at the state level. Such a consensus among the states can then influence federal courts in their own constitutional decision-making. This process can proceed in one of two ways. First, state constitutional decisionmaking can simply influence federal courts by the persuasiveness of its reasoning. If the reasons supporting state constitutional rulings apply at all in the national setting, federal courts may adopt or at least be influenced by such reasoning. The more state courts agree among themselves, the more influence their collective position may have upon federal reasoning in cases arising under the U.S. Constitution. But there is also a second and far more robust way in which state constitutional adjudication affects federal rulings: by contributing to the establishment of a consensus that is then taken by federal courts as a meaningful reference point for federal constitutional adjudication. This phenomenon is seen with increasing frequency in decisions of the U.S. Supreme Court elaborating the meaning of the Due Process Clause.

American courts proceeding in the fashion of the common law have a long tradition of examining judicial decisions from other jurisdictions.[49] Sometimes courts turn to decisions from other jurisdictions out of mere prudence. For example, courts may want to make sure they have not overlooked any significant arguments or considerations, or they may wish to examine decisions from other jurisdictions for the persuasive value of their reasoning. Yet there is another reason why courts consult peer institutions, one rooted in the Blackstonian conception of the common law as the embodiment of truth: the decisions of other courts may furnish important evidence of the "true"—or at least the "best"—content of legal rules. The fact that forty-four states follow one rule of tort liability and only six follow an alternative rule is not conclusive evidence, even in the Blackstonian tradition, that the majority rule is the "correct" one, but it is impressive nonetheless, and courts often respond to such considerations.

Constitutional adjudication bears more than a passing resemblance to common law adjudication.[50] Occasionally, federal courts contemplating some

49. Friedman et al., "State Supreme Courts," 796; Canon and Baum, "Patterns of Adoption of Tort Law Innovations"; Caldeira, "The Transmission of Legal Precedent."

50. Strauss, "Common Law Constitutional Interpretation."

decision under the U.S. Constitution will consult the rulings of state courts in the common law fashion, opening themselves to influence and persuasion. Certainly the premier example of this is *Mapp v. Ohio*,[51] in which the U.S. Supreme Court adopted the exclusionary rule, which requires the suppression of unconstitutionally seized evidence, as a means of enforcing the Fourteenth Amendment's prohibition on unreasonable searches and seizures. In reaching this decision, the Court was deeply influenced by an emerging consensus among state courts, which it carefully and extensively documented, that suppression of illegally seized evidence was the most effective way to deter constitutionally unreasonable searches. "[M]ore than half of those [states] passing upon" the question, the Court noted, "have wholly or partly adopted or adhered to" the rule.[52] The Court placed special emphasis on a ruling by the California Supreme Court adopting the exclusionary rule as a matter of federal and state constitutional and state evidentiary law, in which the California court found that other remedies had "completely failed to secure compliance with the constitutional provisions."[53] Finding California's experience consistent with that of other states, the Court incorporated the exclusionary rule into the Fourteenth Amendment's definition of protected liberty.

Since *Mapp*, and particularly in the last fifteen years or so, the Court has increasingly exhibited this more robust form of reliance on state court decisionmaking. Rather than merely opening itself to persuasion by the reasoning and experiences of state courts, the Court has used the content of state law to provide a baseline against which to measure whether any particular individual right can be considered part of the fundamental liberty protected by the Fourteenth Amendment. In earlier periods, the Court tended to focus on whether a particular right could be considered "implicit in the concept of ordered liberty." In its contemporary due process jurisprudence, however, the Court now tends to utilize a slightly different formulation that focuses on whether the liberty in question is "'deeply rooted in this Nation's history and tradition,'"[54] an analysis that cannot be performed without some examination of the content and evolution of state law. Moreover, in reviewing Ameri-

---

51. 367 U.S. 643 (1961).

52. Id. at 651.

53. People v. Cahan, 282 P.2d 905, 911 (Cal. 1955).

54. Washington v. Glucksberg, 521 U.S. 702, 721 (1997), quoting Moore v. East Cleveland, 431 U.S. 494, 503 (1977).

can legal traditions as embodied in state law, the Court has repeatedly examined whether legal patterns in the states have persisted into the present.[55] This new, heavy emphasis on the recent and contemporary content of state law gives state courts even greater opportunities to influence the shape of national constitutional doctrine.

In *Bowers v. Hardwick*,[56] for example, as we have seen, the Court declined to recognize what it characterized as a due process privacy right to engage in consensual homosexual sodomy. In reaching this decision, the Court relied on a detailed review of the history of state regulation of sodomy, noting that before 1961 "all 50 States outlawed sodomy, and today, 24 States and the District of Columbia continue to provide criminal penalties for sodomy performed in private and between consenting adults."[57] In *Cruzan v. Director, Missouri Department of Health*,[58] the Court recognized a due process constitutional right to be free from unwanted medical treatment, but held that the right had not been violated by a state law that prohibited termination of life support for a person in a persistent vegetative state without clear and convincing evidence that the person, if competent, would so wish. Both aspects of the Court's rulings were heavily informed by its survey of past and present state law concerning the content and application of state doctrines of informed consent. Some of the state cases the Court consulted that recognized a right to refuse treatment, the Court explicitly noted, were based on a combination of state common law and privacy rights recognized under state constitutions.[59]

This trend continued in *Cooper v. Oklahoma*,[60] in which the Court invalidated on due process grounds a state law requiring a criminal defendant to prove his incompetence to stand trial by clear and convincing evidence. The Court held,

55. See Glucksberg, 521 U.S. at 723 ("we are confronted with a consistent and almost universal tradition that has long rejected the asserted right, and continues explicitly to reject it today"); Burnham v. Superior Court, 495 U.S. 604, 615 (1990) ("This American jurisdictional practice is, moreover, not merely old; it is continuing."); Cooper v. Oklahoma, 517 U.S. 348, 356 (1996) ("We are persuaded, by both traditional and modern practice . . . , that the State's argument must be rejected.").

56. 478 U.S. 186 (1986), *rev'd*, Texas v. Lawrence, 123 S. Ct. 2472 (2003).

57. Id. at 193–94.

58. 497 U.S. 261 (1990).

59. Id. at 271 ("most courts have based a right to refuse treatment either solely on the common-law right to informed consent or on both the common-law right and a constitutional privacy right").

60. 517 U.S. 348, 356 (1996).

on the basis of "both traditional and modern practice,"[61] that such an elevated standard was inconsistent with due process. "Contemporary practice," the Court observed, "demonstrates that the vast majority of jurisdictions remain persuaded that the heightened standard of proof imposed on the accused in Oklahoma is not necessary to vindicate the State's interest in prompt and orderly disposition of criminal cases."[62] Similarly, in *Washington v. Glucksberg*,[63] the Court refused to recognize a due process right to physician-assisted suicide based upon a review not only of seven hundred years of "Anglo-American common law tradition,"[64] but also on contemporary legislative and judicial attitudes toward the practice. The Court thus found it relevant that "[i]n almost every State . . . it is a crime to assist a suicide,"[65] and that "the States' assisted-suicide bans have in recent years been reexamined and, generally, reaffirmed."[66] The Due Process Clause cannot be understood to recognize such a right, the Court concluded, because "we are confronted with a consistent and almost universal tradition that has long rejected the asserted right, and continues explicitly to reject it today."[67]

Most recently, the Court in *Lawrence v. Texas* overruled *Bowers,* finding that the Due Process Clause protects a personal right of private sexual autonomy sufficiently broad to encompass homosexual unions.[68] The majority opinion devoted extensive consideration to the historical claims made in *Bowers,* finding them unfounded. Instead, the Court recharacterized the historical record, arguing that "American laws targeting same-sex couples did not develop until the last third of the 20th century."[69] The Court then turned to state practice and policy *following* its 1986 decision in *Bowers,* noting expressly that several states had repealed or ceased to enforce existing sodomy statutes, and that five state appellate courts had construed their state constitutions to require inval-

61. Id.

62. Id. at 360.

63. 521 U.S. 702 (1997).

64. Id. at 711.

65. Id. at 710.

66. Id. at 716.

67. Id. at 723. See also Vacco v. Quill, 521 U.S. 793 (1997) (rejecting equal protection challenge to state law that permitted patients to refuse lifesaving treatment but prohibited physician-assisted suicide on the ground that past and contemporary state law makes a clear distinction between actions that permit death to occur naturally and that unnaturally hasten it).

68. 123 S. Ct. 2472 (2003).

69. Id. at 2479.

idation of state sodomy laws on due process grounds. The Court concluded by proclaiming: "As the Constitution endures, persons in every generation can invoke its principles in their own search for greater freedom"[70]—a surprising acknowledgment of the ability of the instrument to evolve in response to changes in official and public opinion and practice.

Although most of these examples involve the expansion of individual rights, the Court's methodology in due process cases operates without regard to the content of the disputed right, and could in principle result just as easily in the contraction as in the expansion of protected individual liberties. Thus, it seems far from inconceivable that continuation of a current state-level trend away from wholehearted acceptance of the exclusionary rule could eventually cause the Court to reconsider its holding in *Mapp v. Ohio*.[71] As public sympathy for criminal defendants ebbs, other presently incorporated rights of criminal procedure regulating interrogation of suspects, preventive detention, and proportionality of punishment, to name just a few, might be equally vulnerable to federal reconsideration. State courts of course would be required under the Supremacy Clause to continue to observe existing federal standards until they are expressly reversed by the Supreme Court, but nothing prevents state courts in the meantime from attempting to drive lower as well as higher the standards established by the U.S. Constitution through pertinent constructions of parallel provisions of their state constitutions.

Although the U.S. Supreme Court has most often incorporated shared state constitutional baselines into national constitutional doctrine in due process cases, state constitutional rulings may influence the content of national constitutional law in at least some other significant doctrinal areas. For example, the Court has long held that the Eighth Amendment's bar of cruel and unusual punishment "draw[s] its meaning from the evolving standards of decency that mark the progress of a maturing society."[72] This language is virtually an open invitation to states to influence the meaning of the national prohibition by developing state standards of capital punishment. In fact, the coalescence of a state-level con-

---

70. Id. at 2484.

71. The California Victims' Bill of Rights, added to the state constitution by initiative amendment in 1982, eliminates the exclusionary rule as a matter of state constitutional law. Much of the state-level activity in the area of criminal procedure has been in the direction of reducing the constitutional protections available to criminal defendants. See, e.g., Wilkes, "The New Federalism in Criminal Procedure in 1984."

72. Trop v. Dulles, 356 U.S. 86, 101 (1958).

sensus condemning the execution of the mentally retarded prompted the Court in 2002 to reverse a 1989 decision holding that execution of a mentally retarded defendant does not offend the Eighth Amendment.[73] Although the Court's decision relied almost exclusively on standards developed by state legislatures in statutes rather than by state courts in constitutional rulings, the result would certainly have been the same had state legislatures been forced to act in response to state constitutional imperatives articulated and enforced by state courts.

Opportunities for state constitutional rulings to affect national constitutional law may also arise in other areas. It is possible, for example, that the emergence of consensual state-level constitutional principles concerning the nature and permissible uses of property could affect the development of national constitutional protections that are triggered by government regulation of property interests. Such areas might include regulatory takings under the Fifth and Fourteenth Amendments, and procedural due process protections that arise upon the deprivation of property. The evolution of state constitutional principles regarding the relationship between individuals and government might in turn influence the content of the Court's state-action doctrine under the Fourteenth Amendment. And as *Mapp v. Ohio* continues to illustrate, the Court may well remain open to influence by state constitutional practices in the realm of criminal procedure.

In other areas, however, the Court's approaches suggest fewer obvious opportunities for state constitutional consensus to affect the content of national doctrine. The Court's First Amendment jurisprudence of free speech, for example, seems relatively armor-plated against influence by state practices. The same might be said of its jurisprudence of equal protection, and the body of law it has developed concerning democracy and voting rights. In these areas, the Court seems decidedly uninterested in what states do and why; indeed, the Court sometimes seems to understand its role in these areas to be primarily one of invalidating state laws and practices that clash with strongly nationalized principles of constitutional dimension.[74]

Nevertheless, in those areas in which the U.S. Supreme Court has shown itself to be open to state influence, particularly in substantive due process cases arising under the Fourteenth Amendment, state courts clearly have the ability to influence indirectly the content of nationally guaranteed liberties through their rulings under cognate provisions of state constitutions. More to the point,

73. Atkins v. Virginia, 536 U.S. 304 (2002).
74. See Gardner, "Forcing States to Be Free."

it seems possible for state courts to utilize this process as a way of working actively, if slowly, to undermine Supreme Court interpretations of the U.S. Constitution with which they disagree.[75] The possibility of engaging in this kind of resistance, moreover, is only increased by the widespread tendency among state high courts to consult rulings from other states when construing their own state constitutions.[76] Thus, much as the common law evolves and converges by mutual consultation across jurisdictions, so constitutional law may evolve in the same way—particularly when the controlling methodology of interpretation places considerable emphasis, as it does under the Due Process Clause, on the emergence of consensus on the state level. By working to influence the formation of a consensus at the state level, then, state courts may employ state constitutional law as a tool to resist incorrect and abusive interpretations of the U.S. Constitution by federal courts.

Creation of a Protected Space for Prohibitable Behavior

I have focused thus far only on indirect routes by which state constitutional decisions influence the exercise of national power—methods that operate by influencing over the long term the view that the U.S. Supreme Court might take of the scope of federally protected rights. There are, however, at least two ways in which state constitutional rulings granting state citizens heightened individual rights can much more directly and immediately counteract the impact on individual liberties of oppressive federal constitutional rulings: first, by making it more likely that there will be some space for certain kinds of private behavior that the U.S. Supreme Court permits American governments to suppress; and second, by providing space for private behavior that amounts to second-best alternatives to the types of behavior the Supreme Court permits governments to suppress.

75. This process need not be used solely to expand individual rights; it can also operate to contract them. A national overexpansion of individual rights could just as easily be understood as "abusive," especially when it sets up a conflict with other perceived rights such as property or economic rights. A good example is state constitutional protection for speech in shopping malls, which was challenged unsuccessfully as violating nationally protected rights of property owners to exclude unwanted individuals, or to compensation for the loss of the power to exclude. See Robins v. Pruneyard Shopping Ctr., 447 U.S. 74 (1980) (rejecting Fifth Amendment takings claim). A state is free to set its own protection for uncompensated takings at a higher level, and in so doing to attempt to influence the content of federal Fifth Amendment doctrine.

76. Porter and Tarr, *State Supreme Courts,* xxi–xxii; Tarr, *Understanding State Constitutions,* 199–200.

To say that someone holds a right or is free to exercise some liberty generally means that he or she may engage in some kind of private behavior without fear of punishment by the government against which the right or liberty is held. Nevertheless, the fact that some right or liberty may be constitutionally guaranteed does not, in our system, affirmatively grant anyone the right to engage in any particular behavior. On the contrary, under the prevailing American theory of government, the general rule to be presumed is that anyone may engage privately in any behavior whatsoever until such time as some government with the authority to curtail the behavior invokes its power and by law restricts the activity in question. This is the model of negative liberty that dominates American constitutional law.[77] Consequently, to have a constitutional right to engage in some behavior typically means less that one has the freedom to act than it means that government may not restrict one's behavior by prohibiting it. For most practical purposes, these two understandings of constitutional right amount to the same thing, for, in organized society, one is generally free to engage in an activity only insofar as one's government is disabled from restricting it. But once we begin dealing with more than one government at a time, as we inevitably must in a federal system, the difference between these two understandings takes on greater significance.

When a federal court takes a restrictive view of the scope of some individual liberty guaranteed by the U.S. Constitution, it does nothing by itself to restrict in any way the actual ability of any person to engage in any particular behavior. Rather, the main significance of such a ruling is that it authorizes the national legislative and executive branches to enact and enforce laws that prohibit or restrict some kind of behavior in which people would otherwise wish to engage. Moreover, since the 1960s, when the Supreme Court developed the incorporation doctrine under the Due Process Clause of the Fourteenth Amendment, a federal individual rights ruling that authorizes the national government to suppress some kind of behavior usually amounts to a similar authorization to state and local governments to do the same. Thus, a stingy ruling on individual rights by the U.S. Supreme Court for the most part amounts to an authorization to every government in the United States to suppress the behavior in question, should it choose to do so—it declares a kind of open season against the private activity that is the subject of the ruling.

Here, however, is where the difference between constitutional authoriza-

77. Berlin, "Two Concepts of Liberty." For a contrary view, see Hershkoff, "Positive Rights and State Constitutions."

tion to suppress behavior and actual legislative use of that authorization begins to make a difference. If the Supreme Court holds that the Constitution does not forbid governmental power to be used to restrict some particular activity, then the national government and all fifty state governments may restrict it. But, of course, they need not do so. A decision by one state to invoke this authority and suppress the activity typically will not in any way affect the ability of people in any other state to engage in that activity. Thus, the impact of a federal constitutional ruling on individual rights is typically felt by any individual only if the authority to suppress behavior is invoked legislatively either by Congress or by the legislature of the state in which the individual resides.

Because of this architecture of the federal system, state constitutional rulings can thus serve as actual antidotes—of a limited scope, to be sure, but antidotes nonetheless—to abusively restrictive federal judicial interpretations of federally guaranteed individual rights. A ruling by a state supreme court recognizing heightened protection of the very same individual right that the U.S. Supreme Court has already held to be only narrowly protected by the national Constitution is a ruling that revokes the state government's authority to exercise the power that the federal courts have granted it to suppress the behavior. The practical effect of such a ruling is that only one government—the national government—is then permitted to punish the behavior in question. But not all governments are equivalent in their ability to suppress all varieties of constitutionally prohibitable behavior. In practice, the power of the national government to suppress behavior within any given state is often only a fraction of the power that the state government has to suppress the same behavior. National law enforcement resources must be spread around the entire country, and the ability of the national government to detect and punish prohibited behavior is often limited—certainly far less than the ability of the state government to detect and punish the behavior.[78] Moreover, as shown above, the national government often requires the cooperation of the states to achieve its

---

78. According to the U.S. Department of Justice's Bureau of Justice Statistics, federal agencies in 2000 employed 88,496 full-time law-enforcement personnel. Sixty percent of this total worked for the Immigration and Naturalization Service, Federal Bureau of Prisons, FBI, and Customs Service. More than a quarter of these officials were deployed in only two states, Texas and California. See http://www.ojp.usdoj.gov/bjs/fedle.htm. In contrast, state and local law enforcement agencies in 1996 employed nearly a million full-time personnel. Id. at sandlle.htm.

goals, cooperation that will not be forthcoming if state officials are barred under their own state constitutions from providing the requested assistance.[79] As a practical matter, then, to enjoy protection against punishment of some activity by state government is sometimes to enjoy close to complete protection against any governmental punishment at all.

A concrete example may help illustrate the point. Libel laws permit individuals to sue and recover damages from those who publicly circulate defamatory statements about them. In a 1964 case, the U.S. Supreme Court held that libel laws are subject to evaluation under the First Amendment of the national Constitution because they restrict the freedom of speech.[80] Ever since, litigants have clashed over the scope of the First Amendment's protection for speech that has the potential to harm the reputation of others. One question that sometimes arose was whether the First Amendment protected statements of opinion from punishment; many took the position that expressions of opinion, unlike assertions of fact, were sheltered from civil liability rules under the First Amendment. In its 1990 decision in *Milkovich v. Lorain Journal Co.*,[81] the U.S. Supreme Court held that couching a statement in the form of an opinion does not cloak it with any privilege that would make it immune as a matter of constitutional law from libel rules. After *Milkovich,* any legislature in the United States was thus constitutionally free to craft libel laws that punish the expression of defamatory opinions. While most libel rules would be expected to appear at the state level, it is not inconceivable that Congress might also enact a libel law within the scope of its admittedly more limited powers. For example, there might be a plausible argument that Congress could enact libel laws to protect national government officials and candidates for office from unwarranted attacks, especially if it could be shown that highly qualified can-

79. A particularly stark example of this phenomenon is the refusal, mentioned above, of the Portland, Oregon police department to cooperate with the FBI's effort to interview approximately five thousand young men of Middle Eastern descent in the weeks immediately following the September 11, 2001 attacks on the World Trade Center and the Pentagon. Portland police claimed that the FBI's program amounted to a kind of unjustifiable racial profiling forbidden by Oregon law. See Butterfield, "A Police Force Rebuffs F.B.I. on Querying Mideast Men." On the topic of state constitutional restrictions that impede cooperation by state officials with the national government, see Van Alstyne, "'Thirty Pieces of Silver' for the Rights of Your People."

80. New York Times v. Sullivan, 376 U.S. 254 (1964).

81. 497 U.S. 1 (1990).

didates were being deterred from seeking national office because of a fear of smear attacks by their opponents.[82]

A year after the Supreme Court's decision in *Milkovich,* the same issue reached the New York Court of Appeals, New York's highest court. That court disagreed with the Supreme Court's handling of the opinion question. Of course, it could do nothing about the Supreme Court's interpretation of the First Amendment. However, the New York Constitution also has a provision protecting the freedom of speech, and in *Immuno AG. v. Moor-Jankowski*[83] the New York court interpreted that provision to provide broader protection for free speech than the First Amendment—sufficiently broader to create a free speech privilege for expressions of opinion. Consequently, the court held, New York's libel law may not constitutionally punish expressions of opinion. After *Milkovich* and *Immuno AG.,* then, Congress has the authority to enact libel laws that punish the expression within New York of defamatory opinions, but New York State may not.

How safe is it, then, to express defamatory opinions in New York? Very safe. New York itself is constitutionally disabled from punishing such speech. No other state's law, no matter how restrictive, is likely to apply, at least so long as the opinion is expressed within New York and not distributed outside the state. Congress could conceivably enact a libel law that would reach within New York, but it has not, nor is it likely to do so. Even if it did, the applicability of the law would likely be so limited that it could conceivably affect only an extremely small proportion of the defamatory opinions expressed in the state. By choosing to accord defamatory opinions a higher degree of protection under the New York Constitution than they receive under the U.S. Constitution, the New York Court of Appeals thus ensured the survival of a considerable public sphere in which the expression of such opinions would remain unpunishable. In so doing, it undid a great deal of the harm to the public good— if harm there was—caused by the Supreme Court's decision in *Milkovich.*

Again, there is no necessary ideological tilt to this dynamic of intergovernmental relations. State courts might equally attempt to counteract, say, the Supreme Court's due process and equal protection jurisprudence of economic regulation, in which laws regulating ordinary economic and social re-

---

82. Article I, § 4, which grants Congress the power to regulate the time, place, and manner of congressional elections, might authorize an election code containing such a provision.

83. 567 N.E.2d 1270 (N.Y. 1991).

lations receive highly deferential rational basis scrutiny.[84] A state court that believed such a standard to provide insufficient protection for economic liberties or private rights of property might choose to subject state economic legislation to some more demanding level of scrutiny under the state constitution.[85] Similarly, state courts could seek to implement a more stringent regime of protection for private property by expanding beyond bounds established by the U.S. Constitution the circumstances in which the state constitution's takings clause requires state and local governments to compensate owners of property subject to public regulation. The point here is one of system mechanics, not ideology: state courts can use their independence to insulate their citizens from harm caused by abusively narrow national constitutional rulings along a wide range of definitions of what constitutes an abuse of national judicial power.

Protection of Second-Best Liberties

A second way in which heightened state protection of individual rights can serve as a direct, if limited, check on abuses of national judicial power is by ensuring space for private behavior that is a second-best alternative to the types of behavior that narrow federal interpretations of nationally protected rights permit governments to suppress. As a rule, national power tends to be spread thinly throughout the states and to touch the lives of most citizens lightly. There are, however, some areas in which national power penetrates American life deeply, if narrowly. In these areas, national standards prevail and there may be nothing states can do to limit their impact on the activities subject to federal regulatory standards. When national power is deployed in this way, and is used to achieve a purpose antithetical to the public good, liberty is irrevocably lost.

Liberty means, among other things, the freedom to live one's life in a certain way.[86] When national power is carefully targeted and then deployed to maximum effect, it is fully capable of choking off certain ways of life. That is, of course, the very definition of effective power, and the Constitution grants powers to the national government in ways designed to make them effective

---

84. E.g., Nebbia v. New York, 291 U.S. 502 (1934); United States v. Carolene Prods., 304 U.S. 144 (1938); Williamson v. Lee Optical, 348 U.S. 483 (1955).

85. See Kirby, "Expansive Judicial Review of Economic Regulation under State Constitutions," 94–145; Galie, "State Courts and Economic Rights."

86. Cf. Rawls, A Theory of Justice, 407–16.

within their legitimate scope.[87] Thus, in such cases, the exercise of national power can close off certain ways of life, resulting in a loss of welfare to those who value that way of life and wish to pursue it.

A state that views such an exercise of national power as an abusive invasion of liberty has at its disposal no fully legal means to undo directly the particular harm committed by the national government. A lawful exercise of national power, backed by the Supremacy Clause and the threat of enforcement, is enough to make that harm stick. Nevertheless, it may be possible for the state government to ameliorate that harm indirectly by using its lawful powers to expand and protect liberty in other directions. One important way in which the state can accomplish that objective is by providing heightened protection under the state constitution to other liberties that are related to the liberty that national power has denied, or that might in some circumstances plausibly substitute for it.

For example, until 1994 national drug laws that criminalized the possession and distribution of peyote prohibited some Native Americans from practicing their religion in traditional ways.[88] The enforcement of drug proscriptions tends to be heavily federalized. The U.S. Supreme Court, moreover, ruled in 1990 that application of a statutory peyote ban to Native American religious rituals does not violate the Free Exercise Clause of the national Constitution.[89] Until Congress voluntarily chose in 1994 to exempt Native Americans from the reach of the peyote ban,[90] national power was applied systematically and effectively to preclude a group of citizens from living a particular kind of life, one in which they might take part in what they consider to be important sacred rituals. As far as these individuals were concerned, their liberty had been irrevocably impaired.[91] Moreover, should congressional tolerance for the sacramental use of peyote flag and Congress rescind the exemption, Native

---

87. Though limited, the powers of the national government are said to be plenary within their sphere. McCulloch v. Maryland, 17 U.S. 316 (1819).

88. 21 U.S.C. §§ 811–12. However, the Drug Enforcement Administration had by regulation exempted the sacramental use of peyote from prosecution. 21 C.F.R. § 1307.31. Apparently this regulation was respected by the Justice Department in its enforcement policies.

89. Employment Div., Dept. of Human Resources v. Smith, 494 U.S. 872 (1990).

90. American Indian Religious Freedom Amendments Act, 108 Stat. 3125 (1994), codified at 42 U.S.C. § 1996a.

91. McConnell, "Free Exercise Revisionism and the *Smith* Decision."

Americans would again be barred by federal law from practicing their religion as they believe they must.

A state whose people thought such an exercise of national power abusive could do nothing short of outright, escalated defiance of federal law—nothing, that is, by legal, nonviolent means—to win for Native Americans the right to use peyote in religious rituals. It is true that state courts could invalidate *state* anti-peyote laws on free exercise grounds, but federal prosecution of drug crimes is fairly ubiquitous, and Native Americans are a small group who are already subject to extensive federal oversight. Nevertheless, even in these circumstances, it may well be within the power of state governments to use constitutional or statutory means to protect *other* enclaves of religious liberty in the hope that the uncomfortable effects of a contraction of liberty at one point in the system might be offset in some way by an expansion of liberty elsewhere.

For example, virtually every state constitution contains a provision that, like the Establishment Clause of the First Amendment of the U.S. Constitution, requires states to treat all religions neutrally, a requirement that prohibits states from endorsing any particular religion. The U.S. Supreme Court has interpreted the Establishment Clause narrowly in recent years, holding that overtly religious symbols associated with the major religions may be displayed prominently on public property in certain circumstances without violating the clause.[92] Critics of these decisions sometimes claim that they take insufficient account of the context in which such symbols are displayed—a context in which these displays look, to those who do not practice the major religions, very much like official endorsements of Christianity, and occasionally of Judaism and Islam.[93] The idea that the state endorses certain religious ideas and not others may then be perceived by dissenters as marginalizing and oppressive.

A state, however, is free to take a more expansive view of state constitutional prohibitions on government support for religion than the Supreme Court has taken of the First Amendment's Establishment Clause. A state constitutional ruling barring any displays of religious symbols on public property might expand the liberty of Native Americans in a way that could help ameliorate some of the harm they might feel from a federal proscription of peyote use. Native Americans are a tiny minority in this country. Like other religious minorities, they probably feel their identity is put under constant pressure by the ways in which a largely Christian majority unreflectively takes the as-

92. Lynch v. Donnelly, 465 U.S. 668 (1984).
93. See id. at 700–701 (Brennan, J., dissenting).

sumptions and practices of Christianity to be those of religion in general.[94] The unreflective invocation of religious symbols by those who practice majority religions is one of many potential sources of pressure on minority religious identity. A state ruling barring the display of any and all religious symbols on state and local government property might go some way toward easing this pressure. It might send a welcome message of inclusion and understanding. In one way or another, it might use state power to confront and counteract a potentially liberty-impairing use of national power.

State courts might use a similar approach in many other areas. The right to use marijuana for legitimate medical purposes, such as relieving pain suffered by cancer patients, is another contentious arena of drug policy in which the national government has even more adamantly refused to back away from blanket prohibitions. If federal courts make it impossible for state courts effectively to recognize and protect a state constitutional right to palliative care,[95] say, state courts might respond by recognizing a collateral right under the state constitution to physician-assisted suicide. While this would not help every patient suffering from intractable pain, it could at least provide some relief for those with no hope of recovery who find their pain unbearable.

A more difficult example is presented by recent uses of national power to restrict the use of affirmative action in employment and education. In the last decade, the U.S. Supreme Court has interpreted the Equal Protection Clause so as to sharply restrict the constitutionality of national or state laws that extend employment and, to a somewhat lesser extent, educational preferences to minorities.[96] Should the people of a state see the Court's rulings in this area as an abuse of national power, a state court might expand the liberty of racial minorities in other directions by recognizing, say, a state constitutional right to

94. As Justice Brennan observed in his dissent in Lynch v. Donnelly, 465 U.S. at 700–701, these cases "appear[ ] hard not because the principles of decision are obvious, but because the Christmas holiday seems familiar and agreeable." Professor van Alstyne has called the Court's interpretation of the Establishment Clause "secularized Christian ethnocentrism." Van Alstyne, "Trends in the Supreme Court."

95. See United States v. Oakland Cannabis Buyer's Coop., 532 U.S. 483 (2001) (upholding federal criminal prosecution of marijuana possession notwithstanding state law permitting it when prescribed by a doctor).

96. See Adarand Constructors v. Pena, 515 U.S. 200, 230 (1995); City of Richmond v. J. A. Croson Co., 488 U.S. 469, 493 (1989). The Court recently took a somewhat more relaxed view of educational preferences in Gratz v. Bollinger, 123 S. Ct. 2411 (2003), and Grutter v. Bollinger, 123 S. Ct. 2325 (2003).

public reparations for past discrimination (though even here it seems possible that the Supreme Court's construction of the Equal Protection Clause might in some circumstances invalidate such a provision).[97] If the liberty of racial minorities to enjoy educational and employment opportunities cannot be expanded in any direction without violating federal law, perhaps the state constitution could be interpreted to confer upon minorities some kind of right to noneconomic opportunities, such as rights to cultural integrity or cultural expression.[98] There is, to be sure, an important difference between a constitutional right to pursue economic opportunities and a right to pursue cultural ones. The way of life associated with the second path may be quite different from the one associated with the first, and perhaps less widely or intensely desired by those in a position to benefit from the offered liberty. But even when state power is limited to offering liberties that are only substitutes for the liberties national power has denied, state power might nevertheless plausibly be understood as asserting itself against national power in the only way it can.

In making these arguments, I certainly do not wish to be understood to say that liberty is a single or fungible entity. If the national government invades liberty in one sphere in ways that states are powerless directly to affect, it is not necessarily the case that a state expansion of personal liberty in a different sphere automatically counterbalances the harm. To be sure, each liberty is different, and giving people one kind of liberty instead of another will not and should not satisfy everyone. When the denied liberty has structural functions that affect politics, such as free speech or association, the harm may be irremediable. But it may well be that for a great many people, expanding opportunities to pursue one kind of liberty may help even the score for the denial of others. Undoubtedly, some people who highly value the opportunity to live a certain kind of life will not be mollified by the opportunity to live a different kind of life to which they do not aspire. But there may be others who do value that kind of life more than the kind that has been denied, or who are indifferent between the two, and who will thus be made better off by state expansion of a wholly different kind of liberty. For such individuals, a state's use of its constitution to provide heightened protection for individual rights

97. It seems entirely possible that a generalized reparations payment not limited to victims of specifically identified prior discrimination would be viewed by the Court as just another kind of affirmative action program that discriminates on the basis of race. See Adarand Constructors v. Pena, 515 U.S. 200 (1995).

98. See Kymlicka, *Multicultural Citizenship*.

may indeed be a relatively potent tool with which to combat abuses of national power.

ASYMMETRIES BETWEEN STATE AND
NATIONAL POWER UNDER FEDERALISM

As the preceding review has argued, the American system of federalism contemplates the division of all governmental power among the state and national governments. It contemplates that each level of government will use the power so allocated to pursue directly the well-being of its citizenry, to restrain itself, and to check abuses by the other level of government for the common purpose of protecting the liberties of all the people from harm at the hands of any governmental power. While the powers of the state and national governments are thus to be deployed for identical purposes and by equivalent means, important differences nevertheless distinguish the ways in which the state and national governments can actually deploy their powers in a dynamic, well-functioning, operational system of federalism. Some of these differences arise from differences in the precise powers that are allocated to each level of government. Just as importantly, however, they also arise from the fact that the national government has been made supreme: it has been given the authority to use its powers without lawful interference from the states. National power thus may be exercised directly and forthrightly, in those areas to which it extends, when it is invoked to check the abuse of state power. State power, in contrast, must often be used indirectly, subtly, and creatively if it is to succeed in checking abuses of power committed by the national government.

These differences in both the content and "style," so to speak, of state and national power necessarily produce corresponding differences between the state and national constitutions, which are, after all, documents that assign and order the uses of governmental power at each level. Moreover, it stands to reason that constitutions ordering the use of different kinds of power by different means will need to be interpreted in different ways. Chapter 4 examines in greater detail the role that federalism imposes upon state constitutions. Chapter 5 then examines the ways in which a state constitution may be structured to fulfill the functions that federalism assigns it. Chapters 6 and 7 tie together the threads of the argument by proposing a jurisprudence of state constitutional interpretation guided by an overarching goal: to ensure insofar as possible that a state's constitution grants it the power to fulfill the role federalism assigns it.

4

State Constitutions in the Federal Scheme

FEDERALISM PROVIDES a theory of state power, not a theory of state constitutions. In the American tradition, however, constitutions have long played a highly significant role in defining, allocating, and ordering the exercise of governmental power. My project in the remainder of this book is to examine the consequences for state constitutions and state constitutional jurisprudence that result from recognition that state power does not exist in a vacuum—it does not exist, that is to say, solely at the sufferance and for the benefit of the state polity—but rather occupies an important functional position in the nationwide structural apparatus of federalism. If the content of a constitution reflects in any way the functions that constitution is meant to serve, as it surely must, then we ought to expect state constitutions to take up in some way the responsibilities with which the federal system indirectly entrusts them. It follows that the content of a state constitution is unlikely to be dictated solely by the desires and self-understandings of the people of the state, but rather will be influenced, at least to some degree, by imperatives laid at the feet of the state polity by political groupings that are in some sense external to the state.

This is a very different conception of state constitutionalism than is advanced by most constitutional theorists. Because a state constitution goes by the name "constitution," most theorists simply assume that it has all the properties that we typically attribute to the U.S. Constitution. Most often for these theorists, a state is a classic Lockean sovereign, and a state constitution is consequently neither more nor less than the fundamental positive legal enactment of the sovereign people of a state, an enactment that, like the national Constitution, contains only and exactly what the framing polity wants it to contain.[1] In making these choices, the state's people consult exclusively

---

1. This view is most closely associated with the primacy approach. See, e.g., Linde, "First Things First"; Linde, "E Pluribus."

their own preferences and enact them into law. What the national Constitution says is entirely irrelevant to the content of the state constitution, except perhaps to the extent that it might expressly require states to perform certain minimal functions, such as providing for the selection of members of the Electoral College in presidential elections.

The account of federalism sketched in chapter 3 reveals a different picture. State power exists for the benefit of the people of the state, to be sure, and state constitutions exist in part to translate the state polity's wishes into a satisfying plan of state-level self-government. But state power also exists for the benefit of the people of the nation, and it plays a potentially significant role in securing their liberty. This relationship implies an interdependence between state and national constitutionalism that most theories fail to recognize. My welfare, in other words, depends not only on our shared national Constitution and on my state constitution, but also to some extent on your state constitution as well. State constitutions are thus linked in a web of constitutional relations created by the national system of federalism.

This linkage, incidentally, provides yet another reason to reject both the Lockean and Romantic models of nationalism discussed in chapter 2 as conceptual foundations for analyzing state constitutions. Under the Lockean model, a state constitution embodies the choices made by a complete, and completely independent, self-defining polity of rational citizens. Yet because its members submit simultaneously to membership in a national polity of federal design, membership in the state polity is not complete in and of itself; on the contrary, membership in the state polity carries with it obligations to the national polity, and vice versa. Similarly, according to the Romantic model, a state constitution expresses the values and character of an organic people that, precisely because it is organic, is by definition complete and independent of all other peoples. Yet the web of political relationships and obligations established by federalism links the lives and fortunes of the state and national peoples, formally as well as practically, thereby creating an interdependence between them that hardly comports with the existence of an organically distinct political identity.

In exploring the implications of the federal structure for the content of state constitutions, however, it is important to proceed carefully. Constitutions are complex documents that serve many functions simultaneously, and institutionalizing the exercise of state power consistent with the requirements of federalism is only one of them. Consequently, the discussion that follows confines itself to examining on a broad scale some of the more significant functional parameters that influence the form and content of state constitutions.

THE FUNCTIONS OF STATE CONSTITUTIONS

One of the principal purposes of a constitution in the American tradition is to set out the powers that governments may exercise, as well as any limits on those powers. If federalism requires state governments to exercise certain kinds of power in certain ways, it follows that one of the most important purposes of a state constitution is to implement the federal plan by empowering the state government to act in just the ways that federalism demands. In light of the discussion of chapter 3, this means that a state constitution should do at least three things. First, it should grant the state government sufficient authority to permit it to work directly for the public good of its citizens. Second, it should establish sufficient limits on state power to restrain, at least to some extent, the ability of state officials to use state power for unjust ends. Third, a state constitution should grant the state government sufficient power to assert itself with at least some degree of efficacy against abuses of national power by the national government.

Empowerment

Affirmative state power. In seeking to determine the influence national constitutional structures have on the content of state constitutions, let us begin by examining the easiest case: explicit requirements imposed on state power by the U.S. Constitution. It is occasionally argued that the national Constitution requires every state not only to have a government, but to have one structured on the national model. Article I, § 4 of the Constitution, for example, provides: "The Times, Places and Manner of holding Elections for Senators and Representatives, shall be prescribed in each State by the Legislature thereof." Article VI, § 3 provides that "the Members of the several State Legislatures, and all executive and judicial Officers . . . of the several States, shall be bound by Oath or Affirmation, to support this Constitution." These provisions suggest strongly that the U.S. Constitution contemplates that states have governments consisting of legislative, executive, and judicial branches—as most did at the time of the framing.

Even supposing the national Constitution contemplates state governmental structures, it is another question altogether whether the Constitution requires these governments to be able to *do* anything in particular, and if so, what. The explicit national constitutional requirements for state power, if any, are negligible; a state would probably satisfy them by doing little more than taking steps to ensure the selection of senators, representatives, and members of the Electoral College. We could imagine a state polity attempting to comply with the U.S. Constitution by creating a state government that exercised no powers except those upon which the national government directly relies. The people of such a state would in effect designate the national government as their only government. Anything they wished to be done would be accomplished by collective private agreement or by the national government, if it were to be done at all.

Even if such a government would satisfy the technical requirements of the national Constitution, however, it seems grossly at odds with the philosophy of federalism. Federalism contemplates a balance of state and national power. Liberty is adequately protected in this scheme only when power is sufficiently well divided to allow each sovereign both to command popular allegiance and to place itself, in some moderately effective degree, in the way of any tyrannical design of the other sovereign. The national government is powerful, and a state government lacking any significant affirmative powers would be unable to fulfill this role. It would be, at best, more like an administrative subdivision of the national government than a full-blown sovereign power capable of using public power for public ends. Thus, it is safe to say that one of the primary functions of a state constitution is to identify those powers that the state must have to achieve the desired public ends, and to grant those powers affirmatively to the state government.

As things have turned out, every state polity has in fact decided that it wants its state government to possess significant affirmative power. The constitution of every state grants its officials considerable power to act in pursuit of the common good, however the people of the state may happen to understand it. Indeed, it is a commonplace of state constitutional law that constitutional grants of power to state governments are presumed to be plenary except as restricted—a presumption directly opposed to the one governing the construction of national power, which holds that national power is denied except as expressly or implicitly granted.[2]

At a minimum, then, a state constitution must grant the state government

2. Tarr, *Understanding State Constitutions,* 6–9.

sufficient power to do successfully those things the state's citizens wish it to do. It seems safe to presume that the citizens' goals in every state, whatever they may be, require the state to possess some kind of affirmative power to pursue the public good as it is locally conceived. If the citizens were able to achieve all their goals without the application of organized governmental power, presumably they would attempt do so without creating and empowering a government, with its attendant risk of official tyranny. The fact that state polities have seen fit to create state governments at all, much less to endow them with such broad powers, suggests that organized, collective social power wielded by a state governmental apparatus is essential to the achievement of common popular goals. Moreover, as John Marshall observed nearly two centuries ago, a constitution that fails to grant government power sufficient to achieve the goals the people have charged it to achieve would be nothing more than "a splendid bauble"[3]—"a magnificent structure, indeed, to look at, but totally unfit for use."[4]

What counts as sufficient state power will of course vary with citizens' ends, with their views of what state power and private power can respectively accomplish, and with their beliefs about the comparative trustworthiness of government officials and private actors. Federalism does not dictate solutions to any of these problems, and it would go too far to suggest that federalism by itself requires a state government to possess any particular set of clearly defined powers. Nevertheless, federalism certainly contemplates that a state will have power sufficient to do what its citizens think needs doing, and one job of the state constitution is to supply that power.

The power to check national abuses. The requirements of federalism become somewhat more specific when we consider another aspect of governmental authorization and empowerment with which state constitutions must be concerned: the granting of state power for the purpose of checking abuses of power at the national level. The success of a federal system depends critically upon the ability of each level of government to exercise a mutual check on abuses of power by the other. As we have seen, states have numerous means at their disposal to resist exercises of national power they consider abusive or unjust. These range from secession and the use or threat of force, to illegal defiance, to uncooperative foot-dragging, to the refusal of national financial incentives, to provid-

3. McCulloch v. Maryland, 17 U.S. 316, 421 (1819).
4. Gibbons v. Ogden, 22 U.S. 1, 222 (1824).

ing heightened protection for individual liberty, to the use of political pressure and negotiation. If federalism is to operate properly—if state power is to be a potentially meaningful check on national power—a state must have the authority to engage in at least some of these activities. Since the source of such authority is the state constitution, a second function of a state constitution must therefore be to grant state governments a measure of power sufficient to allow them to engage in meaningful resistance to abusive exercises of national power.

The vital need for such powers is clarified by considering what would happen if a state constitution denied them. Imagine, for example, that a state constitution contained a provision requiring the state government to accept all federal funds without regard to the conditions placed by Congress on their use. Or a provision that barred state officials from taking the national government to court when it exceeded the scope of national power granted by the U.S. Constitution. Or a provision that prohibited the state government from accepting delegations of national programmatic authority so that every congressional program operating within the state had to be staffed by national employees answerable only to national authorities. It seems clear that in each of these cases the people of the state would have traded away important safeguards against abuses of national power without having gained anything in return.

It is possible, of course, that national power could be exercised in such a way as to achieve virtually the same results. Congress might create financial incentives so tempting that states would not feel free to refuse the funds no matter how onerous the conditions placed upon their distribution. Or Congress might create national programs and decide to staff them entirely with national employees, raising federal taxes as necessary to pay for what would amount to a duplicate national bureaucracy alongside state administrative organizations. Yet Congress need not, and usually does not, operate in this way, and it would incur significant political costs should it choose to do so. Thus, a state constitutional provision that tied the hands of the state in this manner would, as a practical matter, limit the state's ability to protect the interests of its citizens—perhaps severely so.

When states do occasionally tie their own hands in this way, the result is jarring. For example, Article I, § 12 of the Florida Constitution provides:

> The right of the people to be secure in their persons, houses, papers and effects against unreasonable searches and seizures, and against the unreasonable interception of private communications by any means, shall not be violated. No war-

rant shall be issued except upon probable cause, supported by affidavit, particularly describing the place or places to be searched, the person or persons, thing or things to be seized, the communication to be intercepted, and the nature of evidence to be obtained. This right shall be construed in conformity with the 4th Amendment to the United States Constitution, as interpreted by the United States Supreme Court. Articles or information obtained in violation of this right shall not be admissible in evidence if such articles or information would be inadmissible under decisions of the United State Supreme Court construing the 4th Amendment to the United States Constitution.

This provision prohibits the Florida government from granting to its citizens any rights against unreasonable search and arrest at the hands of Florida law enforcement officials greater than those they already enjoy as U.S. citizens under the Fourth and Fourteenth Amendments of the national Constitution. Apparently, this linkage of state to national individual rights applies no matter how little protection the national Constitution provides. The linkage would seem to apply even if the U.S. Supreme Court, in league with tyrannical national executive and legislative branches, construed the Fourth Amendment to permit, say, suspicionless arrests of political opponents of the regime in power—a practice distressingly familiar in other parts of the world and reminiscent of our own Alien and Sedition Act of 1798, which all three branches of the national government have since repudiated.

It is easy to understand why the people of Florida might choose to reduce the scope of state constitutional protections that limit the ability of the executive branch to catch and convict criminals. They might think that crime had become sufficiently serious and widespread as to require an adjustment to the constitutional balance between the competing goals of successfully protecting the public from crime and protecting the innocent from wrongful conviction. Certainly such an inclination would justify an amendment to the Florida Constitution designed to lower protections against search and arrest to levels Floridians considered more desirable. But it is difficult to see why Floridians would choose to limit the ability of their own state government to protect them from national tyranny in the event, however unlikely, that it materialized. Such a move needlessly surrenders state power that, in a federal system, serves as an important line of defense against abuses of national power.

Because federalism is such a broad and flexible concept, knowing that it requires state constitutions to grant state governments a measure of power sufficient to resist national tyranny tells us relatively little about exactly what powers a state must or should have to fulfill its role in the federal system. State polities surely have considerable latitude in constitutionally allocating and structuring state power sufficient to serve federalism's purposes. On the other hand, faithful adherence to federalism's structural requirements may well preclude state polities from making certain constitutional choices about state power that lie at the extreme minimalist end of the spectrum. A true night-watchman state government that is allocated only enough power to structure and enforce private market discipline, for example, might lack sufficient power to mount the kind of formidable resistance to abuses of national power that states may require to perform their checking function effectively.

Romanticism reconsidered: the state as popular champion. Having in a previous chapter criticized an overly romanticized view of statehood and state constitutional power, I must now offer a significant, though narrow, qualification. As we have seen, federalism contemplates not only that the state and national governments will use their power to check and restrain each other, but that they will do so at the behest of the people whose good they are charged with securing. On this view, the state and national governments are not so much competitors as alternatives. For such a system to work, each level of government must have the capacity to act as the champion of popular liberty and the public good. If the pursuit of these goals should happen to cause one government to come into opposition with the other, then conflict will result—but it will be conflict undertaken for the purpose of achieving, or suppressing threats to, the public good.

The role of the people in this system is to discern which level of government will more faithfully and effectively pursue their interests, and to shift their allegiance to that government as circumstances dictate.[5] In the early days of the Republic, Americans identified most closely with their state governments and routinely assumed that their states would most reliably champion their interests against a new and possibly dangerous national government.[6] Yet, as Madison argued:

> If . . . the people should in future become more partial to the federal than to the State governments, the change can only result from such manifest and irresistible

5. Pettys, "Competing for the People's Affection."
6. Wood, "Foreword: State Constitution-Making in the American Revolution."

proofs of a better administration as will overcome all their antecedent propensities. And in that case, the people ought not surely to be precluded from giving most of their confidence where they may discover it to be most due . . . .[7]

Thus, Madison anticipated not only that the state and national governments might clash, but that popular loyalty itself might shift between them.

Allegiance to a state, however, is a crucially important component of political identity. One does not simply choose allegiance to one sovereign over another the way one chooses a pair of shoes. Such a significant aspect of identity itself is not so easily retooled, and the people might find it at best awkward and perhaps emotionally difficult simply to place their confidence in a government because it would be temporarily expedient for them to do so.[8] To serve as a repository of popular confidence, a government must be the kind of entity to which a polity may plausibly turn and in which it may plausibly place its trust. Here, then, is where constitutional Romanticism has its legitimate place.

The characteristics that a putative government must possess to command popular trust and allegiance cannot possibly be catalogued in the abstract since they are contingent upon such a wide variety of political, social, and cultural factors specific to individual communities. Still, in the political tradition that all Americans have inherited, there is no question that constitutions play a potentially important role in the process of shaping and cementing political identity. In a familiar and widely accepted account of constitutionalism, a constitution is understood to be a self-conscious act of social definition by the polity that creates it.[9] Because a constitution functions as a democratic expression of the polity's aspirations for good and enduring self-government, it therefore by definition embodies the values the people understand themselves to hold. Moreover, as a document commanding governmental obedience to the popular will, a constitution secures the integrity of political life by ensuring that the organs of constitutional government act consistently with

7. Madison, *The Federalist,* No. 46, 295.

8. As Thomas Jefferson observed in the Declaration of Independence: "Prudence, indeed, will dictate, that governments long established, should not be changed for light and transient causes; and accordingly all experience hath shown, that mankind are more disposed to suffer, while evils are sufferable, than to right themselves by abolishing the forms to which they are accustomed." Declaration of Independence, ¶ 2.

9. See, e.g., McCulloch v. Maryland, 17 U.S. 316 (1819); U.S. Const. preamble.

fundamental political norms. A dual relationship consequently arises: the constitution both expresses and shapes political identity.[10]

But to say that a constitution may perform these symbolic and constitutive functions is by no means to say that it inevitably will do so. Before a constitution can fulfill its role in the process by which political identity is actually constituted, two conditions must be met. First, the constitution must be the kind of document that could plausibly serve as a touchstone of political identity. While it is again impossible to reach abstract conclusions about what such a document must look like, it seems safe to say that the constitution must look "constitutional"—it must contain the kind of high aspirations and weighty decisions concerning collective political life that we expect to find in constitutions, and to contain them in sufficient quantity to give it the "heft" a legitimate constitution might be expected to have. As we saw in chapter 1, state constitutions have frequently been criticized for containing too much fluff and trivia of a nature more suitable to legislation than constitutions, and this is sometimes thought to detract from their seriousness.

The second condition of "constitutionality" seems circular, and in a sense it is: a constitution can play no role in constituting a political identity unless it actually does so. A constitution cannot be "made" or "deemed" to constitute political identity; constitutions do not constitute political identity because they have to, or because that is their job. If a constitution constitutes political identity, it does so because it does. An example may help here; strangely enough, the political career of an emperor nicely illustrates the point.

In 1836 Louis Napoleon Bonaparte, having spent his life in exile, decided to attempt to regain his grandfather's throne. Believing that the French people's nostalgia for the glory of empire would cause them to flock to his banner, Bonaparte and a handful of followers landed in a small boat on the beach at Strasbourg. As he was rowed to shore, Bonaparte tried to appear majestic by standing upright in the pitching boat, wearing his royal uniform. On his shoulder perched an eagle, the symbol of the Napoleonic empire. To keep the eagle on

---

10. As Robert Post has written, "Constitutional law is fundamental because it reflects and embodies the essential political ethos that makes governance possible within a particular culture." Post, "The Challenge of State Constitutions," 45. For expressions of similar views, see, e.g., Bobbitt, *Constitutional Fate;* White, *Justice as Translation,* ix, 23, 217; White, *Heracles' Bow,* 34, 80, 169; Delgado, "Storytelling for Oppositionists and Others," 2412; Cover, "Foreword: Nomos and Narrative." The role of the Constitution in American public life is thoroughly examined in Kammen, *A Machine That Would Go of Itself.*

his shoulder, Bonaparte was forced to stick a piece of bacon in his ear.[11] Perhaps he should have viewed this exigency as a poor omen, for although Bonaparte landed on the beach triumphantly, the French people did not spontaneously arise and take up his cause. Instead, he was immediately arrested and deported. By 1848, however, the political climate in France had changed radically. Bonaparte returned and was elected president of the assembly. In 1851, he led a coup that overthrew the Second Republic and had himself crowned emperor as Napoleon III. In an 1852 plebiscite, the French people overwhelmingly approved these actions, thus inaugurating the Second Empire.

Bonaparte was correct in 1836 when he surmised that constitutive symbols play an indispensable role in orienting and defining political identity. But he was wrong to assume that the mere presence of such symbols is sufficient to make them effective. An imperial heir, a uniform, and an eagle had no constitutive power until the people of France decided, after an organic, evolutionary process of political change, that those symbols could in fact serve a constitutive role in the formulation of French political identity. Many theorists of state constitutional law seem to make the Napoleonic mistake. They assume that because a state constitution exists, and seems somehow "constitutional," it in fact serves as a meaningful point of orientation for the political identity of the residents of that state. But nothing could be further from the truth. A constitution that *could,* judging from its form and content, serve as a focal point for a society's political identity is nothing more than a piece of paper until it actually *does* begin to serve that function. When that happens depends upon completely contingent and uncontrollable political processes that can unfold in only one way: organically. The impulse to define political identity in terms of the polity identified and constituted by a particular constitution is one that can emerge only from the natural play of political and social forces within the relevant society.

This principle is equally well illustrated by the ambiguous role of the Canadian Constitution in that country's social politics. Compared with the U.S. case, it is somewhat more difficult to say of what exactly Canada's Constitution consists, although the Constitution Act of 1867, which granted Canada its

---

11. I have this story from Professor John Merriman of Yale, who says it was widely circulated in France at the time. Karl Marx, and more recently James McMillan, claim that a vulture was pressed into service as a pathetic substitute for an eagle, and, alas, they omit any mention of the bacon. See Marx, *The Eighteenth Brumaire of Louis Bonaparte,* 63; McMillan, *Napoleon III,* 14.

independence from Great Britain, is generally understood to furnish the critical documentary component. Yet, unlike the U.S. Constitution, the Canadian Constitution has not served a deeply constitutive role in national politics:

> [T]he ... Act enshrined few if any eternal principles and is singularly devoid of inspirational content. The Canadian constitution was given birth in no revolutionary or populist context, and ... it has acquired little symbolic aura in its subsequent history. The movement toward Confederation was not so much a rejection of the United States or of Europe as it was a pragmatic response to a series of conditions and considerations that were at once political, economic, military and diplomatic.[12]

Indeed, some have questioned whether there is even a "sovereign Canadian people" capable of serving as the referent of a constitutive politics of national identity upon which a constitution might operate.[13]

Here, then, is the salient point. To serve fully the role that federalism assigns to states, a state constitution ought to be drafted in a way that will facilitate and support the coalescence of a meaningful state-oriented political identity. It should describe an attractive collective political life. It should deal with fundamental questions of collective self-governance. It should create a government with sufficient power to implement the political life it describes. But whether the state or its constitution actually will serve as an organizing factor in the political identities of its residents is a contingency that depends, as Madison observed, upon where the people may happen to discover that their trust and loyalty is best placed.

Self-Restraint

To fulfill its function in the federal system, a state must have in some degree the powers just discussed. Assuming that the people of the state intend to make use of a written constitution, the state constitution should thus grant the state the power to pursue through independent means the welfare of its citizens. It should authorize the state to exercise powers sufficient to resist and obstruct abusive exercises of national power. And it would be wise for the state constitution to take a form that could serve, should circumstances so re-

---

12. McKenna, "Introduction: A Legacy of Questions," xvi (internal footnote omitted).
13. See Russell, *Constitutional Odyssey*.

quire, as a constitutive matrix for the coalescence of an independent, state-focused political identity in the event the national government proves to be unworthy of that role.

The granting to state government of any kind of substantial power, however, entails a corresponding risk: namely, that the granted power will be used tyrannically against the people of the state. Under the regime established by the U.S. Constitution, the risk of state tyranny is lessened by the fact that the national government has significant authority to curtail abuses of state power. Nevertheless, the prevailing philosophy of American constitutionalism holds that it is unwise to rely too heavily on any single method for restraining the abuse of official power. This in turn suggests that state constitutions should rely not merely on the external constraint of national intervention, but should, like the national Constitution, institutionalize some kind of internal system of governmental self-restraint. Measures for causing a state government to practice self-restraint include partially disabling it by dividing power horizontally, vertically, or in both ways; creating a bill of rights; and establishing judicial review as an enforcement mechanism.

American political theory, illuminated by subsequent experience, provides substantial reasons to suggest why a state polity might be fearful, or at least suspicious, of state power. Certainly the best-known theoretical justification for fearing substantial grants of power to state governments is Madison's thesis that a polity's susceptibility to faction varies inversely with its size. Madison addressed the problem of factions in *The Federalist,* No. 10, where he defined them as groups that pursue their own private interest at the expense of the common good. Madison argued that the single most critical problem of constitutional design is to prevent the government from being controlled by a majority faction. The solution he offered to this difficulty is a large, national republic.

A large republic is more resistant to majority faction than a small one, Madison argued, for three reasons. First, because an effective legislature can only be so large no matter what the size of the republic, the number of people each legislator represents increases more rapidly than the number of legislators as the size of the republic increases. This means that a large republic will have larger election districts than a small one. If we may assume, Madison suggested, that "the proportion of fit characters be not less in the large than in the small republic"—if, that is to say, wise and virtuous individuals are distributed evenly throughout the population—then each voter in a large republic will have a greater choice of good candidates, thereby leading to "a greater probability of a fit choice."[14] Second, the large size of election districts in a large republic means that any successful candidate must attract the support of more voters than would be the case in a small republic with smaller election districts. This works to the benefit of the better quality candidates, Madison argued, because

> it will be more difficult for unworthy candidates to practise with success the vicious arts by which election are too often carried; and the suffrages of the people being more free, will be more likely to center on men who possess the most attractive merit and the most diffusive and established characters.[15]

Finally, large election districts also impede the ability of factions to coalesce and to elect venal candidates because each election district is likely to be large enough to contain "a greater variety of parties and interests" than would a small election district, thereby reducing the likelihood that a faction will form a majority within any district. Furthermore, the sheer size of such a district makes it "more difficult for all who feel [a factious motive] to discover their own strength and to act in unison."[16] Thus, in Madison's view, the creation of a large republic can be expected to yield three advantages: it will result in "the substitution of representatives whose enlightened views and virtuous sentiments render them superior to local prejudices and schemes of injustice"; it will impede the ability of any minority faction "to outnumber and oppress the rest"; and it will raise "obstacles to the concert and accomplishment of the secret wishes of an unjust and interested majority," should one appear.[17]

It follows from Madison's account that a small republic such as a state will be more susceptible to majority faction than the national government would be, and the smaller the state the worse the risk. Indeed, Madison was not reticent on this point: he opened the essay with a frank and withering assessment of the performance of state governments following the Revolution:

> Complaints are everywhere heard from our most considerate and virtuous citizens, equally the friends of public and private faith and of public and personal lib-

---

14. Madison, *The Federalist,* No. 10, 82.
15. Id. at 82–83.
16. Id. at 83.
17. Id. at 83–84.

erty, that our governments are too unstable, that the public good is disregarded in the conflicts of rival parties, and that measures are too often decided, not according to the rules of justice and the rights of the minor party, but by the superior force of an interested and overbearing majority.... [T]he distresses under which we labor ... [include] that prevailing and increasing distrust of public engagements and alarm for private rights which are echoed from one end of the continent to the other. These must be chiefly, if not wholly, effects of the unsteadiness and injustice with which a factious spirit has tainted our public administration.[18]

In a later essay, Madison went even further, invoking Rhode Island to make his point. "It can be little doubted," he wrote, "that if the State of Rhode Island was separated from the Confederacy and left to itself, the insecurity of rights under the popular form of government within such narrow [geographical] limits would be displayed by ... reiterated oppressions of factious majorities."[19]

Madison was hardly alone in this assessment: the Constitutional Convention of 1787 was called in large part because of a general consensus among leaders of the revolutionary generation that popular self-government in the states was failing to live up to revolutionary ideals of republican virtue.[20] If this argument is sound, then liberty requires even more vigilant protection from state governments than from the national government because it is far easier for an oppressive majority to take over the apparatus of state government, and to turn state power against minorities, than is the case on the national level.

Subsequent experience suggests that Madison was correct: over the long haul, the more serious threats to liberty have tended to come from state governments rather than from the national government. Certainly the most serious of these was the practice of slavery, which the national government ended only after one of the most violent national interventions in the global history of civil war. The American Civil War did not, of course, end state practices of maltreating former slaves and their descendants. Although its position waffled for many decades, the national government ultimately intervened on several occasions during the mid-twentieth century by enacting and enforcing civil rights legislation, and by taking steps to end state-backed racial segregation in schools. While the national government has been responsible for its share of

18. Madison, *The Federalist*, No. 10, 77–78.
19. Madison, *The Federalist*, No. 52, 325.
20. Wood, *The Radicalism of the American Revolution*, 229–31.

invasions of individual liberty, most notably during the Cold War, state governments have much more frequently threatened liberty through such means as prior restraints, criminal and civil punishment of unpopular speech, extracted confessions, invasive police practices, and racial and gender discrimination. Moreover, in many of these cases, the national government has affirmatively protected American citizens from these deprivations of liberty at the hands of the states, particularly through judicial intervention.

These examples suggest that state power is rightly to be feared as much as or more than national power, and that the people of a state contemplating adoption of a state constitution would do well to include in it some set of substantial restraints on the exercise of state governmental powers that, for other reasons, must be affirmatively granted.

TRADEOFFS IN THE DESIGN OF STATE CONSTITUTIONS

From the mechanics of federalism we may infer that state constitutions should empower state governments to perform the functions that federalism contemplates for them. From basic American political theory we may infer that state constitutions also should institute a form of constitutional self-restraint so that state power is not abused by state officials. Although both of these inferences rest upon the same stock of basic assumptions about power and its risks, they point, unfortunately, in opposite directions: one inference calls upon state constitutions to grant state governments significant power; the other calls upon state constitutions deliberately to impair state power by hobbling it with internal self-restraints. State constitutional design thus necessarily involves making tradeoffs between these two goals.

One important way this tension manifests itself is by requiring a tradeoff between the implementation of internal state self-restraint, on one hand, and the grant of state power for the purpose of checking national abuses, on the other. The point of federalism, as with any constitutional separation of powers, is to establish institutions in which power does not merely oppose power, but opposes it effectively.[21] If a state is to check abuses of national power, it needs power of its own. To be sure, not every method that a state might use to resist national abuses requires a substantial authorization of state power. Even the weakest state government may engage in political negotiation with

21. Madison, *The Federalist,* No. 51, 322.

national officials, or refuse financial incentives dangled by the national government. These are, however, fairly passive forms of resistance. Even the more modest affirmative means of resisting national power require a more significant allocation to the state of governmental authority. To manipulate national programs by participating in them while simultaneously varying their terms from national baselines, for example, requires the state to have, at a minimum, the affirmative power to legislate in the area in question. Where the programmatic variations require the state to expand eligibility for a national program, say, or to provide more generous benefits to participants, the state also must have the power to raise sufficient revenue to fund its expanded program; establish and fund a state executive bureaucracy to implement the program; and provide sufficient administrative and judicial oversight to enforce the program's terms. Such actions require, by any measure, a substantial degree of governmental power. A state obviously needs even more power if it is to have the capacity to engage in the more dramatic forms of extraconstitutional resistance. A state that wishes to defy national authority by threats of force, for example, must have sufficient power to raise and maintain a military presence of sufficient size to make the threat credible. Doing so would require a substantial commitment of independent state resources, a commitment that even today few American states could plausibly undertake.

On the other hand, the more power a state is granted, the greater the risk it poses to its own people. A state with the power to mount effective resistance to national tyranny unquestionably has the capacity to turn that power against its citizens. State constitutions must, of course, guard against threats to liberty that emanate from the state itself by creating self-restraint mechanisms such as separated powers, a bill of rights, and judicial review. Moreover, the greater the risk a state government poses to the liberty of its own citizens, the more effective must be any constitutional apparatus of internal self-restraint.

These tensions impose upon state constitutions a structural tradeoff whose parameters are defined by the effectiveness of state power and the effectiveness of limitations on those powers. At one end of the spectrum, a state constitution might create an extremely potent state government enjoying ample authority to impede national tyranny and facing few internal impediments to the effective exercise of those powers. Such a state government would be capable of vigorously protecting the liberty of its people against invasion by the national government, but only at the cost of leaving its citizens relatively vulnerable to invasions of liberty by the state itself. At the other end of the spectrum, a state constitution might create a state government enjoying relatively few powers or facing significant internal self-restraints that impair its ability effectively to exercise granted powers. Such a state government, because it would be weak, would pose few direct threats to the welfare of the state's citizens. It would, however, leave them relatively vulnerable to abuses originating at the national level.

This particular tradeoff is a specific manifestation of a more general problem raised by constitutional drafting. In designing any constitution, designers usually face a tradeoff between making a government effective and making it unthreatening. A state constitution can grant the state government significant affirmative power for the purpose of making it as effective an agent as possible for achieving the public good. Conversely, the state constitution can impose significant mechanisms of self-restraint upon the government to make it as safe as possible to live under. But it cannot do both at the same time; effectiveness can be purchased only at the cost of reduced safety, and vice versa.

How a polity chooses to strike this balance depends upon several factors. A polity's choice between effective government power and effective restraint of that power is necessarily informed by its preferences for public, as opposed to private, solutions to common problems. A polity that chooses to place significant obstacles in the way of its government's exercise of granted powers is one that probably does not wish its government to do much. The fact that a government acts sparingly does not, however, mean that nothing ever gets done; it means only that private responses to social or economic problems rarely will be displaced by collective political action.[22] Any group's preference for public or private action will turn on such factors as its philosophy of governance; its estimation of the comparative trustworthiness of public and private actors; and, often, specific historical experiences or "local conditions" that affect the way in which the group has arrived at its political beliefs. For example, a bad experience with powerful, centralized government may make an indelible impression on a people, leading them to prefer weaker, decentralized forms.[23]

None of this, however, is unique to state constitutions. The designers of the U.S. Constitution faced the very same questions. They had to decide just how strong to make the new national government, and their decision was informed by their understanding of government as far less powerful, and far less

---

22. On the notion of private ordering furnishing a baseline for purposes of constitutional adjudication, see Sunstein, *The Partial Constitution,* 68–92; Sunstein, "Lochner's Legacy."

23. See, e.g., Woodward, *The Burden of Southern History,* 17–21.

of an influence on the day-to-day life of a people, than is common today. Part of the Framers' decision process involved deciding how much of a role the national government ought to play in curbing abuses of liberty by the states. In 1787, the states were powerful political actors. To create a national government capable of impeding state tyranny would have required granting it powers that would have seemed quite substantial in the context of eighteenth-century constitutionalism.

Faced with this equation, the Framers of the U.S. Constitution chose to make the national government comparatively weak, sacrificing its ability to check state abuses in favor of moderating the potential threat it might independently pose to American liberty—or so they publicly proclaimed. In one of his least prescient writings, Madison argued at great length that the national government would be far weaker than the state governments in virtually every respect, and would consequently pose a negligible threat to state power. Conversely, he maintained, the state governments would have ample resources to curb abusive exercises of national power.[24] Indeed, although he recognized the nature of the tradeoff between the grant and the restraint of national power, Madison went so far as to deny that it had any meaningful ramifications for the operation of the federal system: "the powers proposed to be lodged in the federal government," he argued, "are as little formidable to those reserved to the individual States as they are indispensably necessary to accomplish the purposes of the Union."[25] The national government, in other words, would have all the power it needed to pursue the public good effectively, but the amount of power it would require to fulfill its functions would be small and unthreatening to the states because the national government's functions were to be so limited. By the time the Supreme Court handed down its decision in *McCulloch v. Maryland,* however, Madison's account of national power seemed dubious and naive.[26]

Although the structural tradeoffs in constitutional design on the national and state levels resemble one another in most respects, there is one way in which they differ significantly. There is only one national Constitution, and its

24. Madison, The *Federalist,* Nos. 45, 46.

25. Madison, *The Federalist,* No. 46, 300.

26. To be fair, Madison apparently did not really believe the argument he ended up making in *The Federalist.* See Rakove, *Original Meanings,* 197–201; McCoy, *The Last of the Fathers,* ch. 3. He also supported the constitutionality of the national bank, which the Court sustained in *McCulloch.*

content, insofar as the states are concerned, is fixed. In contrast, there are fifty state constitutions that not only vary one from another, but also are variable in the sense that the people of a state may change the content of their state's constitution at any time, by a process completely independent from that by which the national Constitution may be changed. In consequence, national power itself is relatively fixed whereas state power can vary considerably. I shall have more to say about this in chapter 7, but it is worth mentioning in this context as a parameter informing the calculus of state constitutional design.

As we have seen, constitutional design in a federal system requires balancing several different processes at once to create a system in which governments can simultaneously accomplish their assigned tasks, engage in appropriate self-restraint, and mutually monitor and check one another. This is a dynamic system in which alterations to one part have ramifications for the operation of the other parts. Yet the process of constitutional design appears very different when approached from the state rather than the national end of the equation. From the perspective of the states, the national Constitution appears fixed for two reasons. First, its content lies completely beyond the power of any individual state—or even the power of the states acting collectively—to affect. No state, therefore, can influence the extent of national power (although states may be able to influence the way national power is used). Second, although the U.S. Constitution can be amended or even replaced, the amendment process is exceedingly difficult and unlikely to be undertaken successfully, in part because constitutional change on a national scale requires the mobilization of a considerable portion of the entire national polity, a daunting task. Because national power is conferred by the U.S. Constitution, and the content of the U.S. Constitution is unlikely as a practical matter to change, the extent of national power is, from the state point of view, a fixed variable, one that can be counted on to remain relatively constant.

The scope of state power is a different matter. From the point of view of any particular state, the scope of its power is an open question. The people of a state have substantial discretion to grant or deny state power in their state's constitution. The content of the state constitution is completely within their control, except for a few limitations imposed by the national Constitution. Should they choose to mobilize themselves to alter some aspect of state power, they may do so freely. Amending the state constitution is easier than amending the national Constitution not only because the polity is smaller and more easily mobilized, but because most states have chosen to give themselves a constitutional amendment process that is substantially easier to use successfully than the one set out in Article V of the U.S. Constitution.[27] As a result, the scope of state power in the American federal system is, from the point of view of the states, a dependent variable that may be adjusted as circumstances require to alter the balance of state and national power.

This means that state power can be granted or adjusted quickly, flexibly, and most important of all, reactively. It need not and should not be conceived as static, as though it were some kind of fixed constitutional apparatus whose every detail was settled at the inception of the federal system and cannot be changed. On the contrary, the variability of state constitutional power means that state power can be deployed as circumstances require, in just the measure and in just the way it is needed, to establish (or re-establish) a satisfactory balance of power between the state and national governments. As we shall see in chapter 7, this flexibility has important consequences for how state constitutions should be interpreted.

CONSTITUTIONAL ORDERING OF STATE POWER

The final function that a state constitution ought to serve is to set out any necessary details concerning the purposes for which granted powers may be used; state any conditions attached to the use of such powers; identify the circumstances in which limitations on power apply; and lay out any other measures required to translate an otherwise abstract plan of state political self-rule into a workable blueprint for constitutional governance. These are the kinds of considerations that the founding generation of constitutional drafters sometimes referred to as the "ordering" of governmental power. A constitution, on this view, does not merely mete out power and authority willy-nilly; it provides additionally for the orderly exercise of power.

State constitutions generally contain many such provisions, far more so than the national Constitution. They often go into considerable detail—some say too much detail—concerning procedures to be followed by government actors. Consider, for example, the kinds of specific conditions and limitations state constitutions frequently place upon the legislative process. In many states, for example, a bill must be read three times before coming to the floor. The title of the bill must accurately reflect its subject matter. No piece of legislation may deal with more than one subject. No piece of legislation may pro-

27. Tarr, *Understanding State Constitutions*, 34–37.

vide relief to any particular designated individual. State and local legislatures may not impose new taxes or extend existing ones, or borrow money except for certain highly restricted purposes, without popular approval. Provisions such as these typically are understood primarily as limitations on state power designed to protect the liberty of state citizens in specific ways. Indeed, most of these provisions have been included in state constitutions for the express purpose of preventing repetition of specific, historically identifiable acts of governmental malfeasance.

A functional analysis of state constitutions puts these kinds of provisions in a different light by illuminating their functional consequences for state power in a federal system. Any provision that hampers the ability of the legislature to legislate, for example, does more than merely restrain the legislature from abusing its powers. Such a provision also inhibits to some degree the legislature's ability to use its independent constitutional powers in pursuit of the public good. Similarly, limits on the scope of legislative power, or the manner in which it may be used, can reduce the state's ability to deploy legislative power to counteract abuses of national power by Congress, the president, or the federal courts. A state polity considering how best to order the exercise of constitutionally granted powers need not approach the question with these considerations foremost in mind, of course. Nevertheless, such considerations are relevant to the process of state constitutional design, and a full assessment of their ramifications must look to their impact outside the state as well as within it.

5

Patterns of Distrust

IF FEDERALISM IS a structural system that divides governmental power for the purpose of protecting liberty, the goals and mechanics of federalism clearly play a crucial role in defining what states are, what powers they should have, and the purposes for which state power may be exercised. The significance of the federal structure for defining state power is complicated, however, by the fact that state power is not solely a means for securing the welfare of a state's people. As we have seen, state power also threatens the public welfare, for the very powers that a state might use to pursue the public good and to check abuses of national power also can be turned against the state's people. This means that decisions about the scope and extent of state power require that some balance be struck among competing considerations. As the vehicles by which decisions about state power are translated into action, state constitutions unavoidably embody the tensions and tradeoffs that shape decisions about state power. These tradeoffs appear most notably in the balance that a state constitution strikes between empowerment and self-restraint—between granting the state power to pursue the public good and to check national abuses, on one hand, and limiting or creating impediments to the use of those same powers, on the other.

There is no limit to the number of different ways in which a state constitution may strike a balance among the various functions that constitutional federalism assigns it. In this sense, an understanding of the structural and functional framework in which state constitutions operate tells us little about the content of any particular state constitution. A state constitution that grants the state government enormous power subject to very few restraints fulfills its function in the federal system just as much as does a state constitution that grants the state few powers, or one that imposes burdensome prerequisites and conditions upon the exercise of granted powers. Each of these constitutions fulfills its role in a different way, of course, and reflects different judgments about how state power should be arranged and balanced. Each constitution gestures toward a different conception of how the federal system should operate—which level of government should make certain kinds of decisions, which poses the greater threat to liberty, and so on. Yet each state constitution contemplates taking its place in a system that is recognizably federal.

Although the ways in which a state polity may choose to strike the constitutional balance are theoretically unlimited, the considerations that inform that choice are not. In fact, a polity's choices about the content and structure of its state constitution are likely to be influenced by only a small number of critical considerations that, together, define a range of major constitutional possibilities. These considerations are of two types. The first relates to the particular patterns of distrust of governmental power that prevail among the people of any given state. This distrust of governmental power itself falls along two different dimensions: the relative distrust a state's people feel toward public as compared to private power; and the relative distrust they feel for state as compared to national power. The other factor that informs a state's constitutional choices concerns its people's preferences for allocating constitutional decisionmaking authority between themselves and the state's courts. Discussion of this latter dimension, which is especially significant for working out an approach to interpreting the state's constitution, is deferred to chapter 6.

GENERAL DISTRUST OF GOVERNMENT

American constitutional theory rests on the bedrock proposition that no government is entitled to the people's complete trust and faith. The founding generation understood the creation of any constitutional government to be an exercise in both necessity and distrust. Government is necessary, argued Madison, because the governed are not "angels"—they will not, that is to say, always behave in desirable ways unless coercive state power is available to make them do so. As Madison put it, "what is government itself but the greatest of all reflections on human nature?"[1] Yet the creation of a government also requires the governed to indulge a sense of distrust because the governors also are not angels:

> If men were angels, no government would be necessary. If angels were to govern men, neither external nor internal controls on government would be necessary.

1. Madison, *The Federalist*, No. 51, 322.

> In framing a government which is to be administered by men over men, the great difficulty lies in this: you must first enable the government to control the governed; and in the next place oblige it to control itself.[2]

The people thus establish and institutionalize their government, whether by constitutional means or otherwise, against a backdrop of general distrust of governmental power.

Distrust of government is meaningful, however, only in comparison to some alternative. If skepticism of government power has any prescriptive force for societal arrangements, the arrangement it prescribes must be that the role of government in social and political affairs should be relatively modest. But minimizing the level of government involvement in daily life does not itself minimize the activities of daily life; it means only that social rules will be made and enforced by means other than the exercise of government power. In American political thought, the principal alternative to governmental power is traditionally said to be private power. In the traditional view, private power is what exists in the absence of government. People use their private power to enter mutually beneficial economic agreements, such as trade and employment, or to establish social relations pertaining to the family or community. Private arrangements, then, are those into which individuals would voluntarily enter if government did not interfere. A generalized distrust of government thus implies a correspondingly greater faith in private power as a tool for ordering the social and economic spheres—a faith that private power in any form is less dangerous than organized public power and less likely to intrude upon valued liberties.

Because, on this view, private power is the default method by which groups and individuals arrange their affairs and order their lives, private arrangements are understood to be more "natural" than the kinds of arrangements people reach after government power has been applied to alter the range of available choices. This view has been forcefully criticized on the ground that the traditional understanding of the difference between public and private power unjustifiably takes as "natural" a set of contingent political, social, and economic arrangements that, far from being natural and freely chosen, are in fact sustained only by significant exercises of government authority.[3] For example, in the traditional view, private power includes the power to do with one's property as one sees fit. Yet, critics point out, "property" and "owner-

2. Id.
3. See, e.g., Sunstein, *The Partial Constitution,* 68–92; Sunstein, "Lochner's Legacy."

ship" are not features of some private, pregovernmental natural world, but rather political and economic relationships constructed collectively by society and maintained by the force of government power. Those who own property enjoy exclusive personal dominion over particular objects only because a complex system of laws, backed by a judicial system and executive enforcement authority, recognizes and defends such a relationship.

In light of this critique, a better view of the traditional juxtaposition between public and private power understands it as expressing a preference for one form of government-backed sociopolitical arrangements over another, and in particular a preference for the status quo. Those arrangements consistent with the status quo are elevated to the status of "natural" by collapsing them into whatever private, voluntary transactions the existing legal rules already sanction. Government intervention recognizing or enforcing such arrangements is then understood as maintaining a form of natural order. Government intervention that changes the status quo rules, on the other hand, is redefined as artificial and assigned to the realm of public power. Consequently, when we say that people distrust governmental power, or that they prefer private power to government power, what we usually mean is that they value highly some particular set of legally backed economic and political arrangements, and fear turning over to government an amount of power sufficient to enable it to upset the arrangements they prefer.

This critique sheds considerable light not only on the reasons why "distrust of government" has remained a potent force in American politics since the founding, but also on the reasons why the substantive meaning of governmental distrust has continually evolved. Over the last two centuries, the reach of governmental power at every level has expanded far beyond its original boundaries. After an industrial revolution, a civil war, global military ventures, worldwide expansion of trade, the evolution of social welfare policies, and ceaseless technological advances, to name only a few developments, government now regulates aspects of social and economic life to an extent that the founding generation would have found inconceivable. The modern trend, moreover, has been to rely increasingly on government to accomplish collective social and economic objectives, partly because certain goals have proven to be unattainable without the kind of massive marshaling of power that only a strong government can undertake, and partly because Americans have grown more accustomed to and comfortable with continual, direct governmental intervention in many areas of daily life. The pressure for even more reliance on powerful, centralized government power could well continue to increase given the boundary-crossing nature of so many contemporary problems—the globalization of trade, regional and global pollution, and regulation of worldwide economic markets, for example.

Despite these developments, distrust of government power remains a staple of American political discourse, particularly from the political Right. Yet it is clear that the kind of distrust of government power expressed in contemporary notions of minimal government means something very different from what it might have meant fifty or a hundred years ago. At the dawn of the twentieth century, government minimalists would have opposed government intervention in race relations, for example, or interference in the operation of a laissez-faire economy.[4] Today's government minimalist, in contrast, may well accept the propriety of government prohibitions on racial, ethnic, and religious discrimination, and gladly accept any personal benefits such laws provide, but be unwilling to accept the extension of those prohibitions to gays and lesbians. Or the contemporary minimalist may accept and even rely on government financial incentives and subsidies for agricultural businesses, but be unwilling to accept more aggressive forms of regulation that for environmental reasons prohibit certain agricultural products or practices.

COMPARATIVE DISTRUST OF NATIONAL AND STATE GOVERNMENT

The concept of government distrust is further complicated and contextualized by the unlikelihood that any polity will distrust all governments equally. As we have seen, the Framers specifically contemplated that popular trust in the national and state governments would vary over time and according to circumstances. The people, as Madison put it, will "giv[e] most of their confidence where they may discover it to be most due."[5] In a federal system, then, an important variable in the constitutionalization of state power is the extent to which state power is trusted in comparison to national power. This relative degree of distrust influences heavily the amount of power a state polity is willing to grant to state government, as well as the kinds of limitations the polity places upon the state government.

A state polity might be less willing to trust one level of government than the other for several reasons. First, size alone may affect political dynamics in

4. See Plessy v. Ferguson, 163 U.S. 537 (1896); Lochner v. New York, 198 U.S. 45 (1905).
5. Madison, *The Federalist,* No. 46, 295.

different ways on the state and national level. As pointed out in chapter 4, state political processes may well be more susceptible to a destructive, factional politics of self-interest than are national political processes simply because states are smaller, and contain fewer people, than the nation. As Madison argued in *The Federalist,* No. 10, the number of distinct interests that any polity contains increases with its size. The more interests any given territory embraces, the less likely it is that any single interest will be able to dominate and exploit the whole. Madison seemed to believe that when self-interested factions fight one another to a draw, the electoral playing field is left open to the kind of enlightened and virtuous statesmen he favored. In this more cynical age, we might not share Madison's faith that virtuous statesmen stand in the wings, waiting for the various factions to neutralize one another; yet we might still share his conclusion that national politics is likely to be cleaner and more trustworthy than state politics. If no single faction is able to seize control of the apparatus of government, only a coalition may do so, and to form a coalition requires compromise. The more that assuming power depends on compromise, the less the likelihood that the interests of some will be sacrificed outright to satisfy the interests of others. National politics would then be safer than state politics if taking power nationally required broader coalitions, and thus more compromise, than taking power on the state level.

A second way in which the state and national governments are often said to differ in trustworthiness concerns their responsiveness to the popular will. From the founding all the way up to contemporary calls for devolution, the belief that state governments are more democratically responsive than the national government to the will of the people has been an article of faith of American political thought.[6] Indeed, the Framers deliberately designed the U.S.

---

6. The claim that state governments are more democratically responsive than the national government is sometimes meant in two distinct ways. First, the exercise of power on the state level is sometimes said to be more responsive because it better accommodates heterogeneity. Policy preferences often differ from region to region and state to state. While summing individual policy preferences nationwide should produce a policy that is preferred by a national majority, summing and implementing policy preferences state by state may be even more responsive by allowing an even greater number of people to be governed by policies that they prefer, thereby increasing overall social utility. See, e.g., McConnell, "Federalism: Evaluating the Founders' Design," 1493–94; Tarr and Katz, "Introduction," ix–x.

Second, state government is sometimes said to be more responsive than the national government because state governments are simply more likely to do what the people

Constitution to make the national government as unresponsive to the popular democratic will as possible while still preserving the principle of popular sovereignty. Like the ancient Greeks, the Framers feared democracy, associating it with instability and the rule of the mob. "Democracies," wrote Madison, "have ever been spectacles of turbulence and contention; have ever been found incompatible with personal security or the rights of property; and have in general been as short in their lives as they have been violent in their deaths."[7]

For this reason, the Framers drafted a Constitution characterized, as Madison candidly explained, by a "total exclusion of the people in their collective capacity" from the reins of government.[8] Instead, the most democratic feature of the original Constitution was the establishment of popular elections for representatives. Until ratification of the Seventeenth Amendment, senators were elected by state legislatures rather than popularly. The Constitution mandates no popular role in presidential elections: not only is the president elected by the Electoral College, but the Constitution leaves the manner of selecting electors to the state legislatures. The contemporary practice of popular election to the Electoral College is thus a matter of legislative grace rather than constitutional entitlement.

State governments, on the other hand, have always been viewed as far more responsive to public opinion than the national government. In part, this responsiveness may have to do with the way in which state constitutional government is usually institutionalized. With only a few exceptions, the people of the states have always directly elected their representatives and senators, and by the early nineteenth century virtually every state polity directly elected its governor as well. Most states also have a long history of electing at least some of their judges, as well as a variety of lower executive branch officials. Thus, the more extensive institutionalization of direct democratic self-rule on the state level may have contributed to the impression that state officials were more likely than federal officials to be responsive to the public will.

---

want. On this view, state governments are, for some set of institutional reasons, more democratic—more responsive to the will of the relevant polity—than is the national government. These two claims are of course related: the exercise of power on the state level is unlikely to better accommodate heterogeneous policy preferences across state polities unless state governments are at least as responsive to state polities as the federal government is to the national polity.

7. Madison, *The Federalist,* No. 10, 81.

8. Madison, *The Federalist,* No. 63, 387.

There is another sense, however, in which state government is typically thought to be more responsive to the popular will, one that is often captured in a conception of physical proximity between the governed and the governors. Hamilton, for example, clearly influenced by Adam Smith's account of moral sentiment, argued that the ties binding the people to their state officials would be greater than those binding them to their representatives on the national level:

> It is a known fact in human nature that its affections are commonly weak in proportion to the distance or diffusiveness of the object. Upon the same principle that a man is more attached to his family than to his neighborhood, to his neighborhood than to the community at large, the people of each State would be apt to feel a stronger bias towards their local governments than towards the government of the Union.[9]

This phenomenon, however, was said to work in both directions: government officials feel greater loyalty to those who are close at hand than to those who are physically distant. It was thus expected that state representatives, who live among the people of their state, would better know and more dearly care for the interests of their constituents than would national representatives, who would spend their time in a national capital at some great distance from those who elected them. Although delegates to the 1787 Constitutional Convention initially disagreed over the appropriate term of office for members of the House of Representatives, all agreed that it should be comparatively short for just this reason. Roger Sherman, for example, argued that elections should be annual because "the Representatives ought to return home and mix with the people. By remaining at the seat of Gov't they would acquire the habits of the place which might differ from those of their Constituents."[10] Only the great difficulty of long-distance travel in eighteenth-century America ultimately convinced the Framers to discard annual elections as impracticable.

A third factor that might affect the degree to which the people of a state trust the national and state governments concerns the relative competencies of each. Not every government has the power, resources, or incentives to do every job equally well. The ability of the national government to mobilize re-

---

9. Madison, *The Federalist*, No. 17 (Hamilton), 119. Compare Adam Smith, *The Theory of Moral Sentiments*, VI.ii.1–2 .

10. Madison, *Notes of Debates in the Federal Convention of 1787*, 170 (June 20, 1787).

sources around the nation, coordinate information, speak with a single voice, and conduct diplomacy abroad make it a far more sensible candidate than the states for the powers to conduct foreign affairs and to control military forces. Similarly, the national government's interest in the welfare of the nation as a whole makes it a better choice for the power to regulate interstate commerce than the states, which might have difficulty resisting internal pressures to advance the interests of state residents at the expense of residents of other states. Conversely, the greater ease with which state officials can gather and assimilate information about the social practices and customs of the state's citizens might make state government a better agent than the national government to regulate matters concerning the family, such as marriage, divorce, adoption, and wills. Zoning decisions, in contrast, are probably best made by a level of government even more local than the state. Problems that spill across jurisdictional boundaries, such as pollution or traffic congestion, might best be dealt with at a regional level, and so on.

Finally, a state polity might feel different degrees of trust for the state and national governments as the result of its actual historical experience of life under both. This is not a factor amenable to structural analysis, but rather a contingent matter that depends entirely upon the particular actions each level of government may have taken in the past, the effects of those actions on the state's citizens, and the ways in which the citizenry has chosen to interpret those actions. If the people of the state feel that the national government has, on the whole, treated them better than the state government, they may be more inclined to trust national power than state power, and vice versa.

For example, many Americans perceive the national government as more effective and trustworthy in protecting civil rights. Blacks in particular may hold state governments responsible for denying them the rights to vote and to be free from racial segregation in public facilities, and they may credit the national government with producing any gains in those areas. Americans of Japanese ancestry who live on the West Coast, mindful of the national internment policy during World War II, may feel differently. Sentiment in northern and eastern states tends to run in favor of the national government when it comes to environmental protection, yet in western states, where large portions of territory are administered by the national government, environmental initiatives restricting activity on federal lands have usually been regarded unfavorably. In Massachusetts, where intense national efforts prompted a highly successful cleanup of Boston Harbor, trust in the national government may well be greater than it is in Wyoming, say, where restrictions on grazing implemented over the objections of state officials have limited ranchers' access to national lands.

It is easy to overgeneralize here. The content of public opinion is elusive, and its causes even more so. Opinion within a state, moreover, may be deeply divided on any particular issue. Nevertheless, collective public understandings of historical events do sometimes emerge,[11] and such understandings are surely relevant to the reservoir of trust that the state and national governments have accumulated from the people of any state. Were this not the case, it would be difficult to understand how eighteenth-century American colonists came to believe that their local popular governments were far more deserving of their trust and confidence than was the royal governmental apparatus installed by and administered from London.

CONSTITUTIONALIZING DISTRUST

If the people of a state trust or distrust governmental power, or if they trust state power more or less than national power, how might they translate these sentiments into principles of state constitutional law? Generally speaking, trust in governmental power is likely to manifest itself in generous grants of constitutional authority and the absence of limitations on the use of granted powers, whereas distrust will be reflected in parsimonious grants of authority and extensive limitations on the uses of granted powers. Greater or lesser trust in one level of government than another can be inferred by comparing the amount of power and the scope of limitations appearing in state constitutions with those in the U.S. Constitution.

By granting some significant amount of power to a national government, the U.S. Constitution reflects some corresponding degree of trust for national power felt collectively by the American people. Although the polity of a single state is powerless to affect either the level of trust or the allocation of power at the national level, it is nevertheless free to affect the balance between public and private power, and between state and national power, insofar as its own state is concerned. Because state power is usually felt more immediately and routinely than national power within the borders of any given state, these decisions about state power will in all likelihood have a greater impact on the daily lives of the state's citizens than do national decisions about na-

11. See, e.g., Woodward, *The Burden of Southern History*.

tional power. Thus, although a state polity is free to adjust only one variable in the equation by which governmental power is granted, limited, and balanced throughout the federal system, the adjustments it is capable of making can have a meaningful impact on how federalism is practiced and, consequently, on the ways in which the liberties of the state's citizens are protected.

Suppose a state polity, for whatever reason, trusts state power more than it trusts national power. What specific implications might this have for the content of the state constitution? Surely the most likely result will be that the state polity will express its trust in state government by granting it more power than the people of the nation have granted the national government or by placing fewer limitations on the state government's use of granted powers, or some combination of both. It turns out, indeed, that numerous state constitutions grant power in far greater amounts, and in far more concentrated forms, than does the national Constitution. A few state constitutions also place fewer limitations on the use of state power, primarily by having a somewhat less extensive bill of rights than the national one.

What about the opposite situation, where the people of a state trust state power less than they trust national power? How would this pattern of distrust manifest itself in state constitutions? There are numerous possibilities. Heightened distrust of state power might show up in lesser grants of authority to state governments than the national government enjoys, or in a greater dispersion of state power than appears on the national level. Such distrust might also appear in the form of more extensive restrictions on the exercise of state power. These restrictions could be reflected in a farther-reaching bill of rights than appears in the U.S. Constitution, but state power may also be restricted by imposing more conditions on its use than the national Constitution imposes on the use of national power. Again, examples of each of these approaches can be found in various state constitutions.

The interrelationship between the two principal patterns of distrust—public versus private power, and national versus state power—can make it difficult to distinguish the effects of one from the other. Government minimalists, for example, might prefer a state constitution that grants the state a good deal less power than the U.S. Constitution grants to the national government, but their preference might rest more on a generalized distrust of all governmental power than on a belief that state power is less to be trusted than national power. As a result of this overlap, some of the measures that a polity might take because of its trust or distrust of state power, specifically, would also suit a polity motivated to adjust state power by its trust or distrust of governmental power generally. For instance, a state polity that distrusts any form of governmental power as compared to private power might be inclined to create a state constitution that grants state government only limited, specific powers, or that saddles the exercise of such powers with a host of conditions and limitations. The same purpose could also be served by creating a strong and extensive bill of rights, or a potent system of judicial review to enforce constitutional restrictions on state power. Yet these are all measures that would also be appropriate for a polity that generally trusts governmental power, and trusts national power in particular, but trusts state power a good deal less.

The balance of this chapter looks more closely at some of the specific ways in which patterns of distrust of governmental power turn up in actual state constitutions.

More Extensive Grants of Power

The United States is, famously, a government of limited powers: it has only those powers that the U.S. Constitution grants it. In some cases the grants of power are quite specific, as in the laundry list of powers granted to Congress under Article I, § 8. In other cases the grants are vague and ambiguous, as in the grants of executive and judicial power under Articles II and III, which can be adequately understood only in light of a sometimes obscure and often contested historical record. Even powers granted with a good deal of specificity can turn out to be broad indeed, such as the power to regulate interstate commerce. And powers granted in narrow terms can often be expanded by operation of augmenting clauses such as the Necessary and Proper Clause, which authorizes Congress to "make all Laws which shall be necessary and proper for carrying into Execution" all powers granted specifically to Congress or to any other branch.[12]

Despite the actual and potential reach of national power, the clauses that grant it nevertheless do so in limited rather than unlimited measure. The U.S. Supreme Court has made clear in recent years, for example, that there are limits even to the seemingly infinitely expandable power to regulate interstate commerce, and that these limits establish boundaries beyond which Congress may not go. Congress may not, for example, use its commerce power to regulate noncommercial activity that does not substantially affect interstate commerce.[13] It may not use the commerce power in a way that "commandeers" the

12. U.S. Const. art. I, § 8, cl. 18.
13. United States v. Lopez, 514 U.S. 549 (1995).

legislative or executive processes of state governments.[14] Nor may Congress invoke the commerce power, or any other Article I power, to authorize private lawsuits against nonconsenting states in their own courts.[15] The Court has also articulated limitations applicable to other congressional powers. Congress may not exercise its spending power, for example, in a manner that unduly coerces states to accept conditioned spending.[16] It may not use its power to ratify treaties in a way that circumvents the Bill of Rights.[17] And it may not use its power under § 5 of the Fourteenth Amendment beyond what is reasonably necessary to remedy clear violations of the substantive provisions of that amendment.[18]

The principle of limited, enumerated powers is applicable not only to the legislative branch, but to the national judicial and executive branches as well. One of the Court's most important early rulings established that federal courts may not hear or decide cases for which the Constitution does not provide jurisdiction.[19] The Court has also held that Article III judges may not perform certain kinds of nonjudicial duties.[20] In its rulings on executive power, the Court has held, for example, that the president's powers as chief executive and commander-in-chief do not extend to the legislatively unauthorized regulation of domestic industries.[21] Nor does Article II authorize the president to refuse to comply with judicial process in many criminal and civil cases.[22] None of these constitutional limitations on national power is imposed by a general, across-the-board limiting provision of the Constitution, such as the provisions of the Bill of Rights. These limitations, instead, inhere in the constitutional grants of power themselves. Power is granted, but only in circumscribed amounts whose limits may be discerned and, for the most part, judicially enforced.

State constitutions proceed in precisely the opposite fashion. Every single state constitution, without exception, grants power to each branch of state gov-

---

14. New York v. United States, 505 U.S. 144 (1992); Printz v. United States, 521 U.S. 898 (1997).

15. Alden v. Maine, 527 U.S. 706 (1999).

16. South Dakota v. Dole, 483 U.S. 203 (1987).

17. Reid v. Covert, 354 U.S. 1 (1957).

18. City of Boerne v. Flores, 521 U.S. 507 (1997); Florida Prepaid Postsecondary Educ. Expense Bd. v. College Savings Bank, 527 U.S. 627 (1999); United States v. Morrison, 529 U.S. 598 (2000).

19. Marbury v. Madison, 5 U.S. 137 (1803).

20. Mistretta v. United States, 488 U.S. 361 (1989).

21. Youngstown Sheet & Tube Co. v. Sawyer, 343 U.S. 579 (1952).

22. United States v. Nixon, 418 U.S. 683 (1974); Clinton v. Jones, 520 U.S. 681 (1997).

ernment in one immense, undifferentiated, and unlimited block. A typical provision allocating legislative authority, for example, might provide only that "the legislative power of this State shall be vested in the Senate and Assembly."[23] These provisions are uniformly construed to grant state legislatures at one stroke all the legislative power that any government may in theory possess. No state constitution makes even the slightest attempt to enumerate the powers that any branch possesses. No constitution specifically grants the state legislature the power to regulate intrastate commerce, levy taxes, spend revenues, legislate on civil rights, or to do anything else, as the national Constitution does. Instead, state constitutions grant to the state government all the powers that any government could conceivably possess, except as those powers are specifically limited by other provisions of the state constitution. State legislatures may, quite simply, take up any subject at all, without limit. State constitutions thus grant far greater legislative power to state legislatures than the national Constitution grants to Congress.

This approach to state legislative power dates to the earliest days of the American Republic, and seems to have rested originally on the presupposition that the states somehow acquired, without the necessity of specific popular authorization, the general governmental powers previously exercised in the colonies by the British Parliament. In his highly influential 1868 treatise on state constitutional law, *Constitutional Limitations,* Thomas Cooley warned against facile comparisons of American state power with British parliamentary power. The government of no American state, he wrote, possesses the kind of "complete jurisdiction" that Parliament was said to possess in British law.[24] Nevertheless, in laying down what he offered as a general principle of state constitutionalism, Cooley described state legislative power in extremely broad language:

> In creating a legislative department and conferring upon it the legislative power, the people must be understood to have conferred the full and complete power as it rests in, and may be exercised by, the sovereign power of any country, subject only to such restrictions as they may have seen fit to impose, and to the limitations which are contained in the Constitution of the United States. The legislative department is not a special agency, for the exercise of specifically defined legislative powers, but is entrusted with the general authority to make laws at discretion.[25]

23. New York Const. art. III, § 1.
24. Cooley, *A Treatise on the Constitutional Limitations,* 86.
25. Id. at 87.

Cooley's statement reflects his limited conception of the important distinctions between American state governments and the British Parliament. In Cooley's view, there are two such distinctions: first, in the American case unlimited sovereignty resides not in any organ of government but in the people themselves; and second, American governmental power is starkly divided among three branches, whereas Parliament is, as Blackstone held, "omnipotent."[26] Cooley's work was the first systematic treatment of state constitutional law as a distinct subject, and his influence was enormous in an era when law books were few; his was one of only a handful that might have been found with any frequency on the bookshelves of American lawyers. The treatise went through eight editions, the last published in 1927—long after Cooley's death in 1898. To this day, the treatise is frequently cited by state courts, and it is clear from many contemporary rulings that Cooley's formulation of the scope of state legislative power has passed into common learning.[27]

The position taken by the courts and formalized by Cooley is troubling, however, for it is at odds with the principles generally thought to govern American constitutions. As another pioneering scholar of state constitutional law, Walter F. Dodd, noted in 1915, "the political philosophy of 1776 was based very largely on the notion of social compact and did not recognize the existence of inherent government power in either legislative, executive or judicial department."[28] Rather, Dodd went on, when state legislative power is referred to as inherent, what is usually meant is that it has been "granted in general terms," and that such a grant is presumed, as a matter of ordinary textual interpretation, to be complete except insofar as restricted.

Dodd clearly has the better of the argument. The prevailing American theory of constitutions is that they are positive enactments by the people, who together are the supreme sovereign in our system. The people may, because of some preference or as a matter of convenience, grant to state legislatures all legislative power as a matter of positive constitutional law, but such a grant is in no way a necessary feature of a state's constitution; the people could just as easily create a state constitution that enumerates and restricts state legislative power. While enumeration might leave gaps in legislative power so that certain subjects would be off-limits to both the national and the state govern-

26. Id. at 85–87.

27. See, e.g., State ex rel. Schneider v. Kennedy, 587 P.2d 844, 850 (Kan. 1978); Client Follow-Up Co. v. Hynes, 390 N.E.2d 847, 849 (Ill. 1979).

28. Dodd, "The Function of a State Constitution," 205.

ments, and the presence of these gaps might from time to time prove incon-
venient, nothing compels the people to grant legislative power in general
terms to any level of government.

If such grants of power are not required, what best explains their presence
in state constitutions is a greater popular trust in state power than in national
power. A desire for convenience is certainly part of the equation. It would be in-
convenient for the people to be called upon continually to dish out some additional dollop of legislative authority, which they have previously denied to any
government, whenever changed circumstances require the government to possess it. But the desire for convenience does not explain why the general power
has been given to the state governments and the limited power to the national
government, rather than the other way around. Only a better developed sense
of trust and confidence in state power adequately explains that phenomenon.

Extensive state constitutional grants of authority are not limited to state
legislatures, however. State constitutions also typically grant significantly more
power to the state judicial branch than the national Constitution grants to the
federal bench. Article III of the U.S. Constitution extends the national judicial
power to "cases" and "controversies."[29] The U.S. Supreme Court has interpreted
this language to impose numerous limitations on the kinds of matters federal
courts may adjudicate. For example, the Court has developed restrictive doctrines of standing, ripeness, and mootness, all of which deprive federal courts
of the ability to hear various kinds of cases that do not involve an active dispute
between parties with a direct and significant stake in the outcome of the case.

State courts typically do not labor under similar limitations. In the first
place, state constitutions typically grant state courts general judicial power
comparable to the general grants of legislative power made to state legislatures. Thus, unlike federal courts, which are courts of limited and enumerated
jurisdiction, state courts are courts of general jurisdiction and possess judicial
power to the extent of its theoretical limits. Second, state courts frequently
interpret the more generous scope of state judicial power to provide rules of
standing and adjudication that are far more generous than the rules federal
courts have worked out under Article III. For example, whereas federal courts
lack the power to issue advisory opinions, many state courts do so regularly.[30]
In states that permit them, advisory opinions are often sought by the gover-

---

29. Art. III, § 2, cl. 1.
30. See Carberry, "Comment, The State Advisory Opinion in Perspective."

nor or state legislature to obtain preliminary guidance about the constitutionality of contemplated legislation.

Nearly every state court also has the power to answer certified questions from federal courts.[31] Such inquiries do not flow in the opposite direction: like advisory opinions, answers to certified questions are issued when there are no adverse litigants actually before the court, and thus are beyond the power of federal courts to provide. State courts also frequently apply much more relaxed rules of litigant standing than federal courts apply under Article III. For example, the U.S. Supreme Court has held that a person's status as a taxpayer does not by itself permit that person to bring suit in federal court challenging specific expenditures of federal funds.[32] Numerous state courts, in contrast, recognize taxpayer standing in circumstances far broader than the U.S. Constitution allows. In some cases, taxpayer standing has been provided for directly by constitutional amendment, as in Michigan's 1978 amendment granting standing to any taxpayer to enforce constitutional restrictions on state and local taxation.[33] In other cases, state courts have interpreted their own grants of jurisdictional authority to allow them to hear cases initiated by taxpayers. The Idaho Supreme Court, for example, held more than a century ago that a taxpayer had standing to challenge the authority of a local school board to award a teaching contract to the wife of a member of the school board.[34]

In all these instances, the state constitution grants to state courts considerably broader authority to entertain and adjudicate legal issues than the national Constitution grants to federal courts. This broader power, in turn, makes judicial authority more of a force in state governance than it is at the national level, and makes state courts more active players in the ordinary processes of state self-rule.

Greater Concentrations of Power

The degree to which government power enjoys popular trust is revealed not only in the absolute amount of power that a polity chooses to grant its government, but also in the form of the grant. In the American constitutional tra-

---

31. Goldschmidt, *Certification of Questions of Law.*

32. Warth v. Seldin, 422 U.S. 490 (1975); Valley Forge Christian College v. Americans United for Separation of Church and State, 454 U.S. 464 (1982).

33. Mich. Const. art. IX, § 32.

34. Nuckols v. Lyle, 70 P. 401 (Idaho 1902).

dition, power typically is granted in a dispersed form on the theory that con-centrated power is more dangerous to liberty than divided power. Both the horizontal separation of power into three branches and the vertical separa-tion of powers of federalism proceed from this premise. While every American constitution thus divides power to some extent, not every state constitution displays the same degree of suspicion toward concentrated state power that the national Constitution displays toward concentrated national power. Some state constitutions, to the contrary, implement a regime of horizontal separa-tion of powers that is far more relaxed than the counterpart regime on the na-tional level. Nor is there any tradition of vertical separation of powers among state and local governments that remotely approaches in stringency the ver-tical separation of powers established in the national Constitution.

The doctrine of horizontal separation of powers requires the division of government power into different branches, often identified as the legislative, executive, and judicial branches. The historical roots of this doctrine probably lie in classical notions of mixed government, in which different organs of gov-ernment represent different social interests: the people, the aristocracy, and the king, for example, were understood to be metaphorically present in the assembly, the senate, and the magistracy, respectively.[35] In American constitu-tional theory, however, the horizontal separation of powers is thought to play an important functional role in the protection of liberty. Power is dangerous, the theory goes, but concentrated power is the most dangerous of all. As Madi-son argued in *The Federalist,* human nature is weak, and the temptations to use power in the pursuit of self-interest, rather than for the common good, are great. Concentrated power is particularly dangerous because it gives people the means to act with great effectiveness upon their basest instincts.[36] The Framers did not think that government officials would inevitably give in to temptation.[37] But if they ever did succumb, a well-constructed constitution would deny them access to the kind of concentrated power that would allow them to implement successfully their self-interested plans. That is why Madi-son called the accumulation of all government powers in the same hands "the very definition of tyranny."[38]

The U.S. Constitution accordingly sets out a relatively well-defined separa-

35. Vile, *Constitutionalism and the Separation of Powers.*
36. Madison, *The Federalist,* No. 51.
37. Gardner, "Madison's Hope."
38. Madison, *The Federalist,* No. 47, 301.

tion of powers among the three branches of government. The separation is, of course, far from complete. The Constitution specifically authorizes the president, for example, to propose legislation and to veto legislation of which he disapproves, both arguably aspects of the legislative power. Congress has the authority to confirm presidential nominees for executive branch positions and to ratify treaties, both arguably elements of executive power. Federal courts have the power to invalidate both legislative and executive acts as unconstitutional, arguably extending judicial power into the realm of the other branches. Nevertheless, the Constitution spells out numerous ways in which the branches must be kept distinct. It specifically bars members of Congress, for example, from simultaneously holding any office in the executive branch,[39] thereby rejecting decisively the parliamentary model. The constitutional principle of separation of powers bars Congress from transferring its legislative authority to any other branch of government.[40] Similarly, Congress may not countermand executive branch decisions concerning the enforcement of the law through devices such as the legislative veto,[41] nor may it withhold executive authority from the executive branch by vesting it in legislative branch personnel.[42] Article III of the Constitution prohibits federal courts from deciding questions that are by their nature political, and which thus fall within the purview of the legislative and executive branches.[43]

Every state constitution similarly creates a horizontal separation of powers by dividing the power of state government among a legislative, executive, and judicial branch. However, state constitutions frequently divide these powers in a considerably less rigid way, allowing a degree of blending of powers that the national Constitution does not countenance. As a result, state constitutions sometimes grant governmental power in a somewhat more concentrated, and therefore more potent and potentially dangerous, form. For example, in 1999 the Rhode Island Supreme Court held that the state constitution erects no barrier to a long-standing legislative practice of cross-branch appointments.[44] Rhode Island legislators thus may exercise the power to appoint members of

39. U.S. Const. art. I, § 6, cl. 2.

40. A. L. A. Schecter Poultry Corp. v. United States, 295 U.S. 495 (1935).

41. INS v. Chadha, 462 U.S. 919 (1983).

42. Bowsher v. Synar, 478 U.S. 714 (1986).

43. Baker v. Carr, 369 U.S. 186 (1962).

44. In re Advisory Opinion to the Governor (Rhode Island Ethics Commission—Separation of Powers), 732 A.2d 55 (R.I. 1999). A measure to amend the Rhode Island Constitution to reverse this decision was approved in November 2004.

executive branch agencies, including the power to appoint themselves. Several states permit the state legislature to exercise a legislative veto over regulations promulgated by state executive departments. The constitutions of Connecticut and Nevada, for example, explicitly authorize legislative committees to suspend or disapprove agency regulations.[45] The Iowa and New Jersey constitutions do not permit a legislative veto by a committee, but do permit the legislature to disapprove an agency rule by joint resolution.[46] Idaho also permits a legislative veto, even in the absence of specific textual authorization in the state constitution.[47] Several other states allow legislative committees to block the promulgation of proposed agency rules in a way that amounts functionally to a legislative veto.[48] In each of these cases, the state constitution sanctions practices that would violate the constitutional separation of powers under the U.S. Constitution.

Similarly, state courts sometimes feel free to decide questions that federal courts would consider political, and thus beyond the authority allocated to the judicial branch by the U.S. Constitution. A striking example of this phenomenon arises under the Guarantee Clause of the U.S. Constitution, which requires the United States to "guarantee to every State in this Union a Republican Form of Government."[49] In a series of cases, the U.S. Supreme Court has held that issues concerning the legitimacy under the clause of any specific state government, or form of state government, present nonjusticiable political questions concerning which the federal judiciary must defer to the legislative and executive branches.[50] Some state courts, however, have declined to follow the Supreme Court's lead and have adjudicated such questions directly under the Guarantee Clause.[51] For example, in *Pacific States Telephone and Telegraph Co. v. Oregon*,[52] the U.S. Supreme Court declined on political question grounds to decide whether an amendment to Oregon's constitution providing

45. Conn. Const. art. II; Nev. Const. art. III, § 1(2).

46. Iowa Const. art. III, § 40; N.J. Const. art. V, ¶ 6.

47. Mead v. Arnell, 791 P.2d 410 (Idaho 1990).

48. For discussion, see Rossi, "Institutional Design and the Lingering Legacy of Antifederal Separation of Powers Ideals in the States," 1212–16.

49. U.S. Const. art. IV, § 4.

50. Luther v. Borden, 48 U.S. 1 (1849); Pacific States Tel. & Tel. Co. v. Oregon, 223 U.S. 118 (1912); Colegrove v. Green, 328 U.S. 549 (1946); Baker v. Carr, 369 U.S. 186 (1962).

51. See, e.g., Van Sickle v. Shanahan, 511 P.2d 223 (Kan. 1973); In re Initiative Petition No. 348, 820 P.2d 772 (Okla. 1991); Heimerl v. Ozaukee City, 40 N.W.2d 564 (Wis. 1949).

52. 223 U.S. 118 (1912).

for the use of popular initiatives and referenda caused the form of Oregon's government to become insufficiently "republican." Eighty years later, the Oklahoma Supreme Court considered a similar challenge to an amendment to the state constitution requiring approval by popular referendum of all revenue measures. Unlike the U.S. Supreme Court, however, the Oklahoma Supreme Court deemed the matter justiciable, and ruled that the amendment did not render the state's government insufficiently republican under the federal Guarantee Clause.[53]

Separation of powers is not only horizontal, of course: American constitutions also separate powers vertically. On the national level, this measure takes the form of federalism, the division of power between the national and state governments. On the state level, the equivalent of federalism is the division of power between state and local governments, such as counties, towns, or cities. Every state polity has chosen to divide power in this way by creating numerous local governments and by allocating to them some degree of authority and autonomy. In some cases, the state constitution grants to local governments a considerable amount of authority, which localities are free to exercise with some measure of independence from state control. More typically, however, state constitutions provide localities with little ultimate authority. In these cases, the degree of power exercised on the local level, and the forms in which it is granted, fall within the unbounded discretion of the state legislature.

Municipal governments have long been regarded in the United States as administrative subdivisions of the states, "created as convenient agencies for exercising such of the governmental powers of the State as may be entrusted to them."[54] Accordingly, most state constitutions grant the state legislature plenary power to create or dissolve local governments and to delegate to them whatever powers it chooses. The Florida Constitution, for example, provides that "[m]unicipalities may be established or abolished and their charters amended pursuant to general or special law."[55] According to the Florida Supreme Court, "the power of the Legislature over municipalities under our Constitution is plenary. It may not only grant powers to municipalities, but it may regulate them in any manner it sees fit or prohibit entirely the exercise thereof in such instances as it may determine."[56]

53. In re Initiative Petition No. 348, 820 P.2d 772 (Okla. 1991).
54. Hunter v. Pittsburgh, 207 U.S. 161, 178 (1907).
55. Fla. Const. art. VIII, § 2(a).
56. State v. City of Boca Raton, 172 So. 2d 230, 232 (Fla. 1965).

Even where existing local governments require no express grant of authority to legislate on local matters, such as under home-rule provisions of state constitutions, the powers that municipalities may exercise typically are construed narrowly. Dillon's Rule, traditionally followed throughout the United States, holds that the scope of powers granted to local governments should be narrowly construed: courts should recognize such powers only if there has been an express delegation of state authority, or if such a delegation must be found by necessary implication.[57] Moreover, local power is usually subject to a liberal rule of state preemption under which local legislation enacted pursuant to otherwise legitimate local authority is invalid if it conflicts with legislation or rules enacted at the state level. In California, for example, an otherwise validly enacted local measure will be preempted not only if it conflicts with state law, but also if the state has fully occupied the regulatory field, or if the legislature has elsewhere addressed the subject of the measure, and the subject is one of general rather than local interest.[58]

State governments thus usually possess the power to decide which local governments will exist, if any; their precise configuration; the amount of power such governments will possess; and the circumstances in which that power may be used—all of which may be revoked or modified by the legislature at its pleasure. From the point of view of vertical separation of powers, this arrangement is functionally the equivalent of allowing Congress to decide how much authority state governments should exercise. It is not an arrangement, in other words, that can be expected to produce an effective check from below on abuses of state power. To allocate state power in this way is to grant it in a far more concentrated form than the one in which similar powers are allocated to the national government. Yet power concentrated, as Madison warned, is far more dangerous than power dispersed. That a state polity chooses nevertheless to forgo a vertical check and grant power to the state government in this concentrated form once again might suggest a degree of popular confidence in state government that has no counterpart on the national level.

Limited Bill of Rights

The final way in which greater popular trust of state than national power might manifest itself is the imposition of fewer direct constitutional restraints on the exercise of state power than the U.S. Constitution places on the exercise

57. Briffault, "Our Localism: Part I," 8.
58. In re Hubbard, 396 P.2d 809 (Cal. 1964).

of power at the national level. In particular, a state polity might choose to grant its citizens a less extensive bill of rights than appears in the U.S. Constitution. The fewer the rights restricting state action, the greater the flexibility state officials may enjoy in choosing how best to deploy state power for the general good of the state's citizens.

Many of the earliest state constitutions seem to have provided less in the way of individual rights than the U.S. Constitution provided in 1791, after the Bill of Rights was added, although considerable ambiguity and a lack of decisional law sometimes make it difficult to know with any certainty the contours of the rights mentioned by these documents. For example, both Connecticut and Rhode Island chose to retain their royal charters as foundational governing instruments until 1818 and 1842, respectively. Neither charter contained a declaration of rights, although both contained provisions guaranteeing to colonists "all Liberties and Immunities of free and natural Subjects" of the Crown.[59] The actual scope of these traditional liberties of English subjects must of course have meant something very different to the royal officials who granted the charters in the mid-seventeenth century than it meant to successful American revolutionaries a century later. It is not inconceivable, especially given the history of American constitutional universalism discussed in chapter 1, that this brief phrase might have been understood by Americans of 1776 to encompass all the liberties explicitly mentioned in the national Bill of Rights. Other than this ambiguous language, the Connecticut Charter makes no explicit mention of any individual right, unless one counts the right to fish.[60] The Rhode Island Charter, however, contains an explicit royal guarantee of freedom of worship, recognized as integral to the colony's "livlie experiment, that a most flourishing civill state may stand and best bee maintained, . . . with a full libertie in religious concernements."[61]

The South Carolina Constitution of 1776 made no mention whatsoever of

59. Charter of Connecticut, ¶ 6 (1662); Charter of Rhode Island and Providence Plantations, ¶ 10 (1663).

60. "[T]hese presents shall not in any Manner hinder any of Our loving Subjects whatsoever to use and exercise the Trade of Fishing upon the Coast of *New-England,* in *America,* but they and every or any of them shall have full and free Power and Liberty, to continue, and use the said Trade of Fishing upon the said Coast, in any of the seas thereunto adjoining, or any Arms of the Seas, or Salt Water Rivers where they have been accustomed to fish." Charter of Connecticut, ¶ 8 (1662). To the same effect is the Charter of Rhode Island and Providence Plantations, ¶ 9 (1663).

61. Charter of Rhode Island and Providence Plantations, ¶ 2 (1663).

any individual right. Two years later, South Carolina adopted a new constitution that expressly guaranteed only three individual rights: the right of Christians to worship freely, the right to due process of law, and freedom of the press.[62] In its 1790 constitution, South Carolina added provisions barring impairment of the obligation of contracts, prohibiting excessive fines or cruel and unusual punishments, and protecting the right to trial by jury.[63] Other omissions appear here and there. Louisiana's first constitution (1812), for example, mentions several rights but does not appear to provide explicit protection for the right against unreasonable searches and seizures.[64]

Among contemporary state constitutions, very few contain bills of rights less extensive than the federal version. Nevertheless, the practice is not unknown. In 1985, for example, the Massachusetts Supreme Judicial Court held that the Massachusetts Constitution does not require the exclusion of evidence seized by unconstitutional means.[65] In California, the same result has been achieved by initiative. Article I, § 28(d) of the California Constitution, a provision of a 1982 initiative measure better known in California as Proposition 8, the "Victims' Bill of Rights," provides:

> Except as provided by statute hereafter enacted by a two-thirds vote of the membership in each house of the Legislature, relevant evidence shall not be excluded in any criminal proceeding, including pretrial and post conviction motions and hearings, or in any trial or hearing of a juvenile for a criminal offense, whether heard in juvenile or adult court.

The plain import of this provision is to banish from the California Constitution any remaining trace, in search and seizure cases, of the exclusionary rule. The Fourth Amendment of the U.S. Constitution, in contrast, still recognizes the exclusionary rule, albeit in circumstances that seem to diminish with each subsequent ruling of the U.S. Supreme Court. The people of Massachusetts and California have thus chosen to give themselves less protection from state police than they presently enjoy under the Fourth Amendment from federal law enforcement authorities such as the Federal Bureau of Investigation (FBI), the Drug Enforcement Agency (DEA), and the Bureau of Alcohol, To-

---

62. S.C. Const. ¶¶ xxxviii, xli, xliii (1778).
63. S.C. Const. art. IX, §§ 2, 4, 6 (1790).
64. See La. Const. art. VI (1812).
65. Commonwealth v. Upton, 476 N.E.2d 548 (Mass. 1985).

bacco, and Firearms (ATF).[66] Of course, citizens of these states are for the most part unaffected by this decision, since state and local police officers must abide by national standards embodied in the Fourth Amendment and applied to the states by operation of the Due Process Clause. The provision would come into play, however, if the U.S. Supreme Court ever decided to abandon the exclusionary rule as a matter of national constitutional law.

Another contemporary example concerns the type of information that state law enforcement officials must provide to criminal suspects upon arrest. Under the U.S. Constitution, law enforcement officials are required to provide the famous "*Miranda* warning," in which suspects are informed of their rights to remain silent and to an attorney.[67] The Maine Supreme Court, in contrast, has held that the Maine Constitution does not require such warnings,[68] and the Oregon Supreme Court maintained a similar position briefly in the 1980s before reversing itself.[69] In a recent case, the U.S. Supreme Court reaffirmed that the *Miranda* warning is constitutionally required,[70] a result that applies to the states through the Due Process Clause.

Lesser Grants of Authority

As discussed in the previous sections, state constitutions for the most part grant greater power to the organs of state government than the U.S. Constitution grants to the branches of the national government. In some respects, however, many state constitutions limit the power that state legislatures possess. Two of the most prominent of these are the express provision for a part-time legislature and the imposition of term limits. Both limit the potential

66. The California Supreme Court has been strangely reluctant to acknowledge the full impact of Proposition 8 on the state's criminal procedure. In *In re Lance W.*, 694 P.2d 744 (Cal. 1985), and *People v. Luttenberger*, 784 P.2d 633 (Cal. 1990), among others, the court has held that Proposition 8 trimmed state constitutional protections only as far as the minimum level of federal protections. While this will of course be the practical result of any case in which a defendant invokes the exclusionary rule as a matter of both state and federal constitutional law, such a result comes about not because both constitutions provide the same protection, but because the state constitution provides none and the federal Constitution sets a mandatory floor by operation of the Fourteenth Amendment.

67. Miranda v. Arizona, 384 U.S. 436 (1966).

68. State v. Bleyl, 435 A.2d 1349 (Me. 1982).

69. Compare State v. Smith, 725 P.2d 894 (Or. 1986), with State v. Isom, 761 P.2d 524 (Or. 1988), and State v. Magee, 744 P.2d 250 (Or. 1987) (per curiam).

70. Dickerson v. United States, 530 U.S. 428 (2000).

scope of legislative power by undermining the ability of the legislature to become fully professionalized.

The Montana Constitution, for example, provides that the state legislature may meet only in odd-numbered years, and then only for a maximum of ninety legislative days. The legislatures of Arkansas, Kentucky, Nevada, North Dakota, Oregon, and Texas likewise meet only biennially. The Utah legislature meets annually, but its sessions are limited to forty-five calendar days. The Virginia legislature may not meet for more than thirty calendar days in odd-numbered years, and sixty calendar days in even-numbered years.[71] These limitations reduce the potential power of state legislatures in at least two ways. First, because legislators have less time in which to consider and enact legislative measures, a part-time legislature simply cannot accomplish as much as one that is full-time. Second, part-time legislators are necessarily amateurs. Government cannot be their primary means of livelihood; they must hold full-time jobs in other sectors of the economy. This gives part-time legislators less time to learn about issues facing the state, and fewer opportunities to gain experience of the legislative process itself.

Term limits tend to exacerbate these effects. At present, sixteen states have enacted some form of term limits for state legislators, primarily by state constitutional amendment.[72] Even the most generous of these provisions allows legislators to remain in office only for twelve years. California, Michigan, and Oregon limit the amount of time any individual can serve in the state assembly to six years, after which a lifetime bar is imposed. By limiting the amount of time an individual may serve in the legislature, term limits obviously limit the ability of any single legislator—and ultimately the legislature as a body—to develop any particular expertise, either in specific areas of legislative interest or in the legislative process generally.

A state's lack of a fully professionalized legislature has two important potential effects. First, it tends to amplify the power of the state executive branch at the expense of the legislative branch, since the governor serves continuously and has at his or her disposal a fully professionalized executive bureaucracy capable of working year-round. The work of governance continues when the legislature is not in session, and the governor is left to do it. Second, the state legislature is put at a disadvantage in comparison with Congress, which meets

71. Council of State Governments, 33 *The Book of the States,* table 3.2 (2000–2001).

72. See the U.S. Term Limits Web site at http://www.termlimits.org/Current_Info/ State_TL/index.html (last visited 11/6/03).

annually and sits continuously except for relatively unimportant periods of recess. Congress's high degree of professionalization and busy calendar make it a far more potent generator of legislative initiatives than its unprofessionalized, part-time state counterparts, an arrangement that could well make it difficult for state legislatures to develop positions contrary to those adopted by Congress. In a recent article, Indiana's attorney general expressed just such a concern:

> Indiana, for example, prides itself on its citizen-legislature, and our legislature remains part-time. It could be argued that Indiana and some other states have been able to maintain part-time legislatures because Congress, with its enormous staff and research capabilities, has sifted the data, done the research, and written the law in so many areas.[73]

A part-time, largely amateur legislature facing a full-time, professionalized, and highly informed Congress may find it difficult, then, to identify, much less to resist, abuses of national legislative power.

Greater Dispersion of State Power

Another way in which heightened distrust of state as compared to national power might manifest itself in state constitutions is a greater dispersion of state power than appears in the national Constitution. Many state constitutions do indeed divide and disperse state power in ways that the U.S. Constitution does not. Such measures include a highly splintered executive branch in which executive power is divided among multiple officials, each independently elected, and a stricter horizontal separation of powers among branches of state government.

One of the most striking differences between the state and national constitutions is the way in which the former divide and subdivide executive power. Despite Madison's warning that the legislature was more to be feared than the executive,[74] state constitutions typically proceed as though the executive branch is so exceedingly dangerous that its power must be widely dispersed among a multiplicity of officials who are independently elected, and thus politically independent of the governor.[75] No state follows the national model

---

73. Modisett, "Discovering the Impact of 'New Federalism' on State Policy Makers," 145.

74. Madison, *The Federalist*, No. 45.

75. See Kruman, *Between Authority and Liberty*, 110–11; Rakove, *Original Meanings*, 249–50; Wood, *The Creation of the American Republic*, 132–43.

in which the only elected executive branch officials are the chief executive and a deputy—here, the governor and lieutenant governor.[76] More typically, state constitutions provide for the election not only of the governor and lieutenant governor, but also of the secretary of state, attorney general, treasurer, and comptroller. North Carolina and North Dakota additionally provide for independent election of the state auditor and the commissioners of education, agriculture, labor, and insurance—a total of ten elected state executive branch officials.

The president of the United States of course has constitutional authority to guide policy decisions for the entire executive branch. He not only has the power to appoint subordinate executive officials in the first place (albeit subject to senatorial approval), but also may remove the great majority of them whenever he is dissatisfied with their performance.[77] With so many executive officials answerable only to the people, most governors exercise considerably less influence over the shape of state executive policy than the president does over national executive policy.

The constitutions of forty-three states disperse power even further by providing for the election of at least some state judges.[78] Under the U.S. Constitution, the president appoints federal judges with the approval of the Senate. Federal judges then serve for life. In states that provide for an elected judiciary, any power to affect the appointment of judges is denied to the executive and legislative branches. Moreover, elected judges serve for a term of years rather than for life, weakening their independence and, consequently, their power as compared to judges of the United States.

Many state constitutions not only disperse power more widely than does the national Constitution, but also confine the powers so dispersed more rigidly within their assigned spheres. Sometimes these measures are specific. For example, the North Carolina Constitution until 1996 denied the governor any power to veto legislation,[79] a power conferred upon every other governor and

76. However, New Hampshire and New Jersey provide for the election only of a governor, who then appoints all other executive branch officials. In these states, as well as in Maine and Tennessee, a legislative leader is next in the line of succession. Council of State Governments, 33 *The Book of the States,* table 2.9 (2000–2001).

77. Myers v. United States, 272 U.S. 52 (1926). This power is not, however, unlimited. See Humphrey's Executor v. United States, 295 U.S. 602 (1935); Morrison v. Olson, 487 U.S. 654 (1988).

78. Council of State Governments, 33 *The Book of the States,* table 4.4 (2000–2001).

79. N.C. Const. art. II, § 22(1).

the president of the United States. Other measures are more general. Many state constitutions, unlike the U.S. Constitution, contain a provision expressly mandating a constitutional separation of powers and providing that the separation be strictly observed. The Mississippi Constitution, for instance, provides:

> Section 1. The powers of the government of the state of Mississippi shall be divided into three distinct departments, and each of them confided to a separate magistracy, to-wit: those which are legislative to one, those which are judicial to another, and those which are executive to another.
>
> Section 2. No person or collection of persons, being one or belonging to one of these departments, shall exercise any power properly belonging to either of the others.[80]

Other states express this goal in even more stringent language. The Massachusetts Constitution provides:

> [T]he legislative department shall never exercise the executive and judicial powers, or either of them: The executive shall never exercise the legislative and judicial powers, or either of them: The judicial shall never exercise the legislative and executive powers, or either of them: to the end it may be a government of laws and not of men.[81]

Some state courts, to be sure, do not treat such provisions as having any real functional content. Judging by their decisions, such courts appear to view them more as declaratory statements of relationships implemented concretely elsewhere in the constitutional structure than as meaningful constitutional commands.[82] In some states, however, such provisions have more bite. The Mississippi Supreme Court, for example, has interpreted the provision quoted above to prohibit legislators from serving on a budget preparation committee within the executive branch, a practice not otherwise prohibited by any explicit provision of the state constitution.[83]

Another area in which state constitutions sometimes enforce the separation of powers more strictly than does the U.S. Constitution concerns the

---

80. Miss. Const. art. I, §§ 1, 2.
81. Mass. Const. Part the First, art. XXX (1780).
82. See, e.g., Department of Transp. v. Armacost, 532 A.2d 1056, 1064–65 (Md. 1987).
83. Alexander v. State, 441 So. 2d 1329 (Miss. 1983).

nondelegation doctrine. Under federal law, the doctrine provides that Congress may not delegate power to executive branch agencies in such broad or vague terms as to amount to an abdication of legislative authority.[84] The U.S. Supreme Court has struck down only two federal statutes as overly broad delegations, and has not done so since 1935. Moreover, the standards of specificity the Court has required of Congress are so easy to satisfy that the nondelegation doctrine has long been viewed on the national level as moribund. Many states, however, enforce the doctrine much more strictly against state legislatures than the U.S. Supreme Court has against Congress. In at least nineteen states, the state constitution has been held to require the state legislature to guide the discretion exercised by state executive agencies in terms that are far more specific than the national Constitution requires of Congress.[85]

More Extensive Bill of Rights

If a state polity trusted state power less than national power, another measure it could take to reduce the threat of state-level abuses is to attach to the state constitution a more protective bill of rights than appears in the national document. Many states have done so.

In the eighteenth and early nineteenth centuries, state constitutional drafters displayed a good deal of creativity in the identification and enumeration of specific rights, many of which do not appear in the text of, and have never been inferred from, the U.S. Constitution. Some of these rights were opposed to, and later superseded by, conflicting national rights. For example, the Massachusetts Constitution of 1780 enumerated a right of the people

> to invest their legislature with power to authorize and require ... the several towns, parishes, precincts, and other bodies politic, ... to make suitable provision, at their own expense, for the institution of the public worship of God, and for the support and maintenance of public Protestant teachers of piety, religion, and morality, in all cases where such provision shall not be made voluntarily.[86]

84. A. L. A. Schechter Poultry Corp. v. United States, 295 U.S. 495 (1935); J. W. Hampton, Jr., & Co. v. United States, 276 U.S. 394 (1926); Yakus v. United States, 321 U.S. 414 (1944).

85. Rossi, "Institutional Design," 1193–97. An additional twenty-three states enforce the nondelegation doctrine in a more moderate way that is still typically stronger than the enforcement exercised by federal courts. Id. at 1198–1201.

86. Mass. Const. Part the First, art. III (1780).

This practice is of course prohibited by the Establishment Clause of the First Amendment of the U.S. Constitution. The New Hampshire Constitution of 1784 conferred upon jurors the right to receive reasonable compensation, and explicitly protected civilians from being subjected to martial law.[87] The North Carolina Constitution of 1776 gave criminal defendants the right to acquittal in the absence of a unanimous verdict of guilt.[88] Georgia's 1789 Constitution conferred a right against entailment of property, and guaranteed to widows whose husbands died intestate "a child's share, or her dower, at her option."[89] Numerous early constitutions conferred an explicit right of the people "to alter or abolish their government."[90]

In the years since the founding, state bills of rights have tended to converge in content with their national counterpart. Nevertheless, modern state constitutions contain numerous rights that have no federal equivalent. Every state constitution contains, for example, an affirmative right to vote, something the U.S. Constitution does not grant outright to anyone. Most state constitutions also contain an affirmative right to an education, which the U.S. Supreme Court has refused to infer from the national Bill of Rights. Several state constitutions contain an affirmative right to a clean and healthful environment, a right that the U.S. Constitution does not grant. The national Constitution protects the right to privacy, but only implicitly. Several state constitutions make the right express and protect it in more extensive ways.

Numerous state constitutions also contain right-to-remedy provisions that have no national equivalent. These provisions typically require state courts to provide remedies for any injury that an individual may suffer at the hands of another, and have been invoked to bar the legislature from repealing or excessively limiting common law causes of action.[91] A few state constitutions contain provisions setting out an affirmative right to government assistance. For example, New York's Constitution provides: "The aid, care and support of the needy are public concerns and shall be provided by the state and by such of its subdivisions, and in such manner and by such means, as the legislature

87. N.H. Const. Part I, art. I, §§ XXI, XXXIV (1784).

88. N.C. Const. Declaration of Rights, art. IX (1776).

89. Ga. Const. art. IV, § 6 (1789).

90. Fla. Const. art. I, § 2. To similar effect, see, e.g., Vt. Const. ch. I, art. VI (1777); N.H. Const. Part I, art. I, § X.

91. See Schuman, "The Right to a Remedy."

may from time to time determine."[92] The Montana Constitution provides: "The legislature shall provide such economic assistance and social and rehabilitative services as may be necessary for those inhabitants who, by reasons of age, infirmities, or misfortune may have need for the aid of society."[93] All these provisions, then, protect the liberty of state citizens against infringement by their state governments in ways that the U.S. Constitution does not protect citizens from the national government.

More Extensive Restrictions on the Exercise of State Power

Restrictions on the exercise of affirmative state power need not take the form of broad, cross-cutting limitations that apply, as individual rights do, to the exercise of every kind of state power. Restrictions on state power can also take the form of specific provisions, targeted to the use of particular powers, that limit the circumstances when, or purposes for which, the specific power may be used. Most state constitutions are filled with provisions that condition the use of specific, affirmative state powers in just this way.

Many state constitutions, for example, contain a host of limitations on the way the state government may exercise its taxing and spending powers, limitations without equivalent in the U.S. Constitution. Consider the Michigan Constitution, a generally moderate document as these things go. That constitution forbids the Michigan legislature from imposing annual property taxes in excess of "15 mills on each dollar of the assessed valuation of property as finally equalized"; caps retail sales taxes at 4 percent; prohibits the state from incurring indebtedness in excess of 15 percent of "undedicated revenues"; requires two-thirds approval of the legislature to borrow money; and prohibits the state from investing in stocks except for retirement and pension benefit funds.[94] The Alabama Constitution bars the legislature from passing any revenue bill in the last five days of the session; prohibits the granting of salary increases in any appropriations bill; bars appropriations to any charitable or educational institution "not under the absolute control of the state"; and requires the legislature to obtain all its "stationery, printing, paper, and fuel" by contract from "the lowest responsible bidder."[95] The Arizona Constitution specifically exempts from taxation twelve different kinds of property, including "household goods

92. N.Y. Const. art. XVII, § 1.
93. Mont. Const. art. XII, § 3(3).
94. Mich. Const. art. IX, §§ 6, 8, 14, 15, 19.
95. Ala. Const. §§ 70, 71, 73, 69.

owned by the user thereof" and "stocks of raw or finished materials."[96] The constitutions of thirty-six states require that the state budget be balanced.[97]

Most state constitutions also impose numerous conditions on the use of state legislative power of a type with which Congress need not concern itself. In many states, for example, the title of a bill must accurately describe its contents.[98] State constitutions often prohibit bills from dealing with more than one subject at a time, a restriction that is sometimes rigorously enforced and that may inhibit state legislatures from engaging in the kind of logrolling that sometimes greases the legislative wheels in Congress. Some state constitutional provisions restrict the scope of amendments. The Pennsylvania Constitution, for example, provides: "no bill shall be so altered or amended, on its passage through either House, as to change its original purpose."[99] Unlike Congress, most state legislatures are constitutionally barred from enacting so-called special or local laws, a type of legislation that provides relief to particular individuals or communities.[100] State constitutions frequently require as a condition of enactment that bills be read three times, sometimes on different days of the legislative session.[101] As one critic has observed, "state constitutions [commonly] provide that the legislature shall determine its own rules of procedure, and then deny it the effective exercise of that right by providing for the conduct of legislative business in such detail as to leave very little to rulemaking."[102]

Strong Democratic Checks

Popular distrust of state power, or at least of the officials who wield it, may be most vividly revealed in the plethora of measures that the people of numerous states have enacted to give themselves substantial, direct democratic control over the affairs of state government. The best known and most directly democratic of these are the initiative and referendum. An initiative is an item of proposed legislation or a proposed constitutional amendment that is submitted to the voters for approval. Nineteen states presently provide for initiative measures. In a referendum, a law enacted by the legislature is presented to the voters for

---

96. Ariz. Const. art. IX, § 2(4) and (5).

97. Briffault, *Balancing Acts,* 8.

98. See Ruud, "No Law Shall Embrace More Than One Subject."

99. Pa. Const. art. 3, § 1.

100. See Saunders, "Equal Protection, Class Legislation, and Colorblindness," 251–68.

101. E.g., Md. Const. art. III, § 3.27(a); Mich. Const. art. IV, § 26.

102. Grad, "The State Constitution," 961 n.92.

their approval or rejection. Every state except Alabama currently provides for some form of referendum. Needless to say, the U.S. Constitution provides for absolutely no direct involvement by the people in any matter of governance.

While initiatives and referendums are the devices by which the people of a state exercise the most direct democratic check on state officials, they are by no means the only ones. Twelve state constitutions, for example, provide a recall procedure under which the terms of sitting elected officials can be ended prematurely by popular vote, should the voters be unhappy with their performance in office. Nearly half the states impose upon their governors a form of mandatory rotation in office by disqualifying sitting governors from succeeding themselves.[103] In addition, as noted earlier, the great majority of state constitutions provide for the popular election of many more executive branch officials than does the U.S. Constitution, and forty-three states provide for the election of at least some judges. The greater scope of direct electoral accountability to the people thus gives them manifold tools to ensure that state government is conducted in accordance with their wishes.

MIXED EVIDENCE

As we have now seen, state polities have at their disposal numerous tools for constitutionalizing any distrust they may feel toward state power. Given the flexibility and sensitivity with which state constitutions are capable of reflecting these popular sentiments, one might expect any given state constitution to express some coherent and consistent philosophy of trust in government. A state polity, one might think, would adopt a set of constitutional provisions that consistently either empowers or constrains the organs of state government. The state constitution would then settle on some balance point between authorization and limitation, and its provisions would work together to grant state government just the desired amount of power, and to keep it effectively from exercising power to any greater or lesser extent.

In reality, however, it is rare for a state constitution to express anything that could be deemed a coherent philosophy of trust in governance. On the contrary, most state constitutions seem to contain distinctly mixed evidence of popular feelings about government: some provisions may grant the state

---

103. See Gardner, "Devolution and the Paradox of Democratic Unresponsiveness," 766–67.

government more power than the national government; others may grant it less or restrict it more; and some of these provisions may even appear to work at cross-purposes with one another. For example, Nevada's original 1864 constitution contained the following separation of powers provision, apparently intended to create a sharper division of powers among the branches than appears in the U.S. Constitution:

> The powers of the Government of the State of Nevada shall be divided into three separate departments,—the Legislative,—the Executive and the Judicial; and no persons charged with the exercise of powers properly belonging to one of these departments shall exercise any functions, appertaining to either of the others, except in the cases herein expressly directed or permitted.[104]

More than a century later, in 1996, this provision of the Nevada Constitution was amended by adding a new section authorizing legislative committees to review, suspend, and void regulations promulgated by executive agencies:

> If the legislature authorizes the adoption of regulations by an executive agency which bind persons outside the agency, the legislature may provide by law for:
>
> (a) The review of those regulations by a legislative agency before their effective date to determine initially whether each is within the statutory authority of its adoption;
>
> (b) The suspension by a legislative agency of any such regulation which appears to exceed that authority . . . ; and
>
> (c) The nullification of any such regulation of a majority vote of that legislative body.[105]

This legislative veto provision appears to undermine the strict separation of powers that the original provision attempted to create by authorizing the legislature to engage in an activity that is most often considered to be a serious intrusion into the process of executing the laws, a process that the Nevada Constitution otherwise commits exclusively to the executive branch.

This kind of inconsistency, however, should not be surprising. As we have seen, the Framers themselves anticipated that the degree of trust the people would feel in any particular level of government would change over time, some-

104. Nev. Const. art. III, § 1 (1864).
105. Nev. Const. art. III, § 1(2) (1996).

thing that could happen for any number of reasons. The prevailing public philosophy of governance among a state's people, for example, may change for
ideological reasons. A temporary crisis may require granting one or another
level of government sufficient power to meet specific challenges, or it might
require constraining one level of government from interfering with solutions
advanced by the other. National or state power may be felt within a particular
state in new ways that strike the populace as desirable or dangerous. Particular officials at the state or national level may prove untrustworthy in some
way—or several may betray the public trust, or a whole succession of officials
may do so—thus souring the public for a while on that level of government.

The citizens of a state may respond to such events by reevaluating their
feelings about government power generally, or about the relative utility and
trustworthiness of state and national government. But unless enough other
citizens throughout the nation—indeed, an overwhelming number of citizens—share their sentiments concerning the national government, there is
no chance that their evolving opinions will result in any change to the U.S.
Constitution. Consequently, if a state's citizens wish to see their views about
government trustworthiness constitutionalized, they must enact the desired
changes at the state level.

A state polity may reinscribe in the state constitution its trust in the different levels of government in one of two ways: it may replace the state constitution entirely with one better suited to the task; or it may tweak the existing constitution through amendments designed to readjust state power to match the
polity's present opinions regarding its appropriate scope. A few states appear to
have followed the first course. Louisiana, for example, has had eleven different
constitutions since its admission to the union in 1812, the most of any state.
Georgia has had nine constitutions, South Carolina seven, and Virginia, Alabama, and Florida six each.[106] Indeed, according to at least one account,
Alabama's present constitution, adopted in 1901, is the very model of a constitution framed out of "a basic distrust of government."[107] More commonly,

---

106. Sturm, "The Development of American State Constitutions," 75–76.

107. Brewer, "Foreword: A Broad Initiative," 190. Governor Brewer goes on to explain
that the 1901 Alabama Constitution "provided that the legislature would meet qua-
drennially . . . ; the constitution earmarks revenues for specific purposes denying to
elected representatives the right to allocate funds were most needed; and . . . the constitution deliberately denies to local officials the authority to deal with local issues." Id.
at 190–91.

however, state polities seeking to adjust the scope of state power do so by amending the state constitution. Some state constitutions have been amended repeatedly: the present Alabama Constitution, for example, has been amended more than seven hundred times, and the current California, South Carolina, and Texas Constitutions more than four hundred times each.

If state polities resort frequently to constitutional amendment to bring the scope of state authority within limits defined by a constantly changing conception of the appropriate balance of state and national power, then it should not be surprising if a state constitution comes to be a kind of palimpsest, bearing witness in its many tangled and possibly self-contradictory provisions to the course by which the people's constitutional thought has evolved. Even a new constitution that replaces outright its predecessor may retain many provisions that have accumulated over the years and that reflect the waxing and waning of the people's trust in state power. A state constitution, then, may be usefully understood as a kind of record of a series of popular *adjustments* to state power, and an examination of the state constitution may be not unlike an archaeological expedition: one's sense of the state polity's opinions about the trustworthiness of state or national power may depend upon what layer one explores.

6

A Functional Account of State Judicial Power

MY AIM IN this book is to give an account of state constitutional interpretation that takes into consideration the way state power is actually allocated and exercised within the American federal system. Now that much of the groundwork has been laid in the previous three chapters, that goal finally is beginning to come into view. I argued in chapter 3 that the American system of federalism charges states with monitoring and, when possible, resisting abuses of power at the national level, and that to serve this goal effectively states must possess a not inconsiderable amount of power. In chapter 4, I argued that an important function of a state constitution is to establish and institutionalize such powers as the people of the state believe it necessary for their state government to possess to fulfill this vital role in the federal system. In chapter 5, I argued that state power can be balanced and structured in a virtually limitless number of ways that satisfy the requirements of federalism, and that a state polity's decisions regarding the strength and allocation of state power are likely to be influenced significantly by the patterns of distrust of government power that prevail among the people of the state. The present chapter applies these principles to the state judicial branch in a way that points toward a concrete approach to the interpretation of state constitutions.

We saw in chapter 3 that state power can be deployed for at least three different purposes, each of which promotes liberty in a slightly different way. First, state power can be used to advance the public good directly, through the exercise of ordinary governmental power. Second, state power can be granted and deployed for the purpose of resisting abuses of power originating at the national level. Third, state power can be allocated and deployed for the purpose of imposing upon state government some form of internal self-restraint, as through mechanisms such as separation of powers, judicial review, and a bill of rights. State courts have obvious roles to play in exercising the first and third kinds of power. They clearly can use their granted powers to advance the common good directly—for example, by shaping the state's common law to accomplish desirable social and economic objectives. State courts also have a clear role in restraining state power by enforcing the separation of powers established by the state constitution and by protecting constitutionally guaranteed individual rights against infringement by the other branches. The second kind of power, however, presents a more difficult question. Do state courts have any role in maintaining the balance of state and national power contemplated by federalism? Are they mere bystanders to a permanent struggle against national power waged by the state legislative and executive branches? Or are they active participants, charged at least on occasion with exercising their powers to resist national abuses?

I argue in this chapter that the answer to these questions is: it depends. State courts are fully capable of serving as agents of federalism in at least two ways, one direct and the other indirect. State courts may serve indirectly as agents of resistance to national power by construing the state constitution in such a way as to ensure, insofar as possible, that the state legislative and executive branches have powers adequate to resist abuses of national power. At the very least, state courts may avoid using their power as final arbiter of the meaning of the state constitution so as to impede the effectiveness of those branches. As we saw in chapter 3, state courts may also take a more direct role in checking abuses of national power—especially abuses of national judicial power—by interpreting generously the scope of individual liberty under the state constitution when doing so would tend to resist or counteract liberty-invasive judicial rulings issued or government actions taken at the national level.

Capability, however, is one thing and authority another. Just because state courts are capable of playing a role in resisting abuses of national power does not mean that they are authorized to do so. Just as with any other branch of state government, whether a state court has the authority to join this struggle depends upon whether the people of the state have constitutionally authorized it to participate, which in turn depends, as we saw in chapter 5, on the patterns of distrust that prevail among the people of the state. The more the people trust the state judicial branch to protect their welfare actively, through direct resistance to abuses of national power, the more likely they are to grant it the authority to do so, and vice versa.

Significantly for present purposes, constitutional decisions concerning the authority of state courts to act as agents of federalism have important ramifications for the interpretation of state constitutions. The more authority state courts are granted to serve as agents of federalism by monitoring and resisting abuses of national power, the more flexibility they are necessarily authorized to bring to the interpretation of the state constitution. Conversely, the more tightly the people of the state have, through their state constitution, reined in the exercise of judicial power, the less flexibly state courts may approach state constitutional interpretation and the more fastidiously they must observe specific popular decisions set forth in the state constitution. Constitutional decisions concerning state judicial authority thus allocate between the people and their courts the authority to monitor and check abuses of national power. Federalism requires that some state actor monitor vigilantly the actions of the national government. Which organs of government undertake this job—or whether the people reserve it entirely to themselves—is a question to be decided in the adoption of a state constitution. And popular resolution of this question simultaneously resolves a good deal of uncertainty about how state courts should approach and interpret the state's constitution.

STATE COURTS AS AGENTS OF STATE POWER

The Affirmative Use of Granted Powers to Advance the Public Good

The most obvious function of any government is to exercise its granted powers for the direct benefit of its citizens. As one of the three primary branches of state government, the state judiciary typically possesses considerable power, which it may deploy to serve the public good in some very direct ways.

In its most basic manifestation, state judicial power serves the public good when state courts do nothing more than undertake the routine adjudication of individual cases. Deciding cases arising under clearly established legal principles resolves disputes among individual litigants, and reaffirms and reinforces the rule of law. In criminal cases, the conviction and punishment of the guilty does justice and protects the public from further harm. In civil cases, enforcement of the laws of tort, contract, and property not only does justice in individual cases (or so it is hoped), but also gives effect to economic expectations, thereby establishing and maintaining a necessary condition of economic prosperity. Adjudication in its most ordinary and least controversial forms thus promotes the public good in significant ways.

State courts, however, typically have other, more discretionary means at their disposal to advance the public good beyond the somewhat "ministerial" function of applying established law to individual cases. Surely the most prominent of these is the power of a state court to make new law by deliberately shaping and self-consciously improving the state's common law. The common law is generally understood to embrace "[a] tradition of law improvement by creative judicial action."[1] Although the bulk of common law litigation consists of the routine application of existing legal rules to familiar fact patterns, courts engaged in common law adjudication are sometimes in a position to choose quite deliberately among alternative potential legal rules on the basis of "whether those rules will conduce to a good or a bad state of affairs."[2] In these situations, common law courts actively shape and remake the law.[3]

Throughout the twentieth century, and especially in its middle decades, American state courts developed a record of substantial and rapid innovation in numerous areas of common law. In tort law, for example, state courts developed the new torts of "false light" and "disclosure of embarrassing private facts," and greatly expanded the scope, and thus the utility to plaintiffs, of intentional infliction of emotional distress. They drastically restricted the scope of existing tort doctrines of municipal and charitable immunity, thus subjecting to liability numerous entities that had previously been exempt.[4] State courts also during this period developed tort doctrines of strict liability that greatly expanded the ability of injured consumers to recover damages caused by defective products, going so far in some instances as to create a form of "enterprise liability" in which traditional principles not only of fault, but of proof of causation, were displaced.[5] Some tort cases, such as *MacPherson v. Buick*,[6] which set the law of product liability on a course away from restrictive contract principles and toward more generous principles of tort, have become well-known classics, held up within the legal profession as examples of the best and highest expression of judicial craft.

1. Keeton, *Venturing to Do Justice*, 13.

2. Eisenberg, *The Nature of the Common Law*, 43.

3. Common law courts also reshape the law passively, or at least indirectly, insofar as common law rules evolve with each successive decision. See Levi, *An Introduction to Legal Reasoning*, 1–4. This is a process that goes on continually and irrespective of judicial intentions. I am concerned more here with the kind of deliberate shaping of the law that occurs, for example, when courts overrule prior decisions. See Keeton, *Venturing to Do Justice*, chs. 1, 3.

4. Gordley, "The Common Law in the Twentieth Century," 1834–35; Baum and Canon, "State Supreme Courts as Activists." See also Bernstein, "How to Make a New Tort."

5. Keeton, *Venturing to Do Justice*, ch. 7; Priest, "The Invention of Enterprise Liability"; Keating, "The Theory of Enterprise Liability and Common Law Strict Liability."

6. 111 N.E. 1050 (1916).

In these kinds of cases, courts do something more than mechanically apply the law to new sets of facts: they alter the law, in effect making new law, and do so with the deliberate aim of adjusting controlling legal principles to bring about better, fairer, and generally more desirable results. While this function has long been thought to be an integral part of adjudication in the Anglo-American tradition, it is an aspect of the adjudicatory power by which state courts historically have participated directly and actively in the process of state-level governance—much more so than if they routinely took the position that any changes in the common law must be made by legislatures rather than courts.

While the power to shape the common law is the most visible and probably the most powerful way in which state courts participate actively in state-level governance, it is not the only way. For example, many states grant their highest court the power to issue advisory opinions, which the executive or legislative branches are authorized to request. These branches most often request advisory opinions to assist their deliberations concerning the constitutionality of proposed or pending legislation. When a court issues such an opinion, it inserts itself directly into the deliberative process by which law is made, becoming an active player in the legislative process. This is a more direct kind of participation in state governance than a court undertakes when it merely reviews the constitutionality of legislation after the fact.

State courts also participate directly in governance through their power to make rules for judicial proceedings, a power typically granted by state constitutions.[7] While the judicial rulemaking power is most often exercised to make procedural and evidentiary rules the impact of which is confined mainly to regulating the adjudicatory process, judicial rules sometimes can touch upon highly significant subjects. For example, well before the U.S. Supreme Court decided in *Gideon v. Wainwright*[8] that the U.S. Constitution guarantees indigent criminal defendants a right to appointed counsel, several state courts had so provided by ordinary rulemaking.[9] State courts also engage in a form of inde-

---

7. Parness, "Public Process and State-Court Rulemaking"; Williams, *State Constitutional Law,* 702–23. In some states, the power to make rules is considered an inherent and exclusive aspect of judicial power. See, e.g., State ex rel. Kelman v. Schaffer, 290 A.2d 327, 331 (Conn. 1971), *overruled on other grounds,* Serrani v. Board of Ethics, 622 A.2d 1009 (Conn. 1993): "[T]he General Assembly lacks any power to make rules of administration, practice or procedure which are binding on either the Supreme Court or the Superior Court."

8. 372 U.S. 335 (1963).

9. See State v. Delaney, 332 P.2d 71 (Or. 1958); Williams v. Commonwealth, 216 N.E.2d 779 (Mass. 1966); People v. Parshay, 148 N.W.2d 869 (Mich. 1967).

pendent regulatory governance by making and administering rules governing the legal profession, including rules for admission to the bar and lawyer ethics and discipline. Finally, state courts increasingly have come to participate fairly directly in state governance by creating and administering social service programs that are more often associated with executive than with judicial power. Among these are family court mediation programs, domestic violence programs, and victim assistance programs.[10]

Judicial Restraint of State Tyranny

If state courts generally have the authority under state constitutions to advance liberty by using their powers to achieve the public good directly, they also universally have the constitutional authority to use their power of judicial review to protect liberty in another way: by serving as a force for state governmental self-restraint. As we have seen, if a state government is to advance the public good, it must possess a certain amount of power. The more power a state government possesses, however, the more capable it is of threatening the liberties of its people. This threat may be restrained to a degree by institutionalizing some form of internal self-restraint, such as horizontal separation of powers, creation of a bill of rights, and establishment of judicial review. State courts play a significant role in the exercise of state power to achieve this kind of internal self-restraint.

Consider the separation of powers under state constitutions, often said to be an essential safeguard of liberty. In enforcing these principles, state courts have, among other things, barred legislators from sitting on executive branch commissions; prohibited legislative officials from appointing executive branch officials; prevented state judges from being required to serve on administrative mediation boards; prohibited judicial appointment of special prosecutors; barred the use of a legislative veto; and invalidated numerous instances of excessive delegations of legislative authority to executive branch agencies.[11] In the area of individual rights, state courts have issued an enormous number

10. Durham, "The Judicial Branch in State Government"; Peters, "Getting Away from the Federal Paradigm."

11. See Legislative Research Comm'n v. Brown, 664 S.W.2d 907 (Ky. 1984); Application of Nelson, 163 N.W.2d 533 (S.D. 1968); In re House of Representatives, 575 A.2d 176 (R.I. 1990); State ex rel. Stephan v. Kansas House of Representatives, 687 P.2d 622 (Kan. 1984). Many of the nondelegation cases are collected in Rossi, "Institutional Design and the Lingering Legacy of Antifederal Separation of Powers Ideals in the States."

of rulings restraining state legislative and executive officials from infringing liberties protected by state constitutions. Such rulings, far too numerous to mention with any specificity, include decisions protecting free speech, equal protection, due process, and privacy, among many others.[12] According to one recent study, state courts today invalidate more than 20 percent of the state laws they review.[13]

In all these areas, then, state courts have periodically used judicial power to protect liberty by restraining other branches of government from taking actions forbidden to them by the state constitution—forbidden because they have been deemed to pose actual or potential threats to the welfare of the state's citizenry.

STATE COURTS AS AGENTS OF FEDERALISM

The two different uses of state judicial power just described are "internal" to the state in the sense that their exercise neither refers to nor depends upon the activities or goals of any entity other than the state itself. In exercising its power to shape the common law, for example, a state court has no particular reason to consider the good of the citizens of neighboring states or of Americans generally. So long as it acts within any constraints imposed by national law, a state court is free to adapt the state's common law so as to promote the good of the people of the state, a good that need not be assessed in relation to the good of any other group.[14] Similarly, when a state court protects the liberty of the citizenry by enforcing the state constitution against other branches of state government, it is free to consider the liberty of the state's citizens inde-

---

12. Many examples are collected in Williams, *State Constitutional Law,* esp. chs. 3 and 4.

13. Langer, *Judicial Review in State Supreme Courts,* 1.

14. It might be argued that some of the path-breaking commercial common law decisions were motivated by, or at least responded to, an interest in improving the operation of the national economy. See Horwitz, *The Transformation of American Law,* ch. 7. But this is not necessary in a common law decision. It is also consistent with a judicial interest to improve the welfare of the people of the state, who would be expected to benefit from improved economic activity. Indeed, it seems likely that a state court would issue a commerce-facilitating common law ruling precisely because benefits to the nationwide economy would be expected to accrue to the state populace. One would certainly less expect a state court to care about facilitating some kind of commerce nationwide from which the people of the state would *not* be expected to benefit.

pendently of the liberty enjoyed by citizens of other states. In the exercise of these functions, state courts thus act as agents of state power, exercising that power for the good of the state polity.

But organs of state government need not act exclusively in this inward-regarding manner. Federalism requires that state power be available for deployment outwardly, against threats originating at the national level. This raises the question whether state courts have any role to play in the process of using state power to resist abuses of national power—whether, that is to say, they may serve as what I refer to as "agents of federalism." At this point, I wish to set aside for a moment the question of whether state courts in fact have such a role in order to focus on a preliminary question: if state courts *do* have such a role, how can they fulfill it? Is it even possible for a state court to use its own powers to resist national authority, and if so, by what means? We have a pretty clear idea of what this kind of activity looks like when undertaken by the state legislative or executive branch; how would it look if undertaken by the state judicial branch?

Judicial Tools of Federalism Agency

If the federal structure contemplates in theory a role for state courts as agents of federalism, how might state courts perform that function in practice? To answer that question, it is useful to begin by considering how national courts serve as agents of federalism.

Federalism is a two-way street, and courts of the United States serve as agents of federalism when they use their powers to restrain abuses of power by state governments. This is clearly one of their most important functions. Yet federal courts perform this function merely by enforcing the U.S. Constitution according to its terms. That is because the Constitution *by its own terms* restrains the ability of state governments to behave tyrannically. For example, it prohibits states from creating aristocratic forms of government. It prevents them from abridging rights of free speech, freedom of the press, and freedom of religion. It forbids them from violating principles of equal protection or due process. It restrains them from impairing the obligations of contracts, or from impeding economically desirable interstate commerce. To invoke these limits—and thus to serve as agents of federalism—a federal court need do nothing more than enforce the U.S. Constitution as it is written. Indeed, because the structural dynamic of federalism is itself a feature of the governmental system created by the Constitution, to restrain state power for the purpose of preserving an appropriate balance between and state and national power is simply one aspect of enforcing the federal Constitution on its own terms. The national government's role in enforcing the American system of federalism is thus inscribed directly in the Constitution itself; it is woven deeply into the fabric of the document—in its text, structure, theoretical foundations, and history.

State courts, in contrast, cannot serve as agents of federalism merely by enforcing the terms of state constitutions for the simple reason that state constitutions, although they are integral parts of the overall constitutional structure of federalism, do not purport to assert the kind of sovereignty over the national government that the federal Constitution routinely asserts over states. As a result, state constitutions do not explicitly authorize the use of state judicial power for the purpose of restraining national power; indeed, state constitutions typically do not explicitly authorize any branch of state government to act as an agent of federalism, though state officials routinely do so.

Federalism of course contemplates that state power will be deployed when necessary to resist abuses of national power by the national government. Chapter 3 examined numerous ways in which a state's executive and legislative power may be so deployed, including political negotiation, refusal of financial incentives, grudging or uncooperative compliance with federal law, suing the national government in federal court, defiance of national law, and even threats of force. However, no provision in any state constitution explicitly authorizes the governor to attempt to influence national legislation by working closely with the state congressional delegation; or authorizes a state legislature to decline federal funds when acceptance would require compliance with oppressive nationally imposed conditions; or authorizes a state's attorney general to take the national government to court.

This strange silence raises the puzzling question why state constitutional drafters have never seen fit to include such terms in state constitutional documents. Perhaps because state executive and legislative power is typically granted in unrestricted terms, no basis has ever seemed to exist for challenging the exercise of executive and legislative power in this way. Possibly, the protection of a state's citizens against incursions by the national government has seemed sufficiently analogous to self-defense against an external threat as to qualify as an exercise of the power of self-preservation that all sovereign governments typically are assumed implicitly to possess. Or perhaps the power of state governments to resist abuses of national authority has always seemed such an obvious inference from the federal structure as to require no specific mention, which suggests that the power of resistance must be granted in every state's constitution by necessary implication. State officials, in other words, apparently have the power to resist national authority in appropriate circumstances because they *must* have it—because a properly functioning national system of federalism demands that they have it. In this sense, the silence of state constitutions on this crucial point may echo the belief of the drafters of the national Constitution that it was unnecessary to state explicitly the relationship between state and national power—at least until the Tenth Amendment expressly declared it. Indeed, state constitutions might well be thought to contain implicitly a kind of "inverse Tenth Amendment" that authorizes state officials to assert state power against the national government as agents of federalism.

Be that as it may regarding the state executive and legislative branches, the question here is whether any such inference applies with equal force to state judicial branches. Let us again put aside for a moment whether any particular state court has such authority and turn instead to a related, but more practical question. Assuming a state court does have authority to act as an agent of federalism, how might it assert that authority? What tools, in other words, might a state court employ to resist national power? State courts, it must be conceded, possess far fewer resources to deploy against national power than do the state executive and legislative branches. State courts typically lack jurisdiction over organs of the national government, for example, and are subject to direct national judicial oversight on questions of national law.[15] And although state courts are typically more active and involved in policy formation than federal courts, they still are relatively passive institutions. Unlike the governor and state legislature, state courts cannot simply involve themselves voluntarily in pressing disputes, but must ordinarily wait for problems to come to them before acting. Nevertheless, state courts do have one fairly powerful tool at their disposal: their day-to-day superintendency of the state constitution. This aspect of judicial power gives state courts at least two methods by which they may participate in any state struggle against national authority, one indirect and the other direct.

15. The United States cannot be sued in any court unless it waives its sovereign immunity. United States v. Sherwood, 312 U.S. 584, 596 (1941). Even where the United States has waived its sovereign immunity to suit, it has by statute retained the authority to remove to federal court cases filed against it in state court. 28 U.S.C. § 1442(a). State courts also typically lack the authority to issue orders to national officials. M'Clung v. Silliman, 19 U.S. 598 (1821); Ableman v. Booth, 62 U.S. 506 (1858); Tarble's Case, 80 U.S. 397 (1871). The appellate jurisdiction of the U.S. Supreme Court was established in Martin v. Hunter's Lessee, 14 U.S. 304 (1816).

First, state courts may participate indirectly in state resistance to national power by construing the state constitution in such a way as to ensure, insofar as possible, that the state legislative and executive branches have powers adequate to resist abuses of national authority. Within the federal structure, most state acts of resistance to national tyranny will be undertaken by the state executive or legislative branches. To resist national authority with the greatest possible effectiveness, governors and state legislatures require ample powers. What powers these branches possess is a question determined solely by reference to the state constitution, the final meaning of which is settled by the state judiciary. Should state power come into conflict with national power concerning controversial issues, it is possible, and perhaps likely, that legal challenges will ensue, thereby offering state courts opportunities to construe the constitutional authority of coordinate branches of state government engaged in the dispute. In these circumstances, state courts may well play important roles in state–national disputes by being forced to decide whether the state constitution authorizes other state actors to carry out effective forms of resistance to national power.

For example, the degree of centralized state control over federal grant funds has long been a contentious flash point in intergovernmental relations. Congress presently supplies approximately 30 percent of all state revenue.[16] In exercising this responsibility, Congress often has been interested in distributing federal funds in whatever way is best calculated to achieve as directly and efficiently as possible the programmatic goals for which the grant money is intended. This approach has sometimes led Congress to provide grant money directly to state executive agencies. State legislatures, on the other hand, have not infrequently viewed such targeted grants as undermining state legislative control over the ways in which state executive agencies raise and spend funds to achieve programmatic goals.[17] Indeed, Congress has occasionally viewed state legislatures, not entirely without justification, as interlopers bent on undermining congressionally imposed spending conditions so as to divert state funds to unauthorized uses. To avoid this, Congress has sometimes acted in a way that looks very much as though it is attempting to peel off state executive agencies from state legislative oversight so as to accomplish purposes dictated by Congress rather than by state governmental processes. State legislatures, for their part, tend to see this practice as an intrusive abuse of the national spending power.

16. Somin, "Closing the Pandora's Box of Federalism," 462.

17. The federalism implications of this practice are helpfully discussed in Hills, "Dissecting the State."

Congress, of course, has a great deal of freedom to specify the conditions under which federal grant money may be spent, and may specify that grants be made directly to specific state agencies.[18] It does not follow, however, that state executive agencies have the authority to *spend* money that they receive from sources other than the state legislature. Many state constitutions, like the U.S. Constitution, contain provisions requiring that expended funds be appropriated specifically by the legislature.[19] In reliance on such provisions, state legislatures have from time to time enacted laws requiring federal grant funds to be paid into the state's general treasury for subsequent reappropriation by the legislature, and prohibiting state executive agencies from spending federal grant funds that have not been legislatively appropriated.

State courts have on several occasions been called upon to adjudicate the constitutionality of these restrictions on the spending of unappropriated funds. Some state courts have construed the state constitutional requirement of appropriation narrowly, holding that it applies only to spending out of state general treasury revenue, a description that does not apply to federal grant money.[20] Other state courts, however, have taken a different view. The Pennsylvania Supreme Court, for example, has held that the state constitution does limit the spending authority of state executive agencies to the spending of funds that have been appropriated by the state legislature,[21] and it has accordingly upheld legislative restrictions on agency spending of unappropriated

18. See Lawrence County v. Lead-Deadwood Sch. Dist. No. 40-1, 469 U.S. 256 (1985), which holds that the terms of such a grant may, under certain circumstances, preempt inconsistent state law.

19. Compare, e.g., Pa. Const. art. III, § 24 ("No money shall be paid out of the treasury, except on appropriations made by law"), with U.S. Const. art. I, § 9, cl. 7 ("No money shall be drawn from the Treasury, but in Consequence of Appropriations made by Law").

20. See State v. Department of Transp., 646 P.2d 605 (Okla. 1982); Opinion of the Justices, 378 N.E.2d 433 (Mass. 1978) (advisory opinion); Navajo Tribe v. Arizona Dep't of Administration, 528 P.2d 623 (Ariz. 1974); State v. Kirkpatrick, 524 P.2d 975 (N.M. 1974); McManus v. Love, 499 P.2d 609 (Colo. 1972). See also State v. Lamm, 738 P.2d 1156 (Colo. 1987) (holding that the legislative appropriation requirement applies only to those portions of federal block grants for which Congress has allowed state legislative control).

21. Shapp v. Sloan, 391 A.2d 595 (Pa. 1978). *Accord* Anderson v. Regan, 425 N.E.2d 792 (N.Y. 1981). See also Opinion of the Justices, 381 A.2d 1204 (N.H. 1978) (National Health Planning and Resources Development Act did not preempt state legislative authority to require the governor to designate a particular state agency as the agency authorized to receive federal categorical grants under the Act).

federal grants.[22] In so doing, the Pennsylvania Supreme Court has delivered to the legislature a constitutional tool for defending its control over state executive spending from erosion worked by congressional grantmaking strategies.

Even when these kinds of state constitutional issues do not arise in the course of an active, ongoing dispute with the national government, constitutional rulings by state courts concerning the scope of executive and legislative authority can have obvious ramifications for the ability of those branches of state government successfully to oppose abuses of national authority in subsequent clashes. For example, to resist national power successfully, a state legislature may find itself called upon to do two things: enact some kind of legislation and appropriate money to fund its implementation. The legislature's ability to do both these things obviously can be affected by the construction given by state courts to the relevant state constitutional provisions.

Consider, for example, the California Constitution's urgency legislation clause. Article IV, § 8 of the California Constitution prevents laws enacted by the legislature from taking effect sooner than ninety days after enactment. However, this provision has an exception for what it terms "urgency statutes," which it defines as laws "necessary for immediate preservation of the public peace, health, or safety"; such laws may take effect immediately.[23] It is clear that this exception for urgent legislation is intended to give the state legislature sufficient flexibility to deal quickly and effectively with crises. Yet the degree to which the exception will be available to the legislature turns to a great extent on the construction given the clause by California courts. The language of the exception limits its use to situations where there is an immediate "necessity," dealing with "public peace," "health" or "safety." The meaning of these terms is hardly self-evident.

In practice, the California courts have given the language of the clause a generous interpretation and have tended to defer almost completely to the legislature's definition of "urgency" by giving laws enacted under the urgency exception a strong presumption of validity.[24] But nothing has compelled the courts to take such a deferential approach. The ninety-day waiting period for

22. It is not clear that this holding survives the Supreme Court's ruling in Lawrence County v. Lead-Deadwood Sch. Dist. No. 40-1, 469 U.S. 256 (1985).

23. Cal. Const. art. IV, §§ 8(c)(1) and (2), 8(d).

24. See, e.g., People v. Kinsey, 47 Cal. Rptr. 2d 769 (Ct. App. 1995); People v. Pacheco, 27 Cal. 175 (1865).

legislation and the careful wording of the urgency exception presumably have their roots in some popular distrust of the state legislature's judgment concerning the effective date of legislation. Such considerations might just as easily lead a state court to construe an urgency exception narrowly. A narrow construction might thus serve the constitutional purpose of protecting the people of California from the bad judgment of the state legislature, but only at the price of inhibiting the legislature's ability to protect them quickly and effectively from abuses of national power through prompt exercises of state legislative power.

Much the same can be said about funding. In 1998, California voters approved Proposition 98, a constitutional amendment providing that total annual appropriations may not exceed appropriations for the previous year, adjusted for inflation and population growth. Any excess revenues must be refunded to taxpayers. However, the state constitution directs the legislature to establish a "prudent state reserve fund in such amount as it shall deem reasonable and necessary."[25] No California court has yet had occasion to construe the meaning of the term "prudent state reserve," but it seems clear that a restrictive definition of the term could impede the ability of the state legislature to respond rapidly to abuses of national authority that the legislature might deem it important to resist.

In these situations concerning legislation and funding authority, state courts have an opportunity to influence the ability of other branches of state government to resist abuses of national power with the greatest possible speed and effectiveness. Construing the relevant provisions of the state constitution with an eye toward the federalism effects of their rulings might not lead state courts to different results—but, then again, it might.

The second way in which state courts may serve actively as agents of federalism is much more direct: state courts may help check abuses of national power, especially national judicial power, by interpreting generously the scope of individual liberty under the state constitution. When a state court construes the state constitution to provide greater protection for individual rights than is provided by the national Constitution, it is doing more than merely protecting the state's citizens from infringements of liberty at the hands of state government: it is also actively resisting and to a certain extent counteracting unduly restrictive national protection for individual liberty.

25. Cal. Const. art. XIIIB, §§ 1, 2(b), 5.5.

Chapter 3 explained the mechanisms by which generous judicial interpretation of state constitutional rights can resist and counteract liberty-invasive abuses of national judicial power. A recapitulation may, however, be in order, so I shall review this topic here briefly. State judicial divergence from purportedly abusive national precedents concerning the scope of individual rights helps check national power in at least four ways. First, whenever a state court dissents from the reasoning of a U.S. Supreme Court decision, it offers a forceful and very public critique of the national ruling, which can in the long run influence the formation of public and, eventually, official opinion on the propriety of the federal ruling. Second, state rulings that depart from or criticize U.S. Supreme Court precedents can contribute to the establishment of a nationwide legal consensus at the state level, a factor that the Supreme Court sometimes considers in the course of constitutional decisionmaking. Third, generous state interpretations of individual rights can more directly check national power by prohibiting state and local governments from exercising authority permitted them under the U.S. Constitution to suppress certain kinds of private behavior. In so doing, state courts create spaces in which otherwise prohibitable behavior may flourish. Finally, rights-protective rulings by state courts can help ameliorate the harm to liberty caused by narrow national rulings by providing protection for second-best alternatives to the types of behavior that such national rulings permit governments to suppress.

Here, then, is the critical point: in the two ways outlined above, state constitutional interpretation itself can be a tool of resistance to national power. It can be a vehicle by which state courts participate in the project of deploying state power to check abuses of national power, a project contemplated—indeed, demanded—by a properly functioning system of federalism.

This conclusion should not be surprising. Constitutional law is a means by which official power is projected into the political world. As a result, judicial shaping of constitutional doctrine is necessarily a means by which state courts may influence the way that state power is projected against the national government, and, to a lesser extent, the way in which exercises of national power are experienced by the people of the state. As a tool of resistance, judicial shaping of state constitutional doctrine is neither as dramatic nor as likely to be as effective as the tools typically available to a state's governor or legislature, but that is to be expected given the comparative weakness of courts as institutions of governance. Nevertheless, just because state courts are weaker than state executives and legislatures does not mean that they are incapable of playing any role at all in the enterprise of state resistance to abuses of national power.

Federalism Effects as a Factor in State Constitutional Analysis

It is one thing to suggest that the actions of state courts may have some impact on the balance of state and national power, or that decisions of state courts construing the state constitution may happen to have the effect of impeding or resisting abuses of national power. It is something else, however, to suggest that the impact of a state constitutional ruling on national power could itself serve as a ground or justification for a construction of the state constitution—that a court might legitimately interpret a state constitutional provision in a particular way precisely *because* its decision would resist or rebuke national authority, or would permit some other state official to do so. This second kind of usage passes from a description of how state power may be used to a prescription for how it ought to be used. Nevertheless, that is the position I intend to defend in the balance of this chapter and in the next. I argue that a state court contemplating the meaning of a provision of its state constitution may, in certain circumstances, legitimately consider the ways in which its decision will affect national power—the ruling's "federalism effects"—and that the court may, in certain circumstances, construe provisions of its state constitution with the deliberate purpose of producing particular federalism effects that it deems desirable, even when other indicia of constitutional meaning, such as the relevant text, history, or intentions of the framers, might point toward a different result. A decision's federalism effects, that is to say, furnish a legitimate normative ground on which to rest a construction of the state constitution—not the only legitimate ground, to be sure, but one possible ground.

I have more to say in chapter 7 about how a state court might actually go about construing and utilizing any authority it might have to act as an agent of federalism by using its power to interpret the state constitution. Specifically, I argue that state courts should be understood to operate under a rebuttable presumption favoring their authority to resist abuses of national power through counteractive interpretations of the state constitution. For the moment, however, I want to clarify briefly just what this power would entail so as to avoid any misconceptions about its scope and implications.

The power of a state court to act as an agent of federalism involves nothing more than adding to the usual elements of constitutional analysis an additional factor that takes into account the structural role that state power plays in maintaining liberty within a national system of federalism. As previously noted, when a state court acts solely as an agent of state power, it need concern itself only with norms and decisions internal to the state—established, that is to say, by the people of the state and by state government actors working solely to achieve the good of the state's populace. Thus, when a state court interprets a provision of the state constitution dealing with a home rule provision dividing power between the state and local governments, or a procedural restraint imposed on the legislative process, it is dealing with provisions devoted primarily to restraining state power as it is felt by the people of the state, and its decisions have relatively few ramifications for public welfare outside the state's borders. In these circumstances, the usual factors of constitutional analysis— text, drafters' intentions, legislative history, structural analysis, and so on— suffice to give meaning to the provision in question. This, then, is where the primacy approach to state constitutional interpretation (discussed in chapter 1) may with greatest force claim to provide an accurate and relatively complete framework for the interpretation of state constitutional provisions.

However, because federalism gives states a role to play in resisting encroachments on liberty by the national government, state power will sometimes be exercised primarily for the purpose of resisting national tyranny. In those circumstances, it might well be thought appropriate to authorize state courts to consider, when construing the state constitution, an additional factor in the analytic mix—namely, the potential impact of its rulings on present abuses of national power, and on the ability of the state successfully to resist such abuses in the future. A court authorized to approach state constitutional interpretation in this way would thus be authorized to ask, and to construe the state constitution in light of its answers to, the following kinds of questions:

1. Has the national government abused its authority or acted tyrannically in some way to which the outcome of this case is relevant?

2. If so, is there any possibility that a ruling by this court might act to thwart or in some way minimize the effects of this abuse of national authority?

3. Might a ruling by this court affect in any way the authority or ability of any other organ of state government to resist as effectively as possible any present or future abuses of national authority?

To answer these questions, a state court must look beyond the state's boundaries. It must decide *for itself* whether the national government has abused its authority, a process that not only invites but may well demand examination and independent evaluation of federal judicial rulings construing the U.S. Constitution. A state court must recognize and evaluate the ways in which its own rulings may affect the liberty not merely of the citizens of its own state, but of Americans generally. And it must examine the capabilities of other branches of state government with an eye toward maintaining their efficacy as actors in a permanent, nationwide struggle between state and national power. In short, to permit state courts to become active agents of federalism is to recognize that decisions interpreting the state constitution can have ramifications outside the state—indeed, that the power to interpret state constitutional provisions can serve as a weapon in the service of resistance to national authority.

In the next section, I address several potential objections to this account of state judicial power. First, I want to say a few words about what this approach to state constitutional interpretation does *not* entail. First, just because a state court is capable of acting in this way does not mean it possesses some kind of inherent authority to do so. Granting courts the authority to act as agents of federalism entails certain risks that a state polity might be unwilling to undertake. Later in this chapter and in chapter 7 I discuss the question of whether and in what circumstances state courts should be understood to possess such authority, a question that turns, I argue, on the degree to which the people of a state trust their courts as protectors of liberty. But the power to act as an agent of federalism is one that must be granted affirmatively to a court just as it must be granted affirmatively to any other branch of state government.

Second, when it acts as an agent of federalism, the authority of a state court does not somehow become unlimited; it does not acquire the power to "rewrite" the state constitution in its entirety for the purpose of converting it into a more effective framework for the resistance of national tyranny. As indicated in chapter 4, state constitutions must serve several functions at once, and authorizing resistance to the national government is only one of them. Moreover, these functions often conflict: the more power a state government possesses to resist national tyranny, for example, the more it may be capable of threatening the liberty of its own citizens. It is the state's people, of course, who decide how to balance these competing considerations, a decision that state courts are thus obliged to respect whenever they engage in constitutional interpretation.

Finally and relatedly, judicial authorization to consider the ultimate impact of the court's rulings on abuses of national power does not imply authority to reduce the process of state constitutional interpretation to consideration of that single factor above, or at the expense of, all other factors in constitutional analysis. Text, framers' intentions, structural considerations, and other routine elements of constitutional analysis do not somehow become irrelevant just because a court is also authorized to consider the federalism implications of its rulings. On the contrary, the federalism implications of the ruling must be folded into the analysis and should affect the ultimate outcome no more than their relative weight requires. I have more to say in chapter 7 about how a court might go about doing this.

STRICT CONSTRUCTIONIST OBJECTIONS

Before going any further, I want to address a set of related objections to the account of state judicial power I have just given. In the system described above, state courts may be granted the authority, in a set of narrow circumstances, to serve as agents of federalism by self-consciously interpreting the state constitution to achieve a particular result: helping the state resist abuses of national power. This is an account of judicial power that runs against the grain of the dominant contemporary understanding of how courts ought to engage in constitutional adjudication, an understanding that I call "strict constructionism."[26] The reason this account might offend strict constructionism is because it looks, from the strict constructionist perspective, as though it is advancing a form of constitutional interpretation that is self-consciously result-oriented; it seems to give courts permission to interpret provisions of the state constitution not in accordance with what they in some sense "say," but rather in accordance with what it is necessary for them to say for state power to be deployed effectively against the national government under the circumstances of some particular state–national conflict. According to strict construction-

---

26. In the debates over constitutional interpretation, labels tend to bear significant ideological baggage. It is not my intention to stir this pot, and I hope here to use this particular label as descriptively as possible. I resort to the term "strict constructionism" mainly because the cleavages familiar from more recent theoretical debates about constitutional interpretation, such as "interpretivism" versus "noninterpretivism" and "originalism" versus "nonoriginalism," do not match up well with the set of ideas I wish to discuss. For example, although nonoriginalist methodology is often thought to authorize resort to conceptions of the good as an aid to constitutional interpretation, see, e.g., Dworkin, *Law's Empire*, it is still possible even within that methodological context to reject result-oriented decisionmaking on the ground that judicial authority to consult more general conceptions of the good is limited to consulting them in a noninstrumental way.

ism, the very idea of result-oriented judicial decisionmaking, even when consideration of the result and its consequences is only one factor among many in the analysis, introduces into the enterprise of state constitutional interpretation an element of instrumentalism that is simply inconsistent with the appropriate use of judicial authority.

For strict constructionists, the job of a court is always faithfully to interpret a constitution, and the practice of faithful constitutional interpretation, on this view, generally excludes any consideration of the consequences of an interpretation. This is because the meaning of a constitutional provision is something *given* to a court by the polity that made the document; it is not something to be determined by a court on the basis of its discretionary judgment about what the constitution ought to say to achieve some normatively desirable result—even a result desired by the constitution's drafters and ratifiers. The constitution, in other words, says what it says, not what a court thinks it should say. For a court to ignore this rule by choosing among potential constitutional interpretations based even partly on their consequences is to engage in something forbidden: it is to amend, or alter, or update the constitution, actions that the people do not delegate to courts but reserve for themselves.[27] The reason for this rule of constitutional interpretation, strict constructionists typically contend, is that any other rule would be too dangerous: to allow courts to alter the meaning of the constitution would give the people's agents too much power, thereby putting popular sovereignty itself at risk.[28]

Before responding on the merits to these potential objections, I want to mention briefly two ways in which such a response might be unnecessary. First, it may simply be wrong to describe a state court's consideration of the federalism effects of its rulings as a kind of result-oriented decisionmaking. One might just as easily take the view that when a state court considers the federalism consequences of its constitutional rulings, it does nothing more than rest its construction of the state constitution on a routine structural inference, an entirely legitimate technique of constitutional interpretation with

27. See, e.g., Bork, "Neutral Principles and Some First Amendment Problems"; Rehnquist, "The Notion of a Living Constitution"; Scalia, "Originalism: The Lesser Evil."

28. This view probably achieved its best-known expression in Bickel, *The Least Dangerous Branch*, 16, the so-called countermajoritarian difficulty. To similar effect, see Rehnquist, "The Notion of a Living Constitution," 695–96; Berger, *Death Penalties*, 66; Berger, *Government by Judiciary*, 263–64; Bork, "Neutral Principles," 3, 6.

an unimpeachable pedigree that is fully consistent with strict constructionist premises.[29] Still, the kind of structural inference I am suggesting is somewhat different from the most common kinds of structural inferences in constitutional interpretation in that it does not involve reasoning about the relation among different parts of a single constitution, but rather about the relation of provisions of a constitution to some larger legal system of which the constitution is only a part. Although even this kind of structural inference is in fact sometimes used in federal constitutional law,[30] it is largely absent from the practice of state constitutional interpretation and is thus, if nothing else, novel and therefore deserving of a more considered defense.

A second threshold response to strict constructionist objections might be to dispute strict constructionism on its own merits. Strict constructionism, after all, is not a conception of constitutional interpretation that is universally embraced,[31] and in its more extreme forms it presents some serious concep-

29. Black, *Structure and Relationship in Constitutional Law;* Bobbitt, *Constitutional Fate,* ch. 6. Chief Justice John Marshall, for example, often relied on the adverse consequences of proposed constitutional interpretations as a basis for rejecting them in favor of interpretations that yielded more acceptable consequences. E.g., McCulloch v. Maryland, 17 U.S. 316, 421 (1819); Gibbons v. Ogden, 22 U.S. 1, 222 (1824). Even Justice Clarence Thomas, a strict constructionist *par excellence,* acknowledges that certain inferences from the constitutional structure are permissible. E.g., U.S. Term Limits v. Thornton, 514 U.S. 779, 848 (1995) (Thomas, J., dissenting) ("Where the Constitution is silent about the exercise of a particular power—that is, where the Constitution does not speak either expressly or *by necessary implication*—the Federal Government lacks that power and the States enjoy it.") (emphasis added).

30. For example, it is not uncommon for federal courts to draw inferences about the constitutional scope of presidential power based upon the consequences for the exercise of U.S. power in the international arena. Good examples are Chief Justice Vinson's famous dismissal of what he called the "messenger-boy concept" of the presidency in his dissent in Youngstown Sheet & Tube Co. v. Sawyer, 343 U.S. 579, 708 (1952), and Justice Sutherland's opinion for the Court ratifying the president's use of executive agreements in United States v. Belmont, 301 U.S. 324 (1937). Here, a similar process of inference would apply, one in which the authority of organs of state government is construed in part by considering the ways in which that authority could be projected externally from the state against the national government.

31. Justice William Brennan famously disparaged originalism as "arrogance cloaked as humility." Brennan, "Speech," 11, 14. Justice William O. Douglas utilized a distinctly non-originalist methodology in numerous cases including Griswold v. Connecticut, 381 U.S. 479, 484 (1965) ("specific guarantees in the Bill of Rights have penumbras, formed by emana-

tual difficulties and internal contradictions.[32] It is, moreover, a tradition that might be said, even on its own terms, to provide ample room for judicial consideration of the consequences of constitutional rulings.[33] I do not find it necessary, however, to argue against strict constructionism on its merits. The strict constructionist objections fail here for the more pedestrian reason that strict constructionism simply does not speak directly to the practice of *state* constitutional interpretation: it is an account of judicial power that was developed to describe *national* judicial authority.[34] To attempt to apply it without modification to the practice of state constitutional interpretation is to assume the very similarity between state and national constitutions that it is the purpose of this book to deny; it is to elevate the principles of strict construction of the U.S. Constitution to the level of some incontestable "natural law" of judicial power that, needless to say, does not exist.

Accordingly, I turn now to potential strict constructionist objections to any practice that would put state courts in the position of acting as self-conscious agents of federalism. Two objections are possible. First, strict constructionists might argue that such a practice would be incoherent as an understanding of proper judicial authority. Second, they might argue that even if it is not, allowing such a practice would be a bad idea because of the dangers involved.

The Objection from Incoherence

Strict constructionists might first object that the self-consciously instrumental use of the power to interpret a constitution is by definition an abuse of ju-

---

tions from those guarantees that help give them life and substance"), and Harper v. Virginia State Bd. of Elections, 383 U.S. 663, 669 (1966) ("the Equal Protection Clause is not shackled to the political theory of a particular era. . . . [W]e have never been confined to historic notions of equality. . . . Notions of what constitutes equal treatment for purposes of the Equal Protection Clause *do* change."). Contemporary academic critics of originalism are legion, to say nothing of past movements such as Legal Realism and Critical Legal Studies.

32. One of the best critiques of originalism's coherence as a methodology of constitutional interpretation remains Brest, "The Misconceived Quest for Original Understanding." See also Dworkin, *Law's Empire*, 318–20; Brennan, "Construing the Constitution," 7; Levinson, "Law as Literature," 377–96; Tushnet, "Following the Rules Laid Down," 784–85; Rakove, *Original Meanings*, 6, 10, 16, 339–40.

33. Again, the most prominent examples appear in some of Chief Justice Marshall's early opinions for the Court. E.g., McCulloch v. Maryland, 17 U.S. 316, 421 (1819); Gibbons v. Ogden, 22 U.S. 1, 222 (1824).

34. See Hershkoff, "State Courts and the 'Passive Virtues.'"

dicial power. For a court to engage in result-oriented interpretation for the purpose of resisting national power or for any other purpose, it might be said, is deliberately to manipulate the document's meaning rather than to discern it, an approach inconsistent with a proper understanding of judicial power. Rightly understood, strict constructionists might say, judicial power cannot be used instrumentally because it is not a tool to be used self-consciously to achieve ends; rather, the judicial role is merely to apply the law. A court that used its powers instrumentally would be making law rather than applying it, yet courts should never take it upon themselves to make law because doing so usurps power allocated to other organs of government.

This is a respectable and, in the United States, a venerated conception of judicial power. And although this view presents well-known difficulties at the margin in distinguishing improper judicial invention of law from proper judicial application of law,[35] it is fundamentally coherent and supported by a well-developed theory of the allocation of governmental power. This theory, however, is derived from the structure of national power under the national Constitution, a model that need not be followed, and frequently is not followed, on the state level. It is, on the contrary, merely one possible model of judicial power among many.

Even in the Anglo-American tradition, judicial power has been arranged in many different ways. Originally, the judicial function was united with other governmental functions in the monarch, and then in Parliament. South Carolina's first two constitutions, written in 1776 and 1778, provided that the lieutenant governor and a privy council "shall exercise the powers of a court of chancery."[36] Ultimate judicial power was exercised by the governor in Connecticut until 1818 and in Rhode Island until 1842, when those states finally replaced their royal charters. Moreover, although American federal courts today generally adhere to the strict constructionist model, they have not always understood it to create the sharp distinction between lawmaking and interpretation that prevails today. As described in chapter 1, during the long reign of *Swift v. Tyson*, the U.S. Supreme Court freely invented federal common law, which it then used to displace state common law. The Court eventually came

35. There is surely no better example of this problem than Bush v. Gore, 531 U.S. 98 (2000), in which the justices could not agree whether the Florida Supreme Court was merely interpreting Florida law or whether it was judicially amending it. On the Court's flirtations with this issue, see Krent, "Judging Judging."

36. S.C. Const. art. XVI (1776); S.C. Const. art. XXIV (1778).

to see this process as inconsistent with a proper understanding of the federal judicial power and repudiated it in *Erie Railroad v. Tompkins,* but the Court's repudiation was for itself and lower federal courts, not for state courts. As I have repeatedly emphasized, state courts are situated very differently from federal courts. They retain the common law functions that federal courts renounced, as well as other quasi-lawmaking functions discussed earlier in this chapter. It is always possible, of course, that state judicial power has been allocated under state constitutions in exactly the same way that national judicial power is allocated under the national Constitution, but the numerous actual and potential differences between state and national constitutions and between the nature and functions of state and national power make that a conclusion to be demonstrated rather than one to be assumed.

The proper question, then, is whether state constitutions *in fact* authorize state courts to use their powers of constitutional interpretation instrumentally. That brings us to the next potential strict constructionist objection: a state constitution cannot coherently authorize instrumental judicial interpretation of the document itself because such an exercise of judicial power is inconsistent with basic constitutional conceptions of agency. Strict constructionism rests on a positive theory of constitutional law.[37] According to this theory, constitutions are created by the people for certain purposes, and in so doing the people create organs of government as agents to do their bidding. The constitution thus comprises a set of instructions from principal to agent, and, strict constructionists might say, it is by definition inconsistent with the agency relationship for an agent to alter the terms of its instructions or of instructions issued to other agents.

There is, however, no necessary contradiction between agency principles and the instrumental shaping of constitutional doctrine for the simple reason that there is no reason why the state constitution itself could not instruct state courts to use their powers to achieve particular results. At the most general level, there is a respectable argument to be made that an agent should always treat any set of explicit instructions as provisional, and thus as authorizing deviations, when compliance with the strict letter of the instructions would thwart achievement of the principal's purpose in ways unforeseen at the time the instructions were issued.[38] But one need not go that far in this context because the possibility cannot be ruled out that the people of an

37. See Gardner, "The Positivist Foundations of Originalism."
38. Eskridge, *Dynamic Statutory Interpretation,* 52–55.

American state might in fact affirmatively desire their courts to participate by any means possible in state resistance to tyrannical abuses of national power.

It is certainly plausible—indeed, it is virtually certain—that the people of a state would wish to have a state government that is capable of fulfilling its role in the federal system as a potential check on national tyranny; that is the main reason why the national polity, of which each state polity is a part, adopted a constitutional system of federalism. If the state polity further believes that the judicial branch should stand alongside the executive and legislative branch when resistance to national authority becomes necessary, it is by no means inherently self-contradictory to ask whether the people might directly charge state courts with the responsibility to do what they can to make such resistance effective, including issuing facilitative interpretations of the state constitution. In these circumstances, state courts would not really be "using" the state constitution instrumentally, but "interpreting" it according to conventional understandings of positive constitutional law. Their method of interpretation would, to be sure, include in the interpretational mix a factor that plays no role in the federal judicial analysis; but state courts are not federal courts and their actions cannot necessarily be judged by the same criteria.

As noted earlier, federal courts need not self-consciously "use" national judicial power to restrain tyrannical uses of state authority—even though they often do just that—because such a role is inscribed explicitly into the U.S. Constitution. For federal courts, judicial restraint of state tyranny and straightforward application of national constitutional law are usually one and the same. State constitutions, on the other hand, do not explicitly authorize any organ of state government to resist national power, yet such resistance is nevertheless common enough. More generally, the lack of express constitutional authority has rarely been thought to be equivalent to a bar to the exercise of authority even within the federal tradition, much less within the state constitutional tradition, where constitutional grants of government power generally have been understood to be plenary except to the extent expressly denied.

The critical question, then, is not whether state courts *can* be authorized, in appropriate circumstances, to treat the state constitution instrumentally, as a tool of state resistance to abuses of national power. State courts can be so authorized. The real question is whether they *have* been so authorized. And the critical factor in determining whether a state court has been authorized to serve as a self-conscious agent of federalism, I shall argue, is the familiar consideration of trust: do the people of a state *trust* their courts enough to allocate to them the unique and potentially dangerous power of resisting national authority through the introduction into the constitutional analysis of certain possibly result-oriented considerations.

The Objection from Danger

Strict constructionism offers two possible objections to the proposition that any state polity might actually authorize its courts to engage in result-oriented interpretation of the state constitution. Both objections are based on the belief that such a practice would be so inherently dangerous to liberty that no rational state polity would willingly assume the risks.

One possible objection to the idea of authorizing state courts to interpret the state constitution instrumentally is that such an arrangement inevitably delegates to courts the authority to rewrite the state constitution. This creates obvious dangers in that it would deprive the people of control over the constitution, the principal means by which they control their governmental agents. Notwithstanding that the federalism consequences of a judicial decision would amount, at most, to only one factor among many that courts would be authorized to consider, an instrumental approach, strict constructionists might be inclined to say, cannot be confined. Once a court is authorized to interpret the constitution instrumentally, it possesses for all intents and purposes the power to interpret any provision of the constitution however it likes.

This slippery-slope kind of argument, so often implicit in strict constructionist critiques of federal judicial rulings, is analytically unsound. The power to shape judicially the meaning of a state constitution is not a power capable of being granted solely in all-or-nothing terms. Authorizing an instrumental approach in one area need not set a state polity on a slippery slope from popular sovereignty to some kind of judicial enslavement. In this context, to authorize state courts to act as agents of federalism would be to authorize them to shape constitutional meaning only in a very limited and well-circumscribed area, and then only when doing so would serve the purpose of resisting abuses of national authority—a function that federalism in any event charges state governments to perform.

Strict constructionists like to divide constitutional adjudication into two sharply distinct categories: faithful application of the law and faithless invention of the law; judicial obedience to popular will and judicial usurpation of the power to make fundamental law. Yet even on its own terms, the strict constructionist model does not neatly resolve the difference between judicial application of the law and judicial invention of the law. On the contrary, strict constructionism's categories leave a distinct area of uncertainty between the two, especially where the law is ambiguous. A state constitutional instrumentalism responsive to federalism effects of judicial rulings would do nothing more than shift the interpretational difficulties from one location to another. Instead of trying to discern the line between permitted application of the law and forbidden invention of the law, courts would have to discern the line between permitted and forbidden judicial shaping of the state constitution. The authority of state courts would extend only so far as necessary to regulate state power properly, for the successful resistance of national tyranny. State courts would not be authorized to adjust state power more than necessary to achieve this purpose, or for other purposes, or in other ways. There is no reason to suppose that this line would be any more difficult to discern than the one presently defended by strict constructionism. Indeed, such a line might be easier to identify insofar as it explicitly lays on the table a degree of self-conscious manipulation of the law that, many would say, is always present in the adjudicatory process but that the strict constructionist analysis obscures by denying.[39]

Even if the slippery-slope argument is rejected, strict constructionists still might argue that *any* instrumental judicial manipulation of constitutional meaning gives courts too much power and is therefore too dangerous to permit. Every grant of constitutional authority represents an allocation of authority between the people and their government. In our Lockean ideology, the people are understood to have an indefeasible right to govern themselves directly in all matters.[40] They typically delegate much of this authority, of course, but a popular decision to create a government by constitutional means does not transfer in some irrevocable, Hobbesian sense the people's right to self-governance. Rather, the constitution merely embodies a popular judgment concerning which functions will be performed by governmental agents and which functions the people will continue to perform for themselves. Direct popular action in a large republic is, of course, difficult and cumbersome, but it can be and sometimes is accomplished through constitutional amendment.

Consider the allocation of legislative authority. It is conceivable that a polity could so strongly prefer to make all legislative decisions itself, or could so fear allocating authority to a legislative agent, that it reserves for itself all

39. See, e.g., Dworkin, *Law's Empire;* White, *When Words Lose Their Meaning;* Levinson, "Law as Literature"; Tushnet, "Following the Rule Laid Down."

40. See Locke, *Second Treatise of Government,* ¶¶ 4, 87, 89, 95–99, 243. These ideas are clearly echoed in such canonical American texts as the Declaration of Independence (1776), ¶ 2, and McCulloch v. Maryland, 17 U.S. 316, 404–5 (1819).

authority to make laws by creating a direct democracy. Conversely, the decision to create a legislature with unrestricted legislative power (as in Britain) would allocate authority between polity and government in a diametrically opposite way. By the same token, when the people create a legislature but withdraw certain authority from it through constitutional limitation, they allocate some lawmaking power to the legislature and retain some for themselves: the legislature exercises legislative authority in the areas permitted to it, while the people exercise exclusive legislative authority in the areas forbidden to the legislature. This popular retention of legislative authority is undoubtedly cumbersome, since the people can legislate only through constitutional amendment, but the difficulty of exercising direct popular authority does not change the nature of the underlying allocation.

Things stand no differently in principle regarding constitutional grants of judicial power; all that differs is the type of authority allocated through such grants. One authority typically granted to courts in our system is the power to interpret constitutions. The people could of course allocate this power to themselves—one could perhaps envision some kind of mass, Athenian-style popular convocation—but questions of constitutional meaning come up so frequently, and popular decisionmaking of this type would be so cumbersome, that the power to interpret the constitution is inevitably granted to courts.[41]

Nevertheless, strict constructionists hold that federal courts must always confine themselves to interpreting the U.S. Constitution, and must never alter even the tiniest part of it, for any reason.[42] This principle rests on the belief that the Constitution embodies the people's decision to allocate to themselves rather than to courts the power to alter the document's meaning.[43] Any other

---

41. In 1911, Progressive reformers developed a proposal for "recall of judicial decisions," a mechanism that would have allowed popular referenda on judicial rulings of constitutional law. The idea was to allow popular "correction" of erroneous judicial constructions of the constitution. Unlike much of the Progressive agenda, such proposals were successfully opposed by advocates of judicial independence. For an account, see Ross, *A Muted Fury,* ch. 6; Hartnett, "Why Is the Supreme Court of the United States Protecting Judges from Popular Democracy?" 935–37, 943.

42. See, e.g., Bork, "Neutral Principles and Some First Amendment Problems"; Rehnquist, "The Notion of a Living Constitution"; Scalia, "Originalism."

43. As Justice Harlan once put it, "[W]hen, in the name of constitutional interpretation, the Court *adds* something to the Constitution that was deliberately excluded from it, the Court in reality substitutes its view of what should be so for the amending process." Reynolds v. Sims, 377 U.S. 533, 625 (1964) (Harlan, J., dissenting).

approach, they suggest, would create a situation dangerous to popular sovereignty, in which unelected, unaccountable judicial agents would be able to alter the people's constitutional instructions.

Whatever the ultimate merits of this view, it is, however, at most a contingent, contextual judgment concerning the best allocation of *national* judicial authority between the *national* polity and a *national* court system. And although the reasoning underlying the allocation of national judicial power is by no means irrelevant to an analysis of how judicial power should be allocated on the state level, it is hardly conclusive. In fact, when Americans divide themselves into state polities, the problem of how government power should be allocated between the people and their governmental agents looks quite different.

In the first place, the people of the states already have a set of national agents charged with pursuing their collective good and protecting their liberty, both from the national government and from any state governmental agents they choose to create. The people of every state thus engage the state constitutional decisionmaking process possessed of a nationally guaranteed minimal level of liberty, as well as a powerful external agent in the form of the national government charged directly with restraining any state tyranny that might appear. In the second place, the instructions issued constitutionally to the national government, because they have been formulated through a nationwide process of compromise, are beyond the ability of any single state polity to influence. By contrast, each state polity has direct and exclusive control over its own state constitution. This not only gives a state polity an opportunity to improve upon the U.S. Constitution, if it so desires, but, what is more important, gives the state polity the ability to change or correct any aspect of the state constitution whenever it pleases. Consequently, a mistake in the constitutional allocation of power is much easier to fix, as the extensive record of state constitutional amendment attests.

These differences in the context of state and national constitutional decisionmaking have an important ramification: the stakes for liberty are lower in the creation of a state constitution. No matter how the state constitution is structured, and no matter how state government actors behave under it, the national government is always available to enforce a floor of individual rights that has been deemed acceptable to the national polity as a whole. The national government is also available to use its powers of persuasion, preemption, and conditional spending, among others, to prevent states from abusing their own citizens. Moreover, the direct control that the people of the state exercise over their own constitution allows them with much greater facility to control their state government by altering the constitutional allocation of powers. This enhances the ability of state polities to tinker with different constitutional structures because any poor decisions can be much more readily undone than at the national level.

In these circumstances, it is perfectly sensible to ask of any state constitution the very question that strict constructionism assumes away: *how* does it allocate the power to monitor and resist national tyranny? Have the people retained all such power for themselves? If so, then the people of each state will be responsible not only for exercising careful vigilance over the actions of the national government, but also for parceling out repeatedly, by constitutional amendment, just so much power as the organs of state government require on any particular occasion to resist national abuses effectively. This would of course be a cumbersome and probably not very effective arrangement. Assuming, then, that the people of a state have delegated at least some power to state government to monitor and resist national tyranny, to which organs of state government have they delegated it? Presumably, if the people delegate any such power, they will delegate some of it to the state executive and legislative branches, as these are the organs of state government most capable of quickly and successfully resisting national abuses. This leaves the question of whether the people of a state might also wish to delegate to the judiciary some authority to resist national power.

Of course the risks of such a delegation are obvious. If state courts have some authority to interpret the state constitution instrumentally, they may use this authority badly, making poor decisions that the people of the state dislike. The state polity might then have to chase after its courts, regularly amending the state constitution to undo or modify bad judicial rulings. A particularly dangerous problem would arise if state courts, in an effort to give the other branches ample power to resist national tyranny, interpreted the state constitution to give those branches power of a kind or in an amount that enabled them to threaten directly the liberties of the people of the state.

On the other hand, there are also risks involved in *not* granting state courts the authority to stand with the governor and legislature in resisting tyrannical national actions. If the state constitution, strictly construed, bound the executive or legislature so tightly that they were unable in a given set of circumstances to resist national authority effectively, the people's only recourse would be to amend the state constitution to grant the necessary power. It is typically easier to amend a state constitution than the national Constitution, but that does not make it easy: even at its simplest, it is a relatively slow and cumbersome process. In the event of a crisis, it is by no means certain that a state constitution could be amended in time to grant state actors the authority they need to protect threatened liberties from invasion at the hands of the national government.

TRUST AND DISTRUST OF STATE COURTS

To what extent, then, might state polities trust their courts to engage actively in the process of protecting their liberties against encroachments by the national government? Unlike strict constructionists, I do not believe it is possible to come to any universal conclusions on this topic—far from it. Just as state polities differ in the degree to which they trust other organs of state and local government, so they inevitably will differ in the degree to which they trust their courts. Indeed, I argue in chapter 7 that a preliminary task a state court faces when it interprets a state constitution is to determine the degree to which its own state polity has manifested any actual inclination to trust the state judiciary to serve as an agent of federalism.

Generally speaking, two factors might influence the degree to which a state polity might be willing to trust its state courts to act as agents of federalism: the extent to which institutional arrangements are capable of producing a judiciary that will reliably and competently protect liberty against encroachments; and the actual historical record of state courts as protectors of liberty.

Institutional Considerations

The trustworthiness of courts as guardians of liberty is usually defended on one of two grounds. The first is that courts are insulated from politics and are basically unresponsive to popular sentiment. The other is that they are not.

The first argument has been applied most frequently to federal courts—though it is equally applicable to state courts that follow the national model—and is based upon the institutional arrangement under which federal judges are appointed rather than elected, and hold office for life. The belief that unelected, politically unaccountable judges are the best guardians of liberty goes back as far as the founding, if not all the way back to Plato's *Republic*. In a well-known essay, Alexander Hamilton argued that only an independent judiciary could be counted on to dispense justice, and that the necessary independence could be secured only by lifetime appointment. "Judges who hold their offices by a temporary commission," Hamilton claimed, can hardly be counted on for "inflexible and uniform adherence to the rights of the Constitution."[44] On this view, the judiciary's lack of political accountability enables it to resist majoritarian pressure, the very thing that makes it a reliable defender of liberty. Hamilton's position dominated American political thought during the Republic's first few decades: the first twenty-nine states admitted to the Union all created nonelective judiciaries on the national model.[45]

Recent empirical studies provide some limited support for the intuition that electorally unaccountable judges will be more willing to defend liberty from popular passion than judges who must satisfy the voters to gain or retain office. One comparative study, for example, found that judges in nonelective state judicial systems are significantly more likely than their elected counterparts not only to hear challenges to controversial state laws but, when they hear them, to invalidate the laws.[46] Another study found that elected state judges are less likely to dissent in controversial cases when their constituents agree ideologically with the outcome of the case.[47]

Since the Jacksonian era, however, a second and basically incompatible view of judicial trustworthiness has grown up alongside the Hamiltonian position. According to this view, courts are suspect precisely when their judges are electorally unaccountable to the people through democratic processes. Jacksonians, suspicious of the corruptibility of politicians and convinced of the innate virtue and capacity for self-government of the ordinary citizen, rejected the founding generation's republican elitism in favor of a democratic egalitarianism characterized by strong popular control over government.[48] In 1832, Mississippi became the first state to establish a fully elective judiciary, and every state to join the Union between 1846 and 1958 followed suit.[49] The ideological preference for elective judiciaries was reinforced during the early twentieth century by the Progressive movement, which pushed with great success on the state level for democratizing reforms including not only an

---

44. Madison, *The Federalist,* No. 78 (Hamilton), 470–71.

45. Croley, "The Majoritarian Difficulty," 716.

46. Brace, Hall, and Langer, "Judicial Choice and the Politics of Abortion."

47. Hall, "Electoral Politics and Strategic Voting in State Supreme Courts."

48. See, e.g., Van Deusen, *The Jacksonian Era;* Meyers, *The Jacksonian Persuasion;* Remini, *Andrew Jackson and the Course of American Democracy,* vol. 3; Watson, *Liberty and Power.*

49. Croley, "The Majoritarian Difficulty," 716–17.

electorally accountable judiciary but the initiative, referendum, recall, and direct primary election.[50] Today, supreme court judges in thirty-nine states must face voter approval at some point in their careers.[51]

If independence and a lack of political accountability were thought by the founders to be necessary prerequisites for judicial protection of liberty, proponents of democratic control over judges have thought such independence to be a serious threat to liberty in that it frees judges to ignore popular sentiment, invalidate popular laws, and obstruct democratically desired reforms. The Progressives, in particular, believed that appointed judges tended to be drawn from a small class of economic elites and that they often used their powers of judicial review to protect the wealthy and powerful from urgently needed political and economic reforms.[52] On this view, popular control over judges, far from putting them at the mercy of illicit mob passions, subjects them to a form of democratic discipline that maintains liberty by curbing their arrogance. This view stands at the foundation of strict constructionist objections to judicial activism.

The available evidence suggests that electoral accountability accomplishes its goal of keeping judicial decisions in line with popular sentiment at least to some degree and in some circumstances. The main limitation on the effectiveness of popular control is the public's apparently limited interest in monitoring judicial performance.[53] On the other hand, in those election contests where public attention does focus on judicial performance, electoral accountability clearly can affect judicial decisionmaking. Exhibit A for this point is the electoral defeat of three justices of the California Supreme Court in a 1986 retention election. These jurists, including the chief justice, Rose Bird, were turned out of office largely as the result of a high-visibility, negative electoral campaign charging them with being "soft on criminal matters, especially the death penalty."[54] The ensuing replacement of the defeated judges with appointments by a more conservative governor fundamentally altered the California Supreme Court's death penalty jurisprudence: the rate at which

50. See, e.g., DeWitt, *The Progressive Movement.*

51. Council of State Governments, 33 *The Book of the States* 137–39 (2000–2001).

52. See DeWitt, *The Progressive Movement,* 238: "Most judges, before they are appointed to the bench, receive their training in the employ of corporations. . . . [This gives rise to a] tendency to bias the minds of judges in favor of corporations and property interests as against individuals and human interests." See also id. at 23, 158, 160, 239.

53. Croley, "The Majoritarian Difficulty," 730–31.

54. Wold and Culver, "The Defeat of the California Justices," 350.

the court overturned death sentences dropped dramatically after the change in personnel.[55]

Since then, judicial elections have attracted increasing public attention, as well as vastly increased spending by special interest groups dissatisfied with the decisional track record of individual judges.[56] In 2000, total fund-raising by judicial candidates exceeded $45 million, a 61 percent increase from 1998.[57] There are, moreover, indications that "judicial elections are more and more often high-salience events that mobilize large portions of the citizenry."[58] Elected judges seem to be "targeted" more often by political opponents, occasionally for single, unpopular decisions. Following the controversial Florida recount in the 2000 presidential election, for example, some groups that had supported George Bush threatened political retribution against the members of the Florida Supreme Court who had ruled in favor of Democratic candidate Al Gore in procedural wrangling over the recount process.

In reviewing these two opposing accounts of the conditions for judicial trustworthiness, I do not mean to take, or even to suggest, any particular position on the merits of the debate. Indeed, the nature of the dispute reveals clearly that one's position on judicial independence depends critically on fundamental and controversial assumptions about the comparative political virtue and competence of democratic citizens and public officials. Clearly, there is no universal agreement on these principles at the state level. Today, twenty-two states have chosen to elect judges of the highest court; ten use appointment; and sixteen use a system of initial appointment followed by retention elections.[59] In New Mexico judges are initially appointed and then face subsequent partisan elections, and in Virginia all judges are elected by the state legislature. The methods of selection are even more diverse for lower court judges. On the other hand, I *do* wish to suggest by this discussion that there are possible grounds upon which a state polity could decide to invest its

---

55. After Governor George Deukmejian, a Republican, replaced the three defeated justices who had been appointed by Jerry Brown, a Democrat, the California Supreme Court's affirmance rate in death penalty cases increased from 6 to 77 percent. Stumpf and Culver, *The Politics of State Courts*, 50, 149–50.

56. For an account of business-oriented interests spending against judges who have issued rulings favoring environmental concerns, see Environmental Policy Project, *Changing the Rules by Changing the Players.*

57. Goldberg and Holman, *The New Politics of Judicial Elections,* 7.

58. Croley, "The Majoritarian Difficulty," 734.

59. Council of State Governments, 33 *The Book of the States* (2000–2001), 137–39.

trust in state courts as guardians of liberty; that these grounds are potentially serious and substantial; and that they cannot be dismissed out of hand as inadequate to support a rational decision to charge state courts with significant responsibility for protecting the state polity against abuses of power by the national government.

The Record of State Courts as Guardians of Liberty

The institutional considerations discussed above operate mainly at a theoretical level. It is thus worth looking beyond the structural parameters to inquire whether the actual record of state courts in the protection of individual liberty furnishes any additional reasons to trust or distrust them.

Although generalizations in this area can be misleading, it seems fair to say that courts today enjoy a relatively solid reputation in American society as guardians of liberty.[60] Certainly, it is not venturing too much to say that independent judicial enforcement of a protective bill of rights is widely considered to be one of the cornerstones of American liberty.[61] To be sure, this view is not universally held. Critics on the Right often complain that courts usurp popular authority. Those on the left often criticize courts for refusing to go far enough in the protection of individual rights. Even among the general public, perceptions of the judiciary change with time. During the early days of the New Deal, the U.S. Supreme Court was sometimes seen as obstructionist and tyrannical. During the Warren era, the Court gained a reputation as a vigorous protector of individual rights, though in the South it acquired a reputation as insufficiently observant of the liberty-protective properties of federalism. Today, the federal judiciary is sometimes seen as inhospitable to claims of individual right, or at least less hospitable than it was during the Warren and Burger periods.

However, to the extent that courts enjoy a favorable reputation as protec-

60. To the extent that polling data can bear out this impression, it seems to do so. For example, according to a poll taken in June 2001, 62 percent approved of the way the U.S. Supreme Court was handling its job. The Gallup Poll, June 11–17, 2001. See http://www .pollingreport.com/Court.htm. Even in December 2000, just after the Court issued its controversial ruling halting the Florida recount in the 2000 presidential election, 46 percent of respondents said they had "a great deal" or "quite a lot" of confidence in the Supreme Court. An additional 33 percent had "some" confidence in the Court. CBS News Poll, Dec. 2000, at id.

61. See, e.g., Cross, "Institutions and Enforcement of the Bill of Rights."

tors of liberty, it must be acknowledged that such a reputation is probably confined for the most part to federal courts and derives principally from the record of rights protection compiled by the U.S. Supreme Court during the 1960s and early 1970s.[62] Indeed, the Warren Court gained its reputation as a guardian of liberty largely at the expense of state courts, which it repeatedly reversed in reaching many of its most significant rights-protective rulings. In the body of law generated by the Warren Court, state courts all too often appear as insensitive rubber-stamps of rights-invading state legislatures at best, and as outright collaborators in state-level deprivations of liberty at worst.

Much of this has changed. In the last quarter century, state courts have issued hundreds of decisions that not only protect individual liberty, but do so to a degree that exceeds the levels of protection mandated by U.S. Supreme Court rulings construing the Fourteenth Amendment of the U.S. Constitution. Many of the cases in which the Warren Court made its reputation reversed extremely stingy rulings by southern state courts in civil rights cases. Yet today, state courts in the South may be as likely as state courts elsewhere to issue rights-protective state constitutional rulings. For example, in recent decisions the Georgia Supreme Court has barred the use of electrocution for capital punishment on the ground that it is cruel within the meaning of the state constitution, and has invalidated a state sodomy statute as applied to consenting unmarried heterosexuals. The Texas Supreme Court has expanded state constitutional protection for free speech beyond the boundaries of the First Amendment of the U.S. Constitution. Tennessee's highest court has construed the state constitution to hold police to a more demanding standard than does the U.S. Constitution for obtaining a search warrant on the hearsay testimony of an anonymous informant. At the same time, on the national level the Rehnquist Court has decisively halted the expansion of federal protection of individual rights, and in some areas has even contracted the scope of protections that the U.S. Constitution had previously been understood to provide. In this environment, state courts do not look nearly so bad in comparison to national courts as they did forty years ago.

Nevertheless, these changes seem very far from having penetrated public consciousness. If actual litigation decisions are any guide, state courts today appear to be less trusted than federal courts when it comes to the protection of individual rights. Although evidence is difficult to come by, it appears that

62. See, e.g., Dinan, *Keeping the People's Liberties*, ch. 7.

litigants, given a choice between suing in state and federal court, prefer to bring civil rights claims in a federal forum.[63] Even when they proceed in a state court, litigants tend overwhelmingly to raise civil rights claims under the U.S. Constitution rather than under their state constitution,[64] suggesting that they have more faith in the body of constitutional case law developed by federal courts than in the similar body of law developed by state courts construing the state constitution.

Interpreting the record of state courts is made even more difficult by the apparently cyclical nature of rights protectiveness on the state and national benches. If state courts were less willing than federal courts to stand up to state legislatures during the middle-to-late twentieth century, they were far more active than federal courts in striking down state legislation on constitutional grounds during the late nineteenth century. According to one study, the Virginia Supreme Court invalidated about one-third of all state statutes it reviewed during this period.[65] In what may be the only comparative study of the protection of liberty by different organs of state government, John Dinan found that state courts historically have generally done no worse than state legislatures at protecting liberty, and have often done a better job, particularly during periods of political stress.[66] The U.S. Supreme Court, it might be noted, has not always done its best work during such times, as the *Dred Scott* and *Korematsu* rulings attest.

63. It seems reasonably clear that this is the case when the plaintiff possesses a federally protected right. That is to say, plaintiffs tend to prefer going to federal court to enforce federal rights, a premise consistent with the rationale for both federal question jurisdiction and removal. See, e.g., Marvell, "The Rationales for Federal Question Jurisdiction" (finding that plaintiffs hoping to obtain enforcement of federal rights prefer to go to federal court). When this fact is added to the general perception of a lack of "parity" between the state and federal benches—the belief, in other words, that state courts are not as hospitable to claims of constitutional right or that state judges are not as competent to deal with such issues, see generally Solimine and Walker, *Respecting State Courts*—it seems likely that plaintiffs with potential claims under both the state and federal constitutions would be more likely to proceed in federal court, even if that meant forgoing the potential state constitutional claim. For a very quick and dirty inquiry supporting this conclusion, see Gardner, "The Failed Discourse of State Constitutionalism," 784.

64. See Tarr, *Understanding State Constitutions,* 166–68, and sources cited therein.

65. Id. at 124, citing Morton Keller, *Affairs of State: Public Life in Late Nineteenth Century America* (Cambridge: Harvard University Press, Belknap Press, 1977), 362.

66. Dinan, *Keeping the People's Liberties,* 155, 166.

To complicate the picture further, it is not entirely clear that the record of state courts in standing up to other organs of *state* government is particularly relevant for present purposes. Our inquiry here focuses on whether state polities might have reasons to trust state courts to stand up to the *national* government, not the state legislature or governor. On that score, state courts appear to have achieved decidedly, though by no means uniformly, better results.

Before 1850, state courts routinely asserted state judicial power against the national government. It was widely assumed at the time, for example, that state courts had the authority to issue writs of mandamus and habeas corpus to federal officials,[67] a power that state courts exercised with some frequency. For example, in numerous cases state courts issued writs of habeas corpus to national military officers ordering them to release from custody minors who had illegally enlisted in the armed forces.[68] In at least one case, a state court ordered national military officials to release from custody a soldier who, the court found, had been improperly convicted of treason. In ordering the prisoner released from national military custody, the state judge, Chancellor Kent of New York, observed: "It is the indispensable duty of this court . . . to act as a faithful guardian of the personal liberty of the citizen, and to give ready and effectual aid to the means provided by law for its security."[69] In all of these cases, federal officials produced the prisoners upon state court order, and released them when commanded to do so.

In 1821, complaining of "the growing pretensions of some of the State Courts over the exercise of the powers of the general government," the U.S. Supreme Court ruled in *M'Clung v. Silliman* that state courts lacked the authority to issue writs of mandamus to national officials or their agents.[70] Even so, state courts continued for almost forty years to issue writs of habeas corpus releasing prisoners from federal custody until the Court ruled in 1858, in the case of *Ableman*

67. See Vitiello, "The Power of State Legislatures to Subpoena Federal Officials"; Arnold, "The Power of State Courts to Enjoin Federal Officers"; Bishop, "The Jurisdiction of State and Federal Courts over Federal Officers."

68. See Commonwealth v. Harrison, 11 Mass. 63 (1814); Commonwealth v. Cushing, 11 Mass. 67 (1814); In the Matter of Carlton, 7 Cow. 471 (N.Y. 1827); Commonwealth v. Downes, 41 Mass. 227 (1833). See also State v. Dimick, 12 N.H. 194 (1841) (writ of habeas corpus denied on ground that the minor ratified his enlistment upon reaching majority), and United States v. Wyngall, 5 Hill 16 (N.Y. 1843) (plaintiff's alienage does not void validity of enlistment, so writ of habeas corpus denied).

69. In the Matter of Samuel Stacy, Jr., 10 Johns. 328, 333 (N.Y. 1813) (Kent, C.).

70. M'Clung v. Silliman, 19 U.S. 598, 598 (1821).

v. Booth, that state courts lacked the authority to issue such writs.[71] *Ableman* arose out of a dispute under the Fugitive Slave Act of 1850 in which Booth, a Wisconsin abolitionist, had been convicted by a federal commissioner of abetting the escape of a fugitive slave. Booth, imprisoned for the offense, applied for a writ of habeas corpus to the Wisconsin courts, which ordered him discharged. The U.S. Supreme Court reversed, observing pointedly that "no one will suppose that a Government which has now lasted nearly seventy years . . . could have lasted a single year . . . if offences against its laws could not have been punished without the consent of the State in which the culprit was found."[72]

Notwithstanding the ruling in *Ableman,* state courts continued to issue writs of habeas corpus ordering the release of federal prisoners for another decade. Apparently giving *Ableman* the narrowest possible construction, the Wisconsin Supreme Court in 1870 thus affirmed the decision of a lower court issuing a writ of habeas corpus to a federal military officer ordering the release from military custody of an underage enlistee. In *Tarble's Case,*[73] the U.S. Supreme Court delivered what was apparently the coup de grâce to this particular kind of flexing of state judicial muscle.

The struggle waged by state courts over their authority to issue writs of mandamus and habeas corpus was itself the residue of a much more general and at times bitter struggle state courts waged earlier in the nineteenth century against the appellate authority of the U.S. Supreme Court. In the best known dispute, Virginia's highest court refused to acknowledge the authority of the U.S. Supreme Court to overturn its decisions construing federal law. In a case dealing with the effect of a postrevolutionary U.S. treaty on the rights of a landowner, the Virginia court had held in favor of one party and the U.S. Supreme Court reversed, remanding the case with instructions to the Virginia appellate court to enter judgment for the opposite party. The Virginia court refused to do so, arguing that the national Constitution did not confer upon the U.S. Supreme Court the authority to exercise appellate jurisdiction over state courts. On a subsequent appeal, the U.S. Supreme Court was required to issue an additional ruling affirming its authority to exercise such jurisdiction and renewing its order to the Virginia courts to comply with the appellate mandate,[74] which the state court reluctantly did.

71. Ableman v. Booth, 62 U.S. 506 (1858).
72. Id. at 515
73. 80 U.S. 397 (1871).
74. Martin v. Hunter's Lessee, 14 U.S. 304 (1816).

In the first half of the nineteenth century, state judicial resistance to national power was based primarily on principled disagreement over the scope of national power. After 1850, such resistance took on a decidedly different character. In that year, Congress enacted the Fugitive Slave Act, a law designed to strengthen enforcement of the Fugitive Slave Clause of the U.S. Constitution[75] by nationalizing it. An earlier act of Congress of 1793 had given, or at least had been construed by state courts to give, substantial independent responsibility to state judicial systems for adjudicating issues arising in connection with the rendition of escaped slaves. State courts outside the South, occasionally unfriendly to the institution of slavery, had sometimes exercised their independence in ways that impeded the efforts of slave owners to recover escaped slaves.[76] The Fugitive Slave Act was meant to prevent state interference with the rendition of slaves by bypassing state judicial systems entirely. The Act thus created a system of federal commissioners to preside over the rendition process who were authorized to adjudicate any necessary legal or factual issues.

With the appellate authority of the U.S. Supreme Court well established, and Supreme Court rulings on the books substantially limiting the authority of state courts to interfere with the exercise of national power, any state judicial resistance to the Fugitive Slave Act partook more of the flavor of outright defiance of national authority than of reasoned disagreement over first principles of constitutional law. Unwilling to defy apparently lawful national authority, a succession of "independent and high-minded judges" sitting on state courts in Massachusetts, Pennsylvania, New York, and elsewhere upheld the constitutionality of the Act against abolitionist attacks.[77] Not all did so, however; some state judges did engage in defiance of a national law that they believed intolerably to invade liberty through its support for the institution of slavery.

Particularly in Ohio and Wisconsin, the willingness of state judges to defy national authority under the Fugitive Slave Act led to what soon became a well-choreographed routine. Abolitionists in the state helped a fugitive slave

---

75. U.S. Const. art. IV, § 2, cl. 3 ("No Person held to Service or Labour in one State, under the Laws thereof, escaping into another, shall, in Consequence of any Law or regulation therein, be discharged from such Service or Labour, but shall be delivered up on Claim of the Party to whom such Service or Labour may be due.").

76. See Cover, *Justice Accused,* ch. 10.

77. Id. at 178.

escape to freedom. The owner obtained a warrant for return of the slave from a federal commissioner. A federal marshal arrested the fugitive. Friends of the escapee went to state court to obtain a writ of habeas corpus ordering the fugitive released. The marshal refused to comply with the state court order, and was arrested by a state law enforcement official on charges of contempt of court. The marshal then sought and obtained from the local federal court a writ of habeas corpus ordering the state law enforcement official to release him.[78] The U.S. Supreme Court's decision in *Ableman,* combined perhaps with the tactic's overall lack of ultimate success, eventually put an end to this particular method of state judicial resistance.

A century later, some state courts again evinced a willingness to resist national power when it was exercised in a way inconsistent, in their view, with a proper understanding of the requirements of liberty. Although the partisans took different sides on the merits of the issues in question, the nature of the resistance itself was similar. During the 1950s and 1960s, state judicial resistance to national authority often took the form of refusals to comply with or fully to enforce rulings of the Warren Court concerning desegregation and the protection of individual liberty under the Fourteenth Amendment. Although most state courts seem to have tried their best to comply with Supreme Court mandates,[79] examples of defiance, or at least evasion, are plentiful. In clearly meritorious litigation to force desegregation of the University of Florida Law School, for instance, the Florida Supreme Court managed to rule three times against the plaintiff, issuing two of its decisions even after the U.S. Supreme Court's ruling in *Brown v. Board of Education.*[80] A few years later, the Florida Supreme Court again defied the U.S. Supreme Court, necessitating multiple reversals, in litigation attempting to bar prayer in public schools.[81]

In *Williams v. Georgia,* a capital murder case, a black defendant had been convicted by a jury from which blacks had been excluded, the unconstitutionality of which the Georgia Attorney General conceded at oral argument before the U.S. Supreme Court. For procedural reasons and as a matter of comity, the Supreme Court remanded for reconsideration in light of the state's concession,

---

78. Id. at 183–87.

79. See Beatty, "State Court Evasion of United States Supreme Court Mandates."

80. See Florida ex rel. Hawkins v. Board, 347 U.S. 971 (1954), *on remand,* 83 So. 2d 20 (Fla. 1955), *rev'd,* 350 U.S. 413 (1956), *on remand,* 93 So. 2d 354 (Fla. 1957).

81. See Chamberlin v. Board of Public Instruction, 143 So. 2d 21 (Fla. 1962), *vacated mem.,* 374 U.S. 487 (1963), *on remand,* 160 So. 2d 97 (Fla.), *rev'd per curiam,* 377 U.S. 402 (1964).

observing that it felt compelled to "reject the assumption that the courts of Georgia would allow this man to go to his death as the result of a conviction secured from a jury which the State admits was unconstitutionally impaneled."[82] On remand, the Georgia Supreme Court affirmed the conviction and sentence, stating defiantly that "we will not supinely surrender sovereign powers of this State."[83]

In other litigation over individual rights during the 1960s, the U.S. Supreme Court needed two successive reversals to gain compliance from the supreme courts of Virginia, Alabama, Arizona, California, Ohio, and Georgia.[84] A study of the impact of the Court's Establishment Clause jurisprudence found fifteen instances of state court evasion or noncompliance between 1950 and 1972.[85] This kind of resistance was unsuccessful in the long run, but it does demonstrate a willingness among state courts to assert themselves against national power, at least in ways falling short of complete and permanent disobedience.

By the mid-1970s, state courts had begun to develop a different way of defying national judicial authority, one that was far more effective than its predecessors because it could not be thwarted by persistent U.S. Supreme Court oversight. Once again, the state and national roles had reversed on the merits: this time, state courts were the ones giving expansive interpretations to the individual rights protected by the U.S. Constitution, and the U.S. Supreme Court was reversing those state rulings in favor of a less generous view of the scope of federally protected rights. State judicial defiance now took the form of transplanting to the state constitution, and thereby placing beyond federal appellate review, the very rights-protective rulings that the U.S. Supreme Court was rejecting as readings of the U.S. Constitution.

An early example of this approach appears in successive rulings by the South Dakota Supreme Court in *State v. Opperman*. Initially, the South Dakota Supreme Court reversed Opperman's conviction on the ground that his trial had been tainted by the admission of evidence discovered through an "inventory search" conducted in violation of the Fourth Amendment of the U.S. Constitution. On appeal, the U.S. Supreme Court reversed, holding that the search was not unreasonable under the Fourth Amendment, and remanded the case.

82. Williams v. Georgia, 349 U.S. 375, 391 (1955).

83. Williams v. State, 88 S.E.2d 763 (Ga. 1955).

84. These cases are described in Beatty, "State Court Evasion of United States Supreme Court Mandates."

85. Tarr, *Judicial Impact and State Supreme Courts*, ch. 3.

On remand, the South Dakota Supreme Court reaffirmed its initial ruling, but this time under the state constitution.[86] The court reached this result even though the defendant had neither briefed nor argued the state constitutional issue in the first proceeding. This approach, of course, insulated the decision of the South Dakota Supreme Court from further appellate review by the U.S. Supreme Court.

The California Supreme Court employed much the same strategy in *People v. Ramos,* a capital murder case. In its initial ruling, the state's high court invalidated the defendant's death sentence on the ground that one of the jury instructions violated the defendant's due process rights under the U.S. Constitution. The U.S. Supreme Court reversed. On remand, the California Supreme Court held that the same instruction violated the due process clause of the California Constitution and so reaffirmed its original ruling vacating the death sentence.[87]

State supreme courts have sometimes pursued the same strategy in civil cases raising constitutional issues. For example, in a New York case, a biomedical research company filed a libel suit against a scientific journal that published a letter to the editor criticizing its animal research policies. The journal defended on the ground that the letter stated an opinion, not fact, and thus could not constitutionally be the subject of a libel suit under the First Amendment to the U.S. Constitution. The New York Court of Appeals ruled for the defendant and dismissed the case.[88] On appeal, the U.S. Supreme Court granted certiorari, but during the pendency of the appeal decided *Milkovich v. Lorain Journal Co.,*[89] in which the Court held that expressions of opinion enjoy no automatic immunity from libel suits under the First Amendment. The Supreme Court accordingly vacated the judgment and remanded the case to the New York Court of Appeals for reconsideration in light of *Milkovich.*

On remand, the Court of Appeals once again ruled for the defendant, and on the same precise ground.[90] In its opinion, the Court of Appeals not only distinguished *Milkovich* from the facts of the case before it, but went on, apparently gratuitously, to adjudicate the case under the free speech provision of the New York Constitution. It interpreted this provision to create a state con-

86. State v. Opperman, 247 N.W.2d 673 (S.D. 1976).

87. People v. Ramos, 689 P.2d 430 (Cal. 1984).

88. Immuno-AG v. Moor-Jankowski, 549 N.E.2d 129 (N.Y. 1989).

89. 497 U.S. 1 (1990).

90. Immuno-AG v. Moor-Jankowski, 567 N.E.2d 1270 (N.Y. 1991).

stitutional privilege for expressions of opinion—the very doctrine the court had held initially, and erroneously as it turned out, existed under the First Amendment of the U.S. Constitution. Of course, this move prevented a subsequent appeal to the U.S. Supreme Court on the question of whether *Milkovich* actually controlled.

I raise these instances of state judicial resistance to national authority not to demonstrate any patterns of judicial behavior, or to suggest that state courts can or cannot be trusted to stand up to national authority in any particular way, or at any particular time, or in any particular set of circumstances. Rather, I hope to have demonstrated something much more modest: that there is sufficient evidence on the question so that reasonable minds might differ as to whether or to what degree a state polity ought to repose its trust in the state judiciary to protect its liberty from invasions by the national government. In fact, the record of state courts, considered in light of the available institutional arrangements, supports a broad range of possible choices about judicial power. Certainly, it is impossible to conclude *a priori* that a polity's choice to trust its courts would be either irrational or imprudent. Thus, the only question is: what has any given state polity in fact chosen to do?

INTERPRETATION AND THE CONSEQUENCES OF FEDERALISM AGENCY

In this chapter, I have argued that state courts are capable of serving as agents of federalism. Should they occupy such a role, state courts would stand alongside the state executive and legislative branches when necessary by deploying judicial power for the purpose of resisting national tyranny. The principal tool that state courts possess to resist national power is their superintendency of the state constitution—that is, their power to interpret its provisions. State courts can wield this power against the national government by interpreting the state constitution both to ensure, vigorous, effective resistance to national power by the state executive and legislative branches, and to provide more protection for individual rights than does the national Constitution. It is in this sense that my account of state judicial power is "functional": it conceives of state judicial power as serving a distinct purpose in a complex federal system of overlapping powers and responsibilities. I have defended this account of state judicial power against strict constructionist theoretical objections, and I have shown that the actual record of state courts in resisting national power, supplemented by any of a range of reasonable assumptions about institutional constraints on judicial power, provides a sound basis for a state polity to invest its courts with a degree of trust or distrust that might reasonably vary across a broad range. This degree of trust or distrust in turn prompts a state polity to charge its courts—or not to charge them, or to charge them only to some limited degree—with serving as agents of federalism.

A state polity's choice about whether and to what degree to authorize its courts to serve as agents of federalism has important ramifications for the interpretation of state constitutions. The more a polity trusts state courts faithfully to protect liberty by resisting national tyranny, the more flexibility state courts are authorized to bring to the process of construing the state constitution, a flexibility manifested by their consideration, in the course of constitutional analysis, of the federalism consequences of judicial interpretations of the state constitution. Conversely, the less a state polity trusts its courts to bring their independent judgment to bear on questions of state power and resistance to national authority, the more fastidiously state courts would have to discern and obey specific popular choices made in the state constitution, understood in the conventional, strict constructionist sense of instructions to be faithfully construed through the reconstruction of authorial intent.

This relationship is easiest to see—or at least works out in the way that is most familiar from the national setting—when state polities distrust their courts. Here, managing constitutional change is reserved strictly to the people through the amendment process. State courts in these circumstances are forbidden to "update" the state constitution, or even to push its boundaries in the interest of adapting the document to meet present exigencies. All problems of constitutional inadequacy are referred in the first instance to the people for correction. Courts here are servants that operate under very tight supervision, forbidden to use much in the way of independent judgment to solve problems of state self-governance.

Courts operating under such a mandate would most likely be confined to the use of strictly originalist and intentionalist methods of constitutional interpretation. Because such courts would be required to act with the utmost restraint and deference to the popular will as expressed in the state constitution, it would become imperative for courts to discern the precise instructions of the people. Interpretation in this mode thus would focus heavily, perhaps exclusively, on the text of the constitution and the intentions of the drafters and ratifiers. Furthermore, the strictness of this kind of judicial agency would tend to render irrelevant the actions of bodies outside the state, including the national government. Since courts would have little or no independent authority to resist abuses of national power other than through strict compliance with specific instructions contained in the state constitution, they would have no need to be kept apprised of the way in which national power was being used or abused in any given circumstances. To the extent that the people of a state intended to take advantage of the availability of state power as a potential counterweight to national tyranny, they would either grant the responsibility for using state power in this way to the executive or legislative branches, if they trusted those branches more than they trusted their courts; or they would retain this authority for themselves, instructing the various organs of state government through constitutional amendment how precisely to respond to abuses of national power. Should the state constitution provide an inadequate framework for responding effectively to national tyranny on some particular occasion, correction of the problem would have to await popular action.

In contrast, state courts that have been authorized to serve as strong agents of federalism will have been given a special kind of institutional responsibility to oversee the state constitution for the purpose of ensuring that it serves as an effective charter for the deployment of state power to resist invasions of liberty by the national government. Judges who possess this responsibility would then have some degree of freedom to consult their own views about how state power and effective state public policy can best be structured and deployed to serve the public welfare in the context of some particular dispute between the state and national governments. Courts operating under such instructions would thus be authorized, in appropriate circumstances, to engage in a comparatively open, freewheeling kind of constitutional interpretation that might more closely resemble the process of state common law adjudication than it would the strict originalism to which their distrusted counterparts would be confined. The state polity would still retain ultimate responsibility for the content of the state constitution, but this responsibility would in all likelihood be exercised infrequently, and invoked for the most part to correct judicial interpretations of the constitution that stray too far afield from the rough plan of state self-governance contemplated by the state polity.

The responsibility to serve as an agent of federalism, moreover, is not one that need be granted to courts in all-or-nothing terms. A state polity might trust its courts to some extent, but not completely, and might thus wish to grant them only limited discretion to serve as agents of federalism. This decision, too, would have ramifications for the kind of interpretation the state courts would bring to bear on the state constitution. Courts with some sort of intermediate mandate would not be confined to the strictest forms of interpretation. On the other hand, in utilizing more open-ended methods of interpretation that rely on their independent judgment, they would be required to exercise a degree of caution and restraint commensurate with the limits of popular trust in their ability to serve as reliable agents of resistance to national power.

The main point is that there is a direct relationship between judicial function and the methods of constitutional interpretation appropriate to the judicial role. State courts that are charged with playing a strong role in the federal system by actively protecting liberty against national tyranny will find it appropriate to take an approach to interpreting the state constitution that stresses some degree of reliance on independent judicial judgment and comparatively loose, nonoriginalist, and consequentialist methods of interpretation. Courts that are not charged with playing such a role will find themselves constrained to take a different approach to constitutional interpretation, one employing stricter, more originalist methods of interpretation. Other courts may find themselves authorized to employ a mix of such interpretational techniques, or to employ them in some circumstances and not others, or with respect to certain provisions of the state constitution and not others.

Because the appropriate methodology of constitutional interpretation depends upon the nature of the judicial function, and because the function of the state judiciary in a federal system is not fixed but may be structured by the state polity in a great variety of equally appropriate ways, those who would prescribe for all state courts a single method of state constitutional interpretation are at most half right. Some have argued, for example, that state constitutions are best approached using originalist or textualist methods of interpretation.[91] This prescription is itself only a particular instance of the widely made, broader claim, typically associated with the primacy approach, that state constitutions must always be interpreted independently of national constitutional law. Others, such as proponents of the interstitial approach, claim that national constitutional rulings should ordinarily be taken as the starting point for state constitutional interpretation. Yet any of these prescriptions may be appropriate for particular state courts in particular circumstances, and none can presumptively be appropriate for all state courts in all circumstances.

The primary determinant of interpretational methodology is the function assigned by the state polity to its courts in a federal system of divided and com-

---

91. See, e.g., Titone, "State Constitutional Interpretation"; Tarr, *Understanding State Constitutions,* 194–99.

peting power. The nature of that decision is dictated neither by theoretical necessities, nor by some distinctive essence of local character or values, but by entirely contingent considerations of popular preference, local history, and local experience. It follows that the search for a methodology of state constitutional interpretation must begin with the question: what function have the people of the state in fact assigned to their courts? Have they authorized state courts to act as agents of federalism, and thus to employ looser, nonoriginalist and overtly consequentialist methods of interpretation when appropriate to resist abuses of national authority? Have they denied courts this responsibility, thereby directing them to hew closely to popular constitutional decisions by using strict methods of interpretation? Or have they taken some intermediate position, authorizing their courts to act independently in certain limited circumstances, or with respect to a limited number of issues? The initial task of any state court contemplating its state constitution, then, is to tease from the document answers to these preliminary questions about the judicial function. The next chapter charts out an analysis to guide state courts in this critical task.

7

An Approach to State Constitutional Interpretation

Having sketched the outlines of a functional theory of state constitutions, I now consider how the theory may be applied in the actual practice of state constitutional interpretation. My discussion here is necessarily preliminary. Complete approaches to the interpretation of legal documents do not, alas, spring full-grown from the heads of authors; they must develop and evolve over time as the result of the collaborative effort of many people. My aim in this chapter is thus rather modest: I hope only to point out the general direction, sketch in a provisional plan of attack, and try to anticipate a few features of the analysis that loom large enough to discern even at this very preliminary phase of the analysis.

Adapting the functional theory into a concrete approach to state constitutional interpretation requires consideration of two issues: (1) how courts should approach the interpretation of their own authority to serve as agents of federalism; and (2) how courts that understand themselves to possess the authority to act as agents of federalism ought to exercise that power when construing the state constitution. I consider each of these questions in turn.

WHEN IS A COURT AN AGENT OF FEDERALISM?

In chapter 6, I argued that a state polity might rationally and plausibly decide to trust its courts enough to grant them the authority to serve as agents of federalism, and that the existence and extent of such authority raise empirical questions of positive political authorization. Here, I want to go a step further and argue that state courts should understand themselves presumptively to have been granted such authority. This rebuttable presumption rests on inferences derived from the purposes and operation of the federal system.

Whenever a state court faces an issue arising under the state constitution with potential ramifications for the balance of state and national power, its first task is to decide what authority the people of the state have actually decided to give it. This decision in turn, as we have seen, has important ramifications for how the court approaches certain kinds of state constitutional questions. If the people of the state trust their courts enough to consider them able guardians of liberty and have authorized them to act as agents of federalism, then state courts may approach the state constitution flexibly, interpreting it with an eye not only toward achieving good self-governance within the state, but also toward resisting abuses of national power when such resistance is warranted. Conversely, if the people of the state do not trust their courts and have not authorized them to act as agents of federalism, then state courts must interpret the state constitution solely with respect to the internal goals of good state government and without regard to actions taken at the national level. In that case, authority to resist national power is either conferred solely upon the state legislative and executive branches, or reserved by the people for themselves. What authority, then, has in fact been conferred on state courts?

This question, however, immediately prompts another: how do we know what the people have done? The place for providing or withholding such authorization is the state constitution itself. How can we tell from that document what role the people of the state desire their courts to assume? Answering this question is complicated by at least two considerations. First, there are fifty state constitutions. A state polity's decision whether to authorize its state courts to act as agents of federalism is likely to rest on such factors as the polity's particular historical experiences of state and national self-government, and the particular distribution of trust and distrust of specific governmental actors among its populace. These are entirely contingent and inherently unpredictable characteristics, suggesting not only that the ultimate decision will differ from state to state, but that generalizations in this area may be of only very limited utility. Second, state constitutions tend to provide little in the way of concrete guidance concerning the dimensions of state judicial power. Like the U.S. Constitution, no state constitution says anything explicit about the role the judiciary ought to assume in the wholly internal scheme of state self-governance, much less in the nationwide apparatus of federalism. Indeed, the typical state constitution provides only that "the judicial power" shall be vested in some court or group of courts. How are we to make sense of such cryptic language?

The task may not be so daunting as it seems. In interpreting a constitution, one naturally prefers to have direct evidence of authorial intent—explicit textual language regarding the judicial power, for example, or, barring that, some kind of explicit and instructive legislative history. Yet where direct and explicit textual evidence of the popular will is unavailable, indirect evidence frequently will suffice. The U.S. Constitution says nothing more about the power of the federal courts than that "the judicial Power of the United States shall be vested in one supreme Court, and in such inferior courts as the Congress may from time to time ordain and establish."[1] Yet this lack of explicit instruction has not prevented federal courts from developing an elaborately worked out conception of the scope, nature, and function of national judicial power. In developing this conception, federal courts have relied not so much upon the wording of Article III as upon inferences derived from the structure and functions of the national Constitution, supplemented by historical evidence of the beliefs and judicial practices of the founding generation.

There is no reason why the same kinds of structural inferences and other evidence ought not to furnish the basis for an equally well-developed conception of the nature and functions of judicial power granted by any particular state constitution. Such inferences could then provide the context necessary to determine from state constitutional treatment of judicial power the answer to the question posed above: what kind of judiciary have the people of a state chosen to give themselves? State courts, it bears mentioning, already employ this tactic to some extent. For example, state courts have typically inferred from the federal structure of American government and from the historical circumstances of the founding period that, unlike the U.S. Constitution, state constitutions grant state courts plenary rather than limited judicial power. Implementing the functional approach to state constitutional interpretation outlined in previous chapters would thus require nothing more than walking a few additional steps down a path that has already been well marked.

In this section, I argue that such questions concerning the nature and extent of state judicial power should be approached by application to state constitutions of a rebuttable presumption to the effect that the people of the state wish their courts to act as agents of federalism, and constitutionally grant them the authority to do so. That is to say, in the absence of contradictory evidence, state courts ought to presume that they have the authority to join the legislative and executive branches of the state government in monitoring the ways in which the national government uses its powers and, when necessary, to resist abuses of national power and to facilitate resistance by other state ac-

1. U.S. Const. art. III, § 1.

tors. To that end, they should thus understand themselves to be authorized, presumptively, to exercise a certain degree of independent judgment in the interpretation of the state constitution when doing so would help effectuate legitimate state resistance to national abuses.

Such a presumption is justified, I argue below, because it leads state courts, in the absence of contrary evidence, to construe state constitutions to create an institutional structure of collective self-governance that is normatively desirable—more desirable than the institutional structures that application of a contrary presumption would be likely to yield, at least under the circumstances in which most state polities are most likely to find themselves, most of the time. Specifically, my claim is that federalism is likely to work better, and will thus more likely accomplish the liberty-enhancing goals for which it was established, when state courts are authorized to act as agents of federalism than when they lack such authority.

The Presumption of Institutional Flexibility

Underlying this presumption of judicial federalism agency is a lower-order supporting presumption that I call the presumption of *institutional flexibility*. According to this presumption, the constitutional ordering of state power should be understood to be in some respects adjustable rather than firmly fixed. To put this another way, insofar as the state constitutional allocation and ordering of state power affects the capacity of state officials to protect the citizenry's welfare by resisting abuses of national power, it should be approached, presumptively, as in some sense provisional. This ordering should be viewed as neither unalterably fixed, nor based upon principles or choices deeply fundamental to the state polity; on the contrary, the way in which state power is granted and deployed is the one variable in the dual constitutional system of federalism most readily subject to adjustment for purely instrumental reasons.

To understand state constitutions in this way requires abandoning certain preconceptions that we usually bring to the interpretation of any document purporting to call itself a "constitution." According to the standard conventions of American constitutional interpretation—the conventions, that is to say, governing interpretation of the U.S. Constitution—we are required to think of a constitution as a free-standing expression of the fundamental values and significant political choices of a politically free and independent polity. As I have argued throughout this book, a state polity does not, most of the time, fit that description. The members of a state polity are part of the national polity; the institutions of state government they create exist not only to satisfy their own desires concerning the character and content of political life within the state, but also to satisfy the wishes of the national polity of which they are members concerning the character and content of political life throughout the nation. This means that state government power is allocated and deployed not only to ensure good internal self-governance on the state level, but also to ensure the success of the larger federal system of which state government is a part. In other words, the federal system itself makes demands on state polities, demands that sometimes can be best satisfied through the medium of state constitutional law, and in consequence state constitutions should, presumptively, be responsive to those demands.

An analogy may help clarify these considerations. Suppose I step into the shower and turn on the water, which comes out scalding hot. The plumbing system in my house offers me two different ways to cool the water coming out of the showerhead: I can adjust the faucet in the shower to alter the mix of hot and cold water reaching the nozzle; or I can leave the shower faucet setting where it is, go down to the basement, and adjust the thermostat on my hot water heater to bring the temperature down to a more comfortable level. Both methods will work but, obviously, adjusting the mix of hot and cold at the shower head will get the job done more quickly and allow me greater flexibility to adjust and readjust the temperature to precisely where I like it.

Federalism is a bit like a plumbing system. It is designed to maintain a balance of power between the state and national governments suitable for the protection of the public welfare. What is required to maintain that balance may change at any given moment depending upon the circumstances. This means that the relative powers of, or restraints imposed upon, the state and national governments may from time to time need adjustment. For example, the power of the national government may creep up through expansive interpretations of the national commerce power, or the war or treaty powers, or by incorporation of the Bill of Rights into the Fourteenth Amendment. When such changes occur, the federal system itself may need to be rebalanced to ensure that the liberty of all is not unduly threatened. How may this be accomplished?

Like a domestic plumbing system, the system of federalism offers two possible ways to adjust the balance of power. First, one could try to amend the national Constitution, but this is slow, cumbersome, and unreliable—a bit like running down to the basement to adjust the hot water heater to cool the water coming out of the shower head upstairs. In the short term, at least, the provisions of the national Constitution, and consequently the powers exercised by the national government, are more logically treated as fixed variables. The other way to rebalance the system is to make the adjustments at the state end—to increase, decrease, or modify state power—by adjusting the allocations of power established by the state constitution.

Now, if it is usually easier and faster to maintain an appropriate balance in the federal system by adjusting state power than by adjusting national power, by what means ought state power to be adjusted? Thus far, I have said nothing inconsistent with the standard conventions of American constitutionalism. Here, however, I depart from those conventions by arguing that formal constitutional amendment should be understood, presumptively, as only one available method by which the relevant allocations of power established by the state constitution may be adjusted. In addition to popular adjustment of governmental power by constitutional amendment, state courts should also be understood, presumptively, to have the authority to adjust the powers granted to the various organs of state government, at least within certain limits, which I describe shortly.

Agent discretion in a dual-agent system of overlapping authority. According to the dominant conventions of national constitutionalism, when constitutional structures of power require adjustment there is one and only one legitimate method to accomplish the task: constitutional amendment. This is not to say that the allocation of power under the U.S. Constitution has never been altered by other means—by outright appropriation by governmental actors, for example, or by changes in governance customs or in public opinion, or by judicial reinterpretation of the document, and so on. But all these other methods of constitutional alteration pose legitimacy problems that even their sympathizers have sometimes been hard-pressed to defend.[2]

The reason that constitutional change undertaken by means other than formal amendment poses legitimacy problems under the conventions of national constitutionalism is that, according to those conventions, the U.S. Constitution has been framed and maintained under a presumption of continuing popular mistrust of the national government. Americans, the story goes, have always feared their national government; they have always been afraid that it would expand to undesirable dimensions, accumulate too much power, stifle counterbalancing sources of government power—ultimately, that it would op-

2. Bruce Ackerman's theory of "constitutional moments" is a good example of this kind of fancy dancing. See Ackerman, *We the People: Foundations.*

press and tyrannize them in ways no different from those they endured at the hands of the highly centralized British government that they threw off, at great cost, by violent revolution.[3]

Given the assumption of governmental mistrust, the interpretational convention of strict fidelity to the constitutional text, and its accompanying requirement that constitutional change be accomplished exclusively through formal popular approval, makes a great deal of sense. These conventions make the U.S. Constitution presumptively inflexible, of course, since amendment is difficult and unlikely, but rigidity may well be preferable to flexibility when a principal mistrusts its agent.[4] To be sure, reining in agents tightly by requiring strict and nondeviating compliance with instructions imposes certain costs on principals. First, the possibility that the instructions will prove unsuitable or will become obsolete as circumstances change means that the principal may incur costs in the form of the agent's failure to effectuate the principal's goals, costs that might have been avoided had the principal granted the agent more discretion to accomplish its ends through means selected by the agent rather than exclusively mandated by the principal. Second, to minimize the first kind of costs, the principal may need to incur significant oversight costs arising from the need to monitor closely the agent's progress and to adjust its instructions as necessary to keep the agent performing efficiently. But where the agent is mistrusted, and the consequences of agent misbehavior are severe, such costs may be deemed worth paying.

However sensible this arrangement may be in the single-agent context of national constitutionalism, it makes far less sense in the quite different and more complex context of state constitutionalism. As we saw in chapter 3, federalism is a system in which a single principal, the national polity, divides power by creating two distinct governmental agents. Each of these governmental agents is charged with pursuing the same set of goals established by the principal, and does so independently of the other. If federalism were a matter of dividing up the realm of government activity into two distinct, nonoverlapping spheres of authority, it might make sense to think of a state governmental agent the same way we think of the national government—as a single agent pursuing its principal's goals by itself. But that is not a good description of federalism. In fact, federalism is not at all a system in which two distinct agents pursue distinct and nonoverlapping goals in distinct

3. E.g., Bailyn, *The Ideological Origins of the American Revolution*; Rakove, *Original Meanings*.
4. Schauer, "Formalism"; Eskridge, "Spinning Legislative Supremacy."

spheres of authority, but rather a system in which two agents pursue the same set of largely overlapping goals, each exercising independent authority within what is for many if not most purposes essentially the same sphere of activity. To be sure, this overlap is by no means complete. The national government has exclusive authority over most aspects of foreign affairs,[5] for example, and the state governments have exclusive authority over a wide range of subjects such as the size, organization, and revenue raising authority of state and local governments, and dominant authority over many other areas. Nevertheless, over a very wide range of governmental goals and activities, the federal system is best characterized not as two single-agent systems operating independently side by side, but as a single system of dual agents with overlapping authority.

In such a system, what is the optimal way in which the principal should allocate discretion among the agents? There are basically three possibilities: the principal could grant both agents little discretion; it could grant both agents considerable discretion; or it could grant one agent little discretion and the second agent broad discretion. Intuitively, the third possibility seems most desirable. Where both agents lack discretion, the principal will have to incur substantial oversight costs not only because tightly constrained agents are less likely successfully to achieve the principal's goals, but also because, with two agents simultaneously pursuing the principal's goals, and each agent lacking the flexibility to accommodate itself to the actions of the other, conflicts between the two agents are likely to arise with some frequency. Since the agents' instructions are inflexible, the only actor capable of resolving such conflicts is the principal, who will often be called upon to sort things out.

Conversely, where both agents are granted considerable discretion, the principal may reduce its oversight costs, but can expect to incur a different kind of cost—namely, the cost of agent shirking.[6] Shirking occurs where agents

5. Crosby v. National Foreign Trade Council, 530 U.S. 363 (2000); Zschernig v. Miller, 389 U.S. 429 (1968).

6. Although the paradigm of shirking is the literal failure to pursue the principal's goals through lack of effort, economists tend to define the term more broadly to include "defection," or the pursuit of goals that are antithetical to those of the principal, especially private enrichment of the agent at the expense of the principal. Both kinds of shirking, however, involve a kind of stealing from the principal, whether passively, by accepting payment for doing nothing, or actively, by, in addition to taking payment for nothing, appropriating and converting to the agent's use things that belong to the principal. See Noll, "Economic Perspectives on the Politics of Regulation," 1277–78.

act for their own benefit rather than for the benefit of their principal, and is increasingly likely to occur as the agent's independent discretion increases. In a dual-agent system where both agents have substantial discretion, the possibility of shirking is compounded because the agents have the flexibility to collude not only for the principal's benefit, but for their own. The principal, moreover, is less likely to detect shirking in this situation because neither agent, on account of its discretion, is required very often to refer problems or conflicts to the principal for resolution. This kind of an arrangement, then, is highly flexible and potentially efficacious, but risky.

In the third possible dual-agent arrangement, one agent is granted little discretion and the other is granted wide, or at least much greater, discretion. Of the possible arrangements, this one seems clearly superior because it allows the principal to reap both the benefits of loyalty provided by a tightly constrained agent and the benefits of efficacy provided by granting an agent substantial discretion. Indeed, such an arrangement is quite common, and is often found where a principal employs an oversight agent to monitor the performance of a primary agent.[7] Thus, one might employ an auditor to monitor the performance of one's professional or financial manager, or an architectural engineer to monitor the performance of a building contractor, or an inspector general to monitor the performance of a corporation or government agency. In all these situations, both agents are charged with seeing that the principal's goals are accomplished, but one agent is required to hew closely to a comparatively constraining set of basic instructions, while the other is given more scope to poke around, look beneath the surface, and make complex evaluative judgments about the efficacy with which the principal's goals are being accomplished.

In those areas where the federal system decrees that responsibility be shared between the state and national governments, it thus makes sense to grant each agent different amounts of discretion to pursue the principal's goals. It is clear, moreover, that in the American federal system one of the agents—the national government—is by definition granted extremely limited discretion because the principal does not trust it. We thus interpret this agent's discretion—that is to say, we interpret its constitutional powers—narrowly. We deem the national government, for example, to lack all powers except those that are expressly or implicitly granted; we deem it to lack the authority to alter or update its constitutional instructions, no matter how

---

7. Issacharoff and Ortiz, "Governing Through Intermediaries."

desirable such improvements might be, without express approval from the principal in the form of a constitutional amendment, and so on.

With the national agent subject to the constraint of limited discretion, then, the best arrangement would seem to be to grant the state governmental agent a good deal of discretion in how it goes about effectuating the people's goals in those areas in which it shares authority with the national government. Or at least this is so in the abstract. In the event, of course, this may not be the best arrangement. If the state-level agent is untrustworthy, or if some contingent set of conditions or some unforeseen structural impediment arises to cast doubt on the ability of the state government to act loyally and effectively, the people may have no choice but to grant it discretion just as limited as they grant to the national government and simply to incur the attendant oversight costs. That is why, in my view, the presumption of institutional flexibility is just that—a presumption—rather than as an invariable guiding principle of constitutional design. Conversely, in the absence of evidence indicating that the people of a state harbor significant distrust for state-level government, there is every reason to presume that they would prefer to create the most effective arrangement.

The limits of agent discretion. I have said so far that the dynamics of the federal system make it desirable for some aspects of state power to be thought of as adjustable rather than fixed, and that principles of agency suggest that the most efficient way to ensure that state power gets adjusted in an appropriate way whenever adjustments are necessary is to delegate to state governments the discretion to determine, and to adjust as necessary, the scope of their own powers. (I argue below that state courts are the organ of state government best granted the responsibility to perform this function.) This is in some ways an unsettling thought, for it paints a picture of government officials determining the scope of their own powers not by reference to instructions contained in a popularly approved constitution, but by reference to their own sense of how best to achieve collectively held goals. This raises the possibility that the agent may abuse its discretion, which is why, in a single-agent system, especially where the agent is mistrusted, it makes little sense to structure the agent's authority in this way. As explained above, however, the risks of abuse are considerably lessened when (1) the principal employs two agents with overlapping authority, who consequently monitor and check one another's performance; and (2) the principal in fact trusts the agent to whom it grants the broader measure of discretion.

Even with these safeguards in place, however, it is by no means the case that the agent who receives the grant of discretion—the state governmental agent— receives discretion so broad as to permit it to redefine or expand its powers without limit, to the ultimate detriment of the principal. One very important limitation on this discretion arises from the fact that state governments do not typically share overlapping authority with the national government for every conceivable purpose, and thus the dual-agent model simply will not apply to certain aspects of the state constitutional order. One of the consequences of the federal structure is that it permits state polities to engage to a significant degree in the independent pursuit of good self-government on the state level, and one of the functions of a state constitution is to order state power that is deployed toward that end. Because the national government is a government of limited powers, the instructions issued to a state government are unlikely to coincide completely with those issued to the national government, and the state government is thus likely to be responsible for achieving certain popular goals on its own. In these situations, the safeguards of the dual-agent arrangement are absent, and the state acts more like a single agent with exclusive power—more, that is to say, like the national government. In those cases, the presumption of institutional flexibility simply would not apply.

Even in those areas of shared authority where the dual-agency arrangement prevails, however, the state governmental agent is still an agent, and its discretion is consequently limited in significant ways. First and foremost, because they are always agents, and thus working for the people, state governmental actors are bound at all times to pursue as faithfully as possible the goals established by the people of the state, and only those goals. They cannot disregard such ultimate instructions, and consequently their discretion cannot extend to defining their powers in ways that are not calculated to achieve popularly defined objectives. Some sense of how such a constraint operates may be gleaned from an analogous restraint on invocations of power by the U.S. Congress under the Necessary and Proper Clause of the national Constitution.[8] Under that clause, Congress may do many unspecified things, but only those that are rationally related to the achievement of some constitutionally specified objective.[9] The clause, in other words, is not a bootstrap that the national government may use to expand its own powers for any reason it

8. U.S. Const. art. I, § 8, cl. 18.
9. McCulloch v. Maryland, 17 U.S. 316, 421 (1819).

chooses.[10] The same kind of limitation applies inherently to the discretion of state governmental actors to define their own powers when pursuing goals in areas of shared state–national authority.[11]

Second, significant constraints on the way in which state governments construe their authority necessarily arise from the specific mix of goals that the people of the state charge their governments to achieve. Governments are not single-purpose agents, like taxi drivers or lawn-cutting services. They are among the most general of agents, and by any definition are multipurpose agents whose responsibilities extend to achieving a great many of the principal's goals. One of the great risks in granting single-purpose agents wide discretion is that they may single-mindedly, or worse, zealously, fulfill their narrowly defined responsibilities without regard to any of the principal's many other goals, causing the agent to thwart achievement of those goals. Thus, my electrician installs a new outlet, but in so doing tracks mud all through the house, thereby thwarting one of my other goals, which is to keep a clean house, and indeed undermines the work of one of my other single-purpose agents, my house cleaner.

This kind of risk is lessened considerably when the agent is a general agent and thus charged with achieving not merely one of the principal's goals, but many of them simultaneously. Where the principal is a large polity, it will have many goals and at least some of them inevitably will conflict, or at the very least act as constraints upon one another. Because no agent has the discretion to alter the particular mix of goals established by its principal, the requirement that the agent pursue many conflicting goals simultaneously significantly limits its discretion, no matter how broad that discretion might otherwise appear to be. A government whose polity instructs it simultaneously to protect both the physical security and the personal privacy of its members, for example, cannot easily construe its discretion as extending to fighting violent crime through the use of random, suspicionless searches of citizens' homes. The discretion of state governments to expand their powers to dan-

---

10. At least this is so in theory. Nevertheless, the Court's construction of the clause has been criticized on just such grounds. See, e.g., Gunther, *John Marshall's Defense of* McCulloch v. Maryland, esp. the April 2, 1819 letter from "Amphyction" (64–77). A more contemporary version of this argument may be found in Nagel, *The Implosion of American Federalism*, ch. 2.

11. See, e.g., State ex rel. Barker v. Southern, 177 S.W. 640, 642 (Mo. 1915); State ex rel. Cake v. Steele, 65 P. 515, 517 (Or. 1901).

gerous extents is particularly constrained by the conflicting constitutional imperatives described in chapter 4: typically, state power should be sufficient to protect the citizenry from national tyranny, yet it generally should not be so great as to create an undue risk to the citizenry of tyranny at the hands of the state government itself. State governmental agents cannot successfully maintain this balance if they consider nothing but the sufficiency of their powers to resist external threats.

Finally, the discretion of state governmental agents, no matter how broadly granted in general terms, may always be restrained either by the other governmental agent on the scene—the national government—or by the people themselves. The national government has been given direct authority to monitor and restrain the actions of state governments in certain respects, as well as ample power to prevent them from straying too far from popular instructions. And when all else fails, of course, the principal may become directly involved by issuing new and specific constitutional instructions: "Use your discretion to pursue our goals, to monitor the activities of our national agent, and when possible to resist and counteract actions of the national government that fail appropriately to achieve our goals, but don't do *A, B,* and *C.* When pursuing goal *X,* use procedures *E* and *F.*" State constitutions are of course filled with narrow restrictions of this sort, suggesting again that state governments are often conceived as general-purpose agents of wide discretion whose occasional mistaken exercises of discretion must now and then be corrected by a specific countermanding order from the principal. Indeed, one of the difficulties of state constitutional interpretation, discussed later in this chapter, is how to distinguish provisions that are not subject to discretionary interpretation by state courts from those that are.

The dual-agent model in practice. The preceding discussion gives normative reasons why certain aspects of a state constitution's grant, allocation, and limitations of state power ought presumptively to be understood as provisional and subject to adjustment by state governmental agents themselves. Before leaving this piece of the argument, it is worth asking whether the dual-agent model of state constitutionalism sketched above, whatever its theoretical appeal, has any connection to the reality of state constitutional law as it is practiced on the ground. I believe the model not only has considerable descriptive bite, but describes the actual practice of state constitutionalism much more accurately than the traditional, dominant view, which is based on conventions of constitutional thought imported from the national arena.

First, as I have already suggested, the idea that the federal system may usefully be conceived as a dual-agent system with a highly constrained national agent and a relatively unconstrained state agent possessing broad discretion is borne out by several well-established conventions of state and national constitutional interpretation. The national government is conventionally understood to be a government of limited powers. State governments are conventionally understood to be governments of general powers. The national government is understood to be entitled to exercise only those powers granted to it in the Constitution, and no others. State governments are typically understood to be authorized to exercise any powers except those that they are specifically denied in state constitutions. This looks very much indeed like a system in which the national agent is constrained and operates under a set of strict instructions that it must follow without deviation, while the state agent is granted considerable discretion under a set of extremely loose and general instructions.

Second, the state and national constitutions are typically approached and treated very differently by those who deal with them on a regular basis. The national Constitution is treated with veneration.[12] It is understood to be a critically significant document, one that contributes importantly to constituting Americans as a people. It may be changed only by the people themselves, through amendment, and even then is not to be amended lightly, but should be changed only for the weightiest of reasons. A charge of constitutional violation or usurpation is taken as an accusation of the utmost gravity, representing a breach of faith with the sovereign American people. Courts reviewing such claims look deeply into the document and its legal and political context, which form the sole basis of legitimate judicial decision making. The U.S. Constitution, in other words, is conventionally taken seriously both as a blueprint for the exercise of governmental authority and as a statement of deeply held, shared social and political values.

State constitutions, as we saw in chapter 1, are viewed very differently. They are treated with anything but veneration. Most are amended with great frequency, and many of them are repeatedly and even casually stuffed with all manner of trivial provisions. Entire constitutions are periodically discarded and replaced. Large portions of many state constitutions read like a running list of highly specific rebukes to government officials who have in some way, at some time or another, displeased the public. Courts construing state constitutions often behave as though no such distinct document exists, instead

12. Levinson, *Constitutional Faith*; Kammen, *A Machine That Would Go of Itself.*

treating charges that the state constitution has been violated as though the real violation alleged were of the national Constitution. It is clear from this treatment that state constitutions are not widely revered as untouchable expressions of carefully considered political decisions and deeply held, shared social values, but rather are seen as thoroughly pedestrian vehicles for the achievement of instrumental, and in most cases, entirely immediate results. The presumption of institutional flexibility I have sketched here thus is not merely a matter of theoretical speculation: state constitutions are now, in practice, already understood and treated as the pieces of the federal mechanism most properly subject to short-term adjustment, and are in fact most often and most readily tweaked, both by state polities and state courts, to achieve short-term, instrumental ends. To be clear, I do not argue that this is inevitably the case; as explained in chapter 4, state constitutions may be capable of becoming something else, something more like the national Constitution, able to bear the weight of Romantic nationalist aspirations. For the moment, however, they are not plausibly thought of in this way, and thus play a very different role in the federal system.

Disaggregating Governmental Discretion

Accepting the presumption that the state constitution's allocation of powers to the state government is flexible, and therefore subject to adjustment by means other than amendment in circumstances where state governments are acting in a dual-agency capacity in conjunction with the national government, does not end the analysis. We must still consider which organs of state government ought to be understood to have the authority to make the necessary adjustments and to decide upon the extent of power the various state actors possess. In keeping with the argument of chapter 6, I believe the most sensible way to handle this problem is to presume, in the absence of contrary evidence, that courts have a significant role to play in the exercise of such authority.

In the first place, it must be noted that the state executive and legislative branches are likely to exercise this power anyway, regardless of whether courts do so. Madisonian political psychology predicts,[13] and experience seems to confirm, that executive and legislative actors tend to assert whatever powers they think are necessary to resist external threats; that is, undoubtedly, one reason why judicial review is often thought to be so crucial to the ultimate success of a system of horizontally divided government power. If governors

---

13. Madison, *The Federalist*, Nos. 10, 46–48, 51.

and state legislatures may be expected to define their own powers broadly when they seek to resist what they deem to be abuses of national power, the question may well boil down to the one posed in the previous chapter: are courts mere bystanders to the federal process of mutual state and national checking, or do they have some role to play?

There are good reasons to presume that state courts are competent to play this kind of active role in the federal order. Most obviously, questions of state and national constitutional law form a routine part of state court dockets, and state courts thus possess considerable experience in resolving questions of constitutional construction. To say this, however, is not to say very much, for what is at issue here is not simply the authority to construe state constitutions, which state courts are universally understood to possess, but the authority to construe them in a particular way—instrumentally, for the purpose of directly resisting or indirectly assisting other branches to resist abuses of national power. Thus, the pertinent competence concerns the ability of state courts effectively to monitor national power, to recognize when it is abused, and to respond to such abuses through the exercise of official power. Here, state courts have several additional pertinent qualifications.

First, because they so frequently adjudicate cases arising within the state, state courts are exposed continuously to an extremely broad and diverse subset of national law and its impact within the state. Indeed, because they possess concurrent jurisdiction with federal courts over nearly all questions that may arise under national law, state courts have significant opportunities to maintain up-to-the-minute, detailed knowledge of the substance of national law and the way it is applied in concrete settings within the state. Second, state courts presumptively are well positioned to recognize when national power is being abused. Given their experience and legal learning, as well as their concurrent jurisdiction to decide questions of federal constitutional law, state judges may be expected to understand as well as anyone in the state how not only to interpret the constitutional powers of the national government, but how independently to evaluate interpretations of the U.S. Constitution reached by federal courts or by other organs of national government extrajudicially construing their own powers. Moreover, by virtue of their common law and rulemaking functions, state courts often possess considerable experience in making overt, independent policy judgments of the kind they would be called upon to make as agents of federalism. Third, state courts are often able to respond expeditiously to wrongdoing—often more expeditiously than, say, the legislature, which typically must meet, debate, and work out compromises, all of which may take time. Although courts generally do not have the resources available to other branches to resist abuses of national authority decisively, by identifying national wrongdoing and by issuing appropriate orders quickly, state courts certainly are at least competent to engage the national government with whatever resources they may have available to them.

That state courts may be competent to serve as agents of federalism does not necessarily mean, however, that they should be presumed to have the job in preference to some other branch of state government; there remains the question of whether state courts have any better claim to exercise these powers than other organs of state government. In fact, there are good reasons to presume that state courts are better situated than other organs of state government to exercise responsibly the power to determine and adjust the various powers exercised by state governmental actors. First, because state courts generally have fewer resources than other branches to deploy against the national government, they may face fewer temptations, and have fewer opportunities, to construe their own authority unnecessarily broadly under cover of a claim that they require the additional power successfully to resist some purported abuse of national power. The executive's authority to command the state's law enforcement and military forces, and the legislature's authority to raise and spend money and to promulgate binding codes of conduct, for example, may make them in some circumstances worthy adversaries of national power. But those same powers may be deployed internally as well as externally, to the detriment of the state populace as well as to its benefit. This suggests that authorizing the executive or legislative branches to adjust authoritatively the scope of their own powers may entail dangers, including the possibility of agent defection, of a far greater magnitude than are present when the judiciary is authorized to make ultimate determinations concerning the constitutional authority of governmental actors, even its own.

Moreover, even in areas where state courts already exercise significant independent policymaking authority, as in the common law, they have developed and typically observe important conventions of responsible self-restraint.[14] Few state courts could be described, even in their most active periods, as reckless or even frequent adventurers in the development of the common law. By and large, they take stare decisis seriously, and overturn precedent or strike out in substantially new directions only rarely, and then mainly in response

14. These are well described in Calabresi, *A Common Law for the Age of Statutes.*

to considerable social pressure. State courts thus seem to have earned a presumption—rebuttable, to be sure—of an ability to exercise self-restraint.

Second, state courts are probably better able than other constitutional actors to perceive and to enforce the various balances of power effectuated by the state constitution. Under prevailing conventions of constitutional judicial review, state courts are generally understood to possess ultimate responsibility for policing the state constitution's internal separation of powers,[15] a function that may require them on occasion to restrain the other branches. Enforcing the balance between state and national power does not present a task much different from enforcing the balance of power among the various organs of state government. Moreover, because these same conventions make state courts the principal enforcers of state bills of rights, state courts might be expected to show greater sensitivity than the executive or legislative branches to one particular and critically important kind of constitutional balance: the balance that must be struck between the need for state power to be sufficient to resist external threats, on one hand, and the need, on the other hand, to prevent state officials from accumulating so much power that they begin to pose a danger to their own people.

These considerations may not support a firm conclusion that state courts should always be understood to have a role as agents of federalism. Conditions may differ from state to state, as may the experiences and preferences of the state polity. They are, however, sufficient to support a rebuttable presumption in favor of a broad construction of state judicial power, one broad enough to include the authority to participate directly or indirectly in state resistance to national power as an agent of federalism.

Rebutting the Presumption of Judicial Federalism Agency

Like most presumptions, the presumption that courts may act as agents of federalism is rebuttable, and courts applying this presumption must therefore remain carefully attentive to this possibility. How, then, may this be done? There is, unfortunately, no formula that can be invoked to determine when a presumption of constitutional construction should be deemed rebutted; applying presumptions inherently requires the exercise of judgment. Nevertheless, it is possible to identify a few pertinent considerations.

As an initial matter, it is useful to distinguish two different ways in which the presumption in favor of judicial power may be rebutted. First, it may be re-

15. See, e.g., "Symposium: Separation of Powers in State Constitutional Law."

butted across the board by evidence suggesting that the constitution denies state courts any discretion whatsoever to act as agents of federalism. Second, it may be rebutted on an issue-specific basis by evidence that the constitution denies state courts the authority to act as agents of federalism with respect to particular subjects that the people have chosen to settle constitutionally for themselves, although courts retain presumptive authority as to other issues.

What might count as evidence of a complete denial of discretion? It is, of course, impossible to catalog completely the kinds of evidence that might support such an inference, but it seems safe to say that at least one thing courts might look for is evidence, especially recent evidence, of popular distrust of the state judiciary. Does the state constitution contain specific constraints on judicial power, such as limits on the jurisdiction of courts? Has the constitution been recently amended to switch from an appointive to an elective judiciary? Have judicial decisions been overruled frequently by popular initiative? Have judges been impeached or recalled with any regularity? Are elected judges often turned out of office, or do they frequently fall short in retention elections? Other kinds of evidence might be more equivocal. Is jury nullification a problem throughout the state? This might evince distrust of the judiciary, although jury nullification, at least in criminal cases, is perhaps more commonly a sign of popular distrust of the executive or legislative branches. Has the legislature attempted with any regularity to limit judicial review or other powers of the judiciary? Such efforts might respond to a popular distrust of the judiciary, although again the inference is weaker since some degree of self-interested interbranch rivalry, unrelated to popular desires, is to be expected in a state-level system of horizontal separation of powers.

To give a concrete example, it is possible that a case might be made for California as a state whose people harbor a particular distrust for the judiciary. California has a somewhat distinctive history of popular distrust of state government arising largely from the control over state government exercised during the late nineteenth and early twentieth centuries by the Southern Pacific Railroad Company.[16] Progressive reformers, who argued that state officials, including judges, were in the pocket of corporate interests, succeeded in 1911 in placing on the ballot a proposal to amend the state constitution to add a provision allowing popular recall of elected officials. Unlike several other contemporaneous Progressive-backed reforms, this provision provoked at least some public opposition because the proposed recall authority extended to

16. Harris, *California Politics*, ch. 1; Delmatier, *The Rumble of California Politics*, ch. 6.

judges, thus threatening their independence. That same year, President Taft successfully blocked admission of Arizona to the Union based upon the inclusion in its proposed state constitution of a recall provision that extended to judges, which was subsequently deleted.[17] Nevertheless, in a speech supporting the recall proposal, reformist California governor Hiram Johnson said: "There is one question I have put everywhere and that has never been answered yet: why is it that every Southern Pacific politician, every political crook, every lawyer for big interests should declare themselves against us and declare themselves the sponsors and protectors of the judiciary of California?"[18] The recall provision carried, and California remains one of only a handful of states to permit recall of judges. Several states that employ the recall device specifically exempt judges from its reach.[19] More recently, in a surprising popular revolt against the judiciary, California voters in 1986 threw out the chief justice and two associate justices of the California Supreme Court in retention elections, apparently due to mounting dissatisfaction with what was popularly perceived as the court's hostility to the state's death penalty.[20]

These two incidents, of course, hardly demonstrate a continuous history in California of popular distrust of the judiciary, and there might well be other, countervailing evidence showing popular trust in the state's courts. For example, perhaps ironically, the California Constitution also contains a provision that might well be interpreted as a particularly strong expression of the polity's faith in the independent judgment of their state courts. In 1974, the people of California by initiative amended the state constitution to provide: "Rights guaranteed by this Constitution are not dependent on those guaranteed by the United States Constitution."[21] The clear purpose of this provision is to invite state judges to avoid construing provisions of the state declaration of rights to be identical to their national counterparts, and in so doing, to grant state judges a certain degree of freedom. These examples merely show, first, that a wide variety of different kinds of evidence might serve to support or rebut the presumption in favor of judicial authority to act as an agent of federalism; and second, that the relevant evidence, once it is all assembled, may well be complex and equivocal.

17. Sponholtz, "The Initiative and Referendum," 57.
18. *Los Angeles Examiner,* Sept. 28, 1911, quoted in Tallian, *Direct Democracy,* 39.
19. These include Alaska, Idaho, Kansas, Louisiana, Michigan, and Washington.
20. Wold and Culver, "The Defeat of the California Justices."
21. Cal. Const. art. I, § 24.

Aside from evidence of popular distrust of the judiciary in particular, another type of evidence that might suffice to support an across-the-board rebuttal of the presumption of judicial federalism agency would be evidence of popular distrust of state government generally. In some states, such distrust might run so deep, and be so indiscriminate, as to raise an inference that the people are willing to trust no organ of state government beyond the absolute minimum necessary to achieve their (necessarily limited) collective goals. As indicated in chapter 5, evidence of such distrust might include, for example, a refusal to grant power to organs of state government in plenary terms, or the imposition of severe limitations on how the branches of state government may use their powers, or the inclusion in the state constitution of an unusually extensive set of individual rights protecting an especially broad range of private activity from state government control.

If convincing evidence of this type of extremely broad popular distrust seems rare, it is undoubtedly much easier to find evidence supporting rebuttal of the presumption of judicial federalism agency on an issue-specific basis. A rebuttal of the presumption on a discrete issue would revoke otherwise available judicial authority to adjust certain constitutional instructions, but not others. What might count as evidence of an issue-specific denial of judicial authority? Again, because it is impossible to catalog completely all the different kinds of evidence that might support such an inference, I mention only a few examples.

One of the most direct and obvious indications that the people of a state wish to deny state courts any kind of independent discretion on a particular issue appears in provisions specifically withdrawing such independence by linking specific state provisions to their counterparts in the U.S. Constitution. For example, the provision of the Florida Constitution dealing with unreasonable searches and seizures provides:

> This right shall be construed in conformity with the 4th Amendment to the United States Constitution, as interpreted by the United States Supreme Court. Articles or information obtained in violation of this right shall not be admissible in evidence if such articles or information would be inadmissible under decisions of the United States Supreme Court construing the 4th Amendment to the United States Constitution.[22]

22. Fla. Const. art. I, § 12.

Another provision of the Florida Constitution dealing with cruel and unusual punishment similarly provides:

> The prohibition against cruel or unusual punishment, and the prohibition against cruel and unusual punishment, shall be construed in conformity with decisions of the United States Supreme Court which interpret the prohibition against cruel and unusual punishment provided in the Eighth Amendment to the United States Constitution. Any method of execution shall be allowed, unless prohibited by the United States Constitution.[23]

Neither of these provisions establishes any particular level of protection under the state constitution for the rights in question, which are left to expand or contract according to the vagaries of U.S. Supreme Court rulings. Instead, the provisions are finely tuned to achieve a much narrower goal: to deny Florida courts a particular kind of discretion they would otherwise be thought to possess—namely, the discretion to bring their independent judgment to the interpretation of the provisions. Florida courts are not denied the authority to give any particular level of protection to the rights against unreasonable searches and cruel punishments; they may—in fact must—peg the rights at any level adopted by the U.S. Supreme Court, no matter how stingy or generous. Rather, Florida courts are simply denied the discretion to determine for themselves what degree of protection to afford the specified rights. That federal courts might be doing a poor job in protecting these important liberties, and that Florida courts might be able simultaneously both to do better and to protest the injustice of the federal judiciary are simply made irrelevant to the interpretation of the clauses. These provisions thus represent in the clearest possible terms a popular judgment that the national judiciary is more to be trusted than the state judiciary with the specific function of defending the rights against unreasonable searches and cruel punishments.

Another type of evidence that might strongly support a conclusion that the presumption of judicial discretion has been rebutted on a particular issue might be found in provisions of state constitutions that embody a specific popular decision not to embrace, but to reject, some particular aspect of the U.S. Constitution as a matter of state constitutional law. For example, the California Constitution's "Victims' Bill of Rights," added by initiative amendment

23. Id. § 17.

in 1982, provides: "relevant evidence shall not be excluded in any criminal proceeding."[24] In context, the manifest purpose of this language is to reject as a matter of state constitutional law the exclusionary rule, which the U.S. Supreme Court has held since 1961 to be a part of the Fourth Amendment of the U.S. Constitution.[25] Under that rule, evidence in criminal proceedings may be excluded, no matter how probative of guilt, if it was acquired by way of an unconstitutional search or seizure. Here, one might say, the California constitution denies state courts the discretion to determine how to assess, and if necessary, respond to one particular aspect of national search and seizure policy because it embodies a deliberate, popular judgment to reject that aspect of national policy; indeed, it goes further and establishes with some precision one aspect of how the right in question should be administered within the state, thereby squeezing out any inference in favor of judicial discretion.[26] Other rejectionist provisions raising similar inferences might include state constitutional provisions explicitly protecting privacy, which is protected by the U.S. Constitution only by implication, or the environment, which receives no protection at all under the national document.

Finally, the presumption of judicial discretion might be rebutted simply by the sheer specificity of the provision under review. State constitutions notoriously contain many provisions that are striking in their detail. The Texas Constitution, for example, provides that "Fifteen Thousand Dollars ($15,000) of the market value of the residence homestead of a married or unmarried adult, including one living alone, is exempt from ad valorem taxation for general elementary and secondary public school purposes. . . ."[27] The Missouri Constitution provides: "Any city having more than five thousand inhabitants or any other incorporated city as may be provided by law may frame and adopt a charter for its own government. The legislative body of the city may, by ordinance, submit to the voters the question: 'Shall a commission be chosen to frame a charter?' If the ordinance takes effect more than sixty days before the next election, the question shall be submitted at such election and if not, then at the

24. Cal. Const. art. I, § 28(d).

25. Mapp v. Ohio, 367 U.S. 643 (1961).

26. Of course, so long as the Supreme Court continues to construe the Fourth and Fourteenth Amendments to require application of the exclusionary rule, California must continue to observe the rule to the extent the U.S. Constitution requires it. But this is a matter of compliance with federal law unrelated to the content of state constitutional law.

27. Tex. Const. art. 8, § 1-b(c).

next general election thereafter, except as herein otherwise provided...."[28] The New York Constitution provides: "In ascertaining the power of the city of New York to contract indebtedness, ... there shall be excluded ... [i]ndebtedness contracted by the city for transit purposes, and not otherwise excluded, proportionately to the extent to which the current net revenue received by the city from all railroads and facilities and properties used in connection therewith and rights therein owned by the city and securities of corporations owning such railroads, facilities, properties or rights, owned by the city, shall meet the interest and the annual requirements for the amortization and payment of such non-excluded indebtedness."[29] Provisions such as these might well be thought to be so specific, and so targeted to achieve particular results, as to exclude any possibility of significant judicial discretion in their interpretation, even if it could be shown that in some set of circumstances the relaxation of such constraints, despite their apparent triviality, might somehow improve the ability of state officials to resist abuses of national power.

Before leaving this topic, I want to suggest that reading state constitutional provisions such as these to rebut a general presumption of broad judicial discretion in the interpretation of state constitutional provisions provides a better solution than is usually proposed to what might be termed the "two-category" problem in state constitutional analysis. It has sometimes been observed that state constitutions contain, broadly speaking, two classes of provisions.[30] One class consists of the kind of weighty provisions we are accustomed to find in the U.S. Constitution: provisions dealing with fundamental rights, governmental structure, democratic processes, and so on—"real" constitutional provisions, in other words. The other class consists of fluff like the provisions quoted in the preceding paragraph, provisions that deal with regulatory or revenue issues in such detail that they more resemble statutes, or even administrative regulations, than the kind of significant popular decisions most commonly thought to deserve constitutional status

Under conventional understandings of constitutionalism on the national model, provisions of the latter type pose a challenge to associated conventions of national constitutional interpretation.[31] According to those conventions,

28. Mo. Const. art. VI, § 19.

29. N.Y. Const. art. VIII, § 7-a(B).

30. An excellent analysis appears in Pope, "An Approach to State Constitutional Interpretation." See also Vreeland v. Byrne, 370 A.2d 825 (N.J. 1977).

31. Gardner, "The Failed Discourse of State Constitutionalism," 818–22.

courts construing constitutional provisions must when appropriate extract their meaning by considering the underlying values of the polity revealed by the provision, the relation of the provision to the overarching purposes of the document, and the intentions of the framers and ratifiers. Yet with provisions that are not only highly specific but also apparently trivial, the traditional brand of constitutional inquiry seems awkward and forced. Courts and commentators who have noticed this duality have sometimes suggested that it be resolved by taking a two-track approach to constitutional interpretation: those provisions that have weight—the "vital" provisions,[32] or the "great ordinances"[33]—get the full-bore interpretational treatment, while those that do not rise to this level of "constitutionality" may be approached more like statutes.

The difficulty of this solution is that, in attempting to rescue state constitutions from one kind of conflict with interpretational conventions, it causes state judges to violate a different convention. According to the national model, a constitution is a positive enactment of the sovereign people that must be obeyed literally and undeviatingly by all governmental agents, including courts. It is not for mere functionaries, on this view, to decide which provisions of a constitution are more weighty than others, or which are dearer to the people than others; everything that appears in a constitution is by hypothesis dear to the people, else they would not have bothered to include it. That is one reason why courts construing the U.S. Constitution labor under such a heavy, mandatory obligation to give independent meaning to every word of the text.[34]

The reason why the two-category problem of state constitutional provisions does not yield readily to the bifurcated interpretational approach is that this approach clings to the inapt national model of constitutionalism, and thus creates conceptual categories that are not especially useful for guiding state constitutional interpretation. The approach I have outlined here, in contrast, does not require making inherently difficult and jurisprudentially troubling distinctions between weighty and trivial constitutional provisions. Instead, the relevant conceptual line falls along a spectrum of specificity, and divides those constitutional provisions that are specific enough to represent a denial of judicial discretion from those that are not, regardless of their subject. The important question is thus not whether some provision is sufficiently "fundamental" to

32. Pope, "An Approach to State Constitutional Interpretation," 987.
33. *Vreeland,* 370 A.2d at 831.
34. E.g., Marbury v. Madison, 5 U.S. 137, 174 (1803).

deserve full-blown constitutional status, but simply whether the constitution issues a direct and specific instruction, of any kind, to governmental actors.

HOW TO BE A JUDICIAL AGENT OF FEDERALISM

Suppose a court in some particular case applies the presumption in favor of its authority to serve as a judicial agent of federalism, examines the state constitution, finds the presumption unrebutted either generally or with respect to the specific issue under consideration in the case at hand, and deems itself ready to use its granted authority. How should it proceed? Once again, no catalog or algorithm can capture all the possible considerations and variations in this or any other kind of constitutional interpretation; legal interpretation is an art, not a science. Moreover, the degree of discretion that courts are authorized to invoke, even when they are empowered to act as agents of federalism, may differ from state to state, making generalizations even more difficult. Consequently, rather than attempting to discuss the methods of judicial federalism agency in the abstract, this section instead examines several interpretational problems that tend to arise with some frequency in the construction of state constitutions. Discussion of these recurring problems provides, if not a formula, at least some concrete examples of some of the many ways in which state courts might employ their authority to resist national power.

Because the functional approach has its strongest and most direct application to provisions dealing with individual rights, I begin with some commonly encountered issues arising in the interpretation of state constitutional rights provisions, including the problems raised both by rights provisions that are identical or very similar to their national counterparts, and those that have no national counterpart. The discussion then moves to similar questions that arise in the construction of state constitutional structural provisions, and then concludes with a brief consideration of the treatment of old provisions that were adopted in one historical setting and have been carried forward into other, quite different settings. Readers who want even more detail may consult the appendix, which contains a hypothetical opinion by a hypothetical state supreme court applying the method outlined in this chapter.

Individual Rights Provisions

Duplicative rights provisions. One of the most frequently encountered problems in state constitutional interpretation concerns the treatment of provisions dealing with individual rights that duplicate provisions appearing in the U.S. Constitution. Sometimes such provisions mimic their national counterparts word for word, having clearly been copied directly from the national Constitution; in other cases, they are worded so similarly as to be virtually indistinguishable. It is fair to say that duplicative individual rights provisions are responsible for provoking the deepest crises of state constitutional jurisprudence. These are the provisions that Justice Brennan had in mind when he first urged state courts to construe state constitutions expansively, and they remain the most contested battlegrounds in state constitutional interpretation today. The standard primacy and interstitial approaches to state constitutional interpretation encounter a great deal of trouble explaining these provisions, a failure that has sometimes driven state courts to embrace the kind of implausible and unproductive Romantic subnationalism criticized in chapter 2.

The main jurisprudential problem with state constitutional rights provisions that do nothing more than copy and thus duplicate protections afforded under the national Constitution is that, under the incorporation doctrine, the national protections automatically restrain the states by operation of the Fourteenth Amendment. Consequently, if the state provisions mean the same thing as their national counterparts, they serve no obvious useful function. To avoid a conclusion of redundancy, and thus meaningless, some state courts have felt pressured to give such provisions a meaning—any meaning—that differs from the meaning of cognate federal provisions. Yet the fact that such provisions have been modeled on, or even copied directly from, provisions of the U.S. Constitution suggests strongly that they ought to be given the same meaning. Doing so, however, would apparently make them useless, thereby violating the canon of constitutional construction that requires every constitutional provision to have independent meaning. This dynamic has prompted a variety of responses by state courts—ranging from an automatic assumption of interpretative congruence to the invocation of such imponderable and implausible factors as a purported "unique state character"—to find, apparently by any means available, a different meaning for the state provision.

Under the functional approach of this book, duplicative rights provisions pose no interpretational difficulties whatsoever, and indeed are among the easiest cases, for the functional approach permits them to be recognized for what they are: direct invitations to state courts to monitor federal judicial rulings under the corresponding provisions of the U.S. Constitution, and to exercise their independent judgment concerning the way in which the rights in question should be best understood and applied.

Why, after all, would state constitutional drafters include in a state constitution a provision protecting an individual right that is identical, word for word, to one in the U.S. Constitution that already protects that right? Is it because they fear the national polity may repeal the counterpart provision of the national Bill of Rights? That is absurdly unlikely. Is it because they have some secret agenda to smuggle into the state constitution broader protection for the right in question than the U.S. Supreme Court is willing to give to the same language in the national document? If so, this is a very poor and deceptive way to go about it. Surely drafters ought not to copy into the state constitution language that has been interpreted inadequately by the highest court in the land; surely they should say more explicitly what they want if they want something different from the national regime. But these are silly speculations.

The best answer is also the most obvious: state constitutional drafters include such a provision in their state constitution because they think it is a good provision, and they want their state to have one *just like it.* Yet such an action can have only one plausible meaning: state courts are thereby given the responsibility to interpret and to independently enforce the *same* right as appears in the U.S. Constitution—not a different one that only looks the same, and whose differences may be revealed through some kabbalistic interpretational technique—but the same right that means the same thing as its national counterpart. In a federal system, however, state courts are not answerable to national authorities concerning the meaning of provisions of their own state constitutions. This means that state and federal courts might reach divergent interpretations of the same constitutional right, with each interpretation authoritative and enforceable within the respective spheres of state and national judicial power.[35]

35. This analysis is essentially the same even for individual rights copied from the national into state constitutions before the adoption of the Fourteenth Amendment or, for that matter, copied between the ratification of the Fourteenth Amendment and the Supreme Court's development of the incorporation doctrine in the mid-twentieth century. While under the formal holding of Barron v. Baltimore rights adopted during this period were not duplicative of national protections at the time of their inclusion in state constitutions, they still most likely evince a desire to include in the state constitution protection for a right by the same means as the right is protected in the U.S. Constitution. Indeed, this inference may be even stronger given the tradition of constitutional universalism discussed in chapter 1, for in this tradition constitutional language protecting rights merely instantiated universally applicable constraints on governmental power.

This is precisely this situation that so alarms adherents of the New Judicial Federalism, yet it should not be alarming in the slightest, for such divergence is exactly what a well-functioning federal system should be expected to produce. In a true federal system, two independent governmental agents are given independent authority to police the same turf. If the different levels of government disagree about the best way to police some piece of shared turf, so much the better; two agents are no better than one if they feel they must always agree on how best to effectuate the principal's wishes. An agent in these circumstances would abdicate, not effectuate, its responsibility if it felt it must forgo exercising its independent judgment when using it would result in a conflict with the other agent.

This analysis makes very clear that state courts interpreting duplicative rights provisions of their state constitutions have a responsibility to interpret such provisions by using their best independent judgment. In so doing, however, they should not attempt to confine themselves to examining only state precedent, state history, or the intentions of the framers of the state constitution—the materials that Paul Kahn has called "unique state sources."[36] Such a self-imposed limitation proceeds from an important category mistake: it assumes that when state courts interpret provisions of state constitutions, the object of interpretation is by definition different from any object of interpretation that federal courts might construe in the U.S. Constitution. In fact, they are the same; what differs is not the object of interpretation, but the interpreter. Each has authority independent of the other to interpret the same object, and each must use that authority independently if federalism is to protect liberty in the way the system contemplates.

Consequently, a state court interpreting a duplicative rights provision in a state constitution ought to consult all pertinent materials, whether national or state, including constructions of the same provision by other courts, and especially by the U.S. Supreme Court if that court has issued a pertinent ruling. In so doing, a state court is perfectly well justified, if it so chooses, in using the U.S. Supreme Court ruling as a point of departure, and in orienting its analysis toward the question whether the Supreme Court reached the best possible construction of the provision in issue. It may choose, that is to say, to confine itself to deciding whether it agrees or disagrees with the U.S. Supreme Court.

Of course, a state court need not consider the opinions of the Supreme Court; it has the authority to ignore them entirely if it wishes, choosing in-

36. Kahn, "Interpretation and Authority in State Constitutionalism."

stead to build its analysis independently from first-order materials. Even if it pretends that pertinent Supreme Court rulings do not exist, however, a state court's resolution under a duplicative rights provision of a question that has already been decided under a cognate provision of the U.S. Constitution will inevitably serve as a judgment on the counterpart federal ruling: the state court will, implicitly, be agreeing or disagreeing with the U.S. Supreme Court on a subject of shared concern and responsibility. Moreover, there is something to be said for the proposition that state courts do not fully live up to their obligations when they refuse to assess corresponding federal rulings; one of their obligations as agents in a dual-agent system is to monitor the performance of the other agent so that their principal may evaluate its performance. If, as Madison and Hamilton claimed,[37] federalism institutionalizes a competition between the state and national governments for the people's confidence, pointing out the other government's failures is part of what government officials at all levels ought to do.

As I have previously suggested, most state courts already go about the business of interpreting duplicative rights provisions by using Supreme Court rulings as a point of reference and deciding whether they agree with the high court's resolution of the issue. For this they have been routinely, and in some cases viciously, criticized. This criticism is without merit. Duplicative rights provisions openly invite state courts to engage in precisely this behavior, and in taking up this invitation state courts fulfill their role in the federal system.

"Unique" rights provisions. Many state constitutions contain individual rights provisions that have no direct counterpart in the U.S. Constitution. The most widespread and notable of these is the right to a public education, but there are many others. For example, several state constitutions contain provisions expressly protecting a right to "privacy," a word that appears nowhere in the U.S. Constitution. Some state constitutions contain environmental provisions, couched in the language of individual rights, that protect "the right to clean air and water,"[38] or the "right to a clean and healthful environment."[39] Others contain open courts provisions that grant a right to a judicial hearing; some provide a right to bail in criminal cases.[40] A few even contain social wel-

---

37. Madison, *The Federalist,* Nos. 28 (Hamilton), 46 (Madison), 51 (Madison).
38. Mass. Const. amend. XCVII.
39. Haw. Const. art. XI, § 9.
40. For an overview of such rights, see Williams, *State Constitutional Law,* ch. 6.

fare rights, such as the New York Constitution, which provides: "The aid, care and support of the needy are public concerns and shall be provided by the state and by such of its subdivisions, and in such manner and by such means, as the legislature may from time to time determine."[41]

Adherents of the New Judicial Federalism typically treat these kinds of provisions as self-evidently offering the strongest possible case for an adjudicatory approach that is completely independent of federal decisional law. If the U.S. Constitution does not contain a similar provision, they argue, there is simply no possibility that federal constitutional law can be relevant to, much less shed any significant light on, the meaning of the state provision. As Justice Hans Linde of the Oregon Supreme Court wrote, when a state constitutional provision "do[es] not repeat clauses in the Federal Constitution, . . . [s]tate courts and counsel cannot escape facing the issue of what that term means."[42] They cannot, that is to say, simply look to U.S. Supreme Court decisional law to resolve the issue.

While I agree that "unique" state constitutional rights provisions—those that lack obvious national counterparts—are less amenable than are duplicative rights provisions to an analysis that includes consideration of federalism effects, the argument for complete independence from national constitutional law is significantly overstated. In fact, under the functional approach, unique state constitutional rights provisions raise at least two kinds of issues that might implicate the function of state courts as agents of federalism. First, just because the U.S. Constitution lacks text dealing explicitly with a subject does not mean that the document has nothing to say about it. The national Constitution does not mention the word "privacy," yet a constitutionally protected right to privacy inferred from the Due Process Clause has become one of the most powerful and far-reaching aspects of federal constitutional rights jurisprudence, serving as the basis for decisions recognizing individual rights to contraception, abortion, and gay sexuality, among others. In this situation, a state court might well conclude that the most logical way to treat a state constitutional provision expressly protecting a right to privacy is to treat it more like a duplicative rights provision than a unique one.

Several state courts have seemingly moved in this direction. For example, the privacy provision of the Florida Constitution provides: "Every natural person has the right to be let alone and free from governmental intrusion into his

41. N.Y. Const. art. XVII, § 1.
42. Linde, "First Things First," 391.

private life."[43] Despite this textual independence, in a line of abortion rights cases the Florida Supreme Court has regularly used U.S. Supreme Court case law as the point of reference for its analysis, enlisting the text to support its rejection of the Court's due process jurisprudence of privacy.[44] Indeed, it has long been noted that the right to an abortion fits rather badly within the conceptual framework of a privacy right—as then-Justice Rehnquist observed in his dissent in *Roe v. Wade,* little about an abortion is truly private—and that the right to an abortion is probably much more usefully conceived as derivative of some kind of right of sexual or personal autonomy. The fact that the Florida Supreme Court would assume that abortion issues fall within the domain of the state constitution's privacy provision is testament to the degree to which that court conceived its function to be one of responding to federal constitutional jurisprudence.

While the case for the relevance of national constitutional law is perhaps strongest with state privacy provisions, very similar arguments may be made for other state individual rights that are purportedly unique. The U.S. Constitution, for example, does not mention education any more than it mentions privacy. Granted, the Constitution is not now understood to recognize an individual right to education—but that is only because the U.S. Supreme Court in 1973 decided, by a six-to-three vote, that no such right fairly could be inferred.[45] It is well within the province of a state court monitoring the way the national government protects personal liberty to disagree with that decision. The U.S. Constitution likewise contains no express social welfare provisions, yet the Supreme Court has decided several cases prohibiting certain kinds of discrimination against the poor,[46] and it was not so very long ago that scholars debated seriously whether the national Constitution might reasonably be construed to contain an affirmative right to minimal sustenance.[47] For these reasons, it goes too far to say that state judicial decisions under provisions of

43. Fla. Const. art. I, § 23.

44. In re T.W., 551 So. 2d 1186 (Fla. 1989); North Florida Women's Health and Counseling Servs., Inc. v. Florida, 2003 Fla. Lexis 1160 (Fla. July 10, 2003).

45. San Antonio Indep. Sch. Dist. v. Rodriguez, 411 U.S. 1 (1973).

46. Griffin v. Illinois, 351 U.S. 12 (1956) (state must provide trial transcripts to indigent appellants); Douglas v. California, 372 U.S. 353 (1963) (state must provide counsel to indigents appealing criminal convictions); Harper v. Virginia Bd. of Elections, 383 U.S. 663 (1966) (invalidating state poll taxes).

47. E.g., Michelman, "Foreword: On Protecting the Poor through the Fourteenth Amendment"; Bork, "The Impossibility of Finding Welfare Rights in the Constitution."

the state constitution that have no express textual counterpart in the U.S. Constitution bear no relationship whatever to the content of national constitutional law.

Under the functional approach, there is also a second way in which purportedly unique state constitutional rights provisions may implicate the state judiciary's function as an agent of federalism—under the theory of second-best rights set out in chapter 3. I argued there that one way in which state courts may resist what they believe to be abusively constrictive interpretations by the U.S. Supreme Court of rights guaranteed under the national Constitution is to provide protection under the state constitution for some kind of second-best liberty as a way to ameliorate the harms to primary liberties inflicted at the national level. Unique rights provisions might conceivably serve as useful vehicles for carrying out such a strategy. In other words, abusive national rulings under textually unrelated provisions of the U.S. Constitution might provide a state court with justifications for construing broadly a unique and thus quite different provision of the state constitution.

Having now argued against the overstated view that unique state constitutional rights provisions must by hypothesis be understood to be wholly unrelated to national protections of liberty contained in the U.S. Constitution, I do not wish to go so far in the opposite direction as to overstate my own position by suggesting that these connections should in any way dominate the analysis. Express constitutional language must be given its due, as must any kind of idiosyncratic state history or founders' intentions. Attention must be paid to the possibility that a unique rights provision might embody a deliberate and self-conscious popular embrace or rejection of a particular national constitutional norm, or that the specificity of a unique rights provision might be sufficient to rebut the presumption of judicial federalism agency. In this varied stew of factors, the federalism effect of a court's rulings amounts to only one consideration among many.

Structural Features

As I have already indicated, the functional approach has its most direct and powerful application to the interpretation of state constitutional rights provisions. In that setting, state courts may serve most directly as agents of federalism, using the powers available to them to resist as directly as possible what they take to be abuses of national power. Nevertheless, the functional approach also has implications for the interpretation of structural features of state constitutions.

Here, state courts are more often limited to resisting national power indirectly because their rulings will most likely extend no further than influencing the ability of other organs of state government to engage in such resistance.

Parallel structural features. State constitutions routinely duplicate not only rights provisions of the U.S. Constitution, but many of its structural features as well. Every state constitution, for example, divides the power of government into three branches: legislative, executive, and judicial. Every state but one has a bicameral legislature. Where the U.S. Constitution provides that "[t]he executive Power shall be vested in a President,"[48] state constitutions often provide that the "executive power,"[49] or the "supreme executive power,"[50] "shall be vested in" a "governor." Do these kinds of similarities, like duplicative rights provisions, invite state courts to monitor national judicial rulings when adjudicating issues of separation of powers under the state constitution? State courts often act as though they do. As with identical rights provisions, state courts construing structural features frequently rely on rulings of the U.S. Supreme Court construing equivalent features of the national Constitution. Indeed, state courts sometimes seem to go further, at times ignoring obvious differences between state and national structural provisions and treating the two regimes nevertheless as sufficiently alike to justify importation of national principles and doctrines into the state's constitutional jurisprudence of structure.[51] The functional approach suggests that deliberate state mimicry of national structural provisions, as with rights provisions, does invite state judicial monitoring of pertinent national law, but the inference is considerably weaker. Here, the monitoring function must, to a far greater degree than with duplicative individual rights provisions, share attention with other important functions that state courts must perform when construing the state constitution.

Unlike identical rights provisions, structural provisions of state constitutions may imitate their counterparts in the national Constitution, but they cannot duplicate them. This is because there is no national constitutional principle of structure that affects states in the same way as the incorporation

48. U.S. Const. art. II, § 1.

49. E.g., Md. Const. art. II, § 1; Wis. Const. art. V, § 1.

50. E.g., Cal. Const. art. V, § 1.

51. See Gardner, "The Positivist Revolution That Wasn't," 110–17; Schapiro, "Contingency and Universalism in State Separation of Powers Discourse," 87–96.

doctrine; that is to say, the U.S. Constitution imposes no significant structural requirements on state constitutions.[52] As a result, it is much less correct than in the case of individual rights to characterize the horizontal separation of government power as an area in which the state and national governments are given overlapping authority to police the same turf. In fact, the two areas are largely distinct because the constitutional structuring of government power is concerned mainly with internal self-restraint—that is, with preventing a government from threatening its own citizens—rather than with enabling it to protect its citizens from external threats. This suggests that the interpretation of state constitutional provisions allocating and structuring the power of state officials will be concerned primarily with the internal balance of power among the branches of state government rather than with external issues of the way national power bears on either the state government or the people of the state, and that authority to act as an agent of federalism will thus have relatively little bearing on the way a state court approaches these kinds of provisions.

Nevertheless, structural issues concerning the allocation of powers are not wholly unrelated to questions of federalism that might fall within the purview of courts exercising authority to act as agents of federalism: in fact, the horizontal allocation of power *within* each level of government can affect the balance of power *between* them.[53] This relationship might prove of interest to state courts in at least two respects. First, the distribution of power on the national level, under the national Constitution, is potentially relevant to state courts attempting to police the proper distribution of state and national power. On the Madisonian model, the constitutional division of governmental powers, as well as the continued adherence to constitutionally established boundaries, affects the power of the government in question: the more divided and balanced the powers of a government, the less powerful it is and the less of a threat it poses to the public.[54] A national government whose powers become unduly concentrated through breaches of the separation of powers may become excessively powerful, thereby upsetting the appropriate balance of state and national power. Because state courts authorized to act as agents of federalism are

52. "[T]he concept of separation of powers embodied in the United States Constitution is not mandatory in state governments." Sweezy v. New Hampshire, 354 U.S. 234, 255 (1957).

53. See Rossi, "Institutional Design and the Lingering Legacy," 1188.

54. Madison, *The Federalist*, No. 47.

charged with detecting and if possible counteracting abuses of national power, state courts may very well have an interest in monitoring and responding to federal judicial rulings affecting the allocation of power among national officials under the national Constitution. Second, the structural allocation of power under the state constitution is also indirectly relevant to the balance of state and national power created by federalism; this is so because the internal allocation of state power affects both the powers of the various state officials individually, as well as the ability of the state government as a whole to act. As we saw in chapter 6, these aspects of state power have ramifications for the capacity of the state effectively to resist abuses of national power.

These considerations have implications for the interpretation of state constitutional structural provisions or institutions that imitate those found in the U.S. Constitution. If the people of a state deliberately adopt a structure of state government modeled on the structure created for the national government by the national Constitution, we are entitled, as with rights provisions, to assume that they have done so because they like the national model, think it a good one, and want the powers of state government officials to be distributed in much the same way as they are on the national level. Because state courts have federalism-based reasons to monitor the distribution of powers on the national level, it is thus permissible for state courts construing such features of the state constitution, whether contained in express provisions or implied from structural arrangements, to refer to or rely on federal judicial rulings interpreting parallel structural features of the national Constitution, and even to use the occasion to express approval or disapproval of the way the U.S. Supreme Court has resolved such questions as a matter of national constitutional law. Furthermore, in analyzing such features of the state constitution, state courts may also take into consideration the extent to which different ways of allocating power among state officials might affect the ability of those officials to respond expeditiously and effectively to potential abuses of national power.

Normally, however, these federalism-related considerations would be expected to play a comparatively minor role in state judicial analysis of structural features of state constitutions. A much more important consideration is likely to be the way in which structural provisions of the state constitution work to produce an appropriate balance of power internally, among state officials, for the purpose of best protecting the state citizenry from those officials rather than from their national counterparts. Consequently, state courts would probably need to devote careful attention, when construing structural provisions, to state-specific considerations of text and history, even when the provisions are in some respects identical to parallel features of the U.S. Constitution. Here, then, although reliance on federal constitutional rulings may not itself reveal a problem, an excessive or indiscriminate reliance on federal rulings might be inappropriate.

"Unique" structural features. Although most state constitutions, especially the more recent ones, replicate many of the most important structural features of the U.S. Constitution, one of the notable characteristics of state constitutions as a group is the degree to which they depart structurally from the national model. Unlike the national Constitution, for example, most state constitutions do not establish a unitary executive branch under the head of a chief executive, but rather establish a plural executive branch consisting of several independent power centers. Typically, this is accomplished by creating separately elected officials such as an attorney general, comptroller, secretary of state, and sometimes many others. The powers of these officials are then defined, and sometimes subjected to specific limitations. Few of these provisions might plausibly be thought to have counterparts in the national Constitution. State constitutions also often impose procedural restrictions on constitutional officers, and these restrictions can sometimes affect the relations between the branches of state government in ways that have no real counterpart under the U.S. Constitution. For example, limitations on the frequency and duration of legislative sessions, or specifications concerning the process by which legislation is enacted, can create a dynamic of interbranch relations that differs from the national model.

Because of these differences, the functional approach has a correspondingly attenuated relevance to the construction of unique structural features of state constitutions. In particular, there is much less reason to think that the responsibility of state courts to monitor relevant uses of national power would be much implicated in the review of such provisions. While the establishment in the state constitution of governmental power arrangements that differ from those found in the U.S. Constitution may well constitute evidence of state-level rejection of certain aspects of the national model, that rejection has occurred at the popular level by constitutional directive, suggesting that the judicial role may be more circumscribed than it is when state polities deliberately incorporate aspects of the national model. Accordingly, the interpretation of unique structural provisions may offer state courts few opportunities to provide an independent evaluation of structural developments occurring on the national level.

On the other hand, state constitutional provisions dealing with the powers of and relations among state officials still bear some relevance to questions concerning the capacity of state actors to respond in ways contemplated by the federal system to threats posed by the national government. Consequently, while the interpretation of such provisions might be expected to focus on state-specific materials such as the state constitutional text, founding history, intentions of the framers, and broad constitutional principles of internal self-government and self-restraint, there is still a place in the analysis for consideration of the effects these provisions might have on the ability of state officials to act quickly and effectively to resist abuses of national power. Such considerations might rarely be conclusive; perhaps they would most often serve as a tie-breaker when other factors point in conflicting directions.

Old Provisions

Federalism does not define an eternal, unchanging relationship between the state and national governments. Although the principle of mutually checking state and national power remains constant, the way in which the state and national governments implement their checking functions evolves constantly as circumstances change, and as the corresponding moves and countermoves of each constitutional actor emerge. Federalism is thus more than merely a relationship: it is a process that unfolds in time.

By the same token, state constitutions, because they are instruments that in significant respects order the means by which the federal process plays itself out, are also instruments that exist in time. This is especially true given that state constitutions, as indicated earlier, generally offer greater institutional flexibility than the U.S. Constitution, and are thus more likely than the national document to undergo periodic adjustment for the purpose of responding to some immediate contingency affecting the balance of state and national power. In consequence, state constitutions may for some purposes plausibly be understood to contain a kind of record of adjustments made to state power in response to a series of events occurring over time in the federal environment. Reading a state constitution may thus be something akin to reading a set of tree rings or a geological core sample of sedimentary layers; the story of intergovernmental relations is revealed not so much in their immediate orientation as in the entire series of events recorded in the document.

This conception of state constitutions is relevant to state constitutional interpretation in at least two ways. First, there is little reason to suppose that state constitutions cohere internally to the same degree as the national Constitution.[55] In construing the national document, courts typically try to read its provisions *in pari materia*—as though each provision fit logically into a coherent whole. This may be a hopeless task in the interpretation of all but the most recently adopted state constitutions. Second, it suggests that provisions of the state constitution might well become obsolete as time passes and circumstances change. Provisions adopted to adjust state power so as to rectify particular, historically contingent imbalances in the federal system may serve little useful purpose as conditions evolve, the system readjusts, and other imbalances emerge elsewhere.

In light of the temporal aspect of state–federal conflict and the process of predictable obsolescence it entails, state courts authorized to act as agents of federalism might usefully be thought to possess implicit authority to consider the age and original enacting context of those provisions of the state constitution that order the external deployment of state power in the service of federalism, and to give less effect to provisions that time and changed circumstances have made obsolete. While constructing a complete theory of temporality in state constitutional interpretation is well beyond the scope of the present work, it is possible to say this much. First, under any view of the subject, newer provisions should be treated whenever possible as expressing a timely and contextually appropriate popular response to a particular problem, and should thus in general be construed as embodying specific instructions to constitutional agents that an otherwise broad grant of discretion does not permit them to ignore. Second, as provisions age, their relevance to the present circumstances of state–national relation wanes, and they can presumptively be applied more flexibly,[56] meaning that they should be construed in a way that best helps to maintain an appropriate balance between state and national power in the here and now, under presently prevailing conditions. Finally, it must be stressed that this updating authority is limited in scope, and would not apply to every provision of the state constitution. As with any application of the functional approach to the actual interpretation of state constitutions,

---

55. Tarr, *Understanding State Constitutions*, 193.

56. For parallel arguments concerning the judicial treatment of statutes, see Calabresi, *A Common Law for the Age of Statutes*; Eskridge, "Spinning Legislative Supremacy."

this one would involve only those provisions that have some bearing on the external deployment of state power, and which thus implicate the capacity of state government to protect popular welfare by resisting abuses of national power. Those provisions dealing solely with the achievement of good internal self-government or the internal restraint of state power would be unsuitable candidates for this kind of interpretational approach.

OBJECTIONS TO THE FUNCTIONAL APPROACH

Having described the functional theory of state constitutions and some practical means of implementing it, I conclude by discussing briefly some potential objections.

Politicization of Judicial Elections

One possible objection is that the functional approach would contribute to an unhealthy politicization of state judicial electoral processes by encouraging judges to take campaign positions on federal judicial rulings and other actions by national officials. The worst case scenario, one might suppose, is the judicial candidate who announces: "The U.S. Supreme Court (or Congress, or the president) has shown nothing but contempt for the treasured liberties of the American people. If elected, I will do everything in my power to thwart the evil designs of these horrible tyrants."

Until recently, ethical codes of judicial conduct tended to prohibit judges from running overtly ideological campaigns. In 2002, however, the Supreme Court decided *Republican Party v. White*,[57] in which the Court invalidated on free speech grounds certain kinds of commonplace substantive ethical restrictions on what judges may say during political campaigns. After *White*, the kind of campaign statement imagined above would probably no longer be subject to restriction. Nevertheless, the fact that judges are free to campaign in this way does not by itself make it likely that they will do so. For such campaigning to materialize, judicial candidates must believe that criticizing national actions and officials will give them some political traction, a condition that will arise only if national actions are in fact politically salient to, and unpopular with, likely voters in judicial elections. Surely this will not happen

57. 536 U.S. 765 (2002).

very often, especially in these days of governance by public opinion poll, when the federal government rarely does anything that does not command the broad (if often shallow) approval of the general public.

If, on the other hand, popular dissatisfaction with national officials and policies actually does run high enough to make federal actions potentially salient issues in campaigns for state judicial office, it is hard to see what would be so bad about candidate discussions of these issues. If the architecture of the federal system gives state officials a legitimate role in resisting abuses of national power, and if a state polity decides, by adopting a system of judicial elections, that it wants judges to be democratically responsive to public sentiment, there is no sound basis for thinking that issues concerning the performance of national officials are any less appropriate for judicial campaigning than the more traditional, state-focused issues.

Even were candidates for judicial office inclined to campaign hard on these issues, they would still have strong incentives to be moderate in their public statements and positions. A long tradition of restraint in judicial campaigning probably counsels prudence, and excessively politicized campaigning might well devalue the judicial office itself by diminishing its dignity, giving candidates an interest in moderating their own rhetoric. Finally, nothing in the *White* decision prohibits state codes of judicial conduct from barring the most egregiously unethical types of judicial campaign behavior, such as making explicit promises to decide specific cases in particular ways.

The real problem, it seems to me, would not be that some judges might choose to campaign for office by running against Washington, but rather that running against Washington might come to dominate state judicial campaigns. This would certainly be an unhealthy development, but it seems extremely unlikely. Judicial elections are, without doubt, becoming increasingly politicized. More and more money is being poured into judicial elections each year,[58] and elected judges are increasingly being targeted for defeat by interest groups who oppose their decisions on substantive grounds.[59] But these problems are endemic to state electoral processes, and are of such a magnitude that it seems unlikely that a mere change in the public methodological commitments of state judges could have any significant impact on the trend. Moreover, state constitutional decisionmaking could only become a significant political issue in state judicial elections if the state's citizenry started to care about how it is

58. Goldberg and Holman, *The New Politics of Judicial Elections.*
59. See Environmental Policy Project, *Changing the Rules by Changing the Players.*

conducted; and if people cared that much about the issue, it is hard to see why it shouldn't be a subject of public political debate.

Undermining Respect for Law and Courts

Another possible objection to the functional approach is that it might undermine public respect for law and for courts by reinforcing the view that judicial decisionmaking is basically a matter of politics rather than fidelity to law. I think this extremely unlikely. It is true, in the abstract, that result-oriented judicial decisionmaking is capable of creating the impression that judges decide cases simply on the basis of their personal preferences. Under the functional approach, however, judges are not authorized simply to decide constitutional cases to achieve the results they prefer, but to use instrumental methods only in very limited circumstances. Specifically, the functional approach authorizes result-oriented decisionmaking mainly in two situations: (1) when a state court wishes to disagree with or undermine decisions by federal courts that it believes to be incorrect as a matter of substantive national law; and (2) to facilitate resistance by other branches of state government to exercises of national power that the state court considers abusive.

State constitutional decisionmaking in pursuit of the first objective is unlikely to diminish respect for law precisely because it is undertaken in pursuit of fidelity to law; the justification for this method of decisionmaking is the idea that federal courts have an obligation to get the U.S. Constitution right, and that state courts have a role to play in leading federal courts toward the truth. To be sure, the functional approach contemplates a system of constitutional decisionmaking in which intergovernmental disagreements about the meaning of constitutional law are made public. But if public disagreement among government officials is sufficient to undermine respect for law, we are doomed anyway, since judges routinely disagree with officials of other branches, officials of other levels of government, and with one another. What, after all, is a judicial dissent but a publicized disagreement over the meaning of the law?

Given that public disagreement is already commonplace, the real threat to public respect for law and courts arises not when officials publicly disagree with one another over the meaning of the law, but when that disagreement issues in frequent changes in the content of publicly enforceable legal principles. The problem, in other words, is not a lack of agreement on the meaning of a constitution, which will always be contested, but a lack of finality or stability in its official meaning. Yet nothing about the functional approach disturbs the finality of the official meanings given to the state or national constitutions: the U.S. Supreme Court still has the final say on the meaning of the national Constitution, and each state supreme court remains the final arbiter of the meaning of its own constitution.

The problem of instability is implicated to some degree, however, in the second situation—when state courts construe the state constitution with the goal of facilitating resistance to abuses of national power by other branches of state government. Here, a result-oriented approach to the state constitution might sometimes lead to a change in the controlling legal rule, possibly contributing to the impression in the public mind that the meaning of the state constitution changes in step with the views of a majority of the state supreme court. The question, then, is whether any such erosion in public confidence would be significant. I think it would not be, mainly because the legitimate uses of result-oriented decisionmaking methods under the functional approach are so highly constrained.

As indicated earlier in this chapter, a state polity may always decide to withhold altogether from its courts the authority to act as agents of federalism. It may exercise this option across the board or with respect to particular constitutional provisions. Furthermore, the inference in favor of the authority to act as an agent of federalism is weakest for provisions that are highly specific or very new—those provision, in other words, as to which the polity has most clearly expressed its wish to settle for itself, without judicial modification, a course of constitutional conduct. Consequently, courts may engage in the kind of judicial decisionmaking that might most undermine public confidence in law only in those circumstances where it is least likely to have that effect—when the people have authorized it, when they have not themselves issued express limiting directions, and when older, obsolete provisions have been overtaken by circumstances. Any result-oriented decisionmaking of this type would in any event occur against a background understanding of state courts as more actively engaged in state-level governance than are federal courts, thus further dampening any adverse ramifications in the public mind. In short, the risk to public confidence seems slight.

Giving State Courts Too Much Influence

A final possible objection to the functional approach is that it might give state courts more influence over constitutional norms than they ought to have, to the point where everyone's liberties might be adversely affected. State courts, that is, might use their authority to chip away at essential guaranteed rights, resulting in a general erosion rather than enhancement of constitutional protections. Although there is no question that such a risk exists, it provides no sound basis for objecting to the functional approach.

To admit the possibility that state courts might use their authority to expand individual rights requires us equally to admit the possibility that those same courts might also seek their contraction. The idea that states officials, including judges, might use their powers to resist what they in their discretion believe to be abuses of national authority is ideologically neutral. Federalism itself implies no position on whether rights should be expanded or contracted; it is a mechanism, nothing more, and like any mechanism it may be used for ends that fall anywhere along the ideological spectrum. The theory of federalism contemplates, moreover, that governmental actors will respond to the sentiments of the polities they represent, and it is thus no objection to a well-functioning system of federalism that it responds faithfully to public opinion of a particular ideological coloration. A more serious objection is that federalism contains an inherent ideological bias in which national power inevitably favors the achievement of ends preferred by contemporary political liberalism, and state power inevitably favors the achievement of ends that in a contemporary political context would be characterized as conservative. Such a view finds little support in the historical record of intergovernmental judicial relations described in chapter 6, or in the records of the U.S. Supreme Court and state courts in the protection of individual rights over the last quarter-century.

Giving states a clearer voice in the protection of liberty, moreover, is not the same as giving them an exclusive or even dominant voice. Federal courts will still exist, as they always have, to play the role of backstop defenders of the public good. Should state courts become captured by factions, say, and use their authority to press vociferously for a contraction of constitutional liberties that Americans legitimately possess, nothing prevents federal courts from engaging in their own form of resistance by stubbornly refusing to budge. The U.S. Supreme Court may always decline, as it has many times in the past, to bow to majoritarian public sentiment in the protection of important constitutional liberties.

The final difficulty with this objection to the functional approach is that it is based on a misperception of the relation between governmental processes and political ideology. In the long run, changes in national political ideology are inevitable, regardless of how state or national courts choose to exercise their authority. Judicial decisionmaking on the national and state levels inevitably takes place against a backdrop of contingent public political understandings established in and by national political processes. So long as basic democratic freedoms are observed, political ideologies cannot be frozen by adhering to one governmental process over another; the expression in public policy of ideological change may sometimes be delayed by procedural commitments, but it can never be indefinitely prevented. Political liberals thus cannot hope to maintain—or rather recover—the era of the Warren Court merely by insisting on the continued dominance of national judicial power; changes in public opinion are inevitably reflected in the rulings of a hegemonic national judiciary, just as they are in the actions of state judiciaries, regardless of whether state courts are largely subordinate to national power or institutional players of greater stature.

If public ideological change inevitably affects the ways in which courts exercise judicial power, then the functional approach at least has the advantage of institutionalizing the process and, in so doing, making it more transparent. The functional approach, in other words, takes the process by which constitutional norms are contested and shaped out of the chambers of U.S. Supreme Court justices and places it squarely into the pages of state and national judicial opinions. There, the ways in which public political norms are translated into exercises of judicial power can be seen and evaluated, allowing those affected more directly and openly to participate in the process. The functional approach also contemplates a process of evolution in constitutional norms that is attractively pluralistic by allowing it to occur in many forums, where more voices may be heard. Surely those who are made nervous by the idea of an active state judiciary cannot reasonably hold out for more than a fair opportunity to advance their views in a wide variety of different, and competing, judicial forums.

Function and Interpretation

IN LAW AS IN LIFE, how we talk depends upon what we do. We talk, that is to say, in ways that are useful to us, that help us accomplish our purposes. Scratch a person who is confused about what to say, and you will usually find a person who is confused about what to do.

Constitutional jurisprudence is a way of talking about a highly significant social and political activity—the practice of collective self-government in certain kinds of modern societies. American constitutional jurisprudence has long been a deeply contested battleground, not only because the stakes are high, but because so many people disagree so strongly about how we ought to govern ourselves. As the national government has taken on more and more functions and responsibilities, the significance of national constitutional law to the way we live our lives, and the corresponding intensity of the debate surrounding the document, have increased. People today seek to talk about the U.S. Constitution in many different ways, but the way they do so often depends upon their conception of the order they believe the Constitution ought to impose on American life. If people find themselves confused about how to talk about the national Constitution, it is often because they are confused about which side they should embrace in the political contests that so deeply inform national constitutional discourse.

My sense is that things stand somewhat differently where state and other subnational constitutions are concerned. Contestation creates its own kind of confusion, but people seem to be confused about how to talk about state constitutions in a different and much more fundamental way; the confusion seems to concern the very nature and purpose of the state constitutional enterprise itself. No matter how much they may disagree over the proper way to talk about the U.S. Constitution, few seem to doubt that the battle over national constitutionalism is in some sense a battle over the structure and ordering of collective American life. When it comes to state constitutions, however, no such consensus exists. Many people, even judges and lawyers who deal with state constitutions routinely in their professional lives, seem unsure of their subject when speaking about such documents. What is it that state constitutions actually do? What functions do they serve? What, at bottom, is a state constitution? Only when we have answered these more basic questions will we be able to say with any confidence, or even to argue meaningfully over, how we ought to talk about—to interpret—these documents.

For this reason, my goal in this book is to approach what appears to be the more immediate and pressing question of how state constitutions ought to be interpreted by addressing instead the background question to which it refers: what is the function of a state constitution? My analysis thus focuses on what it is we do when we engage in self-government, not collectively as a nation, but within our respective subnational units. This inquiry into function yields an interpretive payoff because, to a considerable extent, interpretation follows function. A constitution that serves as a truly constitutive statement of collective self-definition must be interpreted differently from one that serves as, say, a *modus vivendi* among self-consciously independent sovereign groups, which must itself be interpreted differently from one that serves as the blueprint for exercising power delegated by a commonly recognized central authority, and so on.

Such an approach is admissible, however, only if we reject the tyranny of nomenclature; we must, that is to say, admit the possibility that the word "constitution" might mean different things in different times and places. This is especially important in the American case, since part of the insidious genius of the American scheme of federalism is that its design constantly destabilizes, and thus throws continually into doubt, exactly what function is served, at any given time, by the various constitutional documents that frame and expound it. Federalism describes a governmental system neither wholly centralized, like a unitary nation, nor wholly decentralized, like a true league or confederation. Instead it circumscribes a shadowy terrain between these two extremes where central and peripheral power remain in rough but constantly shifting balance.

It is possible that in our constitutional universe, which is still in many respects the product of an eighteenth-century age of nation-states, there is some kind of immutable law of "constitutional conservation" that decrees that in every polity inheres a fixed amount of "constitutionalness" that can never be diminished, but can only be redistributed from one constitutional object to another. If there is such a law, however, the American system of federalism creates a structure in which that ineffable constitutionalness is continually, if unpredictably, redistributing itself between the national and state governments and their respective constitutional documents. And if the essence of a constitution's constitutionality is in constant flux, then we must abandon the idea of some set of interpretational conventions comprising "the" standard and universal conventions of constitutional interpretation in favor of a conception of constitutional interpretation that is more modest, more local, and more contingent. A jurisprudence of function may not represent the culmination of this effort, but it does, I hope, take us a step or two in the right direction.

Below is a hypothetical opinion by an imaginary state supreme court illustrating how a court might actually apply the approach to state constitutional interpretation described in chapter 7. Any similarity to an actual state constitution or state court ruling is most assuredly coincidental.

SUPREME COURT OF THE STATE OF COLUMBIANA

State v. Russell
No. 03-015

GRANT, C.J.:

Michael Russell was convicted of the brutal murder of Elsie Granger. The District Attorney for Martin County sought and obtained a sentence of death. On this appeal, Russell seeks invalidation of his sentence on the ground that administration of the death penalty in the State of Columbiana is so tainted by racial discrimination as to violate constitutional principles of equal protection. We agree, and thus temporarily enjoin further enforcement of the death penalty in this State and remand for determination of a new sentence.

I

During the night of April 16, 2001, Michael Russell, an African American male then aged twenty-four, broke into the house of Elsie Granger, a seventy-four-year-old white woman who lived alone. As Russell was searching for valuables, Granger awoke and confronted him. In brutal fashion, which need not be recounted here, Russell murdered and dismembered Granger. He was apprehended shortly thereafter and convicted in June, 2002 of murder. At a subsequent sentencing hearing, he was sentenced to death. The conviction and sentence were affirmed below and procedural issues raised there are not now before us.

Russell now claims that his sentence of death must be reversed because of racial discrimination in the way the State administers the death penalty. Although he does not accuse the District Attorney, any of her staff, the trial judge, or any juror of racial discrimination, he does contend that the penalty is administered systematically throughout the State in a way that discriminates on the basis of race.

Although the evidence presented below is voluminous and complex, and the parties disagree on many of the particulars, there is no dispute as to the broad outlines of the salient facts, which may be simply stated. Since the U.S. Supreme Court permitted states to resume imposition of the death penalty in 1976, Columbiana prosecutors have indicted over two thousand people on murder charges. In a portion of those cases, prosecutors have sought the death penalty. In some cases where prosecutors have sought the death penalty, juries have imposed it. According to Russell, a detailed examination of these cases shows that the frequency with which prosecutors seek the death penalty, and the frequency with which juries impose it, differs according to the race of both the victim and the defendant. Specifically, Russell contends that criminal defendants are more likely to be charged with capital murder when the victim is white than when the victim is black; that black defendants are more likely than white defendants to be charged with capital murder for similar offenses; that juries are more likely to impose a death sentence when the defendant is black; and that prosecutors are most likely to charge and juries to find capital murder when the defendant is black and the victim white. Russell claims that these results occur not through any deliberate, race-conscious manipulation of individual cases for the purpose of harming blacks, but systemically, as the result of a built-in racial bias in the administration of the death penalty.

II

We note at the outset that any claim Russell might make under the Equal Protection Clause of the Fourteenth Amendment of the U.S. Constitution is foreclosed by the U.S. Supreme Court's decision in *McCleskey v. Kemp,* 481 U.S. 279 (1987). There, faced with very similar statistical evidence regarding administration of the death penalty in Georgia, the Court ruled that racial disparity in the imposition of the death penalty cannot by itself amount to unconstitutional racial discrimination because it is not "purposeful." Because the defendant there was unable to "prove that the decisionmakers in *his* case acted with discriminatory purpose," id. at 292, he was unable to make the showing required by the Fourteenth Amendment.

Realizing this, Russell brings his claim instead under the Equal Protection Clause of the Columbiana Constitution, which he contends must be construed to bar the present system of death penalty administration in Columbiana.

A

Article I, § 24 of the Columbiana Constitution provides: "No person shall be denied the equal protection of the laws." This language is, in all relevant respects, identical to the language of the Fourteenth Amendment of the U.S. Constitution. Indeed, all the available evidence suggests that it was copied directly and deliberately from the federal Equal Protection Clause.

The original Columbiana Constitution of 1837 contained no language equivalent to the present Equal Protection Clause, nor did the subsequent Constitutions of 1878 and 1913. The present clause was added by amendment in 1975 as part of a package of amendments submitted to the electorate by a Constitutional Revision Commission convened to review the Columbiana Constitution and propose amendments. All of the amendments recommended by the Revision Commission and approved by the electorate seem to have been modeled on provisions of the U.S. Constitution, raising a strong inference that their purpose was to make the two constitutions more closely alike. We have reviewed the Revision Commission's final report and other documentary materials relating to its deliberations, and can find no evidence to suggest that the Commission thought it was recommending anything other than inclusion within the state constitution of a provision substantially identical to the federal Equal Protection Clause. To the extent it is possible to discern a Commission viewpoint, the Commission appeared to view the omission of an equal protection clause from the Columbiana Constitution as a sort of embarrassing oversight that ought to be corrected.

The State argues that because our Equal Protection Clause was deliberately modeled on the Fourteenth Amendment, it must have the same meaning as the federal provision; in consequence, the State contends, we must follow the Supreme Court's ruling in *McCleskey* and dismiss the appeal. Russell argues, in contrast, that the textual resemblance is only superficial, and that the state clause has a different meaning from its federal counterpart because the term "equal protection of the laws" means something different to the people of Columbiana than it does to the people of the United States. As a result, Russell argues, we must decline to follow *McCleskey* and instead adopt a broader and more generous view of the scope of equal protection under Article I, § 24. We think each party is half right: we agree with the State that Article I, § 24 must be given the same meaning as the federal Equal Protection Clause, but we agree with Russell that we should not follow *McCleskey*.

B

Russell's argument that the term "equal protection of the laws" has a distinctive meaning in Columbiana rests on a thorough, elaborate, and generally quite impressive march through the State's social and political history. Russell's brief touches on the beliefs and social arrangements of the territory's earliest settlers, reviews the writings of some of the State's earliest governors and legislative leaders, and discusses pre–Civil War abolitionist movements within the State, before moving on to review numerous pieces of contemporary legislation, the history of the civil rights movement in Columbiana, and many other kinds of information. From this account, Russell infers that Columbianans hold a substantially broader and more generous view of racial equality than do Americans generally, that Article I, § 24 embodies that view, and that in consequence the state provision cannot have the same meaning as its federal counterpart.

Ingenious though it is, Russell's account of the State's Equal Protection Clause is beside the point. We find it simply implausible that the people of Columbiana would in 1975 adopt and incorporate into the State constitution a provision copied directly from a century-old federal model unless they intended it to have the same meaning. Although we have no doubt that the historical experience of the people of Columbiana differs somewhat from the experiences of Americans generally, we cannot accept the proposition that these differences are so profound as to cause the people of the State and Nation to use the same words to signify materially different legal concepts. We therefore hold that Article I, § 24 has the same meaning as the Equal Protection Clause of the Fourteenth Amendment to the U.S. Constitution.

The critical question for resolution, then, is: what follows from this conclusion? In addressing that question, both parties have misunderstood this Court's function in a case such as this.

III

The State argues that if we find Article I, § 24 to have the same meaning as its federal counterpart, then we have no choice but to give it the same meaning here as the U.S. Supreme Court gave it in *McCleskey*. We disagree. This conclusion rests on a false premise: that the meaning of the U.S. Constitution is to be found solely in the rulings of the U.S. Supreme Court. In fact, we have independent authority to interpret the meaning of concepts embedded in the U.S. Constitution. The State points out, correctly, that we are not free to depart from binding Supreme Court rulings in cases to which they apply, but we have already complied with this obligation by rejecting Russell's claim under the Fourteenth Amendment. Here, however, we are engaged in a different enterprise.

The system of federalism established by the U.S. Constitution creates a dynamic structure in which the state and national governments share responsibility for advancing the people's collective welfare. It does so by creating, in James Madison's words, a "double security" in which "[t]he different governments will control each other, at the same time that each will be controlled by itself." *The Federalist*, No. 51 (Madison). Liberty is aggressively protected in the federal system because "the general [national] government will at times stand ready to check the usurpations of the state governments, and these [the states] will have the same disposition towards the general government." *The Federalist*, No. 28 (Hamilton). Federalism thus contemplates not only that the federal government will check abuses by state governments, but that state governments will also monitor and check abuses by the national government. As an organ of state government in a federal system, this Court has a role to play in policing actions taken by the federal government in areas of shared responsibility. The protection of individual rights is clearly such an area.

In light of this structure of the federal system, we read Article I, § 24 differently from the parties. In our view, by expressly incorporating into the Columbiana Constitution an Equal Protection Clause that is in all respects identical to its Fourteenth Amendment counterpart, the people of this State have charged us with the responsibility to do whatever is in our power to protect their entitlement to equal protection of the laws. While we have no authority to disregard, modify, or reverse applications of equal protection by the U.S. Supreme Court under the Fourteenth Amendment, and thus cannot ultimately protect the people's right to equal protection from incursions by the national government, we do have independent and unreviewable authority to see that the people's right to equal protection receives all due and appropriate protection from organs of the State. In our view, then, far from requiring us to follow U.S. Supreme Court interpretations of the Fourteenth Amendment, as the State contends, the identity of meaning between Article I, § 24 and the federal Clause requires us to do just the opposite: to construe the shared principle of equal protection in the way we think best calculated to effectuate the guarantee, and to do so in a way that is most true to the constitutional goals and aspirations of all Americans.

IV

In our view, Article I, § 24 requires us to set aside Russell's death sentence as unconstitutionally tainted by systemic racial discrimination in the administration of the death penalty. To the extent the Supreme Court thought equal protection to require something less, we think it erred tragically.

The most fundamental purpose of the original Equal Protection Clause was to prohibit all forms of invidious racial discrimination, a purpose that has been carried forward and embraced by our State in Article I, § 24 of the Columbiana Constitution. In *McCleskey,* the Supreme Court held that a criminal defendant challenging even the most blatantly disparate racial impact of a state's death penalty is required to produce evidence showing that he himself has been the victim of deliberate racial discrimination, either in his selection by the prosecutor for a death penalty charge, or in his sentencing by the jury. This is of course an impossible burden to meet, as overt racial discrimination will rarely be found in such decisions. Indeed, no individual prosecutor or juror will ever be in a position to formulate an intent to bias the statewide administration of the death penalty since such individuals are capable of influencing the direction of only a tiny number of cases. Russell's point is a different one: he argues that the systemic bias of the system, a bias that is revealed only through statistical evidence over many cases, shows self-evidently that prosecutors and jurors approach capital cases with an *unconscious* racial bias. The only alternative explanation, which the State does not even bother to advance, is that blacks routinely commit more heinous murders than whites, thereby justifying the racially differential treatment. Needless to say, no credible evidence supports such a possibility.

We think Justice Blackmun, in his dissent in *McCleskey,* far better captured the appropriate equal protection analysis: "absent evidence to the contrary, one must conclude that racial factors entered into the decisionmaking process that yielded McCleskey's death sentence." 481 U.S. at 359. McCleskey, Justice Blackmun explained, "demonstrated a clear pattern of differential treatment according to race that is 'unexplainable on grounds other than race.'" Id. at 361, quoting *Arlington Heights v. Metropolitan Housing Development Corp.,* 429 U.S. 252, 266 (1977).

The State argues that to reject *McCleskey* is to embrace a disparate impact cause of action under Article I, § 24 when the Supreme Court has held that disparate treatment, not merely disparate impact, must be shown to make out an equal protection violation. *Washington v. Davis,* 426 U.S. 229 (1976). To do so, the State claims, would mark a break with nearly universally recognized American principles of equal protection, and would thus exceed any mandate this Court might have to determine jointly with federal courts the meaning of equal protection. We find it unnecessary to address this contention. Today, we need not decide whether the Columbiana death penalty may be invalidated because of its disparate racial impact alone, or because that disparate impact provides sufficient evidence of purposeful discrimination somewhere within the system as to satisfy a disparate treatment standard. It is necessary only to say that Russell has shown that the State's administration of the death penalty is unacceptably tainted by racial considerations, and cannot stand.

Reversed. The case is remanded for further proceedings consistent with this opinion.

Abrahamson, Shirley. "Criminal Law and State Constitutions: The Emergence of State Constitutional Law." *Texas Law Review* 63 (1985): 1141–93.

———. "Reincarnation of State Courts." *Southwestern Law Journal* 36 (1982): 951–74.

Ackerman, Bruce. *We the People: Foundations* (vol. 1). Cambridge: Harvard University Press, 1991.

Adrian, Charles R. "Trends in State Constitutions." *Harvard Journal on Legislation* 5 (1968): 311–41.

Advisory Commission on Intergovernmental Relations. *Changing Public Attitudes on Governments and Taxes*. Washington, D.C., 1991.

Amar, Akhil Reed. "Of Sovereignty and Federalism." *Yale Law Journal* 96 (1987): 1425–1520.

———. "Some New World Lessons for the Old World." *University of Chicago Law Review* 58 (1991): 483–510.

Anderson, Benedict R. *Imagined Communities: Reflections on the Origin and Spread of Nationalism* (rev. ed.). New York: Verso, 1991.

Applebome, Peter. *Dixie Rising: How the South Is Shaping American Values, Politics, and Culture*. New York: Times Books, 1996.

Arnold, Richard S. "The Power of State Courts to Enjoin Federal Officers." *Yale Law Journal* 73 (1964): 1385–1406.

Austin, John. 1832. *The Province of Jurisprudence Determined*. New York: Humanities Press, 1965.

Bagdikian, Ben H. *The Media Monopoly* (6th ed.). Boston: Beacon Press, 2000.

Bailyn, Bernard. *The Ideological Origins of the American Revolution* (enlarged ed.). Cambridge: Harvard University Press, 1992.

Baker, C. Edwin. "Media Concentration: Giving Up on Democracy." *Florida Law Review* 54 (2002): 839–919.

Bardach, Eugene. *The Implementation Game: What Happens after a Bill Becomes a Law*. Cambridge: MIT Press, 1977.

Baum, Lawrence, and Bradley C. Canon. "State Supreme Courts as Activists: New Doctrines in the Law of Torts." In *State Supreme Courts: Policymakers in the Federal System*, ed. Mary Cornelia Porter and G. Alan Tarr, 83–108. Westport, Conn.: Greenwood, 1982.

Beamer, Glenn. *Creative Politics: Taxes and Public Goods in a Federal System*. Ann Arbor: University of Michigan Press, 1999.

Beatty, Jerry K. "State Court Evasion of United States Supreme Court Mandates during the Last Decade of the Warren Court." *Valparaiso Law Review* 6 (1972): 260–85.

Berger, Raoul. *Death Penalties: The Supreme Court's Obstacle Course*. Cambridge: Harvard University Press, 1982.

———. *Government by Judiciary: The Transformation of the Fourteenth Amendment*. Cambridge: Harvard University Press, 1977.

Berlin, Isaiah. "Two Concepts of Liberty." In *Four Essays on Liberty*. Oxford: Oxford University Press, 1969.

Bernstein, Anita. "How to Make a New Tort: Three Paradoxes." *Texas Law Review* 75 (1997): 1539–65.

Bickel, Alexander M. *The Least Dangerous Branch: The Supreme Court at the Bar of Politics*. Indianapolis: Bobbs-Merrill, 1962.

Billington, Ray Allen. "Foreword." In *The Frontier in American History*, by Frederick Jackson Turner, vii–xviii. New York: Holt, Rinehart and Winston, 1920. Reprinted with foreword. Malabar, Florida: Robert E. Krieger Publishing Co., 1985.

Bishop, James L. "The Jurisdiction of State and Federal Courts over Federal Officers." *Columbia Law Review* 9 (1909): 397–418.

Black, Charles L., Jr. *Structure and Relationship in Constitutional Law*. Baton Rouge: Louisiana State University Press, 1969.

Blight, David W. *Beyond the Battlefield: Race, Memory, and the American Civil War*. Amherst, Mass.: University of Massachusetts Press, 2002.

Bobbitt, Philip. *Constitutional Fate: Theory of the Constitution*. New York: Oxford University Press, 1982.

Bogue, Allan G. *Frederick Jackson Turner: Strange Roads Going Down*. Norman, Okla.: University of Oklahoma Press, 1998.

Bork, Robert H. "The Impossibility of Finding Welfare Rights in the Constitution." *Washington University Law Quarterly* 1979 (1979): 695–701.

———. "Neutral Principles and Some First Amendment Problems." *Indiana Law Journal* 47 (1971): 1–35.

Brace, Paul, Melinda Gann Hall, and Laura Langer. "Judicial Choice and the Politics of Abortion: Institutions, Context, and the Autonomy of Courts." *Albany Law Review* 62 (1999): 1265–1303.

Braithwaite, Dennis J. "An Analysis of the 'Divergence Factors': A Misguided Approach to Search and Seizure Jurisprudence under the New Jersey Constitution." *Rutgers Law Journal* 33 (2001): 1–47.

Branch, Taylor. *Parting the Waters: America in the King Years, 1954–63*. New York: Simon and Schuster, 1988.

Brennan, William J., Jr. "The Bill of Rights and the States: The Revival of State Constitutions as Guardians of Individual Rights." *New York University Law Review* 61 (1986): 535–53.

———. "Construing the Constitution." *U.C. Davis Law Review* 19 (1988): 2–14.

———. "Speech to the Text and Teaching Symposium." Georgetown University, Washington, D.C., October 12, 1985. Reprinted in *The Great Debate: Interpreting Our Written Constitution.* Washington, D.C.: The Federalist Society, 1986.

———. "State Constitutions and the Protection of Individual Rights." *Harvard Law Review* 90 (1977): 489–504.

Brest, Paul. "The Misconceived Quest for Original Understanding." *Boston University Law Review* 60 (1980): 204–38.

Brewer, Albert P. "Foreword: A Broad Initiative: Alabama's Citizens' Commission on Constitutional Reform." *Cumberland Law Review* 33 (2003): 187–93.

Briffault, Richard. *Balancing Acts: The Reality behind State Balanced Budget Requirements.* New York: Twentieth Century Fund, 1996.

———. "Our Localism: Part I—The Structure of Local Government Law." *Columbia Law Review* 90 (1990): 1–115.

———. "'What About the "Ism"?' Normative and Formal Concerns in Contemporary Federalism." *Vanderbilt Law Review* 47 (1994): 1303–53.

Butterfield, Fox. "A Police Force Rebuffs F.B.I. on Querying Mideast Men." *New York Times,* November 21, 2001, B7.

Calabresi, Guido. *A Common Law for the Age of Statutes.* Cambridge: Harvard University Press, 1982.

Caldeira, Gregory A. "The Transmission of Legal Precedent: A Study of State Supreme Courts." *American Political Science Review* 79 (1985): 178–94.

Canon, Bradley C., and Lawrence Baum. "Patterns of Adoption of Tort Law Innovations: An Application of Diffusion Theory to Judicial Doctrines." *American Political Science Review* 75 (1981): 975–87.

Carberry, Charles M. "Comment, The State Advisory Opinion in Perspective." *Fordham Law Review* 44 (1975): 81–113.

Carter, Stephen L. *The Confirmation Mess: Cleaning Up the Federal Appointments Process.* New York: Basic Books, 1994.

Cauthen, James N. G. "Expanding Rights under State Constitutions: A Quantitative Appraisal." *Albany Law Review* 63 (2000): 1183–1204.

———. "State Constitutional Policymaking in Criminal Procedure: A Longitudinal Study." *Criminal Justice Policy Review* 10 (1999): 521–45.

Chemerinsky, Erwin. "Privacy and the Alaska Constitution: Failing to Fulfill the Promise." *Alaska Law Review* 20 (2003): 29–48.

Choper, Jesse. *Judicial Review and the National Political Process.* Chicago: University of Chicago Press, 1980.

Collins, Ronald K. L. "Reliance on State Constitutions—Away from a Reactionary Approach." *Hastings Constitutional Law Quarterly* 9 (1981): 1–19.

Collins, Ronald K. L., Peter J. Galie, and John Kincaid. "State High Courts, State Constitutions, and Individual Rights Litigation since 1980: A Judicial Survey." *Publius* 16 (1986): 141–62.

Conforti, Joseph A. *Imagining New England: Explorations of Regional Identity from the Pilgrims to the Mid-Twentieth Century.* Chapel Hill: University of North Carolina Press, 2001.

Connor, Walker. *Ethnonationalism: The Quest for Understanding.* Princeton: Princeton University Press, 1994.

Cooley, Thomas M. *A Treatise on the Constitutional Limitations Which Rest upon the Legislative Power of the States of the American Union* (6th ed.). Boston: Little, Brown, 1890. First edition 1868.

Council of State Governments. *The Book of the States,* vol. 33. Chicago: Council of State Governments, 2000–2001.

Cover, Robert M. "Foreword: Nomos and Narrative." *Harvard Law Review* 97 (1983): 4–68.

———. *Justice Accused: Antislavery and the Judicial Process.* New Haven: Yale University Press, 1975.

Croley, Steven P. "The Majoritarian Difficulty: Elective Judiciaries and the Rule of Law." *University of Chicago Law Review* 62 (1995): 689–794.

Cross, Frank B. "Institutions and Enforcement of the Bill of Rights." *Cornell Law Review* 85 (2000): 1529–1608.

Cuddihy, William, and B. Carmon Hardy. "A Man's House Was Not His Castle: Origins of the Fourth Amendment to the United States Constitution." *William and Mary Quarterly* 37 (1980): 371–400.

Dahl, Robert. "Decision-Making in a Democracy: The Supreme Court as a National Policy-Maker." *Journal of Public Law* 6 (1957): 279–95.

Degler, Carl N. *Place over Time: The Continuity of Southern Distinctiveness.* Baton Rouge: Louisiana State University Press, 1977.

Delgado, Richard. "Storytelling for Oppositionists and Others: A Plea for Narrative." *Michigan Law Review* 87 (1989): 2411–41.

Delmatier, Royce D., Clarence F. McIntosh, and Earl G. Waters, eds. *The Rumble of California Politics, 1848–1970.* New York: John Wiley and Sons, 1970.

Derthick, Martha. "American Federalism: Madison's Middle Ground in the 1980's." *Public Administration Review* 47 (1987): 66–74.

———. *The Influence of Federal Grants: Public Assistance in Massachusetts.* Cambridge: Harvard University Press, 1970.

———. *New Towns In-Town: Why a Federal Program Failed.* Washington, D.C.: Urban Institute, 1972.

DeWitt, Benjamin Parke. *The Progressive Movement.* New York: Macmillan, 1915.

Dickerson, O. M. "Writs of Assistance as a Cause of the Revolution." In *The Era of the American Revolution,* edited by Richard B. Morris, 40–75. Gloucester, Mass.: Peter Smith, 1971.

DiIulio, John J., Jr., and Donald F. Kettl. *Fine Print: The Contract with America, Devolution, and the Administrative Realities of American Federalism.* Washington: Brookings, 1995.

Dillon, Sam. "States Are Relaxing Standards on Tests to Avoid Sanctions." *New York Times,* May 22, 2003, A1.

Dinan, John J. *Keeping the People's Liberties: Legislators, Citizens, and Judges as Guardians of Rights.* Lawrence, Kan.: Kansas University Press, 1998.

Dodd, Walter F. "The Function of a State Constitution." *Political Science Quarterly* 30 (1915): 201–21.

Durham, Christine M. "The Judicial Branch in State Government: Parables of Law, Politics, and Power." *New York University Law Review* 76 (2001): 1601–22.

Dworkin, Ronald. *Law's Empire.* Cambridge: Harvard University Press, 1986.

Dye, Thomas R. *American Federalism: Competition among Governments.* Lexington, Mass: Lexington Books, 1990.

Editorial: "Get Government Out of Bedrooms." *St. Petersburg Times,* November 29, 1998, 2D.

Editorial: "Privacy: Leave Adults Alone." *Charleston (W. Va.) Gazette,* December 3, 1998, 6A.

Editorial. "Privacy Prevails: Georgia's Supreme Court Strikes Down a Sodomy Law." *Pittsburgh Post-Gazette,* December 7, 1998, A16.

Eisenberg, Melvin Aron. *The Nature of the Common Law.* Cambridge: Harvard University Press, 1988.

Elazar, Daniel J. *American Federalism: A View from the States* (2d ed.). New York: Harper and Row, 1972.

———. *Cities of the Prairie.* New York: Basic Books 1970.

———. "The Principles and Traditions Underlying State Constitutions." *Publius* 12 (1982): 11–25.

Elazar, Daniel J., and Joseph Zikmund II, eds. *The Ecology of American Political Culture: Readings.* New York: Thomas Y. Crowell Co., 1975.

Elkins, David J., and Richard E. B. Simeon. "A Cause in Search of Its Effect, or What Does Political Culture Explain?" *Comparative Politics* 11 (1979): 127–45.

Environmental Policy Project. *Changing the Rules by Changing the Players: The Environmental Issue in State Judicial Elections.* Washington: Georgetown University Law Center, 2000.

Eskridge, William N., Jr. *Dynamic Statutory Interpretation.* Cambridge: Harvard University Press, 1994.

———. "Spinning Legislative Supremacy." *Georgetown Law Journal* 78 (1989): 319–52.

Esler, Michael. "State Supreme Court Commitment to State Law." *Judicature* 78 (1994): 25–32.

Etcheson, Nicole. *The Emerging Midwest: Upland Southerners and the Political Culture of the Old Northwest, 1787–1861.* Bloomington: Indiana University Press, 1996.

Fairman, Charles. *Reconstruction and Reunion, 1864–88.* New York: Macmillan, 1971.

Faragher, John Mack. *Rereading Frederick Jackson Turner.* New York: Henry Holt and Co., 1994.

Feldman, Stephen M. "From Premodern to Modern American Jurisprudence: The Onset of Positivism." *Vanderbilt Law Review* 50 (1997): 1387–1446.

Fischer, David Hackett. *Albion's Seed: Four British Folkways in America.* New York: Oxford University Press, 1989.

Fish, Stanley. *Is There a Text in This Class?* Cambridge: Harvard University Press, 1980.

Foner, Eric. *Reconstruction: America's Unfinished Revolution, 1863–1877*. New York: Harper and Row, 1988.

"Forum—Albion's Seed: Four British Folkways in America—A Symposium." *William and Mary Quarterly* 48 (1991): 223–308.

Freehling, William W. *Prelude to Civil War: The Nullification Controversy in South Carolina, 1816–1836*. New York: Harper and Row, 1968.

Frieden, Bernard J., and Lynne B. Sagalyn. *Downtown, Inc.: How America Rebuilds Cities.* Cambridge: MIT Press, 1989.

Friedman, Barry. "Dialogue and Judicial Review." *Michigan Law Review* 91 (1993): 577–682.

Friedman, Lawrence M., Robert A. Kagan, Bliss Cartwright, and Stanton Wheeler. "State Supreme Courts: A Century of Style and Citation." *Stanford Law Review* 33 (1981): 773–818.

Fritz, Christian G. "The American Constitutional Tradition Revisited: Preliminary Observations on State Constitution-Making in the Nineteenth-Century West." *Rutgers Law Journal* 25 (1994): 945–98.

Galie, Peter J. *The New York State Constitution: A Reference Guide.* New York: Greenwood Press, 1991.

———. "The Other Supreme Courts: Judicial Activism among State Supreme Courts." *Syracuse Law Review* 33 (1982): 731–93.

———. "State Courts and Economic Rights." *Annals of the American Academy of Political and Social Science* 496 (1988): 76–87.

Gardner, James A. "Devolution and the Paradox of Democratic Unresponsiveness." *South Texas Law Review* 40 (1999): 759–87.

———. "The Failed Discourse of State Constitutionalism." *Michigan Law Review* 90 (1992): 761–837.

———. "Forcing States to Be Free: The Emerging Constitutional Guarantee of Radical Democracy." *Connecticut Law Review* 35 (2003): 1467–1507.

———. "Madison's Hope: Virtue, Self-Interest, and the Design of Electoral Systems." *Iowa Law Review* 86 (2000): 87–172.

———. "The Positivist Foundations of Originalism: An Account and Critique." *Boston University Law Review* 71 (1991): 1–45.

———. "The Positivist Revolution That Wasn't: Constitutional Universalism in the States." *Roger Williams University Law Review* 4 (1998): 109–31.

———. "Southern Character, Confederate Nationalism, and the Interpretation of State Constitutions: A Case Study in Constitutional Argument." *Texas Law Review* 76 (1998): 1219–91.

Gates, Paul Wallace. *Pressure Groups and Recent American Land Policies.* Ithaca: Cornell University Press, 1980.

Gellner, Ernest. *Nations and Nationalism.* Oxford: Blackwell, 1983.

Goldberg, Carey. "Alaska Revels in Frontier Image Though Frontier Slips Away." *New York Times,* August 14, 1997, A1.

Goldberg, Deborah, and Craig Holman. *The New Politics of Judicial Elections.* New York: Brennan Center for Justice, 2002.

Goldschmidt, Jona. *Certification of Questions of Law: Federalism in Practice.* Chicago: American Judicature Society, 1995.

Gordley, James. "The Common Law in the Twentieth Century: Some Unfinished Business." *California Law Review* 88 (2000): 1815–75.

Grad, Frank P. "The State Constitution: Its Function and Form for Our Time." *Virginia Law Review* 54 (1968): 955–73.

Greenhouse, Linda. "Will the Court Reassert National Authority?" *New York Times,* September 30, 2001, 4:14:3.

Greenfeld, Liah. *Nationalism: Five Roads to Modernity.* Cambridge: Harvard University Press, 1992.

Gunther, Gerald, ed. *John Marshall's Defense of* McCulloch v. Maryland. Stanford: Stanford University Press, 1969.

Hall, Melinda Gann. "Electoral Politics and Strategic Voting in State Supreme Courts." *Journal of Politics* 54 (1992): 427–46.

Hansen, Kristin A. *Current Population Reports: Geographical Mobility: March 1995 to March 1996.* Washington, D.C.: U.S. Department of Commerce, Census Bureau, November, 1997.

Harris, Joseph P. *California Politics* (4th ed.). San Francisco: Chandler Publishing Co., 1967.

Hartnett, Edward. "Why Is the Supreme Court of the United States Protecting Judges from Popular Democracy?" *Texas Law Review* 75 (1997): 907–87.

Hegel, Georg Wilhelm Friedrich. *The Philosophy of History.* Translated by J. Sibree. New York: Dover, 1956.

Hershkoff, Helen. "Positive Rights and State Constitutions: The Limits of Federal Rationality Review." *Harvard Law Review* 112 (1999): 1131–96.

———. "Rights and Freedoms under the State Constitution: A New Deal for Welfare Rights." *Touro Law Review* 13 (1997): 631–52.

———. "State Courts and the 'Passive Virtues': Rethinking the Judicial Function." *Harvard Law Review* 114 (2001): 1833–1941.

Hills, Roderick M., Jr. "Dissecting the State: The Use of Federal Law to Free State and Local Officials from State Legislatures' Control." *Michigan Law Review* 97 (1999): 1201–86.

Hobsbawm, Eric, and Terrence Ranger, eds. *The Invention of Tradition.* Cambridge: Cambridge University Press, 1983.

Hofstadter, Richard. *The Progressive Historians: Turner, Beard, Parrington.* New York: Alfred A. Knopf, 1968.

Holmes, Oliver Wendell. *Collected Legal Papers.* New York: Harcourt, Brace, 1920.

Horwitz, Morton J. *The Transformation of American Law, 1780–1860.* Cambridge: Harvard University Press, 1977.

Howard, A. E. Dick. "The Renaissance of State Constitutional Law." *Emerging Issues in State Constitutional Law* 1 (1988): 1–15.

——. "State Courts and Constitutional Rights in the Day of the Burger Court." *Virginia Law Review* 62 (1976): 873–944.

Huntington, Samuel P. *The Clash of Civilizations and the Remaking of the World Order.* New York: Simon and Schuster, 1996.

Ignatieff, Michael. *Blood and Belonging: Journeys into the New Nationalism.* New York: Farrar, Straus, and Giroux, 1993.

Issacharoff, Samuel, and Daniel R. Ortiz. "Governing Through Intermediaries." *Virginia Law Review* 85 (1999): 1627–70.

Janofsky, Michael. "Cities Wary of Antiterror Tactics Pass Civil Liberties Resolutions." *New York Times,* December 23, 2002, A1.

Kagan, Robert A., Bliss Cartwright, Lawrence M. Friedman, and Stanton Wheeler. "The Business of State Supreme Courts, 1870–1970." *Stanford Law Review* 30 (1977): 121–56.

Kahn, Paul W. "Community in Contemporary Constitutional Theory." *Yale Law Journal* 99 (1989): 1–85.

——. "Interpretation and Authority in State Constitutionalism." *Harvard Law Review* 106 (1993): 1147–68.

Kammen, Michael G. *A Machine That Would Go of Itself: The Constitution in American Culture.* New York: Alfred A. Knopf, 1986.

Kaye, Judith S. "Dual Constitutionalism in Practice and Principle." *St. John's Law Review* 61 (1987): 399–429.

——. "A Midpoint Perspective on Directions in State Constitutional Law." *Emerging Issues in State Constitutional Law* 1 (1988): 17–27.

Keating, Gregory C. "The Theory of Enterprise Liability and Common Law Strict Liability." *Vanderbilt Law Review* 54 (2001): 1285–1335.

Keeton, Robert E. *Venturing to Do Justice: Reforming Private Law.* Cambridge: Harvard University Press, 1969.

Keiser, Lael R. "Street-level Bureaucrats, Administrative Power and the Manipulation of Federal Social Security Disability Programs." *State Politics and Policy Quarterly* 1 (2001): 144–64.

Key, V. O., Jr. *American State Politics: An Introduction.* New York: Alfred A. Knopf, 1956.

Kirby, James C., Jr. "Expansive Judicial Review of Economic Regulation under State Constitutions." In *Developments in State Constitutional Law.* Edited by Bradley C. McGraw. St. Paul, Minn.: West Publishing Co., 1985.

Kirk, Russell. "The Prospects for Territorial Democracy in America." In *A Nation of States: Essays on the American Federal System.* Edited by Robert A. Goldwin. Chicago: Rand McNally, 1963.

Kohn, Hans. *The Idea of Nationalism.* New York: Macmillan, 1944.

Kramer, Larry. "Putting the Politics Back into the Political Safeguards of Federalism." *Columbia Law Review* 100 (2000): 215–93.

——. "Understanding Federalism." *Vanderbilt Law Review* 47 (1994): 1485–1561.

Krent, Harold J. "Judging Judging: The Problem of Second-Guessing State Judges' Interpretation of State Law in *Bush v. Gore.*" *Florida State University Law Review* 29 (2001): 493–534.

Kruman, Marc W. *Between Authority and Liberty: State Constitution Making in Revolutionary America.* Chapel Hill: University of North Carolina Press, 1997.

Kymlicka, Will. *Multicultural Citizenship: A Liberal Theory of Minority Rights.* Oxford: Clarendon Press, 1995.

Landau, Jack L. "Hurrah for Revolution: A Critical Assessment of State Constitutional Interpretation." *Oregon Law Review* 79 (2000): 793–891.

Landau, Martin. "Federalism, Redundancy and System Reliability." *Publius* 3 (Fall 1973): 173–96.

Langer, Laura. *Judicial Review in State Supreme Courts.* Albany: State University of New York Press, 2002.

Latzer, Barry. "The Hidden Conservatism of the State Court 'Revolution.'" *Judicature* 74 (1991): 190–97.

Levi, Edward H. *An Introduction to Legal Reasoning.* Chicago: University of Chicago Press, 1949.

Levinson, Sanford. *Constitutional Faith.* Princeton: Princeton University Press, 1988.

———. "Law as Literature." *Texas Law Review* 60 (1982): 373–403.

Levy, Jacob T. *The Multiculturalism of Fear.* Oxford: Oxford University Press, 2000.

Levy, Leonard W. *Original Intent and the Framers' Constitution.* New York: Macmillan, 1988.

Lightman, David. "Poll Tracks National Growth in Trust; A Strong Majority Likes and Trusts the U.S. Government for the First Time Since the Vietnam Era." *Hartford Courant,* November 29, 2001, A1.

Lijphart, Arend. *Democracies: Patterns of Majoritarian and Consensus Government in Twenty-one Countries.* New Haven: Yale University Press, 1984.

———. "Proportionality by Non-PR Methods: Ethnic Representation in Belgium, Cyprus, Lebanon, New Zealand, West Germany and Zimbabwe." In *Electoral Laws and Their Political Consequences.* Edited by Bernard Grofman and Arend Lijphart. New York: Agathon Press, 1986.

Limerick, Patricia. *The Legacy of Conquest: The Unbroken Past of the American West.* New York: W. W. Norton, 1987.

Linde, Hans. "First Things First; Rediscovering the States' Bills of Rights." *University of Baltimore Law Review* 9 (1980): 379–96.

Linde, Hans. "E Pluribus—Constitutional Theory and State Courts." *Georgia Law Review* 18 (1984): 165–200.

Locke, John. *The Second Treatise of Government.* 1690. Edited, with an introduction, by Thomas P. Peardon. Indianapolis: Bobbs-Merrill, 1952.

Loftus, Tom. "Patton Signs Bill Abolishing Vehicle Emissions Tests in Jefferson." *Louisville (Ky.) Courier-Journal,* April 9, 2002.

Long, Larry. *Migration and Residential Mobility in the United States.* New York: Russell Sage Foundation, 1988.

Macgill, H. C. "Upon a Peak in Darien: Discovering the Connecticut Constitution." *Connecticut Law Review* 15 (1982): 7–19.

MacIntyre, Alasdair. *After Virtue* (2d ed.). Notre Dame, Ind.: University of Notre Dame Press, 1984.

Madison, James. *Notes of Debates in the Federal Convention of 1787.* Edited, with an introduction, by Adrienne Koch. New York: W. W. Norton, 1966.

Madison, James, Alexander Hamilton, and John Jay. *The Federalist Papers.* 1787–88. Edited, with an introduction, by Clinton Rossiter. New York: Mentor, 1961.

Maltz, Earl M. "The Political Dynamic of the 'New Judicial Federalism.'" *Emerging Issues in State Constitutional Law* 2 (1989): 233–38.

Marvell, Thomas B. "The Rationales for Federal Question Jurisdiction: An Empirical Examination of Student Rights Litigation." *Wisconsin Law Review* 1984 (1984): 1315–72.

Marx, Karl. *The Eighteenth Brumaire of Louis Bonaparte.* Moscow: Progress Publishers, 1967.

McConnell, Michael W. "Federalism: Evaluating the Founders' Design." *University of Chicago Law Review* 54 (1987): 1484–1544.

———. "Free Exercise Revisionism and the Smith Decision." *University of Chicago Law Review* 57 (1990): 1109–53.

McCoy, Drew R. *The Last of the Fathers: James Madison and the Republican Legacy.* Cambridge: Cambridge University Press, 1989.

McDonald, Forrest. *States' Rights and the Union: Imperium in Imperio, 1776–1876.* Lawrence: University Press of Kansas, 2000.

McGraw, Bradley C., ed. *Developments in State Constitutional Law.* St. Paul, Minn.: West Publishing, 1985.

McHugh, James T. *Ex Uno Plura: State Constitutions and Their Political Cultures.* Albany: State University of New York Press, 2003.

McKenna, Marian C. "Introduction: A Legacy of Questions." In *The Canadian and American Constitutions in Comparative Perspective.* Edited by Marian C. McKenna. Calgary: University of Calgary Press, 1993.

McMillan, James F. *Napoleon III.* New York: Longman Group, 1991.

Mead, Lawrence M. *The New Politics of Poverty: The Nonworking Poor in America.* New York: Basic Books, 1992.

Meyers, Marvin. *The Jacksonian Persuasion: Politics and Belief.* Stanford: Stanford University Press, 1960

Michelman, Frank I. "Foreword: On Protecting the Poor through the Fourteenth Amendment." *Harvard Law Review* 83 (1969): 7–59.

Miller, David. *Citizenship and National Identity.* Malden, Mass.: Polity Press, 2000.

Modisett, Jeffrey A. "Discovering the Impact of 'New Federalism' on State Policy Makers: A State Attorney General's Perspective." *Indiana Law Review* 32 (1998): 141–54.

Mosk, Stanley. "State Constitutionalism: Both Liberal and Conservative." *Texas Law Review* 63 (1985): 1081–93.

Nagel, Robert F. *The Implosion of American Federalism.* New York: Oxford University Press, 2001.

Nienstedt, John. "Social Values Emerging from the Rubble of Sept. 11." *San Diego Union-Tribune,* December 28, 2001, B7.

Noll, Roger G. "Economic Perspectives on the Politics of Regulation." In *Handbook of Industrial Organization,* vol. 2, ch. 22, 1253–87. Edited by R. Schmalensee and R. D. Willig. New York: Elsevier Science Publishers, 1989.

Note. "California's Constitutional Amendomania." *Stanford Law Review* 1 (1949): 279–88.

Note. "Developments in the Law: The Interpretation of State Constitutional Rights." *Harvard Law Review* 95 (1982): 1324–1502.

Nugent, John D. "State Implementation of Federal Policy as a Political Safeguard of Federalism." Paper delivered at Annual Meeting of the American Political Science Association, Washington, D.C., Aug. 31–Sept. 3, 2000.

Owsley, Frank Lawrence. "The Irrepressible Conflict." In *I'll Take My Stand: The South and the Agrarian Tradition,* by Twelve Southerners. 1930. Introduction by Louis D. Rubin, Jr. Biographical essays by Virginia Rock. New York: Harper and Row, 1962.

Parness, Jeffrey A. "Public Process and State-Court Rulemaking." *Yale Law Journal* 88 (1979): 1319–24.

Patterson, Samuel C. "The Political Cultures of the American States." *The Journal of Politics* 30 (1968): 187–209.

Peters, Ellen A. "Getting Away from the Federal Paradigm: Separation of Powers in State Courts." *Minnesota Law Review* 81 (1997): 1543–64.

———. "State Constitutional Law: Federalism in the Common Law Tradition." *Michigan Law Review* 84 (1986): 583–93.

Pettys, Todd E. "Competing for the People's Affection: Federalism's Forgotten Marketplace." *Vanderbilt Law Review* 56 (2003): 329–91.

Pfaff, William. *The Wrath of Nations: Civilization and the Furies of Nationalism.* New York: Simon and Schuster, 1993.

Pierson, George Wilson. "The Frontier and American Institutions: A Criticism of the Turner Theory." In *Turner and the Sociology of the Frontier.* Edited by Richard Hofstadter and Seymour Martin Lipset. New York: Basic Books, 1968.

———. "The Obstinate Concept of New England: A Study in Denudation." *The New England Quarterly* 28 (1955): 3–17.

Pollock, Stewart G. "Adequate and Independent State Grounds as a Means of Balancing the Relationship Between State and Federal Courts." *Texas Law Review* 63 (1985): 977–93.

———. "State Constitutions as Separate Sources of Fundamental Rights." *Rutgers Law Review* 35 (1983): 707–22.

Pope, James Gray. "An Approach to State Constitutional Interpretation." *Rutgers Law Journal* 24 (1993): 985–1008.

Porter, Mary Cornelia, and G. Alan Tarr, eds. *State Supreme Courts: Policymakers in the Federal System.* Westport, Conn.: Greenwood Press, 1980.

Post, Robert C. "The Challenge of State Constitutions." In *Constitutional Reform in California: Making State Government More Effective and Responsive.* Edited by Bruce E. Cain and Roger G. Noll. Berkeley: Institute of Governmental Studies Press, 1995.

Potter, David M. *The South and the Sectional Conflict.* Baton Rouge: Louisiana University Press, 1968.

Priest, George L. "The Invention of Enterprise Liability: A Critical History of the Intellectual Foundations of Modern Tort Law." *Journal of Legal Studies* 14 (1985): 461–527.

Rakove, Jack N. *Original Meanings: Politics and Ideas in the Making of the Constitution.* New York: Alfred A. Knopf, 1996.

Rawls, John. *A Theory of Justice.* Cambridge: Harvard University Press, Belknap Press, 1971.

Rehnquist, William. "The Notion of a Living Constitution." *Texas Law Review* 54 (1976): 693–706.

Remini, Robert V. *Andrew Jackson and the Course of American Democracy, 1833–1845.* New York: Harper and Row, 1984.

Rinard, Amy. "State Pays for Its 0.10 Standard." *Milwaukee Journal Sentinel,* April 21, 2002.

Ross, William G. *A Muted Fury: Populists, Progressives, and Labor Unions Confront the Courts, 1890–1937.* Princeton: Princeton University Press, 1994.

Rossi, Jim. "Institutional Design and the Lingering Legacy of Antifederal Separation of Powers Ideals in the States." *Vanderbilt Law Review* 52 (1999): 1167–1240.

Rubin, Edward L., and Malcolm Feeley. "Federalism: Some Notes on a National Neurosis." *UCLA Law Review* 41 (1994): 903–52.

Russell, Peter H. *Constitutional Odyssey: Can the Canadians Become a Sovereign People?* Toronto: University of Toronto Press, 1992.

Ruud, Millard H. "'No Law Shall Embrace More Than One Subject.'" *Minnesota Law Review* 42 (1958): 389–452.

"'Sagebrush Rebels' Are Reveling in Reagan." *New York Times,* November 24, 1980, D9:2.

Said, Edward W. *Orientalism.* New York: Vintage Books, 1978.

Saunders, Melissa L. "Equal Protection, Class Legislation, and Colorblindness." *Michigan Law Review* 96 (1997): 245–337.

Scalia, Antonin. "Originalism: The Lesser Evil." *University of Cincinnati Law Review* 57 (1989): 849–65.

Schapiro, Robert A. "Contingency and Universalism in State Separation of Powers Discourse." *Roger Williams University Law Review* 4 (1998): 79–108.

Schauer, Frederick. "Formalism." *Yale Law Journal* 97 (1988): 509–48.

Schneider, Saundra K. "Governors and Health Care Policy in the American States." *Policy Studies Journal* 17 (1989): 909–26.

Schuman, David. "The Right to 'Equal Privileges and Immunities': A State's Version of 'Equal Protection.'" *Vermont Law Review* 13 (1988): 221–45.

——. "The Right to a Remedy." *Temple Law Review* 65 (1992): 1197–1227.

Schwartz, Herman. "A Prohibition That Frustrates the People's Will." *Los Angeles Times,* May 20, 2001, M2.

Segal, Jeffrey A., and Albert D. Cover. "Ideological Values and the Votes of U.S. Supreme Court Justices." *American Political Science Review* 83 (1989): 557–65.

Segal, Jeffrey A., and Harold J. Spaeth. *The Supreme Court and the Attitudinal Model.* Cambridge: Cambridge University Press, 1993.

Shafer, Boyd C. *Nationalism: Myth and Reality.* New York: Harcourt, Brace, 1955.

Sherry, Suzanna. "Natural Law in the States." *University of Cincinnati Law Review* 61 (1992): 171–222.

Smith, Adam. *The Theory of Moral Sentiments.* 1759. Edited by D. D. Raphael and A. L. Macfie. Indianapolis: Liberty Fund, 1982.

Smith, Anthony D. *National Identity.* Reno: University of Nevada Press, 1991.

Solimine, Michael E., and James L. Walker. *Respecting State Courts: The Inevitability of Judicial Federalism.* Westport, Conn.: Greenwood Press, 1999.

Somin, Ilya. "Closing the Pandora's Box of Federalism: The Case for Judicial Restriction of Federal Subsidies to State Governments." *Georgetown Law Journal* 90 (2002): 461–502.

Spaeth, Harold J., and Jeffrey A. Segal. *Majority Rule or Minority Will: Adherence to Precedent on the U.S. Supreme Court.* Cambridge: Cambridge University Press, 1999.

"Special Section: The Connecticut Constitution." *Connecticut Law Review* 15 (1982): 7–120.

Sponholtz, Lloyd. "The Initiative and Referendum: Direct Democracy in Perspective, 1898–1920." *American Studies* 14 (1973): 43–64.

"State Constitutions in a Federal System." *Annals of the American Academy of Political and Social Science* 496 (1988): 1–139.

Sterk, Stewart E., and Elizabeth S. Goldman. "Controlling Legislative Shortsightedness: The Effectiveness of Constitutional Debt Limitations." *Wisconsin Law Review* 1991 (1991): 1301–67.

Strauss, David A. "Common Law Constitutional Interpretation." *University of Chicago Law Review* 62 (1995): 877–935.

Stumpf, Harry P., and John H. Culver. *The Politics of State Courts.* White Plains, N.Y.: Longman Publishing Group, 1992.

Sturm, Albert L. "The Development of American State Constitutions." *Publius* 12 (Winter 1982): 57–98.

Sunstein, Cass R. *The Partial Constitution.* Cambridge: Harvard University Press, 1993.

———. "Lochner's Legacy." *Columbia Law Review* 87 (1987): 873–919.

Swindler, William F. "State Constitutions for the 20th Century." *Nebraska Law Review* 50 (1971): 577–99.

"Symposium: The Emergence of State Constitutional Law." *Texas Law Review* 63 (1985): 959–1318.

"Symposium on the Revolution in State Constitutional Law." *Vermont Law Review* 13 (1988): 11–372.

"Symposium: Separation of Powers in State Constitutional Law." *Roger Williams University Law Review* 4 (1998): 4–174.

"Symposium on State Constitutional Jurisprudence." *Hastings Constitutional Law Quarterly* 15 (1988): 391–478.

"Symposium on State Constitutional Law." *Washington Law Review* 64 (1989): 5–132.

Tallian, Laura. *Direct Democracy: An Historical Analysis of the Initiative, Referendum and Recall Process.* Los Angeles: People's Lobby Press, 1977.

Tamir, Yael. *Liberal Nationalism.* Princeton: Princeton University Press, 1993.

Tarr, G. Alan. "Interpreting the Separation of Powers in State Constitutions." *New York University Annual Survey of American Law* 59 (2003): 329–40.

———. *Judicial Impact and State Supreme Courts.* Lexington, Mass.: Lexington Books, 1977.

———. *Understanding State Constitutions.* Princeton: Princeton University Press, 1998.

Tarr, G. Alan, and Ellis Katz. "Introduction." In *Federalism and Rights,* ix–xxiii. Edited by Ellis Katz and G. Alan Tarr. Lanham, Md.: Rowman and Littlefield, 1996.

Taylor, Charles. *Sources of the Self: The Making of the Modern Identity.* Cambridge: Harvard University Press, 1989.

Teachout, Peter R. "Against the Stream: An Introduction to the Vermont Law Review Symposium on the Revolution in State Constitutional Law." *Vermont Law Review* 13 (1988): 13–47.

Thomas, Emory M. *The Confederate Nation, 1861–1865.* New York: Harper and Row, 1979.

Thompson, Frank J., and Michael J. Scicchitano. "OSHA, the States, and Gresham's Law: From Carter to Reagan." In *Intergovernmental Relations and Public Policy.* Edited by J. Edwin Benton and David R. Morgan. New York: Greenwood Press, 1986.

Tibbetts, Donn. "Lift Seat-Belt Sanctions, Merrill Urges DOT Chief." *Manchester Union Leader,* January 28, 1995, A1.

Titone, Vito J. "State Constitutional Interpretation: The Search for an Anchor in a Rough Sea." *St. John's Law Review* 61 (1987): 431–72.

Turner, Frederick Jackson. *The Frontier in American History.* New York: Holt, Rinehart and Winston, 1920. Reprinted with foreword by Ray Allen Billington. Malabar, Fla.: Robert E. Krieger Publishing Co., 1985.

———. *The Rise of the New West.* New York: Harper and Bros., 1906.

———. *The Significance of Sections in American History.* New York: Henry Holt and Co., 1932.

———. *The United States, 1830–1850: The Nation and Its Sections.* New York: Henry Holt and Co., 1935.

Tushnet, Mark. "Following the Rules Laid Down: A Critique of Interpretivism and Neutral Principles." *Harvard Law Review* 96 (1983): 781–827.

United States Census Bureau. *Annual Geographical Mobility Rates, by Type of Movement, 1947–2001.* Washington, D.C.: U.S. Department of Commerce, 2002.

United States Environmental Protection Agency. *Managing Nonpoint Source Pollution.* Washington, D.C.: U.S. Environmental Protection Agency, 1992.

Unruh, John D., Jr. *The Plains Across: The Overland Emigrants and the Trans-Mississippi West, 1840–60*. Urbana: University of Illinois Press, 1979.

Urofsky, Melvin I., and Paul Finkelman. *A March of Liberty: A Constitutional History of the United States*. New York: Oxford University Press, 2002.

Utter, Robert F. "Freedom and Diversity in a Federal System: Perspectives on State Constitutions and the Washington Declaration of Rights." In *Developments in State Constitutional Law*. Edited by Bradley D. McGraw, 239–72. St. Paul, Minn.: West Publishing, 1985.

———. "Swimming in the Jaws of the Crocodile: State Court Comment on Federal Constitutional Issues When Disposing of Cases on State Constitutional Grounds." *Texas Law Review* 63 (1985): 1025–50.

Van Alstyne, William. "'Thirty Pieces of Silver' for the Rights of Your People: Irresistible Offers Reconsidered as a Matter of State Constitutional Law." *Harvard Journal of Law and Public Policy* 16 (1993): 303–26.

———. "Trends in the Supreme Court: Mr. Jefferson's Crumbling Wall—A Comment on *Lynch v. Donnelly*." *Duke Law Journal* 1984 (1984): 770–87.

Van Deusen, Glyndon G. *The Jacksonian Era, 1828–1848*. New York: Harper, 1959.

Vile, M. J. C. *Constitutionalism and the Separation of Powers* (2d ed.). Oxford: Clarendon Press, 1998.

Vitiello, Michael. "The Power of State Legislatures to Subpoena Federal Officials." *Tulane Law Review* 58 (1983): 548–72.

Wachtler, Sol. "Our Constitutions—Alive and Well." *St. John's University Law Review* 61 (1987): 381–98.

Watson, Harry L. *Liberty and Power: The Politics of Jacksonian America*. New York: Hill and Wang, 1990.

Wechsler, Herbert. "The Political Safeguards of Federalism: The Role of the States in the Composition and Selection of the National Government." *Columbia Law Review* 54 (1954): 543–60.

White, James B. *Heracles' Bow*. Madison: University of Wisconsin Press, 1985.

———. *Justice as Translation*. Chicago: University of Chicago Press, 1990.

———. *When Words Lose Their Meaning*. Chicago: University of Chicago Press, 1984.

White, Richard. "Trashing the Trails." In *Trails: Toward a New Western History*. Edited by Patricia Nelson Limerick, Clyde A. Milner II, and Charles E. Rankin, 26–39. Lawrence: University Press of Kansas, 1991.

Whittington, Keith E. "Dismantling the Modern State? The Changing Structural Foundations of Federalism." *Hastings Constitutional Law Quarterly* 25 (1998): 483–527.

Wilkes, Donald E., Jr. "The New Federalism in Criminal Procedure in 1984: Death of the Phoenix?" In *Developments in State Constitutional Law*. Edited by Bradley D. McGraw, 166–200. St. Paul, Minn.: West Publishing, 1985.

Williams, Robert F. "In the Supreme Court's Shadow: Legitimacy of State Rejection of Supreme Court Reasoning and Result." *South Carolina Law Review* 35 (1984): 353–404.

——. *State Constitutional Law* (3d ed.). Charlottesville, Va.: Lexis Law Publishing, 1999.

——. State Constitutional Law Processes, *William & Mary Law Review* 24 (1983): 169.

Wold, John T., and John H. Culver. "The Defeat of the California Justices: The Campaign, the Electorate, and the Issue of Judicial Accountability." *Judicature* 70 (1987): 348–55.

Wood, Gordon S. *The Creation of the American Republic, 1776–1787.* Chapel Hill: University of North Carolina Press, 1998.

——. "Foreword: State Constitution-Making in the American Revolution." *Rutgers Law Journal* 24 (1993): 911–26.

——. *The Radicalism of the American Revolution.* New York: Vintage Books, 1991.

Woodward, C. Vann. *The Burden of Southern History.* New York: Vintage Books, 1960.

Yack, Bernard. "The Myth of the Civic Nation." *Critical Review* 10 (1996): 193–212.